Friends of the
Davis Public Library

Providing Books
and Programs

ALSO BY EVAN OSNOS

*Joe Biden: The Life, the Run,
and What Matters Now*

*Age of Ambition: Chasing Fortune, Truth,
and Faith in the New China*

WILDLAND

WILDLAND

THE MAKING OF AMERICA'S FURY

EVAN OSNOS

FARRAR, STRAUS AND GIROUX
NEW YORK

Farrar, Straus and Giroux
120 Broadway, New York 10271

Copyright © 2021 by Evan Osnos
All rights reserved
Printed in the United States of America
First edition, 2021

Portions of this book originally appeared, in different form, in *The New Yorker*.

Grateful acknowledgment is made for permission to reprint an excerpt from "A Vision,"
by Wendell Berry, from *New Collected Poems*. Copyright © 1977 by Wendell Berry.
Reprinted with the permission of The Permissions Company, LLC, on behalf of
Counterpoint Press, counterpointpress.com.

Library of Congress Cataloging-in-Publication Data
Names: Osnos, Evan, 1976– author.
Title: Wildland : the making of America's fury / Evan Osnos.
Description: First edition. | New York : Farrar, Straus and Giroux, 2021. |
    Includes index.
Identifiers: LCCN 2021022114 | ISBN 9780374286675 (hardcover)
Subjects: LCSH: Osnos, Evan, 1976—Travel—United States. | United States—
    Description and travel. | United States—Civilization—21st century. |
    United States—Politics and government—21st century.
Classification: LCC E169.Z83 .O97 2021 | DDC 973.93—dc23
LC record available at https://lccn.loc.gov/2021022114

Designed by Gretchen Achilles

Our books may be purchased in bulk for promotional, educational,
or business use. Please contact your local bookseller or the Macmillan Corporate
and Premium Sales Department at 1-800-221-7945, extension 5442, or by email at
MacmillanSpecialMarkets@macmillan.com.

www.fsgbooks.com
www.twitter.com/fsgbooks • www.facebook.com/fsgbooks

1 3 5 7 9 10 8 6 4 2

For Oliver and Rose

We see the world piece by piece, as the sun, the moon, the animal, the tree; but the whole, of which these are shining parts, is the soul.

—RALPH WALDO EMERSON, "The Over-Soul," 1841

What followed then was what invariably follows in the wake of every tortured consciousness. From what it dreads or hates, yet knows or feels to be unescapable, it takes refuge in that which may be hoped for—or at least imagined.

—THEODORE DREISER, *An American Tragedy*, 1925

CONTENTS

WILDLAND

PROLOGUE

ON A HILLSIDE three hours north of San Francisco, a rancher waded through a meadow that rustled with golden grass. His name was Glenn Kile, and he lived in a sliver of the American West so blessed by nature that indigenous people called it Ba-lo Kai—the "verdant valley." But on this day, the terrain was merciless. The temperature was 103 degrees, and it had been in the triple digits for days. All of the hottest summers in California history had arrived in the past twenty years, and the fields of the verdant valley had acquired the bone-dry smell and snap of straw.

A hundred feet from his house, the rancher stopped at the sight of a small hole in the gray-black soil at his feet. It was the mouth of an underground wasps' nest. He lifted a steel hammer and pounded a rusty iron stake into the hole to seal it. But the clash of metal on metal spat out a spark, and the spark struck the field, and the field began to burn. At first, the rancher tried to kick dirt on the flames, but the heat of that wicked summer had rendered the soil as hard as stone. He tried to snuff out the fire with an old trampoline, but the fabric was consumed by the flames. He tried to coax water from a hose, but the rubber melted. And by the time Glenn Kile ran to his house and called the firefighters, history had slipped beyond his grasp. In half an hour, the inferno was twenty acres wide and racing toward a horizon of dried-out forests and scattered homes, a terrain that firefighters call "wildland"—a realm of nearly perfect tinder that is less a place than a condition.

The rancher's spark ignited the largest wildland fire in the history of California, a record that would soon be broken and then broken again. They named it the Mendocino Complex Fire, and it raged for a month—a jet engine of wind and flame, consuming an area more than twice the size of New York City, a landmark in the annals of a warming world. When, at last, the inferno was extinguished, the state of California ruled that the rancher Glenn Kile was not liable for the catastrophe. He had lit the spark, but the true roots of the disaster ran deeper. The fire was the culmination of forces that had been gathering for decades.

That story reminded me of an old line about politics, from a book by the Chinese revolutionary Mao Zedong. "A single spark," Mao wrote, "can start a prairie fire." Mao knew little of America, but he knew brutal truths about politics. Living in Washington in the years of Donald Trump, I often thought about that image of a landscape primed to burn. Sometimes it felt like metaphor, and sometimes it felt like fact. But eventually I came to understand it as something else—a parable for a time in American history when the land and the people seemed to be mirroring the rage of the other. I wanted to understand how that time had come to be, and what it would leave behind.

├─────┤

Americans are among the world's most restless people. In the 1950s, a fifth of the American population picked up and moved each year, in pursuit of a spouse or a job or a backyard in the suburbs. My own family followed that path. My father came to America in 1944 as a refugee; he had been born in India, to Jewish parents who were fleeing the Nazis' invasion of Poland. My mother was born in Morocco to American diplomats from Chicago. During the Vietnam War, my parents met in Saigon, where my mother worked in the office of a nonprofit group and my father was a newspaper reporter. When they returned to get married, the occasion had an American eclecticism about it—a Jew born in India, and a WASP born in Morocco, exchanging vows at a courthouse in Michigan.

I left the United States a little over a year after the terrorist attacks of September 11, 2001. The country was preparing to go to war in Iraq, and I reported from Baghdad, Cairo, and elsewhere in the Middle East. A few years later, I settled in Beijing, where I met Sarabeth Berman, from Massachusetts, who had gone abroad as a young producer of theater and dance. We married, and eventually prepared to go home. If we stayed abroad too long, Sarabeth said, we would find it hard to go back at all.

It was 2013, and we made plans to move to Washington. In our years abroad, we had witnessed the global response to Barack Obama's election—euphoric in some places, wary in others—but we knew less about what his victory meant to Americans. I had watched election returns on television, at an event in 2008, surrounded by curious Chinese spectators. The prospect of America's first Black president conveyed an infectious sense of potential, particularly for people who recalled that the United States had once barred them under the Chinese Exclusion Act. When Obama won, Wang Chong, a Chinese newspaper reporter standing near me, let out a quiet whoop of celebration. "Ethnic discrimination exists very deeply in Chinese minds," he said.

Coming home always holds the promise of a new way of seeing. In the 1940s, after covering the war in Europe, the author John Gunther returned to America. At times he felt like "the man from Mars," he wrote in *Inside U.S.A.*, published in 1947. In Gunther's case, some features of his home unnerved him; the segregation of the South "out-ghettoes anything I ever saw in a European ghetto, even in Warsaw," he wrote. But other encounters thrilled him. On his travels across the country, he took to asking people, "What do you believe in most?" He was told: work, children, Thomas Jefferson, God, the golden rule, the Pythagorean theorem, a high tariff, a low tariff, better agricultural prices, happiness, good roads, and Santa Claus. But the most frequent response was, as he put it, "the people, if you give them an even break."

Sarabeth and I landed at Dulles International Airport on July 7, 2013. At passport control, I picked up a brochure with the title "Welcome to the United States." It was published by the Bureau of Customs and Border Protection, and it had a cover photo of the Washington Monument and cherry trees in bloom. The brochure began, "We are glad that you decided to travel to the United States to visit, study, work, or stay."

For a few weeks, we stayed at my in-laws' house on a quiet street in the Washington suburbs. It was a stark change from an alleyway in Beijing, where traveling merchants shouted offers to sharpen your kitchen knives or tell your fortune or buy your hair for a wig factory.

On Craigslist, we found a row house to rent in Washington, and we savored the minor luxuries we had missed in China—potable tap water, clean air, a dishwasher. In the city's most prosperous quarters, it felt like everyone was jogging or power-walking. Washington's poorest streets, Wards 7 and 8, had levels of unemployment among the highest of any urban neighborhoods in America. They were just across the Anacostia River from Capitol Hill, but the distance was vast. In 2013, the average white family in Washington was eighty-one times richer than the average Black family. And the strains on life at the extremes were getting worse. By 2016, a child born in Washington, D.C., would have a life expectancy four years less than a child born in Beijing—seventy-eight years, compared with eighty-two.

⊢——⊣

I started keeping track of changes during my years away, including some tiny details. Walking by the window of Brooks Brothers, the suitmaker, I noticed that it was selling suits with flag pins pre-attached to the lapel. A corporate spokesman told me that it was intended to advertise suits made in America. The company had adopted the practice in 2007, when Republicans were lambasting Obama for not wearing a flag pin.

Other changes felt so vast that it was difficult to grasp their full dimensions. In 2013, the United States passed a threshold in the long evolution of immigration and diversity: for the first time in American history, the number of nonwhite newborns surpassed the number of white newborns. Initially, the gap was barely perceptible, no more than a thousand out of more than 3.8 million babies born that year. But it began to grow. As the son of a refugee, I considered it an exhilarating milestone, a mark of renewal, but I could see that many other Americans did not.

In the case of some changes, I was most startled by how thoroughly people had adapted to them. I was waiting for an Amtrak train one morning when a video screen in the station's boarding area started playing a public-service announcement. If someone started firing at us, the voice-over explained, we should "take flight" or "take cover." On the screen, an actor with white hair and a blue blazer huddled behind a pillar. As a last resort, it said, take action: "Yell, and look for surrounding objects, including your belongings, to throw and use as improvised weapons."

Mass shootings were happening, on average, every nine weeks—nearly three times as often as a decade earlier. Barely six months had passed since the most heart-wrenching: a twenty-year-old in Newtown, Connecticut, had killed twenty children and six educators at Sandy Hook Elementary School. But in American politics, that event had already faded. Politicians had offered "thoughts and prayers," but an effort to pass new gun-control measures had failed in Congress. When I glanced around the waiting area, people were absorbed in other things. I felt like Gunther's man from Mars.

The country had responded in very different fashion to the trauma of September 11, 2001. When Al Qaeda destroyed the towers of the World Trade Center, the historian Tony Judt wrote: "From my window in lower Manhattan, I watched the twenty-first century begin." Twelve years later, the event had acquired a unique symbolic power. In the years since, Americans had been attacked more than twice as many times by far-right terrorists as they had by Islamic terrorists, yet when researchers in 2016 asked people to estimate the share of Muslims in the country, Americans, on average, estimated one in six. The real number was one in a hundred.

Since 2001, the country had been at war in Afghanistan, Iraq, and elsewhere longer than in any stretch in our history. Those who did the fighting represented less than 0.5 percent of the U.S. population. For most Americans, the wars had little impact on life. The closest many Americans came to the wars was a genre of video, featured as a light moment at the end of local news broadcasts, depicting parents in the armed forces tiptoeing into classrooms to surprise their children. The videos became so abundant that they filled a dedicated channel on YouTube, called "ComingHomeTV." When I searched for them online, Google automatically suggested a range of subcategories:

soldiers reunited with their families
soldiers reunited with wife
soldiers reunited with their dogs
soldiers coming home try not to cry

———

I began to notice how far fear was reaching into our political life. Before going abroad, I had lived in Clarksburg, West Virginia, a small Appalachian city where I worked at the local paper, *The Exponent Telegram*. The day after September 11, the editors had published a humble declaration of commitment to a story Americans tell ourselves: "Far be it for a small-town daily newspaper to suggest what the government's reaction should be," they wrote, but one thing must be clear: "We are a free society, which prides itself on its diversity, its exchange of ideas and its willingness to tolerate dissent"; the attacks must "strengthen our ideals rather than shatter them." That month, after someone desecrated a mosque in the West Virginia city of Princeton—the vandals drew the picture of a lynching and the name "Jamaal"—neighbors rallied in the mosque's defense, and the response became a point of local pride.

But by 2008, a poll showed that one fifth of the public in West Virginia believed that Obama was a Muslim, and hate crimes, which had subsided after 2001, were climbing, according to the FBI. In 2013, someone vandalized the mosque again, but the local reaction was quieter that time. Churches condemned the assault, but the sheriff said the incident did not meet the threshold of a hate crime. Muslims who had lived in West Virginia for generations described growing sense of isolation. In 2015, Hazem Ashraf, a doctor, told an interviewer, "Your loyalty is being called out, your worth and value as a person is being called out, that somehow you're less of an American, less of a citizen, for something you have not done." He invoked Woody Guthrie's lyrics: "This land is my land, this land is your land." (Four years later, during a Republican Party rally in the West Virginia Capitol, someone hung a poster of the burning World Trade Center and a photo of Representative Ilhan Omar of Minnesota, one of the first Muslim women in Congress. The caption read, "I am the proof you have forgotten.")

Those fissures in American life were part of a larger fracturing. The United States had the largest economy in the world, with median incomes higher than they had ever been, but the living standards for millions of people had stagnated or declined. Twenty-seven states were so short of cash to fix potholes that they were returning some of their paved roads to dirt. At the same time, three men—Bill Gates, Warren Buffett, and Jeff Bezos—had more wealth than the entire bottom half of the U.S. population combined. Every hour, Bezos earned $149,353—which was more than the typical American worker earned in three years.

When scientists reported the startling fact that life expectancy was declining, it sounded like a national problem. But it was not. In West Virginia's McDowell County, male life expectancy had sunk to sixty-four—a level on a par with Iraq. In neighboring Virginia, men in Fairfax County could expect to live eighteen years longer. The chasms between American lives had become so vast that the vanishing common ground could no longer carry the weight of American institutions, a prospect that the late Supreme Court justice Louis Brandeis warned against when he told a friend, "We may have democracy, or we may have wealth concentrated in the hands of a few, but we can't have both."

America wasn't just losing a story of itself; it was losing a habit of mind, a capacity to envisage a common good, to believe in what Martin Luther King Jr. once called the "single garment of destiny." He wrote, "Whatever affects one directly, affects all indirectly." Eighty years after Franklin Roosevelt decried the temptation of "fear itself," Americans did not deny their fears; they announced them and acted on them. Crime was at historic lows, and yet the number of Americans who obtained permits to carry concealed guns had nearly tripled in two decades, to 13 million people—more than twelve times the number of police officers in America. Long after Obama apologized for saying that small-town voters "cling to guns or religion," those words were no longer received as an insult. Gun shows sold T-shirts with the slogan "Proud Bitter Clinger."

├─────┤

I settled into an office in Dupont Circle, with a view of the soaring dome of St. Matthew's Cathedral, the seat of Roman Catholicism in Washington. I recognized the church from famous photos of John F. Kennedy's funeral in 1963—Jacqueline Kennedy bending down to whisper in the ear of her three-year-old son, who saluted his father's casket. A few years before that moment, the church had held a funeral for a very different figure: the demagogic senator Joseph McCarthy, the maestro of fear and suspicion. From my window, I watched the church pass through the seasons, washed in sunlight and draped in snow, and I thought of those two funerals as a reminder of the full spectrum of Washington's potential to lift Americans up or tear them apart.

When I had moved abroad in 2003, CNN and the Fox News Channel had been competitors with comparable levels of prime-time viewership. Eleven years later, Fox had veered away from its rival; it had triple the ratings each night, and it had helped usher in a new vocabulary of politics, especially around immigration, security, race, and the role of the federal government. On my earliest day back at work in America,

October 1, the government shut down for the first time in seventeen years. Strictly speaking, it shut down because Republican members of Congress were seeking to rescind President Obama's expansion of public health-care benefits, but the real point of the shutdown was to discredit Obama's signature legislation, rally the faithful, and raise money for upcoming campaigns. It was an act of official ideological resistance unlike anything since the 1960s, when segregationist Democrats had rejected the legitimacy of decisions by the federal courts and Congress.

I called the White House switchboard and was greeted by a recording: "You have reached the Executive Office of the president. We apologize, but due to the lapse in federal funding, we are unable to take your call." Across the country, 800,000 federal employees were ordered to stay home. Four hundred national parks were closed. Preschools for low-income children had no funding; Americans could not apply for new Medicare or Social Security benefits, or get a new small-business loan. With nothing else to do, I wandered over to Capitol Hill, where the building was shuttered. The museums were closed, and tourists milled about under a warm autumn sun, photographing reporters doing stand-ups on the lawn. I met a retired couple from Finland, Timo Engblom and his wife, Marita. They were trying to make sense of America's peculiar bout of self-punishment. "When we go to our hotel, we open the TV and it was speech after speech after speech," Marita said. Timo said the whole affair left them baffled. "What does it mean, 'government shutdown'? Does this lead to a new election?" he asked.

Not in our system, I said. We just have to let it work itself out.

After sixteen days, Republicans relented, and the government reopened. The shutdown had cost American taxpayers an estimated $24 billion in lost economic activity, enough money to send a rover to Mars and back—eight times. The only clear beneficiary was the senator behind the idea: Ted Cruz, of Texas. His favorability soared among Tea Party Republicans, from 47 percent to 74 percent. His popularity inspired a children's coloring book—*U.S. Senator Ted Cruz to the Future*—which became the most popular coloring book on Amazon for five months.

Even after Congress resumed, it remained almost entirely paralyzed because many elected Republicans in Washington held that their job of running the government was, at bottom, in conflict with freedom. What had begun as a belief in low taxes and limited government had hardened, under the pressures of profit and political opportunity, into a fundamental disdain of federal power. John Boehner, Speaker of the House, said that lawmakers should not be judged by "how many new laws we create" but, rather, by "how many laws we repeal."

The shutdown struck me as a sign of a deep rupture rising toward the surface of American politics. Day by day, Washington had less and less in common with the country it represented. Congress was 82 percent men, 83 percent white, and 50 percent millionaires. The country was not. When I traveled outside Washington, people reflexively dismissed the words of politicians as self-serving or corrupt. In 1964, 77 percent of Americans had said they generally trusted the government; by 2014, that figure had collapsed, to 18 percent. The terrain of American politics was primed for a wildland fire. Somebody was going to strike a spark.

From the moment Donald J. Trump announced his run for president, he was a symptom of American distress as much as any cause of it. He won by nationalizing politics as much as possible, torquing the most explosive issues into existential showdowns that could unite his supporters across vast distances. Though they rejoiced in his contempt for the norms and culture of politics, many more Americans were appalled by him; they grieved for a nation that seemed to have come unmoored from some of its deepest commitments and was drifting broadside to the judgments of history. The tensions ultimately ignited in 2020, when the coronavirus pandemic visited wildly divergent effects across lines of race, class, and ideology, and the killing of George Floyd beneath a policeman's knee summoned a full-scale confrontation with the disposition of American power. By year's end, politics was succumbing to violence, and Americans were asking if they had lost so much collective faith in the mechanics of democracy that they might never recover it.

The Trump years brought an end to silences; Americans were no longer satisfied by narrow critiques of Wall Street or trade or elite institutions; they expanded their aperture of attack to encompass the full architecture of power—class, race, gender, education—and set out to remake America's social contract in ways that had been impossible a few years earlier. If American history is a story of constant rebalancing—between greed and generosity, industry and nature, identity and assimilation—then the country had spun so far out of balance that it had lost its center of gravity.

———|

This book is the story of a crucible, a period bounded by two assaults on the country's sense of itself: the attack on New York and Washington, on September 11, 2001, and the attack on the U.S. Capitol, on January 6, 2021. It is a period in which Americans lost their vision for the common good, the capacity to see the union as larger than the sum of its parts. A century and a half after the Civil War, America was again a cloven nation. Its stability was foundering on fundamental tensions over the balance between individual freedom and the protection of others, over the reckoning with injustice, and over a basic test of any political society: Whose life matters?

In this narrative, I attempt to tie together the disparate experiences of being American, to determine how the course of lives intersected in ways we often overlooked in the disorienting rush of those twenty years. I focus, most of all, on the connections—often subterranean—that give us a more integrated understanding of our present. I returned to three places I know—three places I've lived, in different parts of the country. Too often, political reporters parachute into unfamiliar territory and interview a few dozen strangers. I've done it many times. But this moment demanded a deeper kind of questioning. I hoped to find some explanations that were larger than the immediate events suggested—in linkages across geography and generations, and in some of the underlying attitudes that people are not quick to tell a stranger.

I returned to Clarksburg, West Virginia, to take stock of what was gained and what was lost when some of America's wealthiest people tapped the natural resources beneath the homes of some of America's poorest people. I returned to Chicago, where my family took root, to understand the compounded effects of American segregation on health, wealth, and the prospect of individual redemption. And I returned to Greenwich, Connecticut, where I grew up and went to school, to learn how a gospel of economic liberty had altered beliefs among leaders of American capitalism and made anything possible, for the right price.

This account is based on thousands of hours of conversation over seven years, from 2014 to 2021. I met some people in the course of my work for *The New Yorker*; I have known others since I was a child. We spoke mostly about their lives, our towns, and the choices they made and the choices that were made beyond their control. We spent far less time talking about the politics on the front page than about the underlying questions that tied these divergent lives together: How did they explain the triumphs and the catastrophes in their lives? Who was responsible, and what were the costs of that responsibility? Who told them the truth, and who lied? What did they expect from their government—and what did they get? How safe did they feel—in their bodies, their homes, their neighborhoods? What, ultimately, did we owe one another as citizens of a political commons?

Every country hands down the stories people tell themselves about will and fate, freedom and belonging. But in the United States, the matter carries an extra burden because our defining myth rests on the prospect of wrestling destiny into submission, the aspiration that all children can rise to the top through work and talent, no matter their background. "France was a land, England was a people, but America," F. Scott Fitzgerald wrote in 1929, is "a willingness of the heart."

In this book, I ask of my own country some of the questions I once asked of China—about the meanings of success, freedom, security, and opportunity, and about our oscillations between dignity and cruelty, tolerance and fear. For all the roiling of daily politics, I was more interested in the sources of the moment we inhabited. In *Ramp Hollow*, Steven Stoll's history of Appalachia, he writes, "Seeing the world without the past would be like visiting a city after a devastating hurricane and declaring that the people there have always lived in ruins." When I started on this research, I thought the most important story was understanding the sources of disconnection between Americans. By the end,

I came to believe that the larger problem was the range of ways, sometimes deliberate and sometimes unintended, that Americans affected one another every day without fully realizing it.

On the road, I often carried John Gunther's book *Inside U.S.A.* I liked to remind myself of what he observed in America at the end of World War II. On the final page, he recorded his faith in America's talent for "the rational approach, reason, the meeting of minds in honorable agreement after open argument." At its core, my project was an attempt to understand how we had lost that talent and how we might recover it.

I spent a decade in parts of the world where people tend to be skeptical about American promises and values, and I often found myself making a case for the United States, urging citizens of Egypt, Iraq, or China to believe that, for all of America's failings, it aspires to some basic moral commitments, including the rule of law, the force of truth, and the right to pursue a better life. When I returned to the United States, I began to wonder if I had been lying all those years to people around the world—and to myself.

The failure of that mythology became spectacularly vivid in Washington. But the deeper origins and effects lay far away, in real lives of intricate drama, in which the events of the capital intrude only occasionally, like flames licking up on the horizon.

ONE

THE GOLDEN TRIANGLE

WHEN HE WAS JUST A KID on the clammy coast of Florida, Joseph Skowron III received a preppy nickname: Chip. His parents liked to say he was a chip off the old block, but they all knew it wasn't true. His father was a franchisee for Long John Silver's, and Chip loved him, but he didn't intend to join the fast-food business.

Chip's grandparents had arrived from Poland in the early twentieth century and settled near the cotton mills of Fall River, Massachusetts, below the elbow of the commonwealth that juts into the Atlantic. Chip's father, Joe Skowron, grew up in an unhappy house; his parents were consumed by alcohol and depression. Even after Joe had children of his own, he kept his emotions obscure. When Chip pressed his father for stories, Joe would say, "You can ask about it when I die."

Joe Skowron finished high school in the mid-1950s, which was fortunate timing; Massachusetts was expanding its state colleges, and he escaped a fraying industrial town to study engineering at Southeastern Massachusetts Technical Institute. Afterward, he was hired by Boeing and sent to a stretch of marshland on Florida's Atlantic coast that was being developed for NASA into Cape Canaveral. He met another recent arrival, Janet Nutter, born to a Scots-Irish clan in Swandale, West Virginia, a company town run by the Elk River Coal and Lumber Co. Janet had married young and divorced young, and set out to reinvent herself in Florida. She found work as a schoolteacher in the heady stretch of the coast that people called the "space towns." Janet and Joe married in 1966 and settled in a neighborhood where kids at the bus stop could watch rockets climb into the lapis sky.

Joe worked as a supervisor on Cold War rocket projects, but by the mid-1970s, he was chafing at the hierarchy and his promotions had slowed. He left the space program for the restaurant business. Also, it was becoming clear how much he and his wife were opposites: he was curt and aloof; she was warm and intense. She traveled and read philosophy, and, in her late forties, embarked on a doctorate in psychology. The couple sometimes fought bitterly in front of their children, but among outsiders, they were adept at avoiding any signs of distress. If the doorbell rang in the middle of one of their battles, Chip's parents would paint on smiles and usher in the guests. Chip took it as a lesson: "That's what we do. We show this to the world, but it's not the whole truth."

Janet doted on Chip. She told him he was unusually bright, and she invoked John F. Kennedy's belief, adapted from Luke 12:48: "To whom much is given, much is required." School was easy for him, and his attention wandered. At twelve, he started smoking pot. At fifteen, he snorted cocaine; at sixteen, before tennis practice, he smoked crack. But his grades never slipped, and his parents let him roam. "As long as you're getting straight A's, you can do what you want," his father told him. Chip graduated second in his class.

He settled on an idea for the future: he wanted to be a doctor. In the social hierarchy of 1980s suburban Florida, doctors were local royalty. They had education, wealth, and respect. "I wanted to be *that*. I wanted to be important. I wanted to be helpful," he said. He enrolled at Vanderbilt University in Nashville, joined a fraternity, and studied math and chemistry. He planned to combine the work of a physician and a scientist, and he applied to a prestigious program at Yale for a joint MD-PhD. For six students a year, it provided a full scholarship.

In late 1990, he learned that he had been accepted. He called his parents in Florida and left a message on the answering machine. His father called back, but he sounded shaken. "Mom has been killed in a car accident," he said. She had been on her way to dinner that evening when she was broadsided by a pickup truck. She died at the hospital. Her family brought Janet's remains back to West Virginia and buried her on the family farm.

⊢——⊣

After the funeral, Chip Skowron returned to college in a fog. Over the next semester, he prepared for medical school and largely avoided grieving.

Yale was absorbing, and one night, a few years in, he was at a bar in Connecticut when he met a young writer named Cheryl Birdsall. She had been an elite gymnast in Southern California and come east after college to find work in advertising. They married in 1996, and two years later, he finished his degrees in medicine and cell biology. He went on to a medical residency in orthopedic surgery at Harvard. On the side, he volunteered with AmeriCares, a disaster relief agency, for international medical missions. During a trip to Kosovo, he removed a tumor from a six-year-old boy that spared him the amputation of his leg. The medical-relief trips provided the combination of service and stature that he had always wanted. Skowron carried a picture of the boy in his briefcase.

But by 2001, two years before the end of his residency, Skowron realized he was losing interest in the practice of medicine. He resented the long hours, the paperwork, and the cost of insurance. Besides, he and Cheryl were quarreling. They had a baby girl, but Skowron's job left him little time to see her. For a person of his ambition, medicine had begun to feel rigid and confining. When he thought of the future, he imagined he might rise to lead a surgical department or, eventually, a hospital; he might even make a run at surgeon general. But none of those options thrilled him anymore.

When he told colleagues at Harvard that he was thinking of leaving, they were appalled; he would squander his training and his future. Still, he started looking for jobs at consulting firms and medical-device manufacturers. Then a friend who worked in finance suggested Wall Street. In the early years of this century, money-management firms were expanding their hiring of doctors, who could help them assess investments in the lucrative health-care industry. Skowron might be especially valuable at a hedge fund, a type of firm that was still obscure to most Americans but was transforming the culture of American finance.

In small numbers, hedge funds had been around since the 1940s, when the investor A. W. Jones came up with the idea of maximizing returns by "hedging" against swings in the market—betting not only on which prices would rise but also on which would fall. Unlike mutual funds, which, by law, could trade only stocks and bonds within narrow limits to avoid the risk of catastrophic losses, hedge funds could bet big. The Securities and Exchange Commission treated them like powerful chemicals—permitted, but kept away from unsuspecting users. Hedge funds could trade almost anything—derivatives, currencies, even the air rights above buildings—as long as they took money from officially "accredited investors," the individuals and institutions with enough resources that they could afford to lose some of them—in other words, the wealthy. For that reason, the broader public knew almost nothing about hedge funds until the turn of the millennium, when it became increasingly obvious that fund managers were earning more money than almost anyone else in America. In 2004, *Institutional Investor* reported that the top twenty-five hedge-fund managers had earned an average of $207 million the previous year. The editors wrote: "Never have so few made so much so fast."

Skowron knew nothing about Wall Street. He had never read a balance sheet or an income statement. But the idea intrigued him and he went to a bookstore to learn more. He bought a how-to guide, titled *Getting Started in Hedge Funds*, by Daniel A. Strachman. The author, a vice president at a money-management firm, offered his encouragement: "The most important character traits needed are an ego, an entrepreneurial spirit, and guts. A track record also helps, but in some cases experience is frowned upon."

The book introduced Skowron to the elementary vocabulary of finance—bull markets, derivatives, standard deviations—and it explained the generous formula by which hedge funds made so much money: they kept 2 percent of every dollar they managed for investors, as well as 20 percent of the profits. (Some funds kept more.) "If managers show up to work and perform," Strachman wrote, "the revenue they can earn from their funds is nearly endless." The book closed with a libertarian flourish that captured the zeitgeist of the hedge-fund world. Politicians and regulators, Strachman observed, "have very little knowledge of money and markets." Addressing them directly, he said, "Keep out of the business and let the chips fall where they may."

The new generation of financiers Skowron set out to join was no longer physically tied to Wall Street. The Internet allowed traders to work from anywhere, and many of them departed lower Manhattan to avoid city income taxes and to work close to their families, in New Jersey, the Hamptons, or southern New England. Before long, ten of the top twenty-five hedge-fund managers settled or worked in a single town: Greenwich, Connecticut.

One of them was Steven A. Cohen, a billionaire who ran a firm named for his initials—S.A.C. Capital Advisors. Through a friend, Skowron got an interview with S.A.C., and when he arrived, he discovered that another friend, who had given up neurosurgery and joined the firm, could vouch for him. In a salary discussion, S.A.C. Capital executives asked Skowron what he was making at Harvard as a surgical resident. Fifty thousand dollars a year, he said. They'd quadruple it— and if he did well, they would throw in a bonus to make it an even larger multiple.

After the meeting, Skowron called his wife, who was at home caring for their two-year-old in West Newton, Massachusetts, and seven months pregnant. "These guys just made me an offer. It's crazy. We've got to move," he said. They considered the Upper East Side of Manhattan, but settled instead on Greenwich. The newspapers had taken to calling it "The Hedge Fund Capital of the World."

├────┤

In the history of money in America, the town of Greenwich has played a recurring role that is older than the republic. The southern panhandle of Connecticut is cradled between the gray-blue waters of Long

Island Sound and the wooded border of New York State. In the summer of 1640, English colonists, sailing south from the Massachusetts Bay Colony, came ashore at a stretch of fertile coastline that local Native Americans called Monakewaygo—"shining sands." It had open pastures, cranberry meadows, and rocky forests that sheltered bear, wolf, and beaver.

In politics and in culture, Greenwich became a mash-up of New England and New York, a place settled by Puritans who agonized over what the historian Missy Wolfe calls "the proper balance between their flock's economic success and the level of success that they deemed would offend God." The Puritans believed in what Ralph Waldo Emerson later described as a "commanding sense of right and wrong," an austere determination to put morality at the center of their politics. But, long after the Puritans were gone, the tension remained in a seesawing battle between the Brahmin and the buccaneer, service and profit, restraint and greed.

For a time, the Brahmin had the advantage. Greenwich made its earliest fortunes from the land and sea: farms shipped produce to New York City, fishermen gathered oysters, and local quarries yielded granite that furnished the footings of the Brooklyn Bridge. But in 1848, the railroad reached Greenwich; instead of a full day by horse, the trip to the city by train was one hour. A developer's brochure pitched the town to "tired mortals of the busy metropolis" seeking "health, happiness, and comfort, not to mention wealth." They built Gilded Age mansions that rivaled the Old World châteaux and palazzi, including replicas of the Petit Trianon at Versailles and Warwick Castle in England.

Many of the new arrivals worked on Wall Street, home to America's fledgling financial industry, which had taken root in the early nineteenth century to collect savings and funnel them to productive entrepreneurs and investments. In 1908, after scientists realized that epidemics were spreading in part through communal tin cups at water fountains, a Greenwich investor named William T. Graham financed the creation of a disposable paper container—called the Dixie Cup—which earned him a fortune and helped save lives. Another new resident, Zalmon G. Simmons II, was the Henry Ford of sleep, having popularized the mass production of mattresses.

Others in town became known for a progressive approach to business. In 1927, Owen D. Young, a Greenwich resident who was an early chairman of General Electric, gave a speech at Harvard Business School in which he scolded businessmen who "devise ways and means to squeeze out of labor its last ounce of effort and last penny of compensation." He encouraged them instead to "think in terms of human beings—one group of human beings who put their capital in, and another group who put their lives and labor in a common enterprise for mutual advantage." Rick Wartzman, a longtime head of the Drucker Institute and a historian of corporate behavior, told me, "This really was beyond rhetoric. We were much more of a 'we' culture than an 'I' culture." On Young's watch, GE became one of the first American companies to give workers a pension, profit-sharing, life insurance, loans, and housing assistance. In 1939, when Young turned sixty-five, he retired and moved back to his native farming village, Van Hornesville, New York—population 125. His friend and ally Franklin D. Roosevelt, the governor of New York, hailed him as a "necessary factor in almost every forward step of the nation."

Greenwich was also home to a number of progressive journalists and novelists, including Lincoln Steffens, Anya Seton, and Munro Leaf. But it was most popular with executives—at General Electric, Texaco, U.S. Tobacco—fleeing high income taxes in New York. Other residents served as their investment bankers, a cohort that was, by today's standards, almost unrecognizably buttoned-down. By and large, local Republicans had come to accept the expansion of government under Franklin D. Roosevelt and were concerned mainly with avoiding excesses and insolvency.

In the years after the Gilded Age, showing off your money had become déclassé. At Morgan Stanley, executives competed to see who could wear the cheapest watch. "Some of the wealthiest people went around dressed like gardeners," a friend of mine who grew up in the nearby town of Darien recalled. The Greenwich coat of arms declared a prim Yankee ethic: *fortitudine et frugalitate*—courage and thrift.

|—————|

My great-grandparents Albert and Linda Sherer moved to Greenwich from Chicago in 1937. Albert was a Republican who worked in advertising for the National Biscuit Company, and Linda raised their two children. They rented until 1968, when they bought a white Colonial with a wide lawn on Round Hill Road, named for the highlands of northwest Greenwich. During the Revolutionary War, the Continental Army had used Round Hill as a lookout, because it had a sweeping view over orchards and meadows to the distant waters of Long Island Sound. The house passed down through the generations, and when I was nine years old, my parents moved my sister and me from Brooklyn to Greenwich, into a world of uncountable advantages. It was safe and overflowing with opportunity. There were public beaches, well-tended parks, and a well-stocked library. In 1994, I graduated from Greenwich High School, which is the rare public school that has a championship water-polo team and an electron microscope. (The microscope was a donation, obtained by an award-winning science teacher.)

People around town have never much cared for caricatures of the place—the starchy patricians, the chinless wonders, the history of exclusion—even when there is truth in them. For decades, many African Americans and Jews were prevented from buying homes. Bigotry, in the words of Timothy Dumas, an author and journalist who grew up in Greenwich, "ulcerated deep in the town's boggy soul and now and then oozed up like a gas bubble." In 1953, when Jackie Robinson was a star for the Brooklyn Dodgers, he and his wife, Rachel, tried to buy a house in Greenwich, but the owner refused to let them see it. In 1961, a Greenwich real-estate agent wrote a memo to colleagues, later unearthed in a lawsuit; if a customer's name, she wrote, "appears to be Jewish, do not meet them anywhere!" In 1975, protesters came to town with signs reading "Cocktail Bigots" and "Share the Summer," because Greenwich barred nonresidents from the local beach—a restriction that lasted until the state Supreme Court overturned it in 2001.

Among the privileges of living in Greenwich was the right to poke fun at it. In 1986, Jane Condon, an author and comedian raised in the hardscrabble city of Brockton, Massachusetts, moved to town with her husband, who worked in banking. Condon told some jokes at a charity fundraiser in Christ Church, a center of high-WASP culture in town. "After the show, this very patrician man came up to me and said, 'You're so funny. I almost laughed out loud,'" she told me. "People in Greenwich are more smilers than big laughers." She wrote some material about the local politics, too, such as "I had a Clinton bumper sticker. People were throwing martinis at my car." ("Those jokes worked better out of town," Condon said.)

As years passed, nobody pretended that barriers had disappeared, but the town became more diverse. In the 1990s, it was nearly 20 percent Asian, Hispanic, and African American. Beyond the old estates, there was a middle class of shop owners, tradespeople, and educators. Bob and Carol Lichtenfeld, both teachers, moved to town in 1976 from a one-room apartment in Yonkers. In Greenwich, they rented a house for $250 a month and eventually built a four-bedroom house. "As middle-income people, you could buy a piece of property and build a house in Greenwich," Bob recalled. "It was a stretch for us, but we were able to do it. What is more middle-class than two teachers?"

In many cases, it was difficult to tell, at a glance, whether a neighbor was a teacher or an executive. One of America's most powerful capitalists, Reginald Jones, who became GE's chairman and CEO in 1972, lived in a brick Colonial in Greenwich. His daughter, Grace Vineyard, told me, "He asked my mom, 'Do you want anything more?' And she said, 'Why would we want anything more?'" Jones took an imperious view of neighbors whose fortunes came not from employing people and making things, but from financial engineering. "He'd ask, 'Are they *creating* anything?'" Vineyard recalled. "That just bothered him that they were sopping money from the economy that wasn't generating anything new."

Leo Hindery worked for Jones as a junior executive. "I earned fifteen thousand, six hundred dollars when I got out of Stanford, and Reg's salary was two hundred thousand dollars," Hindery said. "GE was the preeminent company in America, and the CEO was making twelve or thirteen times what I did." According to the Economic Policy Institute, that ratio wasn't unusual: In 1965, the CEO of an average large public company earned about 20 times as much as a frontline worker. By 2019, that figure was 278 times as much.

———

In June 2001, Chip Skowron drove south from Boston to go "build my empire," as he put it, half-jokingly. Cheryl stayed behind, with their two children, to sell the house, pack, and move.

When Skowron arrived on his first day at work, most of what he knew about his job came from the book *Getting Started in Hedge Funds*. He discovered it was wise to say as little as possible. He also learned quickly that, for all the generous compensation, his job would be in constant peril. "If you don't perform, you're gone," he said. "It's over. There's no 'Great effort. Nice try.' It's all about performance. That's all that matters."

The Skowrons bought their first home: a 1950s ranch-style house in need of renovation, on a winding road through the woods. Greenwich was in the throes of a transformation. Many of the new estates were no longer surrounded by the simple stone walls, stacked to the height of a farmer's hip, that crossed the New England landscape. Instead, the builders introduced more imposing barriers: tall, stately walls of chiseled stone, mortared in place.

The fashion for higher walls had little to do with safety; Greenwich had one of the lowest crime rates in America. To Frank Farricker, who served on the town's planning-and-zoning commission, they symbolized power and seclusion. "Instead of building two or three feet high, people got into six-footers—the 'Fuck you' walls," he said. Nearby municipalities treated the trend like an invasive species; they rewrote zoning rules to prevent the spread of what stonemasons took to calling "Greenwich walls."

The walls were products of one of the most extraordinary accumulations of wealth in American history. In much of the country, the corporate convulsions of the seventies had entailed layoffs, offshoring, and declining union power, but on Wall Street they inspired a surge of creativity. In the last two decades of the twentieth century, financiers and economists had opened vast new realms of speculation and financial engineering—aggressive methods to bet on securities, merge businesses, and cut expenses using bankruptcy laws and other techniques. U.S. stock markets grew twelvefold, and most of the gains accrued to the wealthiest Americans. By 2017, Wall Streeters were taking home 23 percent of the country's corporate profits—and many of them lived in Connecticut.

The dealmakers earned vastly more than the early industrial executives. In Greenwich, the highest-earning hedge-fund manager, Edward Lampert, took home an estimated $1.02 billion in 2004 after orchestrating the merger of Kmart and Sears. Lampert was not one to dress like a gardener. Just offshore, he docked his yacht, a 288-foot vessel that he had named *Fountainhead*, for Ayn Rand's novel about triumphant individualism. (The book's hero, Howard Roark, is a designer of skyscrapers who declares, "I do not recognize anyone's right to one minute of my life . . . No matter who makes the claim, how large their number, or how great their need.")

Lampert was followed by Paul Tudor Jones II, a former cotton trader who had predicted the stock market crash of 1987 and become the highest-paid person on Wall Street. Jones bought the mansion originally built by the Dixie Cup investor William T. Graham. He replaced it with a manor house reminiscent of Monticello, with a twenty-five-car garage. So much individual wealth accumulated in southern Connecticut that tax officials took to monitoring the quarterly payments of a half dozen of the richest taxpayers, because their personal earnings would affect how much the entire state was able to spend on public services.

Around town, Morgan Stanley executives no longer competed to wear the cheapest wristwatch. (The current chairman and CEO, James Gorman, is celebrated on watch-enthusiast blogs for a rare Rolex that can sell for $17,000.) Reginald Jones's successor at GE, Jack Welch, finished his career with a record severance package of more than $400 million. One of Jones's friends, the investor Vincent Mai, was dismayed that many business leaders put short-term interests ahead of long-term vision. "The culture changed into grabbing as much as you can, as quickly as you can," Mai, the founder and chairman of the Cranemere Group, told me. "Restraint just seems to have gone out the window." The vice chairman of a Wall Street bank told a consultant in Greenwich, "Do you know what I did over the last month? I gave out eight billion dollars' worth of bonuses—and not one person in this firm is happy."

The money physically redrew parts of town. On Greenwich Avenue, the main shopping strip in town, Woolworth's was replaced by Saks Fifth Avenue. The Favorite Shoe Store gave way to Lilly Pulitzer. Other storefronts were taken over by Ralph Lauren and Hermès. Financiers built estates on a scale once favored by Gilded Age railroad barons. Steve Cohen, Skowron's boss, paid $14.8 million in cash for a house, then added an ice rink, an indoor basketball court, putting greens, a fairway, and a massage room, ultimately swelling the building to 36,000 square feet—larger than the Taj Mahal. In a final flourish, Cohen obtained special permission to surround his estate with a wall that exceeded the town's limits on height. It was nine feet tall.

⊢——⊣

After less than a year of working for Cohen, Skowron got poached by another well-known hedge fund—Millennium Management, run by Izzy Englander—but soon he was designing a fund of his own.

He had reached the hedge-fund world at an unusually fortuitous time. Until recently, Wall Street had revolved mostly around the first wave of Internet companies and the investment banks that profited by taking them public. The Nasdaq Composite index, which centered on technology stocks, quintupled between 1995 and 2000. But the dot-com bubble burst in the spring of 2000, and after September 11, 2001, the Federal Reserve slashed interest rates, which reduced the yields that investors could expect from bonds. Large investors—pension funds, endowments, sovereign wealth funds—needed new ways to get high returns, while hedging against downturns in traditional stock and bond funds. Many of them turned their focus to "alternative investments" such as private equity and hedge funds.

In 2003, more than $72 billion flowed into hedge funds—more than quadruple the level of the previous year. Ambitious financiers didn't need the vast resources of an investment bank to go out on their own; funds were sprouting up with no more than a computer and a desk, a model that Philip Duff, a Greenwich investor, called "three guys with a Bloomberg in a garage."

Duff had a plan to capitalize on the boom, and Skowron became a part of it. In a sleek black-glass complex in downtown Greenwich, Duff was starting a company called FrontPoint Partners, which would serve as an umbrella for small, ambitious hedge funds. At that point, Skowron's idea was almost literally three guys in a garage. He and two former colleagues had agreed to be partners in a health-care fund. In March 2003, they added their fund to FrontPoint, which was rising fast; its founders, then managing $2.9 billion, hoped to expand to managing $25 billion by 2007.

Worldwide, hedge funds controlled $1.2 trillion—and one tenth of it was in Greenwich. "All of the sudden, you blinked and went, 'Wait a minute. Everybody's a hedge fund now,'" David Rafferty, a columnist at *Greenwich Time*, the town's daily newspaper, recalled. Within five years, they took over two thirds of the local commercial real estate. There were so few office buildings in town that prices rose to $80 a square foot, double the rate in midtown Manhattan. Hedge funds unable to find real estate simply added Greenwich to their names. "Old Greenwich Capital Partners" was, in fact, based on Park Avenue in Manhattan.

The sudden surge of wealth rippled through the community. The Reverend William Evertsberg had moved from Grand Rapids, Michigan, in 1997, to become the minister of First Presbyterian Church in Greenwich. "The biggest difference was the monoculture. I don't mean race. I mean professional experience," he told me. "I've never worked in a place where the local culture is so dominated by one industry. Almost literally, every breadwinner in my congregation worked on Wall Street. Money was on the tip of everyone's tongue all the time."

Those fortunes were buoyed by pivotal changes in the laws around finance. Since the 1970s, Wall Street had lobbied politicians to scale back regulations that constrained the ability to take larger risks; in 1999, President Clinton repealed provisions in the Glass-Steagall Act, which separated commercial and investment banks; in 2000, he agreed to a ban on the regulation of over-the-counter derivatives. The ban was engineered by Senator Phil Gramm, a Texas Republican, whose largest contributors included banks led by Greenwich residents. (John Reed was a cochairman of Citigroup; William B. Harrison Jr. was the chief executive of JPMorgan Chase.)

But the movement to deregulate Wall Street eventually contributed to a catastrophe. When interest rates sank after September 11, housing prices soared, and banks saw opportunities to delve deeper into the world of mortgages, bonds, and derivatives. In late 2007, housing prices peaked, and the world tipped into a financial crisis. Over the next three years, the Great Recession cost American households more than $19 trillion in wealth, from the value of their retirement savings and homes and other assets. By the end of the recession in 2010, at least 46 million people were in poverty, the highest number since the Census Bureau started estimating it in 1959. The official government autopsy on the fiasco concluded that the ban on regulating derivatives was "a key turning point in the march toward the financial crisis," because "derivatives rapidly spiraled out of control and out of sight."

In Greenwich, the crisis put traders and executives out of work. "This is our Katrina," said Ned Lamont, a local telecommunications mogul who later became governor of Connecticut. But the disruption proved temporary—and it was matched by a sense that some were well positioned to take advantage of the opportunity. One of Skowron's colleagues at FrontPoint, Steve Eisman, bet correctly that the housing market would collapse, and he reaped millions. Eisman's success was featured in Michael Lewis's book *The Big Short*, but he was not alone;

Skowron recalled, "We had several other funds that had different ways of exploiting this disaster."

Greenwich made a vigorous recovery, and some parts of town entered a new stratosphere. In 2014, Stephen Higley, a geographer at the University of Montevallo in Alabama, completed a national study of census data and found that a small wedge of land bounded on the east side by North Street, on the north side by the Merritt Parkway, and on the west by Round Hill Road—just five square miles, home to some 4,600 residents—represented the highest concentration of wealth in America. He called it the "Golden Triangle."

├─────┤

Over time, some in Greenwich started to ask an uneasy question: If the money was changing so many visible parts of life in town, what was it doing to the invisible parts—the culture, the values, the moral groundwater beneath the surface? Jane Condon, the humorist, prodded gently at that question in her cartoon series titled "Our Life," which appeared regularly in *The Greenwich Post*, a local weekly. Her friend Bobbie Eggers, an illustrator who lived nearby, drew the pictures. In one scene, a woman asks a friend: "Ever notice the bigger the house, the less the wife weighs?" In another, a mother in a hospital hallway bestows a solemn task on her son: "Grandpa's very sick, dear. Now go in there and ask him his PIN numbers."

As the wealth in Greenwich soared, American inequality was reaching a precarious new height. The phenomenon had been building for decades. Between 1947 and 1979, the pay of the average American worker grew by 100 percent, despite endemic discrimination that steered the benefits mostly to white men. (Visiting the United States in 1959, the Soviet leader Nikita Khrushchev conceded, "The slaves of capitalism live well.") But in 1975, Arthur M. Okun, one of the leading economists in the Johnson administration, warned that the escalator was grinding to a halt. He cited "disturbing" data showing that the top fifth of American families was earning as much as the bottom three fifths. If the trend continued, he wrote, it would "allow the big winners to feed their pets better than the losers can feed their children." In the next three decades, from 1979 to 2009, the average worker's pay rose by just 8 percent.

In retrospect, the gap that disturbed Okun was quaint. By the 2010s, the share of income held by the top 1 percent was the largest it had been since 1928. In the CIA's measurements of income inequality, America's disparities were akin to those in Kenya and Iran. The effects of such dramatic inequality were manifest in the most basic measurements of health: not only did wealthy Americans live dramatically longer, they also were thinner, had stronger eyes and teeth, and had less cortisol in their saliva, a sign that their bodies felt more insulated from threat. Scholars described this period as the Great Divergence—a fundamental parting of American society.

After the election of Trump, much of the attention by journalists and scholars focused on Americans who had been, in the ubiquitous phrase, left behind. But inequality was better explained by the fact that the very rich had raced ahead. A generation earlier, most wealthy Americans were those who earned high salaries—lawyers, accountants, and doctors of the kind Skowron had once admired in Florida. But in this century, extraordinary wealth was coming from the wealth people already had, thanks to the compounding power of investments and tax advantages. Lawrence Summers, the former treasury secretary, concluded that if the distribution of income in America had stayed roughly what it was in 1979, the bottom 80 percent of American households would have gained another $1 trillion—enough to boost their income by 25 percent.

Wealth accrued at such a pace that even after Warren Buffett announced plans, in 2006, to draw down his fortune through philanthropy, it grew faster than he could give it away. By 2007, on the eve of the financial crisis, an estimated $5 trillion to $7 trillion of global wealth was protected in tax shelters, out of reach of government treasuries, a sum far larger than the estimates of how much it would cost to fix America's decaying roads and bridges and ports. Though Americans often talked about the "1 percent," the benefits were even more dramatic for a more exclusive set: the top 0.01 percent (about 16,000 households). In 1974, they earned an average of $4 million each year; by 2007, their annual take-home pay had grown to more than $35 million. Each of those 16,000 households—about 40,000 people in all—held $1 of every $17 earned in America, the highest share since such data was first collected in 1913.

Many wealthy Americans justified those gaps by hailing America's classic faith in upward mobility—the prospect that all could achieve success. But reality no longer matched the myth. On average, 90 percent of American children born in 1940 grew up to earn more than their parents, but by the early twenty-first century, that number had sunk to 50 percent. Mobility was getting swamped by inequality because wealthy families could pay for so much that extended their lead—private SAT tutors, political influence, exclusive investments, and tax advice. The further they pulled ahead, the more likely their children were to go to elite schools, meet similar spouses, and circulate in networks that delivered further access. For all the pride and inspiration wrapped up in notions of the American Dream, the World Bank had calculated that, by 2018, the United States had a lower level of intergenerational mobility than China.

In 2013, the Stanford economist Raj Chetty unveiled a detailed map of opportunity that showed how the course of a person's life was sharply defined by the zip codes in which they happened to grow up. In Salt Lake City, a person born to a family in the bottom fifth of household income had a 10.8 percent chance of reaching the top fifth. In Milwaukee, the odds were less than half that.

Such a lopsided distribution of wealth was actually hurting the long-term growth of the economy. In a landmark report, in 2011, the International Monetary Fund calculated that reducing inequality by 10 percent could extend periods of growth by 50 percent. As the scale of the problem became clear, the origins of American inequality inspired a vast new literature that cataloged the causes, ranging from structural racism to tax policy to executive compensation to environmental pollution. But if the causes were becoming clearer, the effects were only beginning to reveal themselves. It would be several years before Americans would come face-to-face with the full implications.

Until then, the scale of the soaring fortunes at the top only reinforced the ambitions of competitors like Skowron, who measured himself by one value. "The job is to manage risk and make money. I'm not confused about that," he said. "I'm going to push the boundaries as hard as I can, and get away with as much as I can, to make money for my clients."

Even some of America's most alert and adept politicians had not yet adjusted their rituals to the emerging reality. In a radio address in the summer of 2012, Obama told his audience: "This is a country where no matter what you look like or where you come from, if you're willing to study and work hard, you can go as far as your talents will take you. You can make it if you try."

TWO

THOUGHTS AND PRAYERS

WALKING TO WORK in the morning through northwest Washington, D.C., I liked to pass a building that looked as if it had been airlifted from Paris to a row of sterile office blocks. It was a five-story landmark of Beaux-Arts architecture, trimmed in green copper, and best known as the onetime home of Andrew Mellon, the heir to a banking fortune who had been treasury secretary in the 1920s.

In 2013, I noticed that the building was undergoing a renovation. It had been purchased as the new headquarters for the American Enterprise Institute. One of the country's oldest conservative think tanks, AEI had never had a permanent location. Its handsome new home was a revealing change: even as Democrats were celebrating Obama's reelection, his conservative opponents were gaining strength—sponsored, in large part, by the financial industry that was thriving so visibly in Greenwich. The new headquarters for AEI was named in honor of its donor, Daniel A. D'Aniello, a billionaire cofounder of the Carlyle Group, one of America's largest, and most politically connected, private equity firms.

Since the end of the recession in 2010, the private equity industry, which profited mostly by borrowing money to buy out companies and restructure them, had reported record profits. In 2013, it awarded itself and investors an unprecedented $66.2 billion in dividends, on top of fees and payments. Though the industry argued that it streamlined companies and delivered valuable gains for pension funds, it faced growing criticism that its profits came at society's expense. The more criticism grew, the more it spent on lobbyists and donations to candidates. Their business was breathtakingly lucrative. In 2012, D'Aniello had been paid about $140 million, which dwarfed the pay of most CEOs. (By comparison, Jamie Dimon, of JPMorgan Chase, had earned $23 million.) In donating the new building to AEI, D'Aniello called it a gift in the name of "protecting free enterprise and opportunity." He said, "I want all people to have the same shot at achieving the American Dream."

In its self-narrative, Washington has always been the public-spirited sibling of New York and Los Angeles, the sensible city in which the first craftsmen of Congress were directed to build only "neat and plain" furniture with no "superfluous ornament." The early lawmakers had slept on cots, two to a room, in spaces so tiny that the occupants had to take turns getting dressed. In practice, Washington had long ago become one of America's most prosperous places. But, in the twenty-first century, that prosperity had ballooned at a record pace—and the sheer bounty was altering the incentives and unwritten rules that drove American politics.

Between 2000 and 2010, U.S. companies had tripled their spending on lobbying and public relations in Washington, a surge of money fed mainly by three tributaries: financial firms, such as Carlyle, which were thriving throughout a crescent of American capital that stretched from Fairfax County, Virginia, to Fairfield County, Connecticut; defense contractors, in demand since September 11, and pumped up by the wars in Iraq and Afghanistan; and Internet companies surging in Silicon Valley and other technology clusters. In 2011, even as the country was recovering from the financial crisis, Washington had surpassed Silicon Valley to become the wealthiest metropolitan area in the United States.

My wife and I had arrived in Washington at a luxurious moment. The city's restaurants soon received their first Michelin stars, and Zagat declared Washington the nation's most "fashionable" dining city. More than two thousand people in and around the capital met the threshold for ultra-high-net-worth individuals, whose assets exceeded $30 million. Robert Frank, a journalist who specialized in the culture of wealth, surveyed the relevant metrics, including sales of Aston Martins and Bentleys, and concluded that Washington was moving from "affluence into opulence."

The money in politics had reached a level that even practitioners found hard to manage. Ethan Roeder, a Democratic operative who had been the director of data for Barack Obama's presidential campaigns, later observed, "A dirty secret in my industry is how difficult it is for a campaign bloated with too much cash to spend it." The cash fueled an anxiety of influence; donors poured unprecedented sums into politics in part because they worried that if they did not, someone else—a corporate competitor, an ideological opponent—would gain an advantage. "One campaign I worked on was so flush," Roeder recalled, "we joked that we should project our logo onto the moon."

⊢——⊣

There was a reason donors kept giving long after the point that candidates needed the money. It was, by any fair definition, a realm of legal corruption. Long ago, James Madison had envisaged a Congress "dependent on the people alone," but by the twenty-first century, scholars had documented, with precision, that donors and companies who made contributions to members of Congress effectively purchased greater access to them. In a 2015 study of congressional offices, the political scientists Joshua Kalla and David Broockman of Berkeley found that senior congressional staffers agreed to meet three to four times more frequently when they knew the request came from a donor.

To its defenders, the system allowed for an open competition of ideas; if citizens cared enough about a policy, they would fund the lobbying for it. That was always a fantasy. Donors were no reflection of the country. In both parties, they tended to be older, whiter, more male, and more conservative. In other words, they tended to look like members of Congress.

The economy of influence in Washington was unlike that almost anywhere else in the universe of advanced democracies. A few months before I arrived in Washington, a PowerPoint presentation created for internal use by House Democrats to introduce incoming freshmen to Congress was leaked to the *Huffington Post*. Among its advice, it encouraged new members to set aside three or four hours a day for hearings, voting, and meetings with constituents. But they should set aside no fewer than five hours every day in Washington for soliciting money (known by the euphemisms "call time" and "strategic outreach"). Paying for access had become so routine that its journeymen sometimes forgot to make the ritual denials that it affected their decision-making. In a moment of candor that bordered on farce, Mick Mulvaney, a former congressman from South Carolina, told banking executives that there was "a hierarchy in my office." He said, "If you were a lobbyist who never gave us money, I didn't talk to you. If you were a lobbyist who gave us money, I might talk to you."

The flood of cash had accelerated since 2010, when the Supreme Court, in *Citizens United v. Federal Election Commission*, struck down limits on the amount of money corporations, unions, and rich individuals could spend on elections. The decision led to a surge of money even greater than anyone predicted. Between 2008 and 2012, campaign spending rose by nearly $2 billion. Much of that growth came from super PACs, the political action committees that are allowed to spend whatever they want as long as they don't work directly with candidates. In 2012, super PACs spent a billion dollars; 73 percent of the money came from just a hundred people.

Over the years, the relentless rise of money in politics had altered the very definition of corruption. Dan Balz, a veteran political writer at *The Washington Post*, recalled that in 1972, when it emerged that W. Clement Stone, an insurance magnate and philanthropist, had given $2 million to Richard Nixon's campaign, the public outrage was so intense that it contributed to a wave of reforms in campaign financing. In today's dollars, Stone's donation would be $11 million—somewhere in the bottom tier of modern megadonors. In 2012, Sheldon Adelson, the conservative casino tycoon, spent $93 million. In preparation for the 2016 election, the Koch brothers, whose fortune came from fossil fuels, had organized a small circle of friends to dedicate $889 million to influencing the outcome. Together, they deployed their fortunes to groom and elect a generation of leaders who dedicated themselves to preventing tax increases and reducing business regulation.

The money altered which politicians had power in Washington, and which ideas they endorsed. The parties lost coherence as the membership turned into a muddle of individual strategies clamoring for attention and money. The Freedom Caucus—a group of ultraconservative Republican members of Congress who agreed to vote as a bloc—rapidly undermined party leaders such as House Speaker John Boehner. (He considered the Freedom Caucus leader Jim Jordan a "legislative terrorist.") Since the caucus had its own staff and financial resources, Boehner couldn't keep it in line by threatening to cut them off. Nor could he promise President Obama or Nancy Pelosi that he could deliver votes. "It's hard to negotiate," Boehner told Tim Alberta, "when you're standing there naked."

———

As the sums continued to rise, most elected officials in Washington reacted to the distortions of money in politics with versions of "thoughts and prayers," a ritual expression of concern, and little else. "No politicians are even talking about it," *The Washington Post* noted glumly of campaign finance in 2014. That was because nobody with real power was racing to alter a system that undergirded their positions. Lawrence Lessig, a Harvard legal theorist who had become a leading critic of money in politics, described that silence as the "politics of resignation." He told me he believed that the campaign finance system needed the political equivalent of an "atomic bomb." Change would become impossible, he said, "unless we blow it up now and we find some way to make it so that these bones don't set."

In the months before the 2014 midterm elections, Lessig embarked on a quixotic experiment: a political action committee that would spend millions of dollars in an attempt to elect congressional candidates who would, in theory, pass campaign finance reform. In other words, a super PAC designed to drive its own species into extinction. (He adopted the motto "Embrace the irony.") Lessig and his cofounder, the Republican consultant Mark McKinnon, named it Mayday, after the code word for an emergency. Among political professionals, the effort was generally dismissed. *Politico* called it "a farce" and "performance art." Lessig, who was a stranger to Washington but a celebrity in legal circles, acknowledged that it had "the biggest chance to fail of anything I've ever done."

I got interested in Lessig's project not for his chances of success but for his perspective as an outsider. When I met him, he was traveling from city to city, in a way that reminded me of Al Gore's campaign against climate change, trying to make people see money in politics as an emergency. On a weekday morning in August, Lessig was at the Cajundome Convention Center, in Lafayette, Louisiana. At fifty-three, he wore small round glasses, bore an expression of quiet alarm, and projected an air of oracular intensity. When he was featured as a character on *The West Wing* (advising a foreign government on its constitution), he had been played by Christopher Lloyd, the wild-eyed inventor in the *Back to the Future* movies.

He had been invited to Lafayette to speak at a local business event, the ABiz Top 50 Luncheon. He hoped that Louisiana voters might be receptive to his message. After all, he noted to me, Louisiana had convicted more people per capita for public corruption in the past decade than any other state. The former governor Edwin Edwards was best known for having bragged that the only threat to his political future was getting caught with "a dead girl or a live boy." (Edwards later served more than eight years in prison on corruption charges, for extorting payoffs in exchange for casino licenses, and later ran for Congress.)

The Cajundome luncheon had attracted seven hundred people, a slice of the Lafayette elite. The audience was less diverse than Lessig had expected: mostly prosperous-looking white men, taking their seats at round tables marked with the names of local businesses. I chatted with Pearson Cross, a political scientist from the University of Louisiana at Lafayette, who told me, "These are the people writing the checks." When it was Lessig's turn to speak, he began by drawing an explicit connection between racial justice and democracy. "It is an astonishing—one could say humbling, embarrassing—fact that almost one hundred years after the American Constitution effectively granted the right to vote to African Americans, African Americans still didn't have the right to vote." On two large overhead screens, he showed slides of Abraham Lincoln and Martin Luther King Jr., and of German shepherds lunging at demonstrators. "As all of us look back at that history, we wonder: How could they have thought like this?" He asked, "Are there things that will make our kids look back on us and say, 'Seriously?' How could we believe that the thickness of one's wallet is the metric of citizenship?"

He sketched a dire portrait of American democracy. He cited a poll in which 96 percent of Americans said they believed it was important to reduce the influence of money in politics but only 9 percent believed that it was likely to happen. "This is the moral question of our age," he said. "Can we reclaim our democracy?"

When he finished, there was polite applause, but not the standing ovation he sometimes received. He signed a few copies of his book *Republic, Lost: How Money Corrupts Congress—and a Plan to Stop It*, but dozens were left on the table.

├────────┤

When I lived in Beijing, from 2005 to 2013, the Chinese often complained that their government was beset by corruption, and they asked me if the United States had similar problems. I usually replied that our government had its crooks, but the naked exchange of influence for money was minimized by the rule of law and a free press. After a year in Washington, I was less sure.

In 2014, it took, on average, more than double the money to get elected to the House that it required in 1986, so candidates had to be blunter and hungrier in the hunt for cash. In Wisconsin, a consultant working for Governor Scott Walker told him to visit the casino magnate Sheldon Adelson: "Ask for $1m now."

The torrent of cash created by *Citizens United* had energized reformers more than any other event in decades. "You might say big money has always been a factor," Nick Nyhart, the head of Public Campaign, an advocacy group, told me. "But a group of octogenarian billionaires on the front pages of newspapers, pulling the strings of candidates, was simply something we hadn't seen before." Stephen Colbert dramatized the absurdity of super PACs and 501(c)(4) groups when he registered a "social welfare" organization that could donate under the name "Anonymous Shell Corporation."

And yet the exchange of money for influence was so pervasive that it was sometimes hard to know what was criminal and what was routine. Just after Lessig finished his speech in Lafayette, Robert McDonnell, the former governor of Virginia, took the witness stand in a courtroom in Richmond to discuss his relationship with Jonnie R. Williams Sr., a campaign donor and businessman who had cultivated the governor's support for a dietary supplement made from tobacco. Williams and his company had contributed some $80,000 in air travel to McDonnell's campaign. That, it seemed, was legal. But Williams's generosity extended into a grayer area, with loans, shopping sprees, golf outings, a Rolex, and use of a country house and a Ferrari—amounting altogether to $177,000.

Prosecutors, who had charged McDonnell and his wife, Maureen, each with thirteen counts related to public corruption, argued that the governor had returned the favors using the power of his office. In one exchange, McDonnell emailed Williams to ask about a $50,000 loan and, six minutes later, emailed an aide to check on scientific studies that Williams wanted conducted on his product at public universities. McDonnell, a confident presence on the stand, told the jury that his actions were nothing out of the ordinary—"the bare, basic, routine access to government and nothing more."

Lessig, for his part, had awakened to the problem via an unlikely route. He was not a natural politico; he disliked schmoozing and phones and email. His wife, Bettina Neuefeind, a public-interest lawyer who investigated war crimes in Kosovo, projected a practical side that compensated for his preoccupations. "I'm more of a crunchy-granola, homeopathic, nature-based kind of a person," she told me. But his search for a big change in politics matched other realms of his life. In 2007, after gaining weight on a sabbatical in Germany, he adopted a vegan diet and lost sixty pounds. When I met him, he was eating the same super-food breakfast every day: blueberries, a boiled egg, and half an avocado. Neuefeind said that her husband found "a simplicity and an elegance to just doing something all the way."

Growing up in Williamsport, Pennsylvania, where his father was an ardent Republican who owned a small steel-fabricating company, Lessig became a devout member of the National Teen Age Republicans. In 1980, at nineteen, he was the youngest member of any delegation to the Republican National Convention. His budding career in Republican politics ended when he ran the campaign of a candidate for the state senate, and lost. After college, at the University of Pennsylvania, he developed a growing reverence for law, as "this space where it is reason that is supposed to be directing power." He earned a master's degree at Cambridge and a law degree at Yale, and eventually taught at the University of Chicago and at Stanford.

By the late nineties he was one of America's most influential theorists on the intersection of law, culture, and the Internet. The roots of his crusade against money in politics began in 1998, when Congress passed the Sonny Bono Copyright Term Extension Act, a law that retroactively added twenty years to the copyrights of movies and songs and other work. Lessig visited Capitol Hill to argue that a retroactive extension served no purpose other than to lock down profits for copyright holders; it could not inspire William Faulkner or George Gershwin to create more work, because they were dead. Disney, he noted, had donated to the campaigns of eighteen of the original twenty-five House members who sponsored the Sonny Bono Act. He concluded that copyrights would never be allowed to expire, "so long as Congress is free to be bought."

The root of the problem, in Lessig's view, lay in the tendency of powerful Americans to make quiet compromises every day, shrugging off destructive behavior and gradually corrupting the core institutions in economic, social, and political life. He called them "the good Germans." He said, "The foreground in political corruption is Randy (Duke) Cunningham"—the California congressman who was convicted in 2005 of taking bribes—or Bob McDonnell, the former governor who was on trial in Virginia. "That's not the *interesting* corruption. The interesting corruption is the people who live within a system where influence is peddled and reckoned and bragged about as a function of the norms of culture that have evolved. These are the good Germans."

⊢——⊣

The federal jury in Richmond convicted McDonnell that fall on eleven counts of corruption. The man who had occupied the office once held by Thomas Jefferson had exchanged his power for golf trips, dresses for his wife, and rides in a sports car. After the McDonnell verdict was announced, I called Representative Jim Cooper, a Tennessee Democrat who has served on and off in the House since 1983. I asked what his peers would make of the court decision. "I think members will be secretly terrified," he said. "Those sorts of favors are astonishingly commonplace on the Hill."

But in McDonnell's fall, one could see a test of the fragile boundary between the conduct that sends a man to jail and the behavior that helps him get reelected. McDonnell faced prison for promoting a nutritional supplement in return for gifts, while members of Congress were legally entitled to accept tens of thousands of dollars in contributions from the nutritional-and-dietary-supplement industry. For years, Senators Tom Harkin, an Iowa Democrat, and Orrin Hatch, a Utah Republican, had been two of the industry's largest beneficiaries—and two of its strongest spokesmen, opposing regulations intended to protect consumers.

When it came time for the court to punish McDonnell, he appealed for mercy. Federal sentencing guidelines called for ten to twelve years; another former governor, Rod Blagojevich, of Illinois, was serving fourteen, for trying to sell Obama's Senate seat. Michael Dry, a prosecutor, called McDonnell's crimes "unprecedented in Virginia's two-hundred-and-twenty-six-year history." But defense attorneys asked for no prison time. They proposed instead six thousand hours of community service and in court presented eleven witnesses, including another former governor and an NFL star, who argued for leniency. The witnesses testified that McDonnell cared little for material possessions; the Speaker of the Virginia House of Delegates reported that the conviction itself would be a sufficient deterrent to others; the governor's sister said her brother was already so grieved that he had trouble eating and was losing weight. While pleading for the judge's grace, McDonnell's lawyer choked up.

U.S. district judge James Spencer sounded pained at the sentencing: "It breaks my heart, but I have a duty I can't avoid." He gave McDonnell two years, a term of such leniency that outside the courthouse in Richmond, McDonnell thanked the court.

McDonnell's punishment reflected his ability to marshal the power and influence of prominent friends. When the decision was announced, I called Bryan Stevenson, the executive director of the Equal Justice Initiative, a nonprofit that works against mass incarceration, and I asked what he made of it. For comparison, he pointed me to another conviction in Virginia.

The defendant, Travion Blount, of Norfolk, had no former governors or sitting Speakers or NFL stars to testify to his character. Blount had joined the Crips at the age of eleven. When he was fifteen, repeating the sixth grade for the fourth time, his mother asked the truancy court and other agencies to try to get him into a program that might steer him away from gangs. Not long after that, Blount and two older teenagers robbed a drug dealer at a house party. The three pulled guns, though Blount tried to give his pistol to one of the other attackers, who pushed it back into his hands. They stole money, marijuana, and cell phones. While Blount was in another part of the house, one of his fellow assailants hit a victim in the head with a gun, cutting his scalp.

Police caught them within a week. In 2013, the *Virginian-Pilot* described Blount's role in this way: "No shots were fired, and he didn't hit any victims. It did not merit a mention in the morning newspaper." After refusing to take a plea deal, Blount went to trial on fifty-one felonies—including illegal use of a firearm, robbery, and abduction. The jury found him guilty on forty-nine of them. At sentencing, in March 2008, the judge said the gun crimes carried fixed punishments in Virginia, so his sentence for the weapons charge came to 118 years. On top of that, because the crime involved robbing three juveniles at gunpoint, the judge added *six* life sentences. Unless something changed, Blount would be in prison until he was eligible for "geriatric release," on his sixtieth birthday, in 2051.

———

As the weeks ticked down to the midterms, the full forces arrayed against Lessig's ideas were becoming clear. For years, Republican leaders had rejected campaign finance reform as an assault on free speech and an attempt to undermine the party's traditional advantage in fundraising. Nobody was a more committed defender of the status quo than Mitch McConnell, the Senate minority leader with the soft chin and round glasses of a Victorian clerk. He once joked that campaign finance "ranks right up there with static cling as one of the great concerns of the American people."

McConnell had entered politics a half century earlier as a moderate, pro-choice Republican, an aide to Senator Marlow Cook of Kentucky, who backed clean-air standards and limits on strip mining. But his political commitments were always negotiable. He was as blunt about his pursuit of power as financiers in Greenwich were about their pursuit of wealth. In his memoir of politics, *The Long Game*, he wrote, "Personal ambition usually has a lot more to do with it than most of us are willing to admit. That was certainly true for me, and I never saw the point in pretending otherwise."

In 1977, bored with his work as a Republican lawyer, he ran for county executive and set about raising and spending $355,000, far more than any candidate in the county's history. He hired the consultant Tully Plesser, an expensive pollster and strategist, who concluded that

McConnell would never "make a dominant physical presentation." They would turn that to their advantage; they ran McConnell as a genial centrist, supporting public employees' right to bargain collectively, which won him an endorsement from the local AFL-CIO and from Louisville's liberal newspaper, the *Courier-Journal*. ("The biggest mistake we ever made," the publisher said later.) The money paid off, and McConnell became an orthodox believer. "Everything else is in second place," he said in a post-election interview. "I will always be well financed, and I'll be well financed early." He later said money allowed him to get to voters directly. "The only way a guy like me had a chance," as he put it.

He never forgot it. In 1984, when he challenged Walter (Dee) Huddleston, a two-term Democrat in the Senate, he raised nearly $1.8 million, which allowed him to afford Roger Ailes, the pollster and future founder of Fox News. McConnell squeaked through by 5,100 votes. As he put it, "A win is a win." His personal life was improving, too. In 1993, he married Elaine Chao, a shipping heiress who was rising in Republican politics. After her mother died, they inherited as much as $25 million, joining the ranks of Washington's high-net-worth individuals.

In Congress, McConnell focused most on raising money. In 1997, he took on the job that most of his colleagues hated: head of the National Republican Senatorial Committee, effectively the caucus's chief fundraiser, and then he re-upped for a second term. Raising money was "a joy to him," Alan Simpson of Wyoming told a reporter. "He gets a twinkle in his eye and his step quickens. I mean, he loves it." After a bipartisan effort in 2002 to limit the role of money, McConnell even filed suit against the reforms—*McConnell v. Federal Election Commission*—calling them an unconstitutional restriction on freedom of speech, and later he was a plaintiff in the case that resulted in the Supreme Court's *Citizens United* decision. *U.S. News* ran a headline calling him the Darth Vader of campaign finance, and he hung it on his office wall.

Along the way, McConnell discovered another tool of politics that, like money, could give a small group of politicians power beyond their numbers. He became the king of the filibuster, a Senate tradition that

prevented progress on bills by forcing one side to assemble a supermajor-
ity of sixty votes. Between 1941 and 1970, the Senate took only thirty-
six votes to break filibusters; in just the two-year period, 2009 to 2010,
when McConnell was the Senate minority leader, it took ninety-one.

It was a radical break in the nature of representative democracy;
senators representing just one tenth of the American population—in
sparsely settled rural states—had the power to block almost any legislation. During the Obama years, McConnell bet that by keeping Washington flamboyantly inoperative, he could get Americans to blame the
party in the White House. It was the functional equivalent of turning
down the radiators and draining the pipes in the Capitol. Sure enough,
from 2010 to 2012, Congress set a record for the least productive run of
legislating since record-keeping began.

To a degree that was underestimated at the time, McConnell was
reifying a profound change in modern American politics: though he
retained superficial gentilities ("My good friend from the other side of
the aisle"), McConnell cast the opposing party as an illegitimate presence, a force worth risking America's stability and prosperity to defeat.
In 2011, while leading a campaign of political extortion by threatening
to default on the national debt, McConnell called the debt "a hostage
worth ransoming."

The mood dominated Congress, and almost nothing, no matter
how plainly functional, was protected from partisan contempt. The
Nurse-Family Partnership National Service, a program that sent nurses
to the homes of low-income mothers, had served 18,000 families in
twenty-nine states, and the effects were well documented: lower rates
of sickness, substance abuse, and welfare dependency. By the time the
kids turned fifteen years old, they had been arrested less than half
as often as their peers. The cost, $80 million a year, was tiny by the
standards of federal spending. But when an expansion of the program
was proposed as part of Obamacare, House Republicans seized on it.
They issued a statement mocking it as a "nanny-state boondoggle." At
the Heritage Foundation, a scholar warned of a "stealth agenda" to "impose a federally directed, top-down approach to parenting." Glenn Beck

said it would send nurses to homes with fat children. The proposal to expand it died.

As his power grew, McConnell bothered less and less with the gestures of democracy. He rarely spoke to news organizations that would criticize him. "I only talk to the press if it's to my advantage," he wrote. By the final year of Obama's term, McConnell no longer put up the bunting of institutionalism. When he blocked the Senate from voting on the nomination of Merrick Garland, the Democrats' Supreme Court nominee, he said it should not be up to a "lame duck president on the way out the door."

To keep control of his party, McConnell took to parroting some of his rank-and-file's treasured delusions about the workings of government. It was not always easy to remember which fiction he was supposed to expound. In a Fox News interview shortly before the election, McConnell stated that repealing Obamacare would require sixty votes in the Senate, as well as Obama's approval. But saying that fact out loud was regarded, by some Republicans, as heresy. "Mitch McConnell Surrenders on Obamacare Repeal," declared the Senate Conservatives Fund, which backed Tea Party candidates. His campaign rushed to fix the problem, clarifying that he was still eager to embark on a fruitless, symbolic pageant of protest. "He knows it won't be easy," his spokesman told reporters, "but he also believes that if Republicans are fortunate enough to take back the majority, we'll owe it to the American people to try."

Over the decades, a series of great political writers had tried to divine what the man fundamentally believed. It was a fruitless quest. When the journalist Alec MacGillis published a critical biography, *The Cynic*, shortly before the 2014 midterms, he wrote, "What has motivated McConnell has not been a particular vision for the government or the country, but the game of politics and career advancement in its own right." Chris Dodd, a friend who served alongside McConnell in the Senate for a quarter century, considered the question of his motivations and said, "I don't have the vaguest idea."

In the final days of his 2014 campaign, McConnell traveled around his home state with "Team Mitch" stenciled over his heart, and "Eye of the Tiger" on the loudspeaker. His message was uncomplicated; a McConnell bumper sticker achieved an elegant brevity: "COAL. GUNS. FREEDOM."

The midterms became one of the most expensive and opaque races in history. The "dark money" groups, the political and charitable organizations that were not legally required to disclose the names of their donors, were spending more than ever before. In McConnell's home state, a group calling itself the Kentucky Opportunity Coalition was lambasting his opponent, Alison Lundergan Grimes, as a tool of "anti-coal" forces. (Legal disclosures later revealed that the money came from three sources, including Alpha Natural Resources, one of America's biggest coal companies.)

On Election Day, the GOP took back the Senate with a string of victories that ushered in Republicans who were even farther to the right than their predecessors. (The new senator from Iowa, Joni Ernst, sought to ban abortions and same-sex marriage, and to impeach Obama.) More to the point, the election clinched McConnell's long-running ambition to be Senate majority leader. I had thought of Obama as the political icon of his era. But he inhabited McConnell's Washington. McConnell was the ultimate expression of his generation in Congress. In the usual political compliment, he was described as an "institutionalist," an upholder of the creed. But that was a fiction. He was a pure political being, a calculator of victory, indifferent to fact and suffering, who operated on the plain belief that power mattered more than policy or principle.

McConnell had entered politics as a pro-environment, pro-choice Republican in a Democratic state; but, year by year, he had marched with his party farther to the right. If McConnell had any instinct to rise above it all, in a bid for productivity and history, he hid it well. He privileged the scoreboard above all. Asked about his ideological evolution, he shrugged: "I wanted to win," he said.

├─────────┤

Early twenty-first century America looked sound. It was nearing the record for the longest economic expansion in history. The gross domestic product had nearly doubled since the end of the Cold War. The inno-vations of Silicon Valley were driving the stock market to new heights. Unsurprisingly, in Washington, the dominant sensibility—especially in a Congress composed mostly of white male millionaires—was self-satisfaction.

Members of Congress and other figures in Washington were barely acquainted with vulnerability; they lacked the capacity for catastrophic imagination. When Senator Kirsten Gillibrand of New York tried to raise concern about sexual assault in the military, the Senate responded mostly with thoughts and prayers. "Some of these male senators can't imagine themselves being victimized or brutalized," she told me. "But I can imagine this happening to me. I can imagine it happening to my sons. And it drives me crazy."

The atmosphere of gilded success in the capital obscured a pervasive case of rot. Money and concerted obstruction were damming the nat-ural routes of political evolution. This was easy to overlook because it was less a matter of what was happening than what was *not* happening. Historically, Americans had maintained the fitness of democracy by amending the Constitution, on average, at least once a decade. But that pace had stalled for half a century. Other than a minor amendment in 1992, to raise congressional salaries, the last major change to the Constitution was in 1971, when the voting age was lowered to eigh-teen. Despite campaigns for the Equal Rights Amendment, to pre-vent gender discrimination, and for reforming the Electoral College, Americans had entered the longest stretch without a substantive amendment since before the Civil War. The sclerosis extended to the inhabitants themselves. The Senate was the oldest in history, including eight octogenarians, nearly twice the number who had ever served at one time.

To a degree that was only beginning to show, the cynicism of the McConnell era was spreading through America's body politic. For a generation, Americans had been told by party leaders to put their faith in technology, globalization, and market liberalization, even as inequal-ity grew, wages stagnated, and life expectancy declined. But now people were fleeing both the Democratic and Republican parties; the share of independents was rising. The turnout for the election of 2014 was the lowest level of American voter participation since 1942.

Elihu Root, winner of the Nobel Peace Prize in 1912, once told an audience of Americans, "Men must either govern or be governed." A century later, dispirited Americans were effectively recusing themselves from the rituals of governing. And, in the void, the dominant forces in the economy and politics were refining the systems that ensured their success and insulated them from accountability. In Washington, they enjoyed the powers of fundraising, gerrymandering, and influence peddling; in Greenwich, they enjoyed a steady decline in their taxes, and the accumulated advantages of deregulation, lobbying, and compounding wealth. In a 2014 Gallup poll, 7 percent of Americans reported having confidence in Congress, the lowest level that Gallup had ever recorded for *any* institution. When Washington considered a branding campaign to give it a catchy slogan akin to "Keep Austin Weird," a survey found that when Americans were asked what words they associated with the capital, the most popular answers were "corrupt," "educated," and "arrogant."

Some in Washington had begun to warn that constituents were unhappy. "These people are getting screwed by Wall Street interests, by the big money, by the establishment, and they don't like it," Trevor Potter, the general counsel to John McCain's 2000 and 2008 presidential campaigns, told me in 2014. That spring, the House majority leader, Eric Cantor, had been abruptly deposed by a populist challenger named Dave Brat, who had accused Cantor of protecting crony capitalism. "Most of the party establishment is vulnerable on that issue," Potter said. (Cantor effectively embraced the accusation; he started work at an investment bank at a compensation of $3.4 million by the close of the following year.)

As I crisscrossed the country in the final years of the Obama presidency, I was often struck by the sheer contempt for America's political and economic elites. What I saw was not abstract frustration at "big government" or "meddling bureaucrats." People were acutely, vividly aware of the plutocracy and its self-dealing, and that portrait was altering the political culture of the country, weakening even everyday bonds between people. Social scientists recognized the effect. In studies on the impact of inequality, Nicholas Christakis, a Yale sociologist, found that when people saw flamboyant reminders of unfairness, they cooperated with one another roughly half as often. Disparities "subverted group cohesion, making people less cooperative, less friendly, and ultimately less able to work together," he wrote. Outside of politics, people had an intuitive contempt for conditions that reminded them of structural unfairness. A 2016 study published in *Proceedings of the National Academy of Sciences* showed that airplanes with multiple cabins of various classes experienced higher levels of "air rage." When economy-class passengers boarded the flights through the first-class cabin, rather than through the midsection of a plane, air-rage incidents increased even more. To many Americans, the structures of power—politics, law, economics— looked more and more like one long boarding queue through the first-class cabin.

McConnell's win was Lessig's loss. It was no great shock, but Lessig did not disguise his disappointment. One of his friends, Alex Whiting, a fellow Harvard professor, had told me that Lessig was always stunned when one of his projects did not succeed. "He has so much faith in the ability of the mind to figure out its problems—maybe he doesn't account for the irrational and the influence of raw power," Whiting said.

But, within a few days, Lessig shook off the gloom. He went back on the road to continue making his case. He had come to see his project as something more akin to earlier political movements in American history that had begun in the face of overwhelming skepticism. In the 1880s, after some forty years of activism, women's suffrage advocates were dismissed in *The New York Times* as "suffrage shriekers" who were "contemptuously laughed to scorn"; their proposals, the paper observed, were the work of "half-crazy fanatics or weak-minded old women of both sexes." It took seventy years to achieve the Nineteenth Amendment.

Lessig knew one thing: Americans would not wait that long to rebel against the corruptions of American politics. Young people, in particular, believed that politics was rigged. He said, "You've got to blow it up."

THREE

JEWEL OF THE HILLS

IN 1998, during my last year of college, I looked for a job as a newspaper photographer. I wrote to a dozen small papers between Birmingham, Alabama, and Homer, Alaska. One made me an offer: *The Exponent Telegram* in Clarksburg, West Virginia. The editor offered me $230 a week as an intern in the photo department. I packed up my car and headed south.

Clarksburg—population 16,400—lies in the green highlands of northern West Virginia, between the Ohio River and the Allegheny Mountains. It traces its roots to 1785, when ambitious settlers sought to create a regional capital of culture and politics—"the Athens of Allegheny, Virginia," as the historian Stephen W. Brown put it. By the mid-nineteenth century, they were profiting from shipping coal up the West Fork River to steel mills in Pittsburgh. When J. H. Diss Debar, a French traveler, visited Clarksburg in 1846, he found that its people prided themselves on "superior culture and manners," even if their modern buildings "did not exceed a dozen."

Politically and culturally, the city straddled the line between North and South. In Clarksburg, citizens rose to prominence on both sides of the Civil War; the Confederate general Thomas "Stonewall" Jackson became, in Robert E. Lee's words, "my right arm." Nathan Goff Jr., a major in the Union Army, was so valuable that when he was taken prisoner, Abraham Lincoln personally intervened to secure his release. (Goff went on to be a federal judge, a U.S. senator, and secretary of the navy.)

In the twentieth century, the ambitious grandees of Clarksburg set out to build a metropolis. They installed some of the first telephones in West Virginia, and opened eight banks, three hospitals, and a streetcar line. Nathan Goff, the Civil War veteran, built a luxurious hotel called the Waldo (named after his father, Waldo Goff), as well as one of West Virginia's first "skyscrapers," which consisted of two nine-story towers. Elsewhere in the tiny downtown, the Robinson Grand became one of the first theaters in America to be wired for talking pictures. By 1920, the population of Clarksburg had grown to 28,000, and prosperous families built gracious Victorian mansions in a neighborhood dubbed Quality Hill.

Throughout that history, the land beneath their feet provided an abundant source of opportunity. Rich reservoirs of natural gas and vast acres of sand gave rise to a flourishing glass industry, which attracted craftsmen from Europe and lent the small city a worldly air. Artisans from Belgium spoke French in the streets. Hazel Atlas, the largest glass company in America, had a factory in town, as did Pittsburgh Plate, Anchor Hocking, Rolland, and Harvey Glass. Clarksburg was nicknamed the "Jewel of the Hills."

The standard of living rose steadily for three decades after World War II, as it had in much of America, when the national economy doubled in size and the earnings of the average worker doubled with it. Workers in the local glass factories could afford to buy a house and a car and to raise a family. On Main Street, in front of the handsome Art Deco courthouse, the city hung a billboard that said, "You have a right to be proud!" The local government built so many parks and sewers and roads that, in 1957, the National Municipal League named Clarksburg an "All-America City," for its commitment to such values as "civic engagement" and "inclusiveness." (More than forty years later, when I moved to town, the title still appeared proudly on signs hung from lampposts.)

The first time I drove into Clarksburg, it felt like a tiny fragment of a city transplanted to the mountains; it had a grid of downtown streets, tall, corniced office buildings, and elevated roadways. The FBI had recently opened a vast complex nearby, with 2,700 jobs, processing fingerprints and digital records on the site of an old coal mine. People in town were feeling flush.

I rented an apartment downtown for $250 a month. On one side of the building, I looked out at a car wash and a Wendy's; on the other, I had a view of a quiet residential neighborhood, with streets named for native local trees—Sycamore, Beech, Birch, Locust. The houses were wood-and-brick bungalows, with well-kept lawns, inhabited, in many cases, by retired couples who subscribed to *The Exponent Telegram* and attended the United Methodist Temple on the corner.

The nearest house had the most lovingly cared-for car I'd ever seen—a sixties sedan with a white convertible top and a body painted in a brilliant shade of turquoise. The car was always buffed to a luminous shine, and, on my way home from work, I sometimes stopped and snapped pictures of the car. It reminded me of the billboard about being proud.

The Exponent Telegram occupied a small stout headquarters, made of stone, with columns flanking the front door. The paper was almost as ambitious as the rural city it covered. We published two newspapers a day, seven days a week: *The Clarksburg Exponent* in the morning, and *The Clarksburg Telegram* in the afternoon. In one form or another, the papers could trace their roots back to 1861, and in the early years they had represented fiercely partisan positions in local politics; the *Exponent* leaned left, and the *Telegram* leaned right.

The editors had to contend with the passions of their neighbors. "It wasn't a safe occupation," David Houchin, a Clarksburg archivist, told me not long ago. "It was not uncommon for our editors to be stabbed and shot for things they printed." An early editor of the *Telegram*, Wilbur Richards, was shot at "on more than one occasion—and he'd fire back," Houchin said. "By the time you get past the turn of the twentieth century, they're not shooting newspaper editors anymore. They're just clubbing them or whipping them." In 1903, an up-and-coming local

lawyer named John W. Davis flayed the editor of the *Telegram* with
a buggy whip—he was unhappy with the paper's comments about his
father—and then promptly turned himself in to the police. The beating
did not harm the assailant's career; Davis was elected to Congress eight
years later and went on become the Democratic nominee for president in
1924, having launched his campaign with a ticker-tape parade through
downtown Clarksburg. Davis lost to Calvin Coolidge but retained political power—sometimes at the expense of racial progress: in 1954, he
represented South Carolina before the Supreme Court, arguing, unsuc-
cessfully, for "separate but equal" schools. Davis helped establish the
elite Council on Foreign Relations, and is enshrined in the name of the
law firm Davis Polk.

By the middle of the twentieth century, the mayhem in Clarksburg
journalism had subsided, and the local papers had strong economic
reasons to shed their political ideologies: the more subscribers they attracted, the more they could charge for advertising. So they aimed to
be inoffensive. By the time I arrived, the *Exponent* and the *Telegram*
confined their politics to the editorial pages, and those of us who filled
the news pages were barely aware of the politics. The papers shared a
motto—"My Life, My Home, My Newspaper"—and they shared an
editor in chief. His name was Bill Sedivy; he was forty-two and over six
feet tall with a silver goatee and a broad chest. On weekends, he worked
as a whitewater guide, which lent him a casual air that disguised his
intensity.

Sedivy, raised outside Cleveland, had run small papers in Indiana
and Ohio before coming to Clarksburg with the goal of making it the
best newspaper in West Virginia. The owners wanted to boost profits,
and he persuaded them to try raising the quality of the paper instead of
cutting jobs. They agreed, and let him expand the staff of reporters and
editors and photographers to twenty people. He called us "troops," and
on a good morning he would unfurl the front page and announce, "We
kicked ass yesterday."

I loved the job. My task was to shoot any story that the two more
experienced photographers didn't have the time or desire to cover. Most
weeks, I drove hundreds of miles around West Virginia, taking pictures

at schools, farms, junkyards, factories, and coal mines. I covered local boxing matches, bar bands, house fires, and government meetings. Our pages had all of the usual grist of a community newspaper—the schedule at the senior citizens' home and small ads wishing someone a happy birthday—but the paper also reported aggressively and ambitiously, on striking miners, environmental protests, and plans for new prisons.

Now and then, we tried to draw a connection to an event far away. In the spring of 1999, a few months after I arrived, two teenagers in Littleton, Colorado, attacked their classmates at Columbine High School—a massacre then still so rare that it dominated the news for days. We published four stories about it, including reactions from parents in Clarksburg. A mother reassured her daughter that Columbine was an "aberration." She said, "Your school is safe, and you're safe, and our town is safe."

━━━━

Appalachia always had more than its share of small newspapers, for a practical reason: bad mountain roads made it hard to distribute a paper very far. So you rarely went more than twenty miles without seeing a tiny newspaper office—or sometimes two, competing for dominance of a one-stoplight town. In the oil fields, workers could choose among *The Derrick*, *The Volcano Lubricator*, and the *West Virginia Walking Beam*. During the Civil War, local military units commandeered local presses to crank out *The Knapsack* for the North and *The Guerrilla* for the South.

"A good newspaper," Arthur Miller once said, "is a nation talking to itself." Throughout American history, the scrutiny and sustenance provided by local news had been intertwined with democracy. How else, asked Alexander Hamilton in 1788, would Americans "regulate their judgment of the conduct of their representatives"? Local news also had a powerful effect on social cohesion. Studies showed that people who read local papers were more likely to vote and to run for office. Their reading also connected them to their neighbors around shared complaints and triumphs and sensations, the furnishings of what scholars called the "imagined community." Local newspapers played a role akin to the plankton in a food chain of American awareness, feeding the regional, national, and international understanding of the country itself.

Yet local news had been under threat for nearly as long as it had been around. In 1844, Samuel F. B. Morse, the pioneer of the telegraph, conducted the first public demonstration of his invention, with the message "What hath God wrought?" Morse predicted that his creation would unify Americans, making "one neighborhood of the whole country." Indeed, the telegraph brought benefits beyond measure. But it also began a process that pushed news and politics toward entertainment and fear, lighting a fuse that would stretch across generations.

The day after Morse unveiled his device, a newspaper used a telegraph to relay the first squib of news from Washington to Baltimore. By the end of the century, readers were wading through small stories of war, crime, fires, and floods far away. Neil Postman, one of the twentieth century's most prominent scholars of communications, wrote, "The telegraph may have made the country into 'one neighborhood,' but it was a peculiar one, populated by strangers who knew nothing but the most superficial facts about each other."

Postman, in his 1985 book, *Amusing Ourselves to Death*, identified a fundamental change in the nature of American communication that has become only more visible in the decades since he wrote it. The world of information steadily became what Postman called a "peek-a-boo world, where now this event, now that, pops into view for a moment, then vanishes again." Decades before Americans conceived of communicating in snippets of social media, he warned of a world with less time for context and connection—"a world that is, like the child's game of peek-a-boo, entirely self-contained. But like peek-a-boo, it is also endlessly entertaining." In the era of television news, the sense of discontinuity took the form of a small, elegant phrase: "Now . . . this," which newscasters used to signal, as Postman put it, "that what one has just heard or seen has no relevance to what one is about to hear or see . . . The newscaster means that you have thought long enough on the previous matter (approximately forty-five seconds)" and "that you must now give your attention to another fragment of news or a commercial."

In 1968, the average sound bite on a network news broadcast was more than sixty seconds; by 2004, it had shrunk to less than eight seconds. Eventually, the concept of "Now . . . this" became so suited to the era of shortening attention spans that a company even adopted the name without irony. A video news producer calling itself NowThis launched in 2012, offering short videos and articles intended to be read on mobile phones. It became one of America's most popular mobile news sites.

In a small state like West Virginia, reporters took prickly pride in their closeness to their communities. "You have to be careful how you treat someone, because they may know your mom," Vicki Smith, who worked in the local bureau of the Associated Press for nearly two decades, told me. Smith was often offended by out-of-town reporters' caricatures of the state's complicated history of poverty and sacrifice. While covering a mine explosion that killed twelve men, Smith once turned a corner and nearly collided with Nancy Grace, the hypercaffeinated cable television host. "It felt like a violation, like, 'What are you *doing* here? You don't know us, you don't care about this.'"

———

When I arrived, the paper maintained the tradition of taking sometimes gleeful pride in poking at local notables. When Julie Cryser, the city editor, published a story on people grumbling about Clarksburg's long-serving mayor, the man himself walked four blocks from city hall and stormed into Sedivy's office. "He was pounding his cane on the floor," Cryser recalled. "He'd point it out at me in the newsroom, and then he'd pound his cane on the floor again."

Politically, Clarksburg, like most of West Virginia, had been a stronghold of the Democratic Party since the Great Depression. When the economy collapsed and West Virginia coal production sank by 40 percent, Franklin Roosevelt pushed poverty-relief programs into the mountains. In 1960, the state played a pivotal role in the party's nomination contest. Senator John F. Kennedy faced widespread doubts that a Catholic could win votes, but he made a point to tour West Virginia, which was overwhelmingly Protestant. He was often accompanied by Roosevelt's son, Franklin Jr., who was greeted as a celebrity. A coal miner told him "your daddy's picture" was on the family's wall at home.

In 1960, Clarksburg attracted visits by Lyndon Johnson, Hubert Humphrey, and a parade of Kennedys, including three visits from Bobby and one from Ted, who said his brother's "political future is going to be decided in Clarksburg" and towns just like it. JFK came, too; he toured a glass factory and sat for a live broadcast on local television, in which people were invited to call in and ask him questions. His campaign opened an office at the Stonewall Jackson Hotel, the tallest building in town, where you could get free postcards with the unusually specific claim that Clarksburg was "the smallest city in the world with a 200-room hotel." Kennedy gave a speech in the ballroom, calling for a higher minimum wage and a federal health insurance plan for the elderly. "We are the party that started Social Security. And we are going to finish the job," he said. In an admiring story, the *Exponent* reported that the crowd "became so quiet that one could hear a pin drop." Three weeks later, Kennedy won the primary, which defused concerns that anti-Catholic bigotry would thwart his campaign. Were it not for West Virginia, he said as president, "I would not be where I now am."

Now and then, the local far-right fringe made news. In 1996, Clarksburg attracted national attention when federal agents discovered a plot to blow up the local FBI complex. Seven men, including a lieutenant in the city fire department, called themselves the Mountaineer Militia and stockpiled guns and studied blueprints. Yet the stereotype of West Virginia as a racist backwater had a way of effacing years of painful work by local Black activists. Jim Griffin had grown up in Clarksburg, where he was barred from segregated restaurants. As a teenager, Griffin bagged groceries at the A&P, frustrated that nobody who was Black was permitted to work the cash register. On a whim one day, an ally—a white cashier—asked him to sub in for her. A customer said, "I don't want him to run my groceries." But the white cashier held firm: "If he can't check your groceries out," she told the customer, "put them back on the shelf."

Jim Griffin graduated from high school in 1965, just weeks after marchers led by the twenty-five-year-old voting-rights activist John

Lewis were attacked by police on the Edmund Pettus Bridge in Selma, Alabama. Griffin felt the pull of the civil rights movement. At the age of eighteen, he revived a moribund branch of the NAACP in Clarksburg to fight segregation in local courts. Even though West Virginia had sided with the Union and African Americans had moved there to escape the Deep South, some in the state retained sympathies for the Confederacy. Over time, many African Americans had migrated farther north, and West Virginia became one of the whitest states in America.

Griffin sought to change his home state from the inside. He worked as a laborer at Union Carbide, the chemical corporation, while he attended community college. After six years, he became the company's first Black supervisor. In Clarksburg, he helped establish the Human Rights Commission, which investigated discrimination, and the West Virginia Black Heritage Festival. He encouraged a friend named David Kates, a Black pastor, to get into local politics, and when a vacancy opened up on the city council, Kates was appointed to it. In 1999, members of the council elected Kates to be the first Black mayor in the city's history. "Timing is everything," Griffin liked to say.

When Kates became mayor, a nearby branch of the Ku Klux Klan announced plans for a rally, as it put it, to "unite the white people . . . that still believe they have a voice in America." Kates called for a counter-rally to prove that Clarksburg had "more people who desire diversity than there are who desire hatred." The counter-rally became known as "The Unity Project," and *The Exponent Telegram* promoted it for weeks, calling on the people of Clarksburg to reject what it called the "whackos wearing white sheets spouting idiocy." An editorial declared, "People who believe in diversity will stand in the cold to stand up for their freedoms."

The Klan rally was a flop. At noon on November 6, about fifteen people in white robes turned up, and another fifty or so supporters cheered them on. A city rule banned the wearing of hoods and masks, and the Klan's grand dragon complained that it had scared off people who wanted to remain anonymous. The counter-rally across town drew hundreds of people and speeches by local politicians, clerics, and heads of the Italian, Jewish, and Polish communities. Griffin told me, "The

Klan rally probably only lasted a half hour and then they were gone. I felt very proud to say that I lived in the city of Clarksburg."

In *The Exponent Telegram*, Harry Fox, a member of the editorial board, declared, "It's been good for us all, adults and young people, black and white, wealthy, middle class, and poor, husbands and wives, single people and families, to have been challenged—to ask ourselves what we really believe about each other." On that day, he wrote, "we journeyed a little farther on the road to a truly free society." In the weeks afterward, the city installed a sign on the road into town: "Welcome to Clarksburg. We Celebrate Diversity."

———

On days off, I liked to drive into the hills and go walking. You could find trails through stands of pine and cedar, and from the crest of every ridge, hollows descended into the woods. When I met Judy Bonds, a coal miner's daughter who became an environmentalist, she often said the "mountains are in our soul," which sounded, at first, like a bluegrass cliché. It would take me many years to understand what she meant.

People often felt a deeper attachment to the hollows where they grew up than to the cities where they settled. They spoke of themselves as inseparable from the mountains, the water—the "home place." But this was not the same as preserving it. Harvesting profit from the land was as much a part of West Virginians' self-image as the coal miner on the state flag. The historian John Alexander Williams, a professor at Appalachian State University, told me, "If West Virginia has one enduring theme, it was in the words of those first explorers who described it as a 'pleasing, tho' dreadful' land."

Since the nineteenth century, very little of those profits had been directed to local people. In the 1870s, West Virginia established a system that legally separated the ownership of land from the astronomically valuable mineral rights beneath it. As a result, the people who worked the land, and bore its environmental harm, were not the people who enjoyed its profits—an arrangement that cast a shadow for generations. In New York, a pamphlet for investors hailed "The Oil-Dorado of West Virginia," with an untapped hoard of petroleum and coal and ore "which only needs development to attract capitalists like a magnet." West Virginia, the authors wrote, was "destined to become one of the richest sections of this great country."

But that was not its destiny. Out-of-state companies and investors used their profits to buy political influence that prevented the creation of a permanent tax fund of the kind established in Alaska, which distributes a portion of oil revenues to state residents. By the 1890s, local politicians were helping companies put down local strikes. A lumberman from the north said, "All we want here is to get the most we can out of this country, as quick as we can, and then get out." By 1920, timber companies had gutted the ancient forests that once covered two thirds of the state. A. B. Brooks, West Virginia's first game warden, marveled that "nearly the whole population which originally earned its living from the ground has been pushed out from places of seclusion into a whirl of modern industry."

West Virginians lost control of their most precious asset: their land. Miners relocated to coal camps, where they paid their employers for everything, including the drinking water. Crystal Wimer, of Clarksburg and the historian of Harrison County, told me, "It was very hard to fight what our people were up against without having a lot of influence." She said, "A lot of folks didn't know how to read, and they were told, 'If a railroad runs by your house and a spark comes off the train and burns your barn down, you can't sue them.' The laws were always skewed so that common people couldn't get ahead." When John Gunther visited West Virginia in 1945, it struck him as a world apart. "I once heard an irreverent local citizen call it the 'Afghanistan of the United States,'" he wrote in his book.

By 1960, the year that Kennedy made his historic visit to West Virginia, central Appalachia had yielded fortunes for others, but more than half of its homes still had no central plumbing. When people complained, the answer was often the same: If you think it's bad now, imagine how much poorer you'd be without the coal companies. In 1963, the

Kentucky lawyer and writer Harry Caudill drew America's attention to the depth of human suffering in the region. He said, "This is what happens to a great industrial population when you abandon it, give it just enough food to keep it alive and tell it to go to hell."

———

When I arrived in Clarksburg, the state was embarking on a new chapter in environmental history: the coal-mining revolution known as "mountaintop removal." In the 1990s, companies had discovered a cheaper way to reach Appalachia's coveted, low-sulfur coal; instead of sending crews of miners underground, they could blast the tops off the mountains and scrape away the fortune. The method, which was mostly employed in the southern part of the state, yielded two and a half times as much coal per hour as digging underground. Companies started buying rights to knock off vast stretches of the mountains; the biggest mines, a couple of hours from us, grew larger than the island of Manhattan.

My editor, Bill Sedivy, saw mountaintop removal as the makings of a disaster. He wrote a series of skeptical columns and editorials. He worried about the damage to West Virginia's rivers and landscape—"I'm a river guide, for god's sake," he told me—and he questioned the economic mythology that extraction was the path to progress. "I was doing it because I was tired of seeing people saying, 'Coal is going to save us.'"

The industry retaliated against his columns. Lobbyists bought large ads in *The Exponent Telegram* that hailed mountaintop removal as a matter of state pride. "Coal is a necessity of life," the ads said. "West Virginia communities enjoy clean water, better sewer facilities, ambulance and fire service, even lower electric rates than many other states, thanks to the contribution that coal makes to our economy." They ended with a note of reassurance: "Anyone who has built a home understands when it's under construction it's not a pretty sight." But come back in a few years, they promised, and "you'd never know mining had ever taken place."

Around town, Sedivy's campaign was controversial. He told me, "There was a segment of the community that said, 'Wow, it's been a half century since we've had this kind of watchdog reporting.' But then there was another half of the community that was very, very vocal. They missed stories about who came over to whose house for brunch after church." Sedivy wondered if he had pushed too far, too fast. "I had preached the philosophy that if you have a kick-ass local paper, where you're digging at those hard realities, you're going to sell newspapers and make money," he told me. But readers were losing patience. Resistance was growing in town. A few months after I arrived, Sedivy announced that he was moving on. He accepted a job in Idaho, running a nature conservation group.

Around town, it felt as if people were putting ever more of their hopes in coal mining because other pillars of the Clarksburg economy were crumbling. Since the 1970s, the local glass factories had been closing in the face of competition from larger, more advanced plants in Mexico and Japan. So many young people were leaving in search of work, West Virginians joked that local kids learned the three Rs: reading, 'riting, and Route 77—the road out. By 2000, the population of Clarksburg was half of what it had been in 1940.

A familiar spiral took hold: the declining population paid less in taxes, which forced the local governments to cut spending on police, firefighting, public parks, and garbage collection—which, in turn, made it easier for more people to leave. The neighborhood pools ran out of money. In the tiny downtown, stores closed and buildings began to decompose. The Waldo Hotel moldered into a hulking wreck, with weeds climbing out of the upper windows toward the open sky.

We didn't know it yet, but in the final moments of the twentieth century, tiny cracks were forming in the economic foundation of newspapers like ours. The Internet, which would revolutionize the delivery of news and entertainment (and disinformation), was just starting to reach private homes across West Virginia. In 1999, one of our editors, Bob Stealey, wrote a column about the simple act of signing on to AOL and sending his first email—to what he called "a perfect stranger out there in cyberspace." He was hooked. "I'm blazing my own trail of glory," he wrote. When I happened on that column again years later, it reminded me of the message that passed across the early telegraph: "What hath God wrought?"

—————

In the years afterward, when I was abroad, I sometimes signed on to the *Exponent Telegram* website for a glimpse of what was happening in Clarksburg. There was always some good news—year after year, the local high school had some of the state's top math scores. The FBI complex attracted a cluster of small technology companies, which helped Clarksburg's economy grow faster than that of other parts of the region. The city even developed a real-estate claim to fame, of sorts: the largest strip mall in West Virginia.

Yet there were clear signs of trouble. West Virginia was a case study of radical inequality. The southern coalfields were losing jobs and population, while the eastern panhandle was booming, from money radiating out of Washington, D.C. More than half of West Virginians' income growth since 1990 had gone to the state's top 1 percent. Between 2007 and 2017, West Virginia lost 18,000 people, faster than any other state. It had some of the country's highest rates of smoking, obesity, diabetes, and prescription drug abuse; it trailed much of the nation in the rate of college graduation. Four out of five workers lacked a four-year college degree. And with its population sinking, its political power sank with it. If the trends continued, the state would lose one of its three congressional seats by 2022.

All of these trends were visible in the pages of *The Exponent Telegram*. Local stores, which once advertised, were vanishing, and the Internet was consuming the classified ad sections. Between 2000 and 2012, print advertising across American newspapers fell by a catastrophic 71 percent. Digital advertising would never remotely make up the loss. In twenty-seven years, from 1990 to 2017, U.S. newspaper circulation dropped by 50 percent, even as the nation's population grew by 30 percent.

In 2002, *The Exponent Telegram* had announced it could no longer afford to produce two newspapers each day and merged them into one edition. The Highland family, which had owned the papers for decades, wanted to sell. Relatives had moved out of town; eventually, the only remaining family member in charge of the paper lived four hundred miles away, in Ithaca, New York.

As news moved to television and the Internet, the effects extended to politics in ways that resonated starkly with Postman's warnings of a world "populated by strangers" equipped with only the "most superficial facts about each other." In the digital world, the incentives and attractions were unrecognizable from what had governed the local newspaper era. Instead of touting nonpartisanship, digital news organizations promoted precisely the opposite: they attracted attention with explicit, provocative politics. In their 2014 book, *The Outrage Industry*, the scholars Jeffrey Berry and Sarah Sobieraj described the new mode of communications for talk-show hosts and online commentators: they relied on "overgeneralizations, sensationalism, misleading or patently inaccurate information, ad hominem attacks, and belittling ridicule of opponents" because it paid off. "Emotional responses (anger, fear, moral indignation) from the audience" were more likely to keep people watching.

Vicki Smith, the longtime West Virginia reporter, told me that the effect of social media on news was unnerving. More and more, her editors at the Associated Press were encouraging her to dig into items that were popular on Twitter or Facebook. "You'd have to run down things that were gossip or pure fiction, or waste your time shooting down rumors," she told me. "But it's not news. Why are we responding to that? We had bigger, more important, more meaningful stories to tell here." And the audience was changing. "It became painfully apparent that the news consumer no longer wanted as much objective, factual reporting. They wanted news that comported with their worldview."

That tilt was altering the geography of the mind. Americans were learning less about people in their local communities and more about the distant figures, abstract disputes, and entertaining memes of national politics. Daniel J. Hopkins, a political scientist at the University of Pennsylvania, found that the share of Americans who could name their governor declined sharply between 1949 and 2007, even as the share who could name the vice president remained unchanged. By 2012, Americans were directing far less of their donations to politicians in their own states than they had a generation earlier, and when asked to name the politician they hated most, only 15 percent of respondents named someone in their own state; most of their political attention was directed far away.

The "nationalization" of politics and public life was even changing how citizens described themselves. In Hopkins's book *The Increasingly United States*, he analyzed the texts of digitized books to measure the frequency of phrases such as "I am American" compared with "I am Californian" or the like. Earlier Americans had focused on their state identity, but the expression of national identity took the lead around 1968, and has held it ever since. Television, and eventually social media, allowed people to dissociate from their physical communities. They were powerful tools of self-segregation.

———

Between 2005 and 2020, more than 2,100 American newspapers closed down, according to a count by Penny Muse Abernathy, a professor at the University of North Carolina. American newspapers eliminated more than 45 percent of their newsroom staff. Farai Chideya, a journalist who joined the Ford Foundation, framed the decline in ecological terms: a "mass extinction event." In her 2020 book, *Ghosting the News*, Margaret Sullivan, the media columnist at *The Washington Post*, extended the metaphor: "As with issues like the global climate emergency, it is hard to convince a significant chunk of the public that they ought to care deeply about this, or do anything about it." Indeed, most Americans were impressively unaware of it; nearly three quarters of those surveyed by the Pew Research Center in 2019 said local news outlets were in good financial shape.

Although the disappearance of local news generated little public concern, the consequences on voting and government work were very real. Research by PEN America, the writers' organization, found that as local journalism declines, "government officials conduct themselves with less integrity, efficiency, and effectiveness, and corporate malfeasance goes unchecked. With the loss of local news, citizens are: less likely to vote, less politically informed, and less likely to run for office." A study published in the *Journal of Financial Economics* found that in the three years after a paper shut down, local taxes rose by an average of $85 per citizen, and payroll costs climbed by 1.3 percent beyond the usual pace. In other words, when local papers closed, governments became less efficient and more generous to themselves.

For newspapers in distress, the options were unattractive. Some escaped extinction by selling out to conglomerates, which saved money by reducing the ranks of reporters and selling off unused space—a process that Sullivan called "strip-mining." In practice, those papers often ended up as glorified ad circulars, filled mostly with snippets from the national newswires—a disjointed gallery that Postman would have recognized as peek-a-boo news.

I expected that future to befall *The Exponent Telegram* in Clarksburg. But, in 2012, a century and a half after it started publishing, the fate of the paper took a surprising detour. Brian Jarvis, a local tax lawyer with a sideline in the oil and gas business, stepped in to buy it. He was barely thirty years old, but his father, Cecil, had served as president of the paper, and even after going off to college in Tennessee, Brian came home in the summer to intern in the newsroom while his father worked upstairs. Cecil Jarvis was a local institution—a civic booster, a competitor in Ironman triathlons—who died in a bicycle accident in 2007. When I stopped by on a trip to Clarksburg, Brian told me, "My original plan was to move back and practice law with him. But he died while I was in law school." Buying it was a nod to his father's memory. He said, "He absolutely loved the newspaper."

We sat at a long table stacked with ancient bound leather copies of the newspaper, going back to the Civil War. Brian worried that losing the paper would kick away one more pillar that held up the city. "I'm looking at the issue from 1863, before we even became a state," he told me. But he was allergic to grand pronouncements. He said dryly, "I needed to do something else besides sit in a room and write wills and trusts." In business terms, he was realistic. Print, he said, was a "dwindling community." He hoped to stem the decline by drawing in younger readers online and shoring up print subscribers with an appeal to pride of place. He was running ads that cast the paper in the kind of language usually reserved for selling local cuisine: "Hand Delivered & Printed Every Night by West Virginians for West Virginians."

———

I wandered down to the newsroom to see the editor in chief, John Miller, whom I'd known for twenty years. When I was an intern, he had been the sports editor and an assistant managing editor. By now, I told him, you must have ink in your bones. He smiled and corrected me: "My weary, old, tired bones," he said.

In his late fifties, Miller was tall, with dark, attentive eyes and a thick brown goatee. Not much happened in the newspaper, or in the city, that did not cross his desk. He walked with the heavy step of a man with a lot on his mind. Miller had lived in Clarksburg all his life, and had been at the newspaper almost as long. When he was nine, he joined his three siblings on their paper-delivery route. Their terrain expanded, and by the time he was a teenager, the Miller kids were responsible for slinging papers across a vast swath of the city. Miller wanted to be a teacher, but in 1981, during his freshman year of college, his father suffered a heart attack and Miller had to find work. He started writing sports stories for the paper and eventually got hired on at night so he could finish his college classes during the day.

Whenever he talked about happenings in Clarksburg, or in West Virginia, he spoke in numerals. He still had the soul of a sports writer, hoovering up stats that might bring shape to his world; he could tell me the price of an aspirin at the local hospital, and the number of dilapidated buildings scheduled to be demolished. Most of all, always, he knew the number of jobs opening up and disappearing. "Losing fifteen hundred in Morgantown," he said one day. Another time, he announced, "Two hundred and fifty coming from Mitsubishi." When Thelma's Hot Dogs closed down, he said, "Two-person operation. One of my favorites."

After three decades at the newspaper, Miller viewed his life through the stories he published, good and bad—the economic revival that came with the FBI, the election of Mayor Kates, the rebuttal to the KKK. He remained willfully optimistic. "I'm kind of old school; I don't look at having to tell bad news as something to brag about," he said.

In recent years, Clarksburg had more than its share of bad news. The opioid epidemic was intertwined with West Virginia's economic history; in a state where industrial jobs like coal mining meant physical aches and pains, painkillers arrived first as legitimate treatment, then rippled outward across what the economists Anne Case and Angus Deaton called a "sea of despair." The epidemic fed on poverty, stress, and unemployment. Between 2007 and 2012, wholesalers shipped enough hydrocodone and oxycodone painkillers into West Virginia to give 433 pills to every man, woman, and child in the state, according to an investigation by Eric Eyre of the *Charleston Gazette-Mail*. Pills gave way to heroin and fentanyl, and West Virginia led the nation in drug overdoses. By 2012, the state's indigent burial fund, which helps poor families pay for funerals, was bankrupt.

In Clarksburg, the problem was especially acute. The city lies alongside Interstate 79, the main artery though the hills, between two of the largest communities in the state—Morgantown to the northeast, and Charleston to the southwest. The location had once helped spur its economic growth, but in the epidemic the city became a prime way station for drugs moving back and forth. The annual rate of local arrests of all kinds had grown more than tenfold since I lived there.

Over the years, Miller had watched other drugs come and go—cocaine, crack—but the opioid era felt different. "It was affecting people you wouldn't necessarily expect, people that became hooked on prescription meds and then had to turn to street buys," he told me. The epidemic spilled into public view with the arrival of what folks in town called the "backpackers," men and women hauling their belongings or pushing strollers filled with clothes and food.

I drove to my old apartment building. A first-floor window was boarded up with plywood. I looked up at my place, on the third floor, where a window was missing its glass, and a bedsheet, draped across the hole, was flapping in the wind. A first-time visitor could have mistaken Clarksburg for a place that had never caught up, rather than a city that once shared in an American moment of broader prosperity. The turquoise convertible, once buffed to a high shine, was nowhere in sight.

FOUR

MUD CITY

CHICAGO
APRIL 23, 1905

UNDER A MOONLIT SKY, in the moments after midnight, Albert Sherer, my great-grandfather, was walking home on Chicago's South Side. He was twenty-one years old, a senior at the University of Chicago, short and slight, with round wire glasses. That night, he and friends had watched the Ringling Brothers circus at the Chicago Coliseum and returned to their neighborhoods by train. Albert lived a few blocks from Lake Michigan, with his mother and father, who built grocery-store cabinets for a living.

The Chicago streetscape was an assault on the senses—clattering streetcars, screeching trains, the reek of the slaughterhouses. But after midnight, the city quieted into a stupor, and Albert was alone on Drexel Boulevard. As he passed a line of new mansions, a group of armed men stepped from the bushes and blocked his path.

The gunmen were so young that he thought the holdup was a joke: "Don't be foolish, boys; move along," he said. One of them shot him in the chest. A bullet entered his left lung, near his heart, and he lurched backward. He spotted an onlooker entering a house nearby, and he shouted for help, but a second gunshot entered his back, below the right shoulder. Albert collapsed on the sidewalk in the glow of a streetlamp. The robbers rifled through his pockets but made off with only eighty cents.

In 1905, Chicago recorded more homicides than any of the other big cities in America. The muckraker Lincoln Steffens called the city "first in violence, deepest in dirt; loud, lawless, unlovely." But the shooting of Albert Sherer caused a stir, because the university, still in its infancy, was a source of civic pride. The *Chicago Tribune* put the attack on the front page—"ROBBERS SHOOT A STUDENT"— with a photo of the victim and the prognosis that he was "fatally wounded."

Albert survived the attack, and while he was in the hospital, the president of the university, William R. Harper, sent him a letter of encouragement, noting Albert's "large promise of usefulness." He wrote, "We rejoice that your life is spared." The doctors gave Albert the bullets they pulled from his chest, and he held on to them for the rest of his life. After he died in 1973, his son (my grandfather) didn't quite know what to do with them, so he put them in a small envelope and mailed them to the University of Chicago, which filed the bullets away in the archives, along with clippings and records about the case.

When I was a kid, my grandfather mentioned the shooting once or twice, but only later, when I was back in Chicago after returning from China, did I make an appointment to see what the university still kept in its files. Americans had begun to reckon with the nation's troubled history of crime and incarceration, evolving their notions of punishment and forgiveness, and I often wondered about the story of the shooting. At the archives, a librarian produced a manila folder, and I tipped the contents onto the table. Among the papers, I found two dented slugs of lead, which rested in my palm like river stones.

The folder also held a stack of yellowed clippings about the boys who were imprisoned for the crime. One was William Wojtkowski, a sixteen-year-old who had grown up in a tenement on the South Side and worked as a pressman in a print shop. His parents had emigrated from Poland; his father had died when he was twelve, leaving a widow and four children. William had dropped out of school two years before the shooting. When the attack became a front-page story, he fled town and joined the Navy. Chicago detectives tracked him down on a naval base in Rhode Island, and he confessed.

In court that December, he pleaded guilty to robbery and assault. It was his first arrest, but it shifted the course of his life in ways that I discovered only years later. William told the judge that, after the stickup, he had run away "to get away from bad companions, which I knew I could not do as long as I stayed there." The judge sentenced him to reform school in the central Illinois town of Pontiac, with a prison term to follow. When William arrived, the jailers recorded his answers to a series of questions that sketched out a life on the margins of an American city.

Education?

"Read and Write."

Pauper or Criminal?

"No."

Pecuniary condition?

"Poor."

———

My family reached Chicago just as it was rising as a symbol of a nation on the make. Albert Sherer's grandfather William, a saddle maker barely out of his teens, arrived from northern Pennsylvania in the 1850s and became a grocer. He and his wife, Livina, produced eight new citizens of a city that manifested a spirit that the architect Louis Sullivan, another recent arrival, described as an "intoxicating rawness, a sense of big things to be done."

For much of the year, the land abutting Lake Michigan to the southwest was a boggy mess; one of its first nicknames was "Mud City." But Indigenous Peoples had valued it for centuries because of rich soil and a prime location at the mouth of a river, a natural harbor for vessels seeking shelter from storms off the lake. They named it Chigagou, "the wild-garlic place," for the plants that thrived in the low prairie, and it grew into a crossroads humming with ambition and the pursuit of wealth. By the 1830s, Chicago was a gateway to the West, and its real estate was some of the most sought-after in the country. Chicago was growing faster than any American city before it. In 1901, Frederick Jackson Turner, the historian of the frontier, declared Chicago the place where "all the forces of the nation intersect."

The mythology of Chicago was intertwined with America's cult of invention and reinvention, a creed encapsulated by Thomas Paine's statement: "We have it in our power to begin the world over again." It was a city willed into existence on top of a swamp, and to escape the mud, the city council spent two decades lifting the streets and buildings by as much as fourteen feet. Early mansions and stone buildings were relocated across town, rolled through city traffic like giant dessert carts. In his 1898 novel, *The Gospel of Freedom*, Robert Herrick valorized Chicago as a "stupendous piece of blasphemy against nature," a place in which man was "handling existence as you knead bread in a pan." In 1909, the architects Daniel Burnham and Edward H. Bennett released an audacious vision for redrawing the city again, connecting people to Lake Michigan. "The lakefront by right belongs to the people," Burnham wrote. Public space, he declared, was an essential domain of democracy, a place where people of different backgrounds and experience could come together. In *Nature's Metropolis*, a history of the region, William Cronon wrote that the early city became synonymous with change—the journey "from pastoral simplicity to cosmopolitan sophistication, from rural bondage to urban freedom, from purity to corruption, from childhood to adulthood, from past to future."

In the early twentieth century, the Great Migration began: more than 7 million Black people departed the South in search of safety, freedom, and opportunity. The outbreak of World War I in 1914 had heightened demand for new workers in the factories of northern cities, spurring the largest mass movement in American history. *The Chicago Defender*, the city's leading Black newspaper, launched a campaign to encourage migration, publishing lists of organizations that coordinated travel and housing, and Chicago became known, with fragile optimism, as the "Promised Land." Before the migration, African Americans had made up 2 percent of Chicago's population; by 1970, they constituted 33 percent.

But the migration stirred a powerful backlash. White neighborhoods formed "restrictive covenants," which barred homeowners from renting or selling to Black residents. Migrants were primarily limited to a stretch of the South Side known as the "Black Belt," and the city government was indifferent to overwhelmed schools and tenements. The mansions on Drexel Boulevard, which Albert glimpsed in the moments before the robbery, were divided into boardinghouses and nursing homes. During a visit, the Swiss architect Le Corbusier wrote that a "villa becomes a village." In his telling, "There are weeds in the rubbish-filled gardens, behind rusting iron fences. There is misery there." Segregation was taking hold. In her 1921 novel, *The Girls*, Edna Ferber, who went on to win a Pulitzer Prize, wrote of a family of South Siders determined to get to the North Side: "Anyone who has lived in Chicago," she wrote, "knows that you don't live on the South Side."

In the 1930s, federal agencies such as the Home Owners' Loan Corporation prevented the issuance of mortgages in Black neighborhoods under the policy that became known as "redlining," named for maps with red zones marking areas considered too risky for loans and insurance. By 1940, Chicago was more racially segregated than Richmond, Virginia, the capital of the Confederacy, and then civic planners and politicians made it official. They enshrined segregation in an architecture of exclusion, a set of powerful policies expanding across the country.

Interstate highways built in the 1950s and '60s carved boundaries between the races from Buffalo to Atlanta to Kansas City. In Chicago, real-estate speculators known as "panic peddlers" urged white homeowners to sell cheaply before it was "too late," and then flipped the homes to Black buyers who had limited options in a discriminatory market. The result was accelerated white flight and almost uniformly Black neighborhoods.

Mayor Richard J. Daley took office in 1955, the same year that Rosa Parks refused to move to the back of a bus. But he never embraced the civil rights movement. He lived by what his biographers Adam Cohen and Elizabeth Taylor called a "flinty conservatism," which was popular with Chicago's working-class ethnic whites: "Daley believed that poor people should pull themselves up by their bootstraps, as his Bridgeport neighbors struggled to do." From cradle to grave, Daley lived within a few blocks in a single neighborhood, and, as his adviser Edward Marciniak later put it, his position was "If you grew up in a place, why do you want to come into mine?" He opposed desegregation in schools and affirmative action in the police department, and he used urban-renewal funds to build vast empires of public housing. Though he voiced concerns about building the public high-rises that became symbols of Chicago segregation, he approved the construction, and they eventually became "filing cabinets" for the poor, as a federal commission put it.

In 1966, Martin Luther King Jr. came to Chicago to protest housing discrimination. He called it part of a campaign "to eradicate a vicious system which seeks to further colonize thousands of Negroes within a slum environment." He and his followers marched through the Marquette Park neighborhood of the South Side, home to the white ethnic working class, Poles and Lithuanians, who had invested their life savings in their homes. They feared losing their investments and their neighborhood, as they saw it, to integration. And so when King and his followers arrived, the residents hurled stones and bottles. King was hit in the head with a rock, and said afterward, "I have seen many demonstrations in the South, but I have never seen anything so hostile and so hateful as I've seen here today."

By the end of August, King and Mayor Daley had struck a "Summit Agreement," which pledged an end to housing discrimination, but it was unenforceable, and Daley later shrugged it off as a "gentleman's agreement." Nevertheless, by the end of the decade, King's generation had achieved a series of moral and legal breakthroughs—the 1963 March on Washington, the Civil Rights Act of 1964, the Voting Rights Act of 1965—that gave liberals confidence that barriers to equality were giving way. In 1973, two of Lyndon Johnson's advisers, Ben J. Wattenberg and Richard M. Scammon, declared, "For the first time in the history of the republic, truly large and growing numbers of American blacks have been moving into the middle class." It was, they wrote, a "massive achievement," and by "all appearances it is here to stay."

———

In the summer of 1999, I packed up my apartment in Clarksburg and headed to Chicago for a glorified internship on the city desk of the *Chicago Tribune*. It was among the lowest rungs of the newsroom, but it paid enough to cover the rent for a one-bedroom apartment in Bucktown, a neighborhood on the near northwest side that took its name from the goats, or "bucks," that Polish settlers had grazed there. By the time I arrived, the Poles were almost gone, having followed the highways to the suburbs. For decades, redlining had stopped Black homeowners from moving in, and empty homes had fallen into decay. Eventually, a generation of Mexicans and Central Americans arrived, heaving themselves up the ladder that was off limits to Black people, another turn in Chicago's long history of striving and thwarting.

A few miles away, downtown Chicago was flush with evidence of the fortunes coursing through the local finance industry. For all of the city's unfussy pride, Chicago had sprouted so many new luxury town houses and condos near the lake that the *Tribune* had created a real-estate column about the rich and famous called "Upper Bracket." I arrived at the newspaper in the final abundant years before the Internet upended the business. The *Tribune* had a firm, if controversial, hold over America's third-largest city. "To write about the Middle West and leave the *Tribune* out is like playing Hamlet not only without the prince of Denmark but without Polonius," John Gunther wrote in 1944, on the return to his hometown. At the time, the *Tribune* had the highest circulation of any broadsheet in America. "A great many Chicagoans despise the *Tribune*. But they buy it every day," he wrote.

Their contempt surrounded the owner and editor, Robert "Colonel" McCormick, an ardent conservative described by an opponent as "the greatest mind of the fourteenth century." Six feet four and austere, with a white mustache, McCormick was partial to the grand gesture. During a picnic at his estate, he greeted his guests by emerging from a van on horseback. McCormick's paper railed against liberalism, the New Deal, Roosevelt, and labor unions, but in the decades after his death in 1955, the news pages shed the ideology and reported aggressively on the city, the suburbs, and beyond.

I learned the rhythms of a big-city paper. In the morning, I'd check the schedule of assignments, each listed with a one-word shorthand known as a "slug": MAYOR, PROTEST, or SNOW. Without fail, there was always a slug for MAYHEM, a roundup of shootings and other violence that had transpired overnight. Its presence every morning, as reliable as a metronome, reflected a deeper fact: writing honestly about a place—any place—means writing about power, who has it and who does not, and what some people will do to get it or deprive others of it. In practice, that was expressed in the city's endless struggle over matters of race, money, and violence. I came to see that combination as Chicago's unofficial refrain.

Sometimes, if the MAYHEM story included a big murder, the editors would assign one of the rookie reporters to track down enough detail to make it a story of its own. More often than not, for reasons of tragic similarity, that new story was slugged BOYSHOT. I was often struck by the agonies contained in those two syllables, the newsroom version of "Jesus wept." I spent many days climbing the stairs in the public housing towers, whose names had become symbols of a crumbling system—Cabrini-Green, Stateway Gardens, the Robert Taylor Homes. They represented ten of the fifteen poorest census tracts in America, and the populations were 92 percent Black.

In the fall of 1999, the city announced that it was demolishing all fifty-one of the decaying public housing towers, with plans to build thousands of new homes. Cranes clawed at the shells of the high-rises, under a plan intended, as the city put it, to "promote self-sufficiency for public housing residents." It involved moving fifty thousand people, a logistical undertaking akin, in scale, to knocking down almost every home in Greenwich and rebuilding it elsewhere. As part of the fanfare, Andrew Cuomo, the U.S. secretary of housing and urban development, flew to Chicago and declared that it was time to "stop putting bandages on bullet wounds."

├────────┤

That winter, I was assigned to cover my first political campaign, a contest the editors considered so simple and lopsided that it didn't require the attention of a seasoned political hand. The longtime congressman Bobby Rush was running against an obscure young law professor, Barack Obama. (It would be another five years before the speech at the Democratic National Convention made Obama a celebrity.)

Rush was an icon of local politics. He had grown up in public housing, dropped out of high school, and joined the Black Panthers. In 1968, Chicago police killed his friend and fellow Panther leader Fred Hampton during a raid on Hampton's home; Rush accused them of an "assassination" and became a symbol of resistance to the city's Democratic "machine," the white-led political network that dominated power in Chicago. He went to prison on weapons charges, but was elected in 1992 as the representative of the First Congressional District. It was a uniquely symbolic patch of political terrain. In 1929, the First District had sent Oscar Stanton De Priest, the son of freed slaves, to Congress, where he was the only African American for three terms. Since then, it had been represented by a Black politician longer than any other district in America.

Obama was thirty-eight years old, a transplant from Hawaii, Indonesia, and Harvard who had less than three years of political experience as a member of the Illinois Senate. He hated the hierarchies and paralysis in Springfield, the state capital, and after Rush lost a run for mayor,

Obama decided to mount a challenge. In recent years, he had attracted attention on the edges of politics for making a case that greater unity was possible around the right ideas. "The political debate is now so skewed, so limited, so distorted," Obama told a reporter in 1995, during his first run for office. "People are hungry for community; they miss it. They are hungry for change." Conservative Christians were ascendant, and Obama was trying to seize the language of morality. "Right now we have a society that talks about the irresponsibility of teens getting pregnant, not the irresponsibility of a society that fails to educate them to aspire for more," he said. He had picked up high-powered admirers among political columnists and "Lakefront liberals"—but, in the district he needed to win, he remained an outsider. Rush's name recognition was 90 percent; Obama's was 9 percent.

I called Obama at his office to ask for an interview, and he invited me to the Valois Restaurant, a cash-only cafeteria near the University of Chicago. He arrived alone and waited in a line of senior citizens for a cup of tea. Then he squeezed in behind a small Formica table near the front door, his long legs protruding from the side. He loosened his tie, and I pushed my tape recorder closer to him, to drown out the clatter of dishes in the kitchen.

For an hour, Obama tried to critique the condition of the district and its elected leaders without sounding imperious. "I see so much potential in the First District," he told me. "And I can design a program, not just fund one." It was the technocratic case that his aides hated. Ron Davis, a campaign field coordinator who also taught math at Kennedy-King College, had been trawling the barbershops and churches for support. He had taken to needling Obama: "Motherfucker, you got to talk better, you got to talk to the people!"

Ted Kleine, who covered the campaign closely for *The Reader*, a weekly newspaper, captured how Obama's opponents saw him: an egghead and a tool of white liberals, cutting the line of Black leaders ahead of him. State senator Donne Trotter, who was also vying for Rush's seat, told Kleine, "Barack is viewed in part to be the white man in blackface in our community." During a talk-radio forum on WVON, as Rush described his role leading a march against police shootings,

Obama interjected: "It's not enough for us just to protest police misconduct without thinking systematically about how we're going to change practice." Rush was incensed. "Barack Obama went to Harvard and became an educated fool," Rush told Kleine. "Barack is a person who *read* about the civil rights protests and thinks he knows all about it."

When we spoke, I expected self-defense, a flash of productive rage, but Obama sidestepped the brawl over class, education, and racial credibility. He was convinced that his future rested on the power to make voters and politicians less rigid in their identities, not more. "Less than halfway into the campaign, I knew in my bones that I was going to lose," Obama wrote years later in *The Audacity of Hope*. "Each morning from that point forward I awoke with a vague sense of dread."

I wrote up a story on the race, calling Obama "a rising Democratic star," but I didn't know enough to write anything worthwhile. I quoted almost nothing from the future president. A few days later, I recorded over his interview.

Over the next several weeks, I followed him to community centers and coffee shops and retirement homes. He liked to greet people outside without a hat or gloves. The "Kenyan Kennedy," aides joked. He was still mastering his narrative and rhetoric; he had not yet perfected the story of his own biracial ancestry as an analogy for an encompassing vision of America. But he gave deep, thoughtful answers about policy, including his hopes for providing universal health insurance, cutting juvenile crime, and changing police practices. Some of his answers were so thoughtful that, during one speech, the man beside me fell into a deep and audible sleep.

But even I sensed that Obama was no ordinary contender. He was making a sustained case against cynicism, an argument for a new generation of politics that would be a rebuke to the jowly old wise guys in city hall and their creaking, racist machine. He was exhilarating to be around, even if he didn't stand a chance of winning that race. On the night of the primary, March 21, Obama got walloped by thirty-one points, a larger loss than even he expected. ("I was completely mortified," he later told one of his biographers, David Remnick.) I wrote up a few paragraphs on his loss. It was an unceremonious end to an inspiring encounter.

In 2001, after two years on the city desk, I was assigned to the *Tribune*'s bureau in New York. I arrived in Manhattan in August. In retrospect, those late-summer weeks in New York feel like the weightless instant when a ball has reached the top of its arc and not yet begun to plunge.

On the morning that the planes hit the World Trade Center, I happened to be en route to West Virginia, to visit Clarksburg and write an article about the coal industry. I found a train back to New York the next day. For three months, I did not leave the city. I wrote about the origins and the aftermath of the attacks, which eventually led me to assignments in the Middle East, China, and a decade abroad. When I finally came home in 2013, I found myself drawn back to stories that had been interrupted by history. I headed back to Chicago.

———

A decade into the twenty-first century, Chicago's leaders still voiced a bumptious pride. Richard M. Daley, the mayor, eventually surpassed his father's record as the city's longest-serving ruler and was intent on muscling Chicago into the company of what he called "the New Yorks and LAs and all that."

The pockets of luxury that appeared in the 1990s had grown into a city within the city. Daley had planted new trees and flower beds downtown, and replaced a wasteland of old rail lines with a spectacular expanse called Millennium Park, twenty-five rolling acres of grass and trees, a place for art, music, and lounging. It came in so far over budget that the *Tribune* wondered if Chicago was, officially, "the most corrupt city in America," but white-collar Chicago was thriving; the number of wealthy census tracts had quadrupled since 1970. International companies had moved to town—Motorola Solutions, Beam Suntory, GE Healthcare—and unemployment across the metropolitan area soon dropped to 4.1 percent, the lowest since the government started tracking it in 1976. Like much of the country, Chicago had registered a decline in homicides to levels not seen since the 1960s. Most neighborhoods became safer, including for Blacks and Latinos, though in some places it had gotten far worse.

It was easy to get seduced. In the mid-2000s, *The Economist* magazine hailed Chicago as "humming with prosperity, sparkling with new buildings, new sculptures, new parks, and generally exuding vitality." Visiting from China in 2010, I wrote a piece about Daley in *The New Yorker*, but I spent too much time in his limo and not enough time with his critics. *The Reader*, the weekly paper, rightly criticized the story under the headline "Taking *The New Yorker* for a Ride." I had focused so much on Daley's fixations with London and Beijing that I failed to recognize how much he was driving the city's nutrients to its core, while the extremities starved.

When Daley retired in 2011, he was succeeded by an ally, Rahm Emanuel, who had served as Obama's chief of staff. Emanuel inherited a city of untenable economic contrasts—a quintessential case of American inequality. The scale of Chicago's inequality reflected two basic facts. The first was familiar in the U.S. economy writ large: the collapse of industrial jobs. Though Americans often thought of industrial collapse as the problem of the white working class, it was no less acute in predominantly Black neighborhoods of Chicago. On the South and West sides, the evidence of crisis was inescapable, a collision of Americas that the historian Andrew Diamond, in his 2017 book, *Chicago on the Make*, called "Manhattan smashed against Detroit."

Half a century ago, a giant Western Electric plant employed more than 43,000 workers; International Harvester had a staff of 14,000; Sears, Roebuck and Company kept 10,000 people on the job. Acme made steel; General Mills produced breakfast cereal. The sheer scale of the loss since the 1960s, as the factories started to move abroad or to the suburbs, is shocking. The electric plant was gone by the end of the decade; Sears moved its headquarters, followed by International Harvester, Acme, and General Mills. Not only did those closures eliminate tens of thousands of jobs for people with few educational credentials, but they also cut off the revenue that went to local banks, grocery stores, and gas stations. William Julius Wilson, the Harvard sociologist who studied a Chicago neighborhood for his 1996 book, *When Work Disappears*, estimated that it lost 75 percent of its businesses between 1960 and 1970. The die-off in employment was even more dramatic. In 1970, the Back of the Yards neighborhood, on the near South Side, had 11,646 retail jobs. By 2015, only 1,849 remained. The neighborhoods affected most were predominantly Black and Latino.

———

The other source of Chicago's epic inequality was segregation. I'd sometimes pull over next to the old sites of the vanished housing projects, which had been demolished with such fanfare a decade earlier. Redbrick town houses now filled the space at some sites; others were still vacant lots of dusty grass, with plastic bags fluttering from the weeds.

The optimism around those relocations had curdled. Nobody mourned the loss of Cabrini-Green or Robert Taylor, but, for many, resettlement had only deepened the divides over race and income. Residents had been promised counseling to identify safer, more promising neighborhoods, as well as small infusions of cash to help them put down deposits. Neither fully materialized. For years after, some former residents converged each summer on the empty grass lots for reunions. For all the pain that echoed through the old project, they missed the social connection and camaraderie their prior homes had provided.

A decade after the end of the high-rise projects, Chicago was still considered the most segregated big city in America. Paul Fischer, a political scientist at Lake Forest College, tracked more than three thousand families who moved out of public housing from 1995 to 2002, and found that virtually all of them wound up in heavily Black census tracts. A 2014 study by the Chicago Lawyers' Committee for Civil Rights Under Law documented frequent discrimination against those people who tried to rent using subsidized vouchers from the Chicago Housing Authority. In the city's northwest, landlords refused to rent to them 58 percent of the time.

As a result of that discrimination, Black residents clustered in concentrated pockets of the city, where they were consistently cut off from the economic boom downtown. Chicago did not lack for employment; up to 700,000 jobs were within a thirty-minute commute from thriving neighborhoods in the Loop and the North Side, according to a report by the Great Cities Institute. But on the South Side, there were just 50,000 jobs within that distance. The distance from those jobs stymied the generation of other forms of employment as well; in theory, economists say, each new white-collar job should have generated employment for five more people—the waiters, builders, and dog walkers of the city. But, in Chicago, segregation interrupted that cascade.

Overall, white and Black families in Chicago were moving in fundamentally opposite economic directions. The first generation of African Americans to come of age after civil rights was losing ground. According to a 2007 study, white members of the middle class earned, on average, almost $20,000 per year more than their parents; Black members were earning $9,000 *less* than their parents. Patrick Sharkey, a Princeton sociologist, found that more than 70 percent of African Americans living in the poorest, most racially segregated neighborhoods in 2010 came from the same families that were there four decades earlier. He traced the pattern to a legacy of political decisions that maintained segregation, disinvested in the economy, and drove people deeper into the criminal justice system. As Sharkey put it, they had become "stuck in place."

—

Tenesha Barner called it "the bubble"—"Unless you step outside of it," she said, "you know nothing else." Barner, a single mom with two children, was constantly adjusting her mental map of where the kids could go safely. The public library a few blocks east? No way. Kids from her neighborhood didn't walk more than four blocks in that direction because of a feud among the gangs. "It's stupid, it's crazy, but the only way they can leave the community is if they're in a vehicle," she said.

Barner had a low tolerance for foolishness. In her late thirties, she was an assistant at Dulles Elementary School, her alma mater, where she monitored the hallways, prodded kids into class, and helped them through the agonies of homework, adolescent life, and the world outside. She commanded intense respect, in part, because of her local credentials. "I don't get off work and get in a fancy car and drive to a beautiful house," she said. "No, baby, we're going to walk these same sidewalks with this ice and snow. We're going to slip together."

Born in 1978, Barner had lived in Parkway Gardens her entire life. The apartment complex was conceived in the 1950s as a rebuttal to housing discrimination: Chicago's first co-op owned by Black families. Sandwiched between the Woodlawn neighborhood and a vast rail yard, Parkway had immediate cachet—a home to judges, journalists, and factory workers, as well as a young Michelle Obama, who lived there as a toddler in the 1960s. Barner's grandfather Eddie Barner, formerly of Tchula, Mississippi, had a fifth-grade education but a reliable career at the factory that made the Solo brand of plastic cups, on the South Side. Her grandmother Susie was a seamstress for the suit-maker Hart, Schaffner & Marx.

Barner recalled that when she was little, "You didn't need security in front of the building; you didn't need gates." Each spring, residents held a cleanup week. "We had these big flower beds where we would go out and plant. We would paint the benches, and each building would have bake sales." The complex fielded its own cheerleading team, which competed against cheerleading teams from other housing complexes. But by the late 1990s, the factories were gone and violence drove buyers away. The co-op was converted into a low-income rental complex. Barner's parents struggled with drugs. Her father contracted HIV and died when she was eighteen. Over the years, the road beside Parkway Gardens acquired a singular reputation for violence. Between 2011 and 2014, the area had more shootings than anywhere else in Chicago.

Inside that world, Barner found her own role models. At fifteen, pregnant with her son and thinking of dropping out of high school, she grew close to Jennifer Thomas, a young Black police officer who patrolled Englewood High School. Officer Thomas was nineteen years older, but she took to calling Barner her daughter. "I knew that going to school every day, I would see someone who I knew loved me, who would show me the attention that I need. So I was like, 'I *have* to continue,' not just because she's there, but because now I'm carrying someone who needs me."

After Barner had Antwan, she had to make up classes at night and in the summers. Antwan's father was scarce. "Financially, he would try to help out, but physically, he didn't know how to be a father because his father wasn't in his life. But I'm like, 'I have to raise my son, regardless of if the father's there or not.' It's a saying, 'Mama's baby, daddy's maybe.' So it's on me." Even though Antwan's father was rarely around, his family became indispensable; they and her sister watched the baby so Barner could go to school. "Once I came home from school, I had my son, and I was doing homework and having dinner with him right there with me. But I was determined, 'I'm *going* to finish.' And I did. I finished school in June of 1996, on time."

In the decades since, Barner became only more determined to control what she could in her life. Her apartment was spare and immaculate—a minimalist's dream. "I don't like *junk*," she said. She was a generous but exacting neighbor. "I take it upon myself to buy these little air fresheners, and once the janitor cleans up and mops and sweeps, I put one on each floor," she said. For better and worse, Barner's roots were so deep in Parkway that she rarely considered life outside the bubble. On the wall in her living room, she hung a big panoramic photo of the city. "There's no other place but Chicago," she said proudly. "No other place." Deirdre Koldyke, a licensed therapist who coordinated activities for mothers in the neighborhood, had given her the photo as a present. "Barner is sort of the unofficial mayor," Koldyke said. "You can't go anywhere on the South Side where she doesn't know someone."

But Barner put rigid boundaries around her mental map of the city she loved. The expensive stores on Michigan Avenue, Chicago's most famous shopping strip, were foreign territory. "As a Black person you get looked at. You go into Neiman Marcus, and everybody wants to know, 'Can I help you?' What they really want to know is, 'What are you doing in here?'"

Nobody had expected the election of the first Black president to bring a rapid end to centuries of bigotry in America. But, as Obama's administration wore on, the divergence between the hopes for his era and the enduring realities of discrimination delivered an added sting. In July 2013, a Florida jury acquitted a gunman, George Zimmerman, who claimed self-defense in the killing of Trayvon Martin, an unarmed Black teenager. Outside the courthouse, young activists staged a massive sit-in and first popularized the slogan "Black Lives Matter." The birth of Black Lives Matter marked a turn in progressive politics; five years into Obama's tenure, activists spoke more bluntly about their disillusionment with his vision of long-range change; they wanted Americans to "stay woke" to injustice, a spirit of awakening that reached back to Martin Luther King Jr., who said in 1965, "There is nothing more tragic than to sleep through a revolution."

The enduring reality of segregation, the growing awareness of immobility, were so at odds with the story America told itself that people were slow to absorb the full reality. But the evidence was unmistakable: not only had Americans stopped moving as often up the income ladder, but they had stopped moving geographically as well. Since the 1940s, the ranks of those who relocated in a given year had dropped by half, to 9.8 percent, the lowest rate since the census had started measuring it. Educated, prosperous Americans were still moving for jobs and spouses and larger homes; others were not, even if they couldn't find work. In many cases, they remained trapped in the shadow of the financial crisis, because their homes never regained enough value to exceed the cost of their mortgages. The country, as one report put it, had become "divided between the mobile and the stuck."

The canyons between Chicago's high-income white communities and low-income Black communities had become so vast that researchers struggled to put them into relation with each other. Robert Sampson, a Harvard sociologist, spent more than twenty years leading a study of human development in Chicago neighborhoods. He discovered that in virtually every measure of a life's distress—low birth weight, infant mortality, teen pregnancy, physical abuse, homicide—the gaps constituted, in Sampson's terms, a "difference of kind, not of degree."

No measure showed a starker contrast than the distribution of violence. Since 1990, homicide rates in New York, Los Angeles, Dallas, and Washington, D.C., had dropped by at least 70 percent. Even in Chicago, the subject of frequent discussions of violence, the homicide rate had dropped by a third since 1990. That was hard-won progress, though it was easy for Americans to misunderstand how truly out of sync they were with the rest of the advanced world. "More people are murdered in Chicago in a single year than over the last fifty years in Stockholm," Sampson observed in his 2011 book, *Great American City*. Moreover, he told me, for a subset of the city, life had grown more dangerous. Sampson detailed how the distance of just a few blocks determined the basic probabilities in life—the chances of hearing a tip on a job prospect, or receiving a first-time loan, or being hit by crossfire. In predominantly Black neighborhoods, homicide rates were thirteen times higher, on average, than in better-off white areas.

The cumulative effects of disinvestment, violence, and neglect had become so pronounced that a generation of Black Chicagoans felt little connection to the government and politics that attracted so much attention downtown. During the Great Depression, the country had mobilized to stem unemployment of 25 percent, but in some predominantly Black neighborhoods of Chicago, the unemployment for young men was double that—and politicians weren't doing anything about it. For many, the only encounter they had with the government was through the criminal justice system. "The incarceration rate in the highest-ranked Black community in Chicago is forty times higher than the incarceration rate in the highest-ranked white community," Sampson told me. "You can't even compare them."

For all of the city's purported faith in transformation and renewal, it had slipped into a political and economic torpor that left people stuck in place. A century and a half after my family had arrived, Chicago was once again as Frederick Jackson Turner had described it: the place where "all the forces of the nation intersect." But not in a way that anyone wanted.

FIVE

EVERYONE IS DOING IT
(TAKE 1)

FROM 2007 TO 2010, Chip Skowron's hedge fund paid him $31,067,356. He and Cheryl built a house on three acres of a Greenwich hilltop, a New England shingle-style home with generous proportions: seven bedrooms, eleven bathrooms, a wine cellar, a billiards room, a spa, a pool house, an eight-car garage, and a handsome stone wall. He collected rare sports cars—a Ferrari 458, an Aston Martin Vanquish, an Alfa Romeo 8C Spider, and an Ariel Atom II. He joined the Monticello Motor Club, a private racetrack nearby, whose members included the comedian Jerry Seinfeld and the professional driver Jeff Gordon.

Sometimes he laughed at the scale of it all, but houses like his were going up all over town. In a single year, Greenwich had issued permits for the demolition of 176 homes—triple the level five years earlier. Lining the backroads were lunar-like canyons, with yellow bulldozers carving holes for underground movie theaters, squash courts, and wine cellars. Many of the new homes conformed to a style that wags called Stockbroker Georgian. Mark Mariani, a local developer who built many of them, was earning so much that he acquired two private jets and houses in Anguilla and Telluride, as well as a mansion on Round Hill Road adorned with cherub statues depicting his wife and children. He was unsentimental about the old houses he demolished. "I don't even walk inside them," he told a reporter. "I could care less."

The appetites seemed to reach an even higher orbit when, in 2008, a Russian businessman named Valery Kogan announced plans to demolish his $19 million mansion—which once belonged to the mattress king Zalmon Simmons—and replace it with a 54,000-square-foot château with twenty-six toilets, a patio in the shape of a Les Paul guitar, and a stadium-like mechanized dome for inclement weather. That was too much, even for Greenwich; Kogan, facing resistance from his neighbors, scaled back his vision to a home with fifteen bathrooms. But concerns remained, and eventually he gave up and moved elsewhere.

As the fortunes in Greenwich climbed, a pattern emerged. After residents had secured the major markers of wealth—the home, the right schools, the serenity of private aviation—they turned their attention to the real game in town: the *refining* of advantage, the expansion of the margins, the hedging against trouble, real and imagined. If you knew where to look, you could hone every edge of your life—from your life expectancy to your tax avoidance to your child's performance on the SATs. You could, in other words, make sure that the winners keep winning.

In Skowron's case, his fortune gave him sudden entrée to politics; he became a major donor to John McCain's 2008 presidential campaign. He also joined the board of AmeriCares, the group that had sent him to Kosovo in his days as a doctor. He and Cheryl cochaired the annual benefit, which raised $1 million in a single night, setting a record for the group. Among the new generation of financiers, philanthropy and politics often went hand in hand. They could deploy their fortunes to advance their visions of policy in education or poverty alleviation, without having to wade into the scrutiny of public political debate. To critics, wealthy philanthropists were subverting the democratic process. In bypassing the public sector, in the belief that it was incompetent or inefficient, they were hastening a decline of trust and investment in government, and foreclosing society's collective discussion of how to govern itself.

At times, Skowron couldn't help but marvel at how rapidly his wealth had accumulated. During a visit to Geneva, where he and other fund managers were courting wealthy European investors, he visited the restroom, where he ran into two of his former employers, Steve Cohen on the right, and Izzy Englander on the left. In less time than Skowron had taken to earn a medical degree, he had gone from studying *Getting Started in Hedge Funds* to relieving himself between billionaires. "I'm just standing there, thinking, 'This is crazy,'" he recalled.

In ways both explicit and unannounced, the extraordinary concentration of fortune in Greenwich had a way of distorting one's perception. Even for people who traveled and read broadly, it was easy to lose sight of how the rest of the world experienced things like influence, power, and money. Cliff Asness, a Greenwich hedge-fund manager, once told an interviewer, "In some parts of the world, if you said, 'My daddy runs a hedge fund,' they'd say, 'What's a hedge fund?' In Greenwich, Connecticut, the kids say, 'What kind of hedge fund is your daddy running? Is he event arbitrage? Trend following?'"

———

The story of how Greenwich—and the broader U.S. economy—became wrapped so tightly around finance can feel like the kind of change so vast that it defies concrete accounts of cause and effect. In fact, it hinges on some identifiable changes that most Americans barely noticed at the time. They are decisions that transformed not only the culture of wealth—how it was built, taxed, and spent—but also what America itself values and what it ignores.

For most of the first two centuries of Wall Street, the American finance industry occupied a narrow slice of the economy and focused mostly on funneling savings into new businesses, mortgages, stocks, and bonds. Historically, the bylaws of the New York Stock Exchange required trading firms, such as Goldman Sachs, to be private partnerships. "When it was time for you to go, you sold your share to the next generation," William Wechsler, a former managing director at Greenwich Associates, a consulting firm, told me. "It was culturally acceptable to get to a certain level of success and retire happy." The arrangement discouraged wanton risks: "In managing the firm, you always had to think, How do I not blow up the entire thing?" But in 1969, the stock exchange, pressured by firms that wanted to grow and modernize, scrapped the requirement for partnerships, and the banks began a transformation. Over the next thirty years, all the largest banks in America went public, which eliminated the old restraint on risk by unlocking vast stores of other people's money. They used it to hire thousands of traders and experiment with exotic new securities. Traders speculated far more aggressively, because they were no longer risking their partners' money, and if they bet right, they could score a windfall.

Another far-reaching decision was unfolding at the same time. In the first decades after World War II, big American businesses presented themselves as responsive to customers, shareholders, workers, and society at large. Abuses abounded—companies excluded women and people of color, factories fouled the environment, and Big Tobacco lied for decades. But executives generally believed that they would profit over the long term if they helped the United States maintain basic assets, including a sound legal and political system, a modern infrastructure, aggressive research and development, and a healthy workforce. As the CEO of General Motors, Charles Wilson, put it to the Senate in 1953, "What was good for our country was good for General Motors, and vice versa."

But by the late 1960s, companies faced growing competition from a revived Japan and Germany. Milton Friedman, a libertarian economist at the University of Chicago, called for a fundamental change: on September 13, 1970, in *The New York Times Magazine*, Friedman published a piece titled "The Social Responsibility of Business Is to Increase Its Profits." Friedman argued that American competition was imperiled by "subversive" notions that business should be expected to help "restrain inflation, improve the environment, fight poverty and so on and on." On the contrary, he wrote, "there is one and only one social responsibility of business—to use its resources and engage in activities designed to increase its profits so long as it stays within the rules of the game, which is to say, engages in open and free competition without deception or fraud."

Friedman, who won the Nobel Prize in 1976, succeeded more than he might have dreamed. His work spawned several influential new theories of corporate governance. In 1976, Michael Jensen, one of Friedman's former students, coauthored one of history's most influential scholarly papers under the bland title "Theory of the Firm." It argued that companies will grow fastest if CEOs stop trying to please so many "stakeholders"—including employees, customers, and society at large; instead, they should aim to serve shareholders' interests above all others. To encourage executives to put shareholders first, Jensen proposed turning the executives into shareholders by shifting their pay from salary to stock. "The stock portion of a CEO's compensation used to be a few percentage points," Rick Wartzman, of the Drucker Institute, told me. "Today, it's fifty to eighty percent. Suddenly, maximizing shareholder value is in their *personal* interest. And what's the easiest way to make the stock go up in the short term? Cut expenses like training and wages. And inequality has exploded."

The vision of "shareholder capitalism," as it was called, set the course for a generation of business leaders. At General Electric, the company once led by Owen Young and Reg Jones of Greenwich, Jones's successor, Jack Welch, slashed a hundred thousand jobs, earning him the admiring Wall Street nickname "Neutron Jack." Welch and his lieutenants prospered. "When the market as a whole took off, I made more in the late nineties than I deserved," a senior executive told me. "Depending on stock, you could make five times your salary. It was amazing. It was ridiculous, too, but it was amazing. I'm all for performance bonuses, but I had nothing to do with what was driving the stock price."

That executive watched the board of directors, composed of fellow CEOs and advised by "compensation consultants," give GE executives ever higher pay packages. "There was a limited feedback loop where these people were all dealing with each other and the compensation consultants. There was an enormous conflict of interest. It went wild."

But truly maximizing shareholder value required one more decision. In 1982, shortly after John Shad, a banker who was inspired by the Chicago economists, became chairman of the Securities and Exchange Commission, he loosened a limit that had been in place since the 1930s, which prevented companies from boosting their stock price by buying stock off the open market. Shad instituted esoteric-sounding Rule 10b-18, which cleared the way for stock "buybacks." In the decades since then, American companies have spent more and more of their money propping up the price of their stock. Between 2008 and 2017, companies in the S&P 500 spent 53 percent of their profits on buying their own shares—and gave another 35 percent to shareholders in the form of dividends, according to the economist William Lazonick. In other words, for every dollar in profits, eighty-eight cents went to benefiting shareholders and senior executives instead of toward research, retraining, equipment, or wages and benefits.

The cumulative effect of those changes, over a half century, rendered the world of finance far more profitable—and far less useful to the real economy. In 1982, Wall Street had taken home 6 percent of America's corporate profits. In 2017, it took home 23 percent. With so much money going to trading and bonuses, banks spent far less on lending to create new jobs and businesses. Between 1978 and 2012, the percentage of American businesses that qualified as new declined by 44 percent, according to an analysis of census data. In all, the stock-option revolution transformed corporate behavior so radically that Michael Jensen, the professor who launched it, eventually lamented that it had become, as he put it, "managerial heroin."

———

As the fall of 2007 gave way to winter, Chip Skowron was working on a big bet. For months, he'd been accumulating stock in a biotech company—Human Genome Sciences, Inc.—that was developing a new drug to treat hepatitis C. The drug, Albuferon, had the potential to save millions of lives and generate billions in profits, if clinical trials could prove that it was effective and safe.

Like other health-care investors, Skowron spent much of his time trying to divine what would become the next big drug. He attended medical conferences; he visited labs in Europe and Asia; he spent millions on "expert networks," the referral services that allowed investors to speak with industry researchers at rates of up to a thousand dollars an hour. "There's a community of doctors that are talking all the time about these trials and what's going on. They want to, and need to, know what drugs are good in development, what are not good. They want to be able to share that insight with people and get paid for it."

Hedge funds were always looking for the shred of insight that traders called "informational edge"—any tidbit of information on an event that might boost or depress the price of a stock. It's illegal to pay a senior company employee to trade information that's unavailable to the public, but, as with the borderlands between corruption and campaign finance, a good lawyer could debate and contest the definitions of "pay" or "trade." From Skowron's perspective, ruminating about the fine-grained distinctions was not his job: "For me, that line of demarcation around something that is 'material nonpublic information' from someone with 'a fiduciary duty'—that was like, '*Whatever.*'"

Ever since early 2007, when the clinical trials for Albuferon looked promising, Skowron had been building his hoard of shares. By December, they were worth $65 million. If the drug worked, he guessed that the value would soar another 70 percent. In truth, it was more than a guess; he had carefully developed a reason to be confident. The previous year, while attending a conference in Vienna, he had asked to be introduced to Dr. Yves M. Benhamou, a prominent liver-disease expert whose research was widely published in medical journals. Benhamou, who was in his late forties, lived in Neuilly-sur-Seine, an affluent Paris suburb. Benhamou was one of five members of the steering committee for a clinical trial that was testing Albuferon on patients around the world.

Skowron started spending more time with the doctor. In the spring of 2007, he flew to Barcelona, where Benhamou was attending a conference. They gathered in Skowron's suite at the hotel, and he asked Benhamou to work for FrontPoint as a consultant. As a "present" from the firm, Skowron handed Benhamou an envelope containing five thousand euros—a measure of their appreciation for his expertise. That fall, Benhamou contacted Skowron to say he was planning a trip to New York with his wife; he asked for advice on hotels. Instead of giving advice, Skowron told his assistant to book the couple, at Skowron's expense, at the Mandarin Oriental. In November, they met again, this time in Boston, where Skowron gave the doctor a tour of the city and of Harvard Medical School, and treated him to dinner. "I hope that I will have one day the opportunity to do the same for you, your wife and all the family," Benhamou wrote in a grateful email. Skowron replied: "It's just the beginning."

A few weeks later, however, the drug trials for Albuferon hit a setback. One patient in the drug trial died, and a second was hospitalized. Benhamou spent the next several days in discussions with the company about the future of the drug. He and Skowron spoke repeatedly by phone, and Skowron started to sell his stock. Over the course of eleven days in December, while most of the world was unaware that the drug was in trouble, Skowron's firm dumped 46 percent of the stock, known by its ticker symbol, HGSI. On January 18, 2008, researchers decided to discontinue part of the trial. Benhamou shared the news with Skowron, and even while they were on the phone, Skowron sent instant messages to his colleagues: "Sell the HGSI," he wrote, "all of it." Days later, once the news of the drug's problems became public, the share price plummeted by 44 percent. Skowron had avoided losing $30 million.

The timing of Skowron's trades drew suspicion. The Securities and Exchange Commission launched an investigation. Skowron's firm, FrontPoint, wanted to talk to Benhamou, but Skowron called him first in Paris and encouraged him to say they only talked, in general terms, about a "basket of drugs." Benhamou followed the plan, and his talk with the firm went smoothly. A few days later, Skowron flew to Boston, where Benhamou was attending another conference. They had lunch, and Skowron gave him a ride back to his hotel. In the car, Skowron pulled out a bag containing two stacks of cash, wrapped in paper bands. Benhamou turned it down. But when they met again, weeks later, at a hotel bar in Milan, Benhamou accepted $10,000 in cash. Skowron wasn't worried about the SEC case. He and Benhamou just had to remain vague about the details. "It's simple," Skowron told him. When investigators asked if they discussed specific drug trials, all they had to say was "I don't remember. *I. Don't. Remember.*"

———

In various ways, Skowron's well-ordered life had started to unravel. During his travels, he took to hiring prostitutes and meeting women in bars. He always carried two thousand dollars in his wallet; some nights, he spent double or triple that amount. With so much money changing hands, he barely took notice when he started giving bribes to Benhamou. "Giving him five thousand dollars was just like my wallet, plus a little more," he told me. When he paused and thought about his behavior, he alternated between being ashamed and coolly cynical. Was paying for sex, or stock tips, the scandal that people made it out to be? "It's a pattern that we live with all the time that we just mask in different ways," he said. "What do you think Tinder is?"

At FrontPoint, he was arguing with colleagues as he fantasized about trying to remake the firm. He ricocheted between projecting invincibility and feeling hollow and purposeless. At home, late at night, he lay in bed and thought, "I'm a lie everywhere I go. Nobody knows me."

After the initial flurry of attention from the SEC, the case died down. Investigators interviewed people involved, but Skowron went back to trading, and his earnings continued to soar. By November 2010, even as much of the country was just emerging from the recession, Skowron had earned another $11 million. He was thinking about buying a boat. He mentioned the idea to a colleague, who asked what he thought it would cost. "I'm just thinking about spending like eight or nine hundred thousand," Skowron said.

His colleague laughed. "Why are you even thinking about it? Just do it."

A few hours after the conversation about the boat, Skowron noticed his colleagues huddled around a phone. Unusually, the firm's general counsel was there, too. The newswires had just reported that the FBI had arrested Dr. Yves Benhamou at the Boston airport. The doctor was charged with securities fraud, for tipping off "a hedge-fund manager." The article mentioned no names, but suspicion immediately fell on Skowron.

He walked out of the office, and, like a bookend of his first day in the hedge-fund world, he called his wife. He told her he was on his way to see a lawyer. "It's going to be bad," he said. By the following spring, in 2011, Benhamou had pleaded guilty to insider trading and lying to investigators. He agreed to give information to the government, and he was allowed to return to his wife and two daughters in France.

When the FBI arrests white-collar defendants around New York, the agents usually arrive between Tuesday and Thursday, in case the accused spend weekends in the country. The raids come at dawn, to catch people before work. When it appeared likely that Skowron would be arrested, he and Cheryl sent the kids to her parents' house so that they wouldn't see their father in handcuffs.

But, before that moment arrived, Skowron asked for the chance to turn himself in. On April 13, he was charged with securities fraud, conspiracy, and conspiracy to obstruct justice. He faced twenty years in prison and millions in fines. In a press conference announcing the charges, Preet Bharara, the U.S. attorney for the Southern District of New York, accused Skowron of "blatant cheating of both the market and the ordinary investor." His lawyer made the ritual denials, telling the press, "Dr. Skowron is proud of his work as a physician, investor, and philanthropist. He denies receiving confidential information."

That position did not last long. On August 15, 2011, Skowron

pleaded guilty and agreed to pay more than $13 million in fines and res-
titution. At sentencing, prosecutors called him a "fundamentally decep-
tive and dishonest person." (In a civil case, Skowron was later ordered to
repay Morgan Stanley $31 million in compensation.)

When it came to calculating prison time, his friends and family
wrote letters to the judge, arguing for leniency. Cheryl wrote, "He says
he had no idea prison was a possibility otherwise he never would've
done it. I believe him." Finally, Skowron spoke on his own behalf:
"Your honor, I was not aware of the changes that were happening in
me that blurred the line between right and wrong. They came slowly
over several years. I allowed myself to slip into the world of relativ-
ism where the ends justified the means." He was sentenced to five years
in prison.

———

Until recently, my hometown earned little mention in the annals of
white-collar crime. Our contributions were easy to recall: when I was
in high school, a stockbroker from Toledo named Mike King bought
two houses on opposite sides of the street and bragged to a neighbor
that if he wanted a glass of ginger ale, he had one servant hold the glass,
another fetch a chair, and a third pour his drink. King, it turned out,
was an accomplished grifter named Martin Frankel. In 1999 he set fire
to one of his houses and fled with nine passports and $10 million in di-
amonds. He was arrested in Germany and charged with stealing $200
million in insurance schemes. He tried to saw his way out the window of
a German jail but eventually pleaded guilty to fraud and was sentenced
to seventeen years in a U.S. prison.

Historically, the criminal justice system has given prosperous citizens
a wide berth. As George Bernard Shaw put it in 1922, a man snatches
bread "from the baker's counter" and goes to jail; but if he "snatches bread
from the table of hundreds of widows and orphans and similar credulous
souls . . . he is run into Parliament." For much of the twentieth century,
American scholars and politicians viewed criminality as an outgrowth of

poverty. Businessmen were governed at the state level by a weak web of "blue sky" laws, named because they were supposed to stop unsavory speculators from selling the blue sky.

Over time, Americans became more aware of the crimes committed with a pen rather than a gun. When the stock market crashed in 1929, Congress faced public pressure to prevent the repetition of the market manipulation that had ruined millions of Americans. Richard Whitney, the patrician president of the New York Stock Exchange, a graduate of Groton and Harvard, tried to reduce the pressure with an appeal to clubby understanding, telling visitors from Washington, "You gentlemen are making a great mistake. The exchange is a perfect institution." Whitney, it turned out, had reasons to be uncomfortable with scrutiny. In 1938, he was revealed to be embezzling from the New York Yacht Club, Harvard, and his father-in-law, among others. He went to Sing Sing still dressed in a double-breasted suit. Criminals like Whitney led the sociologist Edwin Sutherland to retire the assumption that malfeasance flourished mostly in the lower classes. In 1939, he invented the term "white-collar crime."

In the decades that followed, every great cycle of boom and bust exposed a new realm of wrongdoing, as whistleblowers and disgruntled investors reported the latest innovations in deceit. In 2001, after accounting scandals at Enron and other firms, a publication called *CFO Magazine* quietly abandoned its annual "Excellence Awards" after the final three winners went to prison. (Scott Sullivan of WorldCom, Andrew Fastow of Enron, and Mark Swartz of Tyco International were sentenced to a combined eighteen years for fraud, money laundering, and other crimes.)

By the time Skowron went to prison, Greenwich had gained an unwanted place in the portrait of American corruption. When the tide began to turn against Wall Street, you could follow it from my family's front door. Up and down Round Hill Road, neighbors became known for one imbroglio after another. If you took a right turn from our place, you could wander by the stone Colonial house of Walter Noel, a money manager with a gracious Nashville accent, who funneled billions of his clients' dollars to the grifter Bernie Madoff. Though Noel and his partners kept fees estimated in court at more than $1 billion, they claimed that they, too, were duped. After legal battles, they agreed to give $80 million to investors who had been cheated, but they faced no jail time.

If you turned left, you reached the estate of the hedge-fund manager Raj Rajaratnam, who had come to Wall Street in the 1980s with plans to retire once he had a million dollars. That goal became ten million, then a billion. He later celebrated his birthday by flying in Kenny Rogers to sing "The Gambler" over and over, until Rogers finally refused. In 2009, after tapping the phones at Rajaratnam's hedge fund, the FBI arrested him in an operation it called "Perfect Hedge." A jury convicted him of fourteen counts of securities fraud and conspiracy, and Judge Richard J. Holwell gave him the longest sentence ever recorded for insider trading—eleven years—saying his crimes "reflect a virus in our business culture that needs to be eradicated." Other neighbors on Round Hill had troubles: in 2009, Frederic A. Bourke Jr., of the handbag maker Dooney & Bourke, was convicted of violating the Foreign Corrupt Practices Act after an ill-fated energy venture with a man known as the "Pirate of Prague." And Dominick DeVito, a developer with the slogan "We Build the Dream," went to prison for fraud and obstruction of justice. Eventually, so many neighbors were ensnared in financial scandals that a local blogger started calling our street Rogues Hill Road.

No case attracted as much attention as that of Steven Cohen, the investor with the nine-foot wall who was once Skowron's boss. In one of the biggest indictments of a financial firm since Arthur Andersen, prosecutors said that Cohen's hedge fund had become a "veritable magnet for market cheaters." The fund closed in 2013 after pleading guilty to insider trading and being sentenced to pay $1.8 billion in fines and restitution. For two years, Cohen was suspended from running a hedge fund. (Afterward, he founded another hedge fund, and he spent $2.4 billion to buy the New York Mets, the highest price ever paid for a baseball team.)

When the charges against S.A.C. Capital became public, David Rafferty, the *Greenwich Time* columnist, published a piece headlined

"Greenwich, Gateway to White-Collar Crime." He wrote, "A few years ago you might have been proud to tell your friends you lived in 'The Hedge Fund Capital of the World.' Now? Not so much." He described a "growing sense of unease in certain circles as one hedgie after another seems to be facing the music." In town, he wrote, there was a creeping discomfort: "They are cheating, and getting caught, and now Greenwich may need to decide where we go after hedge funds."

Most people in town bore no connection to the crimes of Rogues Hill Road; they were embarrassed by it. But their disdain could not erase the unpleasant fact that their neighbors were cheating, bribing, stealing, and wiping out people's savings in ways that hastened the decline of American confidence in capitalism. It was an awfully long way from Emerson's "commanding sense of right and wrong," from the ethic of "courage and thrift," from Owen Young's odes to "common enterprise for mutual advantage." It was impossible not to wonder: Was my hometown attracting rogues or grooming them?

⸺

The late John C. Bogle, an iconic investor who founded the Vanguard Group and spent more than six decades in finance, wrote in 2012: "When I came into this field, the standard seemed to be 'there are some things that one simply doesn't do.' Today, the standard is 'If everyone else is doing it, I can do it too.'" The following year, a survey of financial industry professionals by the law firm Labaton Sucharow found that a quarter of them said they would "engage in insider trading to make $10 million if they could get away with it." An equal share said compensation and bonus structures at their companies "incentivize employees to compromise ethical standards or violate the law." Seventeen percent said they expected their leaders were "likely to look the other way if they suspected a top performer engaged in insider trading."

A Greenwich resident named Jeff Grant landed on an idea: a support group he called "ethics rehab" for white-collar criminals who were heading to jail or getting out of it. Grant, who is big and garrulous, with a sweep of silver hair and intense blue eyes, had been a prosperous lawyer in Rye, New York; a member of a school board; and co-owner of a restaurant called the Good Life. After a knee injury, he became addicted to opioids and started stealing from his clients' accounts to pay for personal expenses. Eventually, he lied on a loan application and pleaded guilty to wire fraud and money laundering. He spent eighteen months at a federal correctional institution in Allenwood, Pennsylvania. Then he went to seminary, and word got around Greenwich that he was willing to share advice with people who needed it.

"My phone would ring in the middle of the night," Grant told me. In one case, a Wall Street financier whose case had burst into the news called him from under his desk. He couldn't bring himself to leave the office. "He said, 'I'm afraid that people will recognize me on the street,'" Grant recalled.

Over the next several years, Grant spoke to hundreds of white-collar defendants across the country. He offered practical advice and reading tips: *Letters and Papers from Prison*, by Dietrich Bonhoeffer, and *The Gulag Archipelago*, by Aleksandr Solzhenitsyn. He advised them that, before reporting to prison, they should mail themselves a list of phone numbers for family members and friends on their visitors' list, because "you'll be too discombobulated to remember them once you're inside." And most of all, he said, remind your wife never to touch paper money on the morning of a prison visit; almost every bill out there has a trace of drug residue, which will set off the scanners.

Grant believed that many of the men he met in the Greenwich support group had lost sight of integrity in their pursuit of success. Greed is as old as the Ten Commandments, but twenty-first-century America had made it more lucrative and permissible. "You have an epidemic of behavior that Italians call *maleducato*," Grant said. "We're raising a characterless society, bred not to cherish the right things in life. As recently as a hundred twenty years ago, ethics was still the central required education course. But the liberal arts core of the schools lost influence to the professional schools.

The business schools created this concept called 'business ethics,' which supplanted ethics."

Luigi Zingales, a business professor at the University of Chicago, agreed; his profession had found "every possible way to avoid the moral questions," he told me. All too often, he said, business schools made only a grudging nod to social responsibility. Zingales told me that in the half century since Friedman described profit as the "one and only social responsibility of business," his profession had failed to emphasize the less-famous half of Friedman's argument—that businesses must profit "in open and free competition without deception or fraud." When business schools provided academic arguments to promote massive growth in stock options, Zingales said, it "legitimated" the runaway growth in executive pay. "The moment you start to grant yourself enormous option payments, then why not other things? The monetization of all the relationships within a firm becomes more and more acceptable. I don't know of any alum that has been kicked out of the alumni association for immoral behavior. There are trustees of business schools today who have been convicted of bribery and insider trading, and I don't think people notice or care." He said, "The opportunities are enormous, people are getting more and more comfortable in the gray area, and there's been very little desire to go after prominent people."

———

Behind the embarrassments of Rogues Hill Road lay an uncomfortable question: Had one of America's most prosperous stretches lost its way—or had it always been this way, but only without the scrutiny? Eugene Soltes, a professor at Harvard Business School, believes white-collar malfeasance has become more common. "Strictly speaking, the answer is yes," he told me. "There *is* more white-collar crime today because there are more things that are criminal today than fifty years ago." Bribing a foreign official, for instance, was legal until the Foreign Corrupt Practices Act of 1977, and insider trading was rarely prosecuted until the 1980s. Today, those are two of the most common offenses. But, Soltes went on, "I suspect that you might be asking the more intuitive version of this question—given the same laws, same number of people, et cetera, is the proclivity for someone to engage in white-collar crime higher than it was fifty years ago? That's a much harder question."

On balance, there is no evidence of a growing "inclination" to break white-collar laws. What *has* changed is what Soltes calls the "psychological distance" between perpetrators and their victims. "Business is done with individuals at greater length now, which reduces the feeling that managers are harming others," Soltes told me. In lab scenarios, people sacrifice the life of someone they can't see far more readily than someone who stands before them. In Soltes's interviews with dozens of white-collar criminals, he found that many almost never had reasons to meet the people who lost money through price-fixing or fraud.

Others who worked on cases of financial harm observed a similar pattern—an abstraction from the consequences that a routine financial move can have in the real world. Stanley A. Twardy Jr., a former U.S. attorney for the District of Connecticut, became a partner in the law firm Day Pitney, where he defended white-collar clients in Greenwich and elsewhere. Earlier tycoons, as Twardy put it, "designed and created the railroad." Or they popularized modern mattresses and Dixie Cups. "These are people making money by trading *on* money, or trading information about what's going on in an industry. The lines get blurred a little bit. Where is it legal and where is it illegal?" He added, "Heaven knows, there's a lot of folks in this industry who don't cheat. At the end of the day, if people get into trouble, it's often about greed. If they're making hundreds of millions, somebody is making billions. I think it's changing morals and ethics. Do they just forget the rules when they get caught up in the moment, because they want to win at all costs?"

The Greenwich GE executive Owen Young warned in his 1927 speech at Harvard, "The sale of a spavined horse to one of his own community may have been a moral delinquency. The sale of a spavined motor to people quite unknown may have been regarded locally as a clever piece of business."

Over the decades, the lament that moral constraints have weakened has not just been voiced by critics of Wall Street; the practitioners themselves talk about it. In 2012, Greg Smith, a midlevel executive director at Goldman Sachs, announced his resignation, decrying a "decline in the firm's moral fiber." Writing in *The New York Times*, he observed, "Over the last twelve months I have seen five different managing directors refer to their own clients as 'muppets' . . . You don't have to be a rocket scientist to figure out that the junior analyst sitting quietly in the corner of the room hearing about 'muppets,' 'ripping eyeballs out' and 'getting paid' doesn't exactly turn into a model citizen." In 2016, Goldman agreed to a record $5.6 billion fine, part of more than $200 billion that major banks paid in fines for their role in the financial crisis. The institutions were seen as guilty of causing vast harm, yet top managers never went to prison.

In recent years, researchers have gained a sharper sense of how immoral behavior moves through a community. In the mid-2000s, the federal government brought criminal and civil cases against people at American companies who had been "backdating" stock options—secretly manipulating their records so that executives could take home a larger return than their options really delivered. Studies of the backdating scandal later found that the practice had started in Silicon Valley and then infected the broader business world; the vectors of transmission could be traced to specific individuals who served on the boards of multiple companies. The practice leaped from one company to another.

An unethical habit travels much like a virus, spread in encounters among neighbors and colleagues, through the subtle cues that psychologists call "affective evaluations." If people are rising on one measurement (profit) even as they are falling on another (ethics), the verdict about which matters more will hinge on the culture around them—on which values are most "exalted by members of their insular business communities," Soltes observed. "If you spend time with people who pick locks," he told me, "you will probably learn to pick locks."

SIX

EVERYONE IS DOING IT
(TAKE 2)

TO UNDERSTAND HOW POWER WORKS in Chicago, it pays to consider the case of the Gangster Disciples, the city's largest criminal gang.

The Gangster Disciples originated in the 1960s, when some street-corner drug dealers came together on the South Side. By the mid-1990s, the peak of the crack era, it had grown to an estimated 30,000 members, with franchise gangs in seven other states. The leader, Larry Hoover, had been locked up for murder in 1973 but oversaw operations and strategy from behind bars. While in prison, he read the book *Boss*, Mike Royko's classic portrait of Richard J. Daley, the Chicago mayor who rose from the Hamburgs, an Irish gang on the South Side that, in 1919, ignited the deadliest race riot in Chicago history, to the peak of the Democratic Party machine. Hoover set out to get his gang into politics.

The Gangster Disciples created a political action committee called Growth and Development, a play on its initials. In 1994, one of the PAC's officials, a longtime gang enforcer who said he had left violence behind, ran for alderman and met with President Bill Clinton in the

White House for a group discussion about crime. In a bid for political legitimacy, the gang and its front groups organized community cleanups, "Stop the Violence" rallies, and events to feed the homeless; they went into the music business, and restaurants, and fashion—while running one of America's largest drug distribution operations. According to Andrew Papachristos, a sociologist at Northwestern University who studies the Gangster Disciples, its members were accused of involvement in at least 827 murders—roughly 300 more than the number attributed to organized crime during the heyday of Al Capone.

By the end of the twentieth century, the gang was splintering: the federal government had arrested top leaders, and the demolition of public housing was scattering the rank and file. Instead of sixty dominant groups, Chicago gangs broke into hundreds of "cliques," often as small as a dozen members who controlled a few blocks. The Gangster Disciples devolved into at least seventy-five separate cliques, and the competition among them sparked a surge in violence. In one case, two factions—G-ville and Killa Ward—controlled neighboring patches of the Auburn Gresham neighborhood on the South Side. Within the span of twelve months, they were responsible for the killing of twenty-seven people, according to police.

Late in the winter of 2016, I attended the funeral for one of the victims, Phillip Dupree, a twenty-six-year-old father of four who was ambushed when he pulled up for dinner at a restaurant in a car driven by his grandmother. Under fire, his grandmother managed to drive three blocks before crashing into a guardrail. The shooter approached them and kept on firing. Dupree died in the car. His grandmother was grazed by a bullet on the top of her head, and later found five bullet holes in the hood of her coat. After the paramedics pulled her out of the wreck, she sent her daughter, Alfreida Cobb, two text messages. The first said "Phillip." The next said "Dead."

Phillip Dupree had wanted to be famous. On his Instagram account, he identified himself as an Actor/Rapper. He posted pictures of himself holding guns, along with photos of cash and marijuana. But the wealth was a mirage; he didn't have much. When I spoke to his mother, she said, "I'm not going to get on the news and say, 'My son was a perfect son.'" She wanted people to know, however, that he "was a loved person." She said, "I don't want nobody to say he took that life because he had nobody to help." His funeral attracted hundreds of people. At the front, Dupree lay in a silver casket with white satin lining. His wounds had been concealed. He wore a pristine gray Chicago White Sox hat.

When Dupree's funeral was over, I drove to the spot where he was killed. It was January, and friends had brushed away snow on the sidewalk for a makeshift shrine, which consisted of a white teddy bear and eight empty bottles of cognac and tequila. On the wall behind it, poster board was adorned with notes, including the comment "This shit feel so unreal." While I was writing in my notebook, a man about my age who was walking by paused to ask what I was doing. Writing about the killing of Phillip Dupree, I said.

When he learned I wrote for *The New Yorker*, he paused for a moment. "The one with the cartoons?" he asked, and I nodded.

He smiled. "I used to read that in the joint," he said. He introduced himself: Maurice Clark. "But everyone calls me Reese," he said. "Around here everyone just knows me as Reese the Villain." He reached into his jacket and pulled out a copy of the program from Dupree's funeral. He had just left the church, too. He lived next door to the deceased for years. "Ash to ash, dirt to dirt," he said.

Clark was forty-four years old. He had high cheekbones and a carefully trimmed goatee. He wore a gray knit hat, a hoodie, and two thin black windbreakers, layered against the cold. In conversation, he swerved between slang and grandmotherly asides. ("God gives you blessings in disguise," he said at one point.) I asked why he'd gone to prison, and he answered matter-of-factly: attempted murder. He had joined the Gangster Disciples as a teenager and shot a rival gang member. "I came out when I was thirty. Missed all of my twenties," he said. He no longer had to adhere to the boundaries around gang turf. "I'm from a different era," he said. The teenagers left him alone. "I'm what they call a Triple O.G."—meaning an original, original, original gangster.

On the day that Dupree was killed, Clark had been at a store nearby; he heard the shots and the car peeling away, and he came out to find Dupree's grandmother sprawled across the seat. White cotton stuffing spilled out of the bullet holes in her coat. I asked Clark how the dispute between G-ville and Killa Ward had started. He said, "I'll take you on the tour." In my car, we headed west for a few blocks, past a hair salon and a check-cashing store, until we reached the busy corner of Ashland Avenue. "This is where it all started, at this damn gas station," he said. "It all started over a jacket."

FalconFuel was a popular hangout that marked the border between Killa Ward to the west and G-ville to the east. The gas station was supposed to be neutral ground, but on this occasion some guys on one side decided to try to steal the expensive new jacket from a guy on the other. "They jumped on him, and his pride was too high," Clark said. "He went over there and shot one of the guys. It just kept on escalating like a motherfucker."

For the next two hours, we drove around, up and down side streets, climbing in and out of the car, while Clark offered an account of the small, nameless war. He ran his hands over bullet holes in a boarded-up storefront and the spidered glass of a bodega, tracing an intricate trail of insults and gunfire. On a map, our route would have looked like a swirl of spaghetti, crisscrossing no more than ten blocks in any direction. In the 1980s and '90s, when gangs were vast enterprises controlling miles of territory, a single corner had been less valuable. But if that was all a clique had, they fought hard to keep it. Chicago has seventy-seven official neighborhoods, but, in a typical year, half of all shootings took place in no more than a dozen of them, according to city statistics. "They're boxed in," Clark said.

Moreover, he said, there were far more guns now. "Back then, you probably had one gun, and you've got to go through a lot of chains and proper channels to get this gun." As violent as it had been in his day, there were unwritten rules about who became a target and why. "Someone was going to be like, 'Who you trying to shoot?' If you say, 'I got to go kill my stepdad because he's raping my sister,' they're going to say, 'Okay, fella, get that gun, pop him in his ass for us, and take these extra bullets.'" Indiana gun laws were notoriously lax. "It's fifteen minutes away," he said. There was always someone willing to make a shopping trip. "Maybe you give him a hundred fifty dollars extra, and, bam, you got your brand-new pistol."

—————

Clark and I stopped at his house, a two-story brick home he shared with his mother. In the living room, I met his girlfriend, Rudy, and their one-year-old son, Jeremiah, who was standing in a crib in the living room, watching a cartoon on television. Clark apologized that the apartment was cold. "I didn't know I was going to have a *guest*," he said, with mock formality. To save money, they had turned down the radiators and turned up the gas burners on the stove; blue flames licked up into the air. It did not look safe, but they worried less about a fire than about freezing.

Clark pulled the funeral program from his pocket and tucked it carefully into an old-fashioned photo album. It was full of funeral programs and obituaries for young men in the neighborhood. Each was protected beneath a clear sheet of plastic, like an artifact in a museum. I had been in and out of the neighborhood for months, and I recognized the names. Shawndell Harris, one of Dupree's friends, had been killed in March 2012 in a shootout near a convenience store, and his funeral program included a note from his mother: "Shawndell my son, the third child I've lost." Taken together, the contents felt like a yearbook-in-reverse—a record of who was not there, the shooting victims who had no prospect of what my great-grandfather had been told would be his "large promise of usefulness." In the previous twelve months, 468 people had been killed in Chicago, higher than in any other American city, and up 13 percent from the previous year.

On every page of his book, Clark had a story interwoven with ones before, and a prelude to stories that came after. To him, the drama was intimate and interconnected. Over time, the effect of each killing reverberated and compounded beyond the death itself; survivors moved away, and strivers looked for homes in safer neighborhoods. Between 2000 and 2010, Chicago lost 181,000 Black residents, many of them from middle-class households. It only deepened the distorting isolation of those left behind. "Who's going to be your role model?" Clark said. "The thief down the street? The bum that lost his family, and now he's on the corner telling us what we ought to do?"

Young people found solace in social media, which provided a simulacrum of community, but they were confined to an ingrown set of contacts and relationships. Clark drew a connection to the demolition of the public housing towers. People missed the sense of community they fostered, what political scientists call "social capital." "That's when the crime rate went up because, see, we ain't going to rob you if we've *known* you for a hundred years! But 'them'? They're *strangers*. So we're going to rob them."

I watched Jeremiah in his crib. At home in Washington, Sarabeth was pregnant with our first child, a boy. He was entering the world under very different circumstances, including some of the most basic conditions of health. To take one example, Auburn Gresham had the highest rate of asthma of any neighborhood on the far southwest side of Chicago. Researchers had identified the sources: segregated, low-income neighborhoods like Auburn Gresham, which was 96 percent Black, tended to be closer to highways and busy roads; people had less money to spend on removing mold and dust and pests, and the adults around were more likely to smoke cigarettes. Even gun violence raised the risks of developing asthma, because parents in unsafe neighborhoods preferred to keep kids indoors, where they were exposed to those other risk factors. Growing up in Auburn Gresham, in other words, was a preexisting condition.

Violence affects kids' health in many other ways, too. Research showed that, as early as preschool, an atmosphere of danger imposed a level of background stress that hampered verbal development by the equivalent of a full year of schooling. Schools in Jeremiah's neighborhood also struggled to recruit strong teachers, and, over time, the effects of that would be stark: a 2014 study led by Raj Chetty, a Harvard economist, found that the best teachers could help a student earn an additional $50,000 in the decades that followed. It also shaped the course of their communities. Scale up those lost earnings to a full classroom, and it amounted to $1.4 million in lost income that those kids would never invest in their homes and neighborhoods. (Chetty suggested that school districts retain the best teachers by linking pay and bonuses to performance.)

Clark also had a four-year-old son, Caleb, and he worried about raising his boys in the city. "Back in the day, every summer the city came up with a program to send kids out of the neighborhood. Something to do. Then they took the programs out." Clark didn't know all the details of the state's finances, but he figured it must have something to do with the corruption that filled the headlines. "We had the governor who sold a Senate seat. Blagojevich!"

├───────┤

Preston Maurice Clark's ancestors had been the property of a slave owner on the outskirts of Birmingham. In her twenties, his grandmother Lillian made the trip to Chicago, where she married a mechanic named Floyd Sanders, originally from Tennessee. Floyd opened an auto shop on State Street, Floyd's Tires. They raised two girls, Liz and Anita, and the family eventually bought a brick bungalow in South Shore, a proud, predominantly Black neighborhood with a coveted location near Lake Michigan.

Clark was born in 1971, the youngest of four siblings. His stepfather, Robert Howell, had a reliable city job, riding a garbage truck for the Department of Streets and Sanitation. He and Clark were close—so close that Clark assumed he was his biological dad. Eventually, his mother told him that his real father had been abusive and was no longer alive. Later, she conceded that his father *was* alive, and he lived a few blocks away. When Clark was a teenager, he knocked on his father's door. A woman answered, and Clark introduced himself. She eyed him warily and said his father wasn't home. Clark never got up the courage to go back.

He grew up on the far South Side, in the West Pullman neighborhood, a remnant of a storied Black community that once thrived around the Pullman train-car factories. In the seventies, in contrast to public housing nearby, his neighborhood was stable and close-knit. There were block clubs and softball games and parties with multiple generations. "The parents would be upstairs, and they'd let you go until eleven thirty and then kick everybody out of the basement. It was peaceful." In the summers, his half brothers, Daren and Daryl, who were five years older, left each morning for a day camp that took them out to forest preserves in the suburbs. They'd come home every night with feathers they'd picked up in the woods, and tales of derring-do.

In elementary school, Clark showed a knack for numbers. When he tagged along with his mother to the grocery store, he entertained himself by tracking the prices of things in the cart and trying to calculate the total before they reached the cashier. "I'd even do the tax on it," he said. His mother saw that the neighborhood school had textbooks with broken bindings and torn pages. "Uh-uh. No way," she told him. "You're not going to that school."

In 1981, as he approached fifth grade, his mother enrolled him at a school in the Mount Greenwood neighborhood, an Irish Catholic enclave in the far southwest corner of the city. For decades, white politicians and parents in Chicago had resisted efforts to integrate its schools. But by 1980, schools in some Black neighborhoods were so overcrowded that students could attend only in shifts, while in white neighborhoods schools were emptying out as families fled to the suburbs. That year, the Justice Department sued the Chicago schools, and the two sides signed a consent decree that committed the city to make greater efforts at integration.

Many Chicago cops, firefighters, and other city workers who were required to live within the city limits chose Mount Greenwood, four miles from Clark's home. The neighborhood was as close as you could come to life in the suburbs: a mix of Irish pubs and mom-and-pop stores with Catholic-school uniforms in the window. It was also, not incidentally, overwhelmingly white, bordered by a cemetery that separated it from more racially diverse neighborhoods around it.

Mount Greenwood had an infamous history of racism. When the first group of Black eighth-graders had tried to enroll in 1968, they had been met by rock-throwers and placards, a display of such hostility that *The Chicago Defender* nicknamed Mount Greenwood "Chicago's Little Rock." Even decades later, the fear and hostility endured. "I don't mind them, but I don't want them living next to me," Peggy O'Connor, a Mount Greenwood waitress and wife of a police officer, told a reporter in 1992, in an article about segregation. "I don't want to be too close to them. I think they've been whining too long, and I'm sick of it." She said, "Blacks buy porterhouse steaks with food stamps, while we eat hamburgers," conceding that she had never actually seen someone buy a steak with food stamps.

After the desegregation agreement, Clark was in an early group whose bus was met, once again, by jeering crowds: "They were throwing rocks and apples at me, on the bus. When we turned to go down our block to go to the school, we had to have the police escort us. And then, all of a sudden, you get to picket signs and parents saying, 'N——s go home!' and 'This is not your community!'"

Despite the protests, Clark stayed in the school and loved it. The textbooks were new and spotless. He made diverse friends—Hispanic, Black, Greek, Irish—and as he approached ninth grade, many of his classmates went on to Morgan Park High School, which scored well on standardized tests. He went on a tour of Morgan Park and imagined himself there. "I see this nice fresh school. It's integrated. White, Black. It's kind of upscale." Then his parents were informed that the school bus he had been riding stopped at eighth grade. His parents didn't have the money for the public bus fare, so Clark enrolled, instead, at his local school—Fenger High, which was known for terrific football and terrible violence. Looking back at that moment, Clark gave a short, rueful laugh. "And that started my life of crime."

———

In 1987, the year Clark turned sixteen, William Bennett, the U.S. secretary of education, pronounced Chicago's public schools the worst in the nation. The dropout rate was 40 percent, and half of the high schools in the city ranked in the bottom 1 percent on college admissions tests. From Clark's vantage point at Fenger High, he saw no reason to disagree.

When he arrived, one of the first things he noticed was the presence of older gang members who did not attend the school but used it as an organizing space. "There's a dude who's been out of school two or three years, and he's hanging out eating lunch," Clark said. The chaos in the lunch room was the product of a specific decision to cut funding for supervision, which, like so much of the city's education policy, was a trade-off about money. School budgets were shrinking, and Fenger was paring back in some drastic ways. In a letter to the board of education in 1991, worried parents and faculty listed the other elements that had been slashed in recent years: "student fee collection, free and reduced lunch programs, locker control, security emergency drills, commencement exercises." So much of the foundation was eroding that the school could barely function. "While we recognize the need for fiscal responsibility," they wrote, "we wonder if the persons making these budgetary decisions really know what high schools need in order to operate."

By 1991, even the prized football team was ravaged. The football coach could name six players, current and former, who had been killed in the past twelve years. And the sports budget was on the brink of extinction; according to the parents' letter, money for sports was scheduled to fall by 88 percent, to just $750. So many teachers were cut that year that when a reporter from the *Chicago Sun-Times* visited Fenger in the fall, a student said, "Our yearbook man is gone. Our newspaper teacher is gone. The man teaching advanced computers is gone. Our French teacher is teaching Spanish."

Clark tried to screen out the havoc and dysfunction. Most of all, he looked forward to math. But he was assigned a teacher who spent so much time tamping down disruptions in the classroom that he seemed to have no energy left to teach. "He said, 'Just put your head down, man. And I'm going to pass you,'" Clark recalled. "I think he was just burned out."

When schools lose the ability to cultivate talent, the implications filter across society. A study of patents, codirected by Chetty, the Harvard economist, found that children of the top 1 percent were ten times more likely to become inventors than comparably intelligent kids from poorer backgrounds. The researchers estimated that if talented children of low-income and minority families—the "lost Einsteins," they called them—were trained for inventive work as readily as well-off white men, the United States would register four times the level of innovation.

Once Clark no longer left the neighborhood every morning for school, or had reasons to look forward to math class, his world shrank, a narrowing reinforced by his encounters with police. At night, he watched the police cars take up positions at the corner of Ninety-fifth Street and Western Avenue—the boundary between Black and white neighborhoods. They would wave over Black kids on bikes who were heading into white territory and direct them to detour around it. "They'd pull you straight over and harass you," Clark said.

The more time he spent on his own block, the more he watched the older guys hanging out on the stoops and working on their cars—men like "Big D," the biggest drug dealer on the block, who drove a gleaming Corvette and a tricked-out Lincoln Mark VII. "We would come outside and just be bored," Clark said. "Then, here we got these guys out here, nice cars, they're selling drugs, and the cops weren't doing nothing. Cops would look at you, like, 'Hey, cool, we don't give a fuck about you killing off your own.'"

Even as a kid, Clark noticed the pillars that held up his community vanishing. "I remember the day my brothers said there ain't no summer camp anymore. My mom and dad said, 'What are we going to *do*?'" To Clark's mind, the closing of summer camp felt like a milestone. "It was programming us in those summer camps to be better people. How to read, learn different languages. Spanish and stuff. It was funded by the government to get the guys off the street. So, when they snatched that, what do you think these guys are going to do?"

———

As Clark got older, he noticed that it wasn't only teenagers who seemed to lose their moorings when rituals and connections fell away. One of the fathers on his block trooped past Clark's house every morning, wearing the uniform of a city bus driver—a tie and short-sleeve shirt in the summer, a tie and coat in winter. Then he lost his job and set himself up as a small-time drug dealer, "selling ounces," as Clark put it. "He kept his shirt and tie on," Clark noticed. The man couldn't seem to bring himself to dress down.

Clark's brothers joined the Gangster Disciples, and eventually he did, too. He started out doing odd jobs; on Mother's Day, he was told to take flowers to the wives of gang leaders—but most of the work was destructive, and often cruel. An older member once called him from prison with instructions to approach a specific house and "hit this bitch in her motherfucking face." Clark walked to the front door and knocked. A woman answered. "I said, 'Is Regina here?' She said, 'This is me.'" He paused. Then he told her, "'I was supposed to be hitting you in your face.' But she's a woman, and I didn't do it." His visit had sent the message, he figured. "Letting your ass know I could reach out and touch you. It's not just on TV."

In February 1987, shortly before his sixteenth birthday, Clark was arrested for the first time and charged with possession of a controlled substance. He had been selling cocaine. It didn't slow him down. By the time he was seventeen, he was making enough money selling drugs that he bought a convertible Mustang with souped-up speakers and white leather interior.

Before long, he was buying cocaine directly from a supplier in Hawaii, who shipped kilos in round cookie tins. "It was called 'mother of pearl.' Pure Peruvian flakes." Around the neighborhood, Clark became known for selling large batches—quarter kilos, at $24,000 each. "They were calling me the 'quarter-key bandit,'" he said. "I was running out of that shit so quick, I was running around asking, 'Hey, man, you got seven keys I could sell?'" He liked the money and the cars and the organization and maneuvering. At home, he carefully divided the cocaine into small bags and grouped them in shoeboxes, ready to sell on the street. He wanted to be seen as disciplined and generous. "I overpaid my crew," he said.

For a time, Clark caught a glimpse of an alternative path. His sister, Deanna, had graduated from high school and found work in the coatroom at the Chicago Mercantile Exchange, keeping track of jackets and luggage. Before long, she moved up to working the phones on the edge of the exchange and talked the bosses into giving her little brother Reese a chance in the coatroom. He got a part-time job there, but it was no match for the influence of his brothers, and the profit and status he took from the drug trade.

One night in July 1990, shortly before he turned nineteen, Clark and a few other members of the Gangster Disciples ("my security," Clark called them) were walking his girlfriend back to her house. The Four Corner Hustlers, a rival gang, controlled the area, and Clark's group encountered them in an alley. Looking back on the several minutes that followed, Clark tried to walk me through a confusing series of insults and counterinsults, before declaring, with mock formality, "My security up and shot those motherfuckers." Two days later, police arrested Clark and charged him with attempted murder for the shooting of another teenager, Naghi McGlaston.

Clark had accumulated so much money selling drugs that he could post his own bond. For much of the next year, his case worked its way through the system, and he made no effort to lie low. He drove around town in a golden BMW, modeled on the car favored by Ice-T in *New Jack City*.

But his upcoming trial was starting to feel like a ticking clock, and on a whim one afternoon he decided to try once more to meet his father. Clark knew the park where he hung out most of the time and found him sitting alone on a bench. Clark adopted the pose of a stranger. "I said, 'Excuse me, sir. Do you know what time it is?' He gave me the time. And I said, 'Thanks.'" Then he dropped the act. "I said, 'Man, you don't even know who I am, do you?'" His father studied him and then a look of recognition crossed his face: "Oh my God. My man!" he said. He greeted Clark by his baby nickname: "Two." ("He was One and I was Two," Clark explained.) "I hugged him, shook hands with him, kicked it with him, had a good time." They made a plan to see each other again.

"Then I fucked up," Clark said. He and some friends raised pit bulls to fight for money, and one night that summer, their team was squaring off against a rival gang. "Total take was one hundred and eighty thousand cash, and six kilos"—a haul worth nearly half a million dollars. Clark's side won. "I jumped in the ring," he said, giving everyone a chance to envy his Christian Dior jumpsuit and a new pair of Nike Air Maxes. But preening in front of the losers was a mistake, and he knew it. A few days later, the losing side sent "the stick-up crew," Clark said. They found him at a friend's house, and in the melee that followed, Clark couldn't even be sure who shot whom. A few days later—July 30, 1992—he was rearrested and sent back to jail.

This time, with his charges piling up, he didn't have the chance to bail himself out. On May 19, 1993, he went to trial on attempted murder, and he was convicted and sentenced to fifteen years. What would feel like a catastrophe to some people struck Clark differently. Prison was almost inevitable, he figured; both of his brothers were already behind bars, and though he didn't know the numbers, Black Americans were incarcerated at six times the rate of whites. More to the point, Black men who didn't finish high school were ten times as likely to have spent time in prison by their early thirties as Black men who finished college. Also, he wondered how long he would survive in the gang life if he continued to attract attention.

"I needed to sit down for a while," he said. He never saw his father again. Preston Maurice Clark died at the age of forty-six, while his son was in prison.

SEVEN

YOU PEOPLE

OVER THE NEXT DECADE, Reese Clark was transferred from one Illinois prison to another—Stateville, Centralia, and Mount Sterling, as well as Pontiac, the prison that once held William Wojtkowski, the sixteen-year-old who shot my great-grandfather. Clark had been absorbed by another epochal migration in American history, one with disastrous effect—the nearly one third of Black men who had entered the criminal justice system. Between 1973 and 2020, the number of Americans in prison grew six times over, from 200,000 to more than 1.4 million. While he was behind bars, the United States entered the twenty-first century with more prisoners than farmers.

The flicker of relief that Clark had felt on his way to prison did not last. Inside, the sheer wanton brutality terrified him. He was no stranger to violence, but in the confines of prison, the gang rivalries intensified; he watched men around him disfigured by beatings and stabbings; they became "pumpkin heads," in prison slang, because they were cut up like jack-o'-lanterns. When he was two years in, his mental health started to deteriorate; he was gripped by a sudden panic he had never known. His hair fell out in patches. "I'd see guys hang themselves because they were weak," he said. He wondered if he was losing his mind. "I stayed in my cell. I prayed to the Lord, 'Save me,'" he said.

Over time, Clark accommodated as much as he could: he learned to avoid the main areas of the prisons, he spent time with the chaplains, and he looked for prison jobs that would keep him occupied. An older man who arrived each morning from outside to work as a barber taught him how to cut hair. "He said, 'This is how you'll make your money.'" He was learning a trade for the first time in his life. "I couldn't wait to go to the barber shop to get away from the crazy motherfuckers." He left prison on May 1, 2001. "It was my new birthday—the day I came out a grown man."

In practice, Clark reentered society without the remotest idea of how to make a legal living. He wondered if a parole officer might point him to jobs or training, but the man assigned to his case was overwhelmed and barely responsive. "They just watch you," he said. He was also one of 5 million Americans on parole or another form of supervision. Through a temp agency, he found a job at a warehouse in Bolingbrook, a suburb southwest of the city. He liked the work; keeping track of shipments appealed to his fondness for math. "After ninety days, they've got the option to sign you on. Get a 'staff' title." As the date approached, they called the temp workers together. "The next morning at seven, they said, they're signing everybody on. But they pulled me to the side and said, 'We can't sign you on because corporate says we can't hire a felon.'" This was a frequent problem in his world. According to a study sponsored by the Department of Justice, when job applicants are required to disclose a criminal record, their chances of getting an interview fall by half.

Clark felt defeated—and, also, a bit exploited. "Wait a minute, so you mean to tell me I could work in this warehouse as a temp, and do all this nice shit, and keep their products going, with no accidents in so many days? I don't mean no disrespect." He continued, "They felt bad for me. They'd seen my heart was broken. So they said, 'We're just going to switch your title and duties.'" And that's what they did—shuffling him among departments as a temp worker. For a while, it was okay, but he was constantly reminded that he had no future there. "Everyone else shot up to eighteen or nineteen bucks, but I'm still stuck in this bullshit." Eventually, he quit. "I just said, forget it, man."

He drifted back to the neighborhood. Some days, he made money sweeping up at local stores. When he couldn't find that, he collected tin cans and recycled them for loose change. The "regular hustle," as he called it. But the temptations were everywhere. "I ain't got no job. I'm back hanging with the wrong crew. And these guys are in the same boat. We're all fucking felons, and what else are we going to do? Sell some goddamn drugs!" he said. "Because, guess what: the rent is due. We don't stick up people and we're not going to rob you. We hustled in the back of the Currency Exchange, so when people get their check, they get their little stuff and they go home." He said, "When we come out after we served our time, we try to get a good job. But no, you're an outcast. You can't go here. It's the scarlet letter."

Clark moved back in with his mother and his grandmother. While he had been locked up, they had made a financial bet: they had moved a few miles away to the neighborhood of Auburn Gresham, where they could afford to buy a modest brick two-story house that would allow them to earn money from the rent on one floor while they lived on the other.

And then an opportunity arrived. In fact, it came right to his mother's front door on a summer afternoon in 2004. Two enthusiastic men were going house to house, encouraging people to consider applying for loans. They represented a company called Countrywide Financial Corporation.

⊢———⊣

The men pointed out dilapidated gutters and cracks in the mortar at Clark's house. "You could refinance," they told his mother; repairs would allow the family to charge more rent; it would more than pay for itself, they said. It sounded a bit like "fancy gibberish," Clark said, but it also seemed too good to pass up. "They said, 'You'll never know it's there. It'll just go up a little bit, but nothing excessive.'"

By now, the outlines of the disaster gathering around them are well known. Between 2000 and 2005, the number of mortgages from subprime lenders in Chicago more than tripled. They were proliferating in low-income neighborhoods across America, as part of a Wall Street frenzy. Financial alchemists had discovered that they could pool risky subprime loans together, divide them into "tranches," and sell them on to investors—in some cases, absurdly rated as AAA bonds with safe, regular yields. The system to prevent abuse and recklessness was failing; regulations had been pared back since the Clinton administration, and government oversight had relaxed under George W. Bush. Banks and traders assembled a pyramid of opaque financial entities, including derivatives, mortgage-backed securities, collateralized debt obligations, and *synthetic* collateralized debt obligations—all built on the loose sand of places like the South Side, where pushy salesmen were trawling for customers.

Nobody issued more of them than Countrywide, which advertised using a photo of a Black hurdler, sprinting ahead of the competition, above an intriguing appeal: "Is something standing in the way of your homeownership dreams?" Countrywide had been founded in 1969, and in its early years it avoided aggressive lending policies. But, after big Wall Street banks entered the mortgage business and competition increased, Countrywide kept up in part by introducing commissions to spur its salesforce. Revenue soared, and so did the company's share price. In 2003, *Fortune* magazine named it the "23,000% stock," for the nearly impossible speed of its growth.

Not long after the Countrywide men came to the door, Anita and Lillian held a small signing ceremony in the den to celebrate the refinancing. They had agreed to a thirty-year adjustable-rate mortgage, for $133,000, at a starting interest rate of 6.34 percent; under the terms, that rate could double, but the risk seemed remote. Clark remembered, "My mom just thinks we're getting a deal. 'They're about to fix the house up.'"

Some of the most prominent architects and beneficiaries of the subprime bonanza were in Greenwich. In the 1990s, Michael Vranos had led a team on Wall Street that popularized mortgage-backed securities; later, his firm, which occupied two floors of an office building in town, was one of their major traders. Greenwich was also home to heads of banks that had embraced the mortgage bonanza: Dick Fuld, the chairman and CEO of Lehman Brothers, made $350 million between 2000 and 2007, a period when Lehman made record profits; Chuck Prince, the chairman and CEO of Citigroup, lived in a Tudor-style manor house that could seat forty guests for dinner. Prince had helped Citigroup become a "financial services supermarket," as it was known, in part by packaging highly risky subprime mortgages into securities. Prince later told an interviewer that even as the risks grew, he could not let Citigroup miss out on profits: "As long as the music is playing, you've got to get up and dance," he said.

By late 2007, the music had stopped—disastrously. Home prices had peaked, and low-income owners were defaulting on loans they could not afford. The failures cascaded through mutual funds, pension funds, and the corporations that owned derivatives. Lehman Brothers collapsed; Bear Stearns was absorbed by JPMorgan Chase, and Citigroup received the largest bailout in U.S. history—$476 billion. Prince, the CEO, left the company with an exit package worth $68 million.

Chicago was left with more high-cost mortgages than any other big city in America. Not long after they signed the papers, Anita came to Clark with a mortgage bill in her hand. She was in a panic.

"Look at it," she said.

From $900 a month, their bill had started to climb—first to $1,000, then to $1,900, before settling back to $1,500—50 percent more than they had expected to play. Clark called the phone numbers listed on the bill, but the experience only made him angrier. "I was talking to someone in Idaho, and then I'm talking to some dude named Jimmy, and I said, 'You sound like your ass is a Hindu.' He said, 'My name is Jimmy Thompson.' I said, 'Man, your name ain't no damn Jimmy Thompson.'"

But then, all of a sudden, Clark had a more urgent problem than the mortgage. In the fall of 2004, he was arrested for selling crack to an undercover cop. According to the police report, the estimated value was ten dollars. He was sent back to prison for three more years.

———

As their interest rate climbed, Clark's family tried to keep up with the bills. They turned down the heat and turned up the stoves. But before long, they were further behind. After he got out of prison again, he looked at the numbers and concluded it was hopeless. "I'm saying, 'Damn, we can't make this mortgage.' And then, one day, I was sitting down watching CNN, and I remember this couple was on there and they said they were suing. I said, 'What? That's my mortgage company!' I jumped straight the fuck up."

In his neighborhood, he attended a free workshop for homeowners in distress. Only there did he begin to realize the scale of the housing crisis reverberating through the Black community. All around him, he saw his neighbors. "I was like, 'You, *too*?'" They had been ashamed to talk about the problems they were facing. "Nobody wants you to know they're losing their house," he said.

In 2010, the Illinois attorney general sued Countrywide for discrimination, accusing it of systematically steering minority borrowers to predatory loans while offering prime rates to comparable borrowers who were white. At Wells Fargo, which used similar policies, internal documents revealed that loan officers had referred to subprime mortgages as "ghetto loans" and to Black borrowers as "mud people." Writing in *The Atlantic*, Ta-Nehisi Coates called it a strategy of wholesale wealth theft. "This was not magic or coincidence or misfortune. It was racism reifying itself," he wrote.

But like so much in America, the story was not just about what happened to the people at the bottom; it was also about what was happening to the people at the top. At the same time that Countrywide was pulling borrowers into unsustainable loans, the CEO, Angelo Mozilo, was dispensing specially discounted loans to friends and powerful politicians, including Senator Chris Dodd of Connecticut, chairman of the Senate Banking Committee. The list was known internally as the "FOAs"— Friends of Angelo. By 2007, Mozilo was one of the highest-paid executives in America, having earned $138 million in two years from the sale of his company stock.

In 2009, the U.S. Securities and Exchange Commission charged Mozilo with insider trading and securities fraud; he agreed to pay tens of millions in fines and was barred from ever leading another publicly traded company. In 2011, Bank of America, which had acquired

Countrywide three years earlier, agreed to pay $355 million to settle claims—the largest residential fair-lending penalty in American history.

Clark applied to a Bank of America program that promised to modify loans that people could no longer afford. For a high school dropout, the paperwork was daunting, but Clark took it as a challenge. He didn't want to hire a lawyer; he did the application himself. "I got that through the system and I was fighting their ass like a motherfucker," he said. Then he missed a payment. And another. Before long, he owed four back payments of $1,700 each. He felt a growing sense of helplessness and resentment at the process—at the abstraction and facelessness of his opponent. "Who the fuck *are* you?" he thought. "I went to war with Bank of America."

On the South Side, unlike in Greenwich, the financial crisis did not feel like a hurricane that came and went. It was more akin to climate change—altering the basic conditions of daily life for years to come. As Clark and I walked down his street in 2016, he pointed out the number of houses that had been abandoned or were subject to foreclosure. Some of his neighbors had fought for better terms, but others just walked away. "In Black neighborhoods, the recession never ended," he said. A decade after the 2008 financial crisis, one out of every six homes on the South and West sides was vacant, according to research by the Woodstock Institute, a research-and-policy nonprofit. "Your education is only going to take you so far. And people didn't understand, so they got scared and bailed," he said.

Clark did not pretend that subprime loans were the only problems bearing down on him and his neighbors; he knew his own mistakes in life, and he spoke candidly of them. But he also marveled at those who had helped plunder his community. "It caused all kinds of mayhem, just because of the greed of their soul," he said. "And they're already rich! It's agents for chaos, that's all it is. Greed."

In the end, after trying to get help and meet payments, Clark's family was too far behind to make it up. They had paid in tens of thousands of dollars over the years on their mortgage. That wealth was gone. On January 29, 2016, Clark's family was evicted, and a "No Trespassing" sign was placed on the door. His mother moved down to Peoria, to be close to Clark's brother, who had found work at a logistics hub. She urged Clark to join her there. But he resisted; he was a Chicago guy, born and raised. "I got another turn at the wheel," he told her. But she was blunt. "Baby, all your wheels are flat. Come on."

He gave in. There wasn't much to wait for. He could hardly afford to rent an apartment anymore. By 2016, the share of apartments available for very low-income families had sunk, in six years, from 11 percent to 4 percent of city housing. Before Clark left, a priest gave him enough money for bus fare to get to Peoria, and McDonald's gift cards he could use for food. "He said to me, 'It's time for you to go. You need to get your head cleared up. Chicago ain't got nothing for you no more.'"

After the eviction, Reese's house was soon on the market. I saw it in real-estate listings described as a fixer-upper, "a great investment for the savvy buyer who wants to own a money maker." If you knew the house's history, it was impossible not to read the description as a version of exactly what Clark's family had hoped to do with it—a bit of investment to create a money maker. A kernel of wealth for the next generation. Instead, a new owner picked it up for $60,000. He did some renovations, then flipped it to another buyer for $225,000.

———

The financial crisis, and the rush to prop up the economy, triggered a wave of political repercussions. On February 19, 2009, a dozen miles north of Clark's house but a world away, a minor CNBC personality named Rick Santelli delivered a monologue from the floor of the Chicago Mercantile Exchange. It was less than a month after Obama's inauguration, and the administration was working on a $75 billion plan to help struggling homeowners refinance. Santelli had grown up in the western suburbs of Lombard, Illinois, studied economics, and worked at the exchange ever since; he had traded gold, lumber, T-bills, livestock, and other goods before becoming a commentator on the financial news network in 1999. And on this day, he was incensed.

Standing in a pit of traders, Santelli voiced an angry contempt for relief programs and the people they were intended to help. He wheeled around and shouted, "How many of you people want to pay for your neighbor's mortgage that has an extra bathroom and can't pay their bills?" The crowd groaned. "President Obama, are you *listening?*" he demanded. Those at risk of foreclosure were "losers," Santelli said. On the set at CNBC, Santelli's colleagues and other guests laughed with nervous enthusiasm at his rant. He continued, "We're thinking of having a Chicago *Tea Party.*" The traders around him cheered, and he hailed them as a "pretty good cross-section of America—the silent majority," he said, invoking Nixon's phrase for conservative voters who recoiled at the rise of the left. On-screen with him, Wilbur Ross, a billionaire who would later join the Trump administration, said, "Rick, I congratulate you on your new incarnation as revolutionary leader."

Santelli's speech was a sensation. By day's end, it was the most-watched video in CNBC's history, and calls for Tea Party protests were circulating on Facebook across the country. The concept took on the scale of a phenomenon, and to some who heard it, the rhetoric contained an ominous political tone. Paul Krugman later called it "an almost pathological meanspiritedness," a quality that was gaining volume on the American right. "If you're an American, and you're down on your luck," Krugman wrote, "these people don't want to help; they want to give you an extra kick."

At first glance, Santelli seemed like a revolutionary. In fact, he had just lit the spark; the makings of a tax rebellion had been gathering for years. Ever since the 1970s, conservative activists and wealthy patrons had sought to beat back the expansion of the federal government. They contended, as Robert LeFevre, an influential libertarian radio host, put it, that "government is a disease masquerading as its own cure." LeFevre's ideas circulated with the help of his acolytes, including the billionaire Charles Koch, who, with his brother David, presided over a conglomerate that stretched from ranching to oil to paper products (including the manufacture of Dixie Cups). The Kochs became political philanthropists in the belief that, as Charles Koch argued in the *Libertarian Review*, "ideas do not spread by themselves; they spread only through people. Which means we need a movement." The brothers underwrote a network of think tanks, academic programs, lobbyists, and candidates. (Hours after Santelli's rant, one of the first websites that spread his message was TaxDayTeaParty.com, which was registered by a Chicago man who had previous ties to the Kochs' political operation.)

The movement to delegitimize federal power would never have succeeded if it stayed on the libertarian fringe. In the 1990s, it gained a powerful new megaphone in Rush Limbaugh, the talk-radio star who built his celebrity around contempt for the Democratic elites represented by Bill and Hillary Clinton. Liberals, as Limbaugh put it, sought to "use the plight of the poor to advance their goal of dominating society." On his radio and television shows, and in a string of bestselling books, he used the tools of comic entertainers to present a case for cynicism and suspicion: "I am here to tell you that liberals don't give a rat's tail about ending discrimination," he said. "Do you know what liberals really mean by 'fighting discrimination'? Getting even." Environmentalism, he warned, was just "another way to panic people into ceding their own personal freedom and wealth and to allow the left to grab even more power and control over the lives of individuals." Schools, in his telling, were a cesspool of wasted tax dollars: "We're spending enough money per classroom today to provide chauffeured limousines to the teachers and the kids."

The campaign was breathtakingly successful. Even though government spending had advanced some of American capitalism's most precious assets—semiconductors, vaccines, nuclear power, wireless communications, aerospace, and the Internet—the conservative movement succeeded in demonizing government as a concept. By the time Santelli gave voice to the Tea Party sensibility, research into public attitudes showed that many Americans expressed abstract hostility to "the federal government," even if they were satisfied with the actual service they received. In a 2015 Pew survey, the vast majority of both Democrats and Republicans said the government did a good job of managing natural disasters (82 and 78 percent, respectively) and of setting fair, safe standards for workplaces (79 and 77 percent, respectively). Roughly half of each party said the federal government did well in maintaining roads, bridges, and other infrastructure and ensuring access to high-quality education.

Most remarkably, Americans had contempt for the very subsidies and benefits they relied upon. In a 2008 study, Suzanne Mettler, a Cornell political scientist, asked Americans whether they had "ever used a government social program" such as Social Security, Medicaid, or the home mortgage interest deduction. More than half—57 percent—said they had never used one, when, in fact, 92 percent of them *had* used government social programs. On average, Americans were enrolled in five federal social programs, such as Medicare and Social Security.

In the weeks after Santelli's speech, there were hundreds of Tea Party rallies, and within eighteen months, the movement had hardened into two thousand local branches. They embraced the slogan "Take It Back," which encapsulated a politics of threatened status—a fear of decaying power and the prospect, however abstract, of losing influence.

From the beginning, the Tea Party did little to hide the current of racial resentment running through it. At some rallies, posters depicted Obama as an African witch doctor or a character from *Planet of the Apes*. On the air in 2009, Limbaugh told his audience, "How do you get promoted in a Barack Obama administration? By hating white people, or even saying you do, or that they're not good, or whatever. Make white people the new oppressed minority." Limbaugh, who called the stimulus bill "reparations," taunted fellow Republicans for "going along with it," as he put it. "They're moving to the back of the bus. They're saying I can't use that drinking fountain, okay. I can't use that restroom, okay." In 2010, protesters against Obama's health-care plan accosted and surrounded Congressman John Lewis, the civil rights icon and Georgia Democrat, on the plaza at the foot of the U.S. Capitol. As Lewis walked slowly to his office, they taunted him and other Black representatives and hurled racial epithets. A demonstrator spat on them.

That racial animosity had been building throughout Obama's campaign. He had received so many death threats that the Secret Service gave him protection. Even before he had clinched the nomination, he was compelled to sleep behind bulletproof barriers in his bedroom. As

John McCain's campaign headed for defeat, his running mate, Sarah Palin, was creating a path for her political future by using a powerful new lexicon of hostility; she combined the xenophobia of the post–September 11 era with McCarthyite warnings about hidden traitors. Of Obama, she told a campaign crowd, "I am just so fearful that he is not a man who sees America the way you and I see America."

In the days after Obama was elected, Stormfront, the leading white-supremacist Web forum, crashed from heavy traffic. Other indicators were more subtle. Dozens of studies of voters found that opposition to Obama was associated with "racial resentment, anti-Black stereotypes, opposition to intimate interracial relationships, ethnocentrism, anti-Muslim attitudes, and even living in areas with many racist Google searches," according to Michael Tesler, a political scientist.

Over the next several years, when Obama spoke even briefly about racism, the reaction was swift and measurable. In July 2009, the Harvard professor Henry Louis Gates Jr. returned home to Cambridge after a trip to China, and found the front door of his home jammed shut. He and his driver tried to force it open, and a witness called police. Gates was arrested by a white officer, Sergeant James Crowley, and charged with disorderly conduct, a charge that was later dropped. Obama said that "the Cambridge police acted stupidly in arresting somebody when there was already proof that they were in their own home." Obama and his pollsters later discovered that those comments triggered the largest drop in support among white voters of his entire presidency.

⊢———⊣

Obama inspired a range of increasingly exotic conspiracy theories, beginning with the "birther" fiction, promoted by the real-estate developer and reality-TV star Donald Trump, which held that Obama was born abroad. (A 2014 study found that birthers were almost entirely white, mostly Republican, and reported high levels of racial resentment.) But birtherism was only the best known of the anti-Obama conspiracy theories. The writer Ta-Nehisi Coates inventoried others that emerged from the imaginings of his opponents: "Obama gave free cellphones to disheveled welfare recipients. Obama went to Europe and complained that 'ordinary men and women are too small-minded to govern their own affairs.' Obama had inscribed an Arabic saying on his wedding ring, then stopped wearing the ring, in observance of Ramadan. He canceled the National Day of Prayer; refused to sign certificates for Eagle Scouts; faked his attendance at Columbia University; and used a teleprompter to address a group of elementary-school students."

By the end of 2009, his first year in office, after a decade-long lull in militia activity across the country, the number of anti-government "patriot" groups more than tripled, according to the Southern Poverty Law Center. Daryl Johnson, a domestic-terrorism analyst at the Department of Homeland Security, warned that year that a slumping economy and the election of the first Black president were being used to fuel anti-government sentiment and "the potential emergence of terrorist groups or lone-wolf extremists." But his report, titled "Right-Wing Extremism," attracted fierce criticism from Republican lawmakers and conservative commentators, who said it unfairly described legitimate grievances. After issuing the report, Johnson's unit at DHS, the Extremism and Radicalization Branch, was dismantled.

Some of the new right-wing activists embraced a realm of martial fantasy and merchandising. Alex Jones, the host of InfoWars, attracted millions of followers with conspiracy theories that September 11 was a "false flag" operation perpetrated by the U.S. government, and that the 2012 massacre at Sandy Hook Elementary School used "crisis actors" to play murdered children and their grieving parents. In his telling, tainted drinking water made frogs gay, and juice boxes were making men infertile. On his website, he sold the emblems and elixirs of his tribe: T-shirts and stickers, dietary supplements intended to boost strength and virility, and emergency supplies in case of a disaster.

Even before Trump entered politics, the apocalyptic ravings on the far right had been edging into mainstream conservative media. In 2014, five years after Santelli's rant, the talk-show host Michael Savage, who amplified white-nationalist and antisemitic conspiracy theories, published a book called *Stop the Coming Civil War*, in which he argued that Obama's presidency "might represent the final nail in the coffin of freedom."

—————

So much of the Tea Party's contempt was focused on Obama that it was easy to overlook a portentous theme that would ultimately shape public life long after Obama was out of office. In Santelli's rant, he invoked a specific image of American failure. "Cuba," he said, "used to have mansions and a relatively decent economy. They moved from the *individual* to the *collective*. Now they're driving '54 Chevys!"

Over the centuries, Americans have tacked between sanctifying the individual and celebrating community, between self-interest and social obligation, between the imagined ideals of the lone cowboy on the frontier and of the wagon train that relies on mutual aid. Alexis de Tocqueville took note of that tension and saw their coexistence as an American talent, which he called "self-interest rightly understood." The pattern endured; in the town of Greenwich, it played out as a tug-of-war between the Brahmin and the buccaneer.

Striking that balance has been a permanent challenge. During the Gilded Age, individualism surged to the fore; some American industrialists invoked Darwin's new theory of evolution to explain, and rationalize, the suffering of the poor. In the words of William Graham Sumner, a sociologist, efforts to protect the vulnerable were attempts to "overrule evolution." In his view, "alleviating the plight of the poor" was "both immoral and imprudent."

By the 1910s, the exploitation exposed by the likes of Upton Sinclair in Chicago had generated a backlash; the balance tipped toward community during the Progressive Era, and the damage of the Great Depression fortified that by undermining arguments that individuals were consistently strong or weak in the face of economic forces. During the depths of the collapse, the historian Charles Beard declared, "The cold truth is that the individualist creed of everybody for himself and the devil take the hindmost is principally responsible for the distress in which Western civilization finds itself." Faith in the community was valorized in John Steinbeck's *Grapes of Wrath* and on-screen in Frank Capra's *Mr. Smith Goes to Washington.*

During my years abroad, I had written about rising individualism in modern China, where greater faith in the individual had developed partly from the distrust of political parties, corporations, and other powerful institutions. In the United States, I'd come upon an even starker version of that trend—a hyperindividualism that rested on fantasies of self-reliance and a cult of winning and losing. It was the crest of an idea that had been growing for decades. In a digital analysis of American books over the past two centuries, the Harvard scholar Robert Putnam and his coauthor Shaylyn Romney Garrett found a steady decline, beginning around 1970, in references to "agreement," "unity," and "compromise."

By the 2010s, social and political innovations intended to balance individual ambition with the public good were in retreat. Labor unions had been declining since the 1950s; taxes had been growing more regressive since the '60s, and antitrust legislation and financial regulation had been unraveling since the '70s. There were efforts to push back; in the '80s, new capital-adequacy rules on banks were intended to prevent another financial crisis; and in the 2000s, after the Enron scandal, accounting reforms known as Sarbanes-Oxley sought to prevent further abuses. But these regulatory efforts proved hard to enforce, and besides, Republicans were moving in the opposite direction, wrapping economics in the semi-sacred language of liberty.

The Tea Party was not the only populist uprising to emerge from the financial crisis. In late 2011, left-leaning protesters set up camp in Zuccotti Park, in Manhattan's financial district, driven by frustration with inequality, money in politics, and Washington's toothless response to financial abuse. Occupy Wall Street inspired hundreds of similar actions across the country around the slogan "We are the 99%." The prosecution of financiers, such as Skowron and the Rogues of Round Hill, had done little to combat the perception of injustice; in fact, those cases only seemed to draw attention to the conspicuous absence of any top Wall Street CEOs in the dock. Though Obama voiced sympathy for the protests, some participants did not hide their disillusion with the spirit of transformation that accompanied his election. "We tried to get the best liberal we could, and then we got more of the same shit," an organizer told *Jacobin*, the socialist magazine. "Then it's either cynicism or we're going to try something completely different."

As public disaffection became more visible, on both the left and the right, politicians found ways to navigate it. At a Republican conference in Florida in late 2011, the conservative political consultant Frank Luntz offered advice to state governors. Instead of the usual odes to "capitalism," he urged them to refer instead to "economic freedom" or the "free market." Avoid mentioning Wall Street "bonuses," he said; it sounded better to call those rewards "pay for performance." And, in a moment of rising anger, never talk about "compromise"; it sounded like failure. Most of all, he added, deflect any incoming anger toward Washington, making all political disagreement into a national drama of existential conflict.

Among its influences, the Tea Party gloried in the legacy of Ayn Rand. At Tea Party rallies, protesters waved signs asking "Who Is John Galt?" (a nod to the hero of *Atlas Shrugged*) and cited Randian ethics to argue that universal health care was immoral. Until recently, mainstream conservative intellectuals had left Rand mostly to her dorm-room devotees, who found a neat moral vindication in her ethics of "rational selfishness," and her fierce division of the world into "producers" and "looters." Jennifer Burns, a historian who wrote *Goddess of Market: Ayn Rand and the American Right*, observed that Rand conjured a "dream world of the successful striver surrounded by equals and unencumbered by the poor, the weak, or the unlucky. Only in this fictional world could her heroes duck the hard questions of fate and chance, for in Rand's novels, everyone gets what they deserve."

In its most pointed form, that change manifested in public life as a flamboyant contempt for mutual aid, a near celebration of suffering. During a Republican primary debate on CNN in the 2012 presidential race, the moderator proposed a hypothetical case: If a man without insurance falls ill, could it be true that society "should just let him die"?

Before the candidates answered, a man in the audience shouted "Yes!" and others hooted in approval. The crowd laughed.

———

The modern cult of individualism was especially stark in the context of the wars that followed September 11, 2001, because it broke with how Americans imagined their instincts for sacrifice and generosity in times of conflict. During World War II, 16 million Americans entered the armed forces, businesses accepted price controls to prevent inflation, and families bought war bonds and rationed everything from meat to firewood to penicillin. Encouraging a spirit of sacrifice for the greater good was considered so essential that some of the measures were symbolic; small towns made a show of rounding up tin cans, purely to give Americans a shared sense of purpose. The sacrifices, of course, were controversial: Roosevelt's enemies called wage controls un-American; in some instances, Black and Latino men were attacked by U.S. sailors for wearing zoot suits, which deliberately flouted wartime limits on fabric as protests against discrimination. But overall the system held.

During the latest wars, there was very little of that ethos. After September 11, while President Bush mobilized the military, he believed that the best answer to terrorism was the projection of normalcy. ("I have urged our fellow Americans to go about their lives," he said.) In the years afterward, there was no pressure for a war tax or rationing, to say nothing of a draft, in part because the military feared that conscription would erode professionalism. By the end of the 2010s, the War on Terror—which began on September 11 and extended to Afghanistan, Iraq, Pakistan, Somalia, Syria, and at least nine other countries where U.S. troops were dispatched—would become America's longest war, surpassing Vietnam by twelve years. It would claim more than 7,000 American lives and leave more than 50,000 wounded—a burden that was borne by less than 1 percent of the population.

Over time, the toll of endless war put stress on American political culture—but it was chronic, not acute. Bush was reelected, and two successive administrations waged war without paying a clear price at the ballot box. Elliot Ackerman, a marine who fought in Iraq and Afghanistan, later observed: "If after 9/11 we had implemented a draft and a war tax, it seems doubtful that the millennial generation would've abided 18 successive years of their draft numbers being called, or that their boomer parents would've abided a higher tax rate to, say, ensure that the Afghan National Army could rely on U.S. troops for one last fighting season in the Hindu Kush."

Without those levers of accountability, the conflicts proceeded in a political bubble, insulated from the pressures that would normally shape the decision to expose Americans and their families and their hometowns, to say nothing of their enemies, to harm. "The history of American warfare—even the 'good' wars—is a history of our leaders desperately trying to preserve the requisite national will because Americans would not abide a costly, protracted war," Ackerman wrote. In this instance, however, the effects of endless war were too diffuse, across geography and class, too muddled by the peek-a-boo distractions of our time, to generate a coherent political meaning beyond the hollow mantra "Thank you for your service." To those who did the fighting, Americans effectively offered "thoughts and prayers" and not much else.

The era of endless wars had gone on so long that it was sometimes easy to overlook entirely. In some parts, the effects were barely visible. But in others, the damage was becoming inescapably clear. On a per-capita basis, Americans from small towns were more than twice as likely to die at war in the years after September 11 than Americans in big cities were. In Clarksburg, West Virginia, where the military had been a proud feature of local life for generations, the veterans' hospital at the bend in the river kept a sign out front with the words "The price of freedom is visible here." In the silent, predawn darkness of a summer morning, that price would become unimaginably vivid.

EIGHT

GETTING LOADED

SHORTLY BEFORE HIS TWENTIETH BIRTHDAY, Sidney Muller enlisted in the U.S. Marines. For generations of West Virginians, the military had been a way up and a way out. The state ranked among the most populous states for veterans, which was a source of pride, and also a reminder of its poverty. In Clarksburg, the markers of military service were everywhere—three war memorials, lodges for the American Legion and the Veterans of Foreign Wars, and, largest of all, the Louis A. Johnson VA Medical Center, which loomed over a bend in the West Fork River.

Muller had grown up in Clarksburg, with difficulty. His father, Arturo Muller, bequeathed him a middle name—Arthur—and little else. By the time he was four, his father was gone. His mother, Linda, co-owned a local sandwich shop for a time but drifted in and out of drugs and alcohol—"my troubles," as she put it. When Muller was in third grade, his mother overdosed on pills and he saved her life by performing CPR. When he was fifteen, she did a stint in prison. Growing up, he loathed what drugs had wrought in her life, but he had his own troubles; he drank too much and got in fights and stole things. ("I was so mad at my life," he said later. "I was letting that madness and hatred out.") Eventually he stole a church van and landed at the Salem Industrial

Home for Youth, a juvenile-detention facility near Clarksburg. Muller got his GED, and, in 2004, when he turned eighteen, he was released from Salem and found a job at Walmart. It was powerfully dull. On television, he watched scenes of marines in Iraq, and he took to mentioning an uncle who had served abroad. He visited a Marine recruiter and asked to join the infantry. His girlfriend, Taylor Durst, sensed the deeper origins of his interest in the military. "It was a form of stability," she told me.

In January 2006, Muller departed for boot camp at Parris Island, South Carolina. He was big—six feet tall, 256 pounds—so they made him a machine gunner, a job reserved for those who can carry the extra weight in weapons and gear. After training, the Marines sent him to Iraq for seven months, and back again the following year, for another eight months. In his third year, he landed a quiet deployment to Kuwait, and eventually, after returning home, he was honorably discharged on February 13, 2010. By then, he and Taylor had married; they had a one-year-old son and a daughter on the way. He was settling down.

But after a few months, Washington came calling. It was 2010, and the war in Afghanistan was faltering; the Taliban had seized the momentum, and Obama had announced a surge of 30,000 additional troops, with plans to bring them home after eighteen months. The Marines asked Sidney to come back, and he agreed. He departed West Virginia and arrived in Afghanistan just before Christmas. He was assigned to a river town in southern Afghanistan called Sangin—a name that would soon become notorious.

To all sides of the war, Sangin was coveted territory, a crossroads of the opium trade and a gateway to Kandahar, the country's second-largest city. The Taliban was fighting hard to gain control of Sangin. Since 2006, British troops had lost more than a hundred lives defending it—nearly a third of all British combat deaths in Afghanistan since September 11. British troops nicknamed it "Sangingrad," after the worst siege of World War II. Shortly before Muller arrived, the British handed off that grim assignment to the U.S. Marines.

Over the next seven months, his unit, the Third Battalion of the Fifth U.S. Marine regiment, suffered a historic toll: 29 dead and 184

wounded, including 34 who lost a limb. It was the highest casualty rate
of any Marine unit since September 11. The casualties were so heavy
that Secretary of Defense Robert Gates made an unusual trip; he flew
from Washington to the dusty outpost at Sangin and made a personal
pledge. "Our nation owes you an incredible debt for the sacrifices you
have made," he told the marines. "If there's anything you need at all,
anything I can do to help you, don't hesitate to ask."

When Muller's battalion ended its tour in April, he asked to stay in
Sangin with another unit. For all of the ordeal, he was doing a job well
for the first time in his life. A commanding officer recommended him
for a medal, writing that his "initiative, tactical proficiency and courage under fire epitomized that of a war fighter." Another officer wrote
that Muller "should be retained and promoted." From Sangin, Muller
emailed a fellow West Virginian named Herman Lubbe, a Marine sergeant who was preparing to join him there soon. Muller warned Lubbe
to brace himself. "Remember Iraq?" he wrote. "Take the worst parts of
Iraq and make it worse. That's what this is." When Lubbe arrived in
January, he discovered that the sensation of vulnerability was relentless.
Day after day, the marines patrolled the same claustrophobic warren of
rutted paths, digging up newly implanted bombs intended to kill or disfigure them. On patrol, Lubbe found that the fear of the next explosion
played sinister tricks on your mind. "You walk single file, like ants, and
you just wonder if the first guy in line steps on it," he said.

There were other dangers: early one morning in May 2011, Lubbe was
in a large canvas tent when he heard the telltale whine of an incoming
mortar. "It shredded the tent like Swiss cheese," he said. At the moment
of explosion, Muller and one other marine had been the only people
standing up. "It missed Sidney, and it hit the other guy right in the face,"
Lubbe recalled. "If you've seen the Batman movie *The Joker*, he looked
like that. Cut from the corner of his mouth, up the side of his face."

That mortar was the opening blast of a firefight that dragged on for
hours. At one point, after Lubbe and Muller had made their way to a
front line at the edge of their base, they were huddled at the bottom of
a staircase. They heard the whine of another incoming mortar. When
it struck, it threw shrapnel and dirt against the wall where Muller had

been standing. "I jump up screaming, 'Sidney! Sidney! Sidney!'" Lubbe said. "And I hear nothing. And then he walks out from underneath the stairs, white as a ghost." Muller slumped down next to Lubbe and said, "I have no idea how that did not just kill me."

Three weeks later, Lubbe was on patrol when a marine near him stepped on a bomb that tore off his legs from the thigh down. In the chaos after the explosion, Lubbe crouched over the stricken marine and started to light a smoke grenade that might be able to guide an incoming helicopter. That's when another marine stepped on another IED. This second blast blew Lubbe into the air. When he landed, he felt a wave of pain and heat settle, like a blanket, across his face. The explosion had torn open his chin and nearly amputated his right ear. Down below, his legs were a tangle of broken bones and flesh. A lieutenant crouched over him. Lubbe pleaded for morphine, and then blacked out. He spent the next two years at the Walter Reed Medical Center. Doctors repaired his face and ear, and mended his legs. He learned to walk again. He felt lucky; most of his fellow patients had no legs.

Lubbe had come to expect a bewildering distance between himself and many Americans in the decades after September 11. However, he said, "I never encountered anything like what the Vietnam vets did; most people would give you their support and would be appreciative of your service, so I am very grateful for that." But the wars were abstractions for the vast majority of people; they offered thoughts and prayers, but they had been asked to give nothing of themselves. "You'd have the same questions and conversations that folks felt they needed to ask," Lubbe said, "even though I knew they wouldn't understand or care five minutes later."

In September 2011, Muller returned from his tour in Afghanistan and drove to Lubbe's hospital room at Walter Reed. He spent a month sleeping in a chair beside Lubbe's bed. During the day, they talked about what they had seen and what lay ahead. Muller was optimistic. "I'm going to go back to school," he said. He had taken some online courses. He thought of becoming a cop with a focus on troubled young people, much as he had been. Lubbe was glad for him. "All these grand ambitions," he said.

Muller drove back to Clarksburg and stayed in touch with Lubbe by phone and email. But over time, Muller's messages grew scarce. Their phone calls became more infrequent. When they did speak, Muller sounded vague and rushed. Lubbe didn't know precisely what was happening, but he knew it couldn't be good. "I didn't ask, and he didn't say," Lubbe said. "It was like a slow-moving avalanche."

⊢———⊣

Over the years, one could track the long-range effects of the wars since September 11, even in a place as far from the attacks as Clarksburg; it was visible in the pages of *The Exponent Telegram*. The paper covered the send-off ceremonies at the airport, when West Virginians set off for Afghanistan—and it published detailed obituaries when some of them died in combat. As the years passed, the paper chronicled the growing strain on members of the national guard who struggled to keep their businesses afloat as the army relied more and more on part-time soldiers. The stresses continued to accumulate; a tone of resignation crept into the writing. While Muller was in Iraq, a story about the departure of another planeload of the West Virginia National Guard noted dryly, "For many of them, it will not be their first deployment."

A few weeks after getting back to Clarksburg, Muller visited the big VA medical center up on the hill. It was one of the biggest employers in the region, with roughly a thousand workers, serving some 70,000 veterans from as far away as Ohio. In a meeting with a doctor, he complained of "issues with anger control and insomnia," according to the doctor's notes. Muller confessed that he was drinking too much. In the doctor's judgment, he also showed "subthreshold symptoms" of post-traumatic stress, but they did not meet the criteria for an official diagnosis. The doctor prescribed mirtazapine to help him sleep, along with hydroxyzine for anxiety, and sent him home.

The problems grew. In the ten months that followed, Muller returned to the VA on two more occasions, with increasingly disturbing symptoms. He "finds himself on the floor and does not remember how he got there," a doctor wrote on September 7, 2012. The "dreams and anger are getting worse," he added. Muller had given up taking the mirtazapine because he thought it was giving him nightmares about the war.

The report ticked off other symptoms: Muller "feels detached and tends to isolate" himself from friends; he "gets anxious if he has to wait, he gets startled easily, has back to walls, mood swings, and irritability. He reports intrusive thoughts of trauma all the time." Muller was given two new prescriptions—fluoxetine (an antidepressant) and prazosin (for nightmares)—and he was tested on a checklist for PTSD. He received a score of 52, which qualified his condition as "severe." The VA put him on disability payments of $1,889 per month.

At twenty-nine years old, Muller was coming undone. He had separated from his wife. "He was very rarely there," Durst told me. "He had been so excited to be the dad he never had, but he didn't know how to do it." Less than a month after the September visit to the VA, he wrecked his car and was arrested for driving drunk. He lost his license. Weeks later, he was arrested for driving without a license. So much for becoming a cop; his record would make that impossible for years. Moreover, his paranoias had become overwhelming. He told the doctor he had "stopped trusting all my friends."

Muller had returned from Afghanistan at precisely the moment that Clarksburg was emerging as an epicenter in America's opioid epidemic. Around town, Muller had no trouble buying Xanax, the anxiety drug, and opioids such as Percocet, as well as Subutex and Suboxone, which are supposed to combat the addiction to opioids. He drank bottles of prescription cough syrup.

Eventually, to fund his habit, he became a small-time dealer, buying painkillers from a supplier in Detroit and selling them in Clarksburg. When a doctor asked him how he spent his time, he made no effort to conceal his life; he was usually at home, he said, "getting loaded." When Durst, his ex-wife, met him to arrange his next visit with their kids, she was startled by the sight of him. "It was creepy. He just had this blank stare in his eyes," she said. "He was on another planet. He couldn't remember our children's birthdays."

The morning of July 25, 2013, started in Muller's usual fashion. He took his prescriptions, then started drinking beer and vodka. Then he took Xanax and Percocet and smoked pot and waited for the sun to go down. In the evening, he went to a bar, where he had, by his count, ten drinks. After midnight, he drank half a bottle of Everclear, a 151-proof grain alcohol. He got into his car, a Buick sedan, and headed to Locust Avenue, one of the streets named for trees, near my old building. Asked later to rate how drunk he was by then, he put the number at "8 to 9" out of 10.

———

In the years since I moved away, the neighborhood had been transformed by the pressures bearing down on West Virginia. Many of the retirees I'd met had died or moved away. One by one, their descendants converted the houses on Locust Avenue into rental properties, which changed the feeling of the place; renters were transient, less familiar with their neighbors, and less inclined to pay for repairs. The signs of collapse accumulated; at one house, the roof shingles sloughed off in the wind; at another, a colony of mold crept up the vinyl siding. At another, a broken window was replaced with plywood. By the time Sidney Muller pulled up at the curb, it had become what a lawyer in town later called "a street that you don't want to walk down in the daytime, much less after dark."

At 743 Locust, a two-story wooden house painted swimming-pool blue, Muller paid a call on a friend, Christopher Hart, whom everyone knew by his nickname: Body. Hart, twenty-six, was a former bodybuilder who weighed more than three hundred pounds. He was in his bedroom, which was decorated with childhood memorabilia—the Green Bay Packers, professional wrestling, zombies from *The Walking Dead*. Body was with another of their friends, Todd Amos; the two of them were known to sell pills and heroin. Sidney Muller was sometimes a customer and sometimes a supplier. On this occasion, Muller was a disgruntled supplier. He had "fronted" them a load of pills to sell and wanted his share of the profits. An argument escalated, and Body pulled out a pearl-handled 9 mm Beretta that his mother had given to him on Father's Day.

Muller was unarmed, but marines like to say there is no such thing as an "ex-Marine." The sight of the gun pulled him out of his stupor, and he knocked it out of Body's hand. The men scrambled for it on the floor. In that moment, Muller would later tell a doctor, he was acting on "instinct." He said, "They became the enemy." Muller picked it up and shot Body in the face. Then he shot Amos, who slumped, dead, onto the couch, his neck on his chest, as if he were napping. From down the hall, Body's housemates were awoken by the blasts and came bounding in. They found Body on his hands and knees, near death but still able to speak. "Sidney did this," he said. (He later died on the way to the hospital.)

By then, Muller had bolted through the front door and out into the street, still holding the pearl-handled 9 mm. It was 4:30 a.m., and in the predawn gloom Muller saw two figures approaching in his peripheral vision. They were in a void between the streetlights, and he couldn't see their faces. He assumed they were people from the house or someone else "against me." He fired at them and drove away, heading for home.

The figures in the darkness were not from the house. They had nothing to do with it. They were delivering *The Exponent Telegram*. A father and son on their paper route. The father, Fred Swiger, was seventy years old; his son, Freddie Jr., was forty-seven and developmentally disabled. They were one of the newspaper's last delivery teams that still worked a route on foot. For thirty years they had done it; always before dawn, to avoid the heat. Along the route, older customers would leave notes for them, asking "the Swiger boys," as they were known, to come back for odd jobs—painting, fixing a lawn mower, trimming a hedge.

In the instant that Muller fired the gun, Minnie Swiger lost her firstborn child and her ex-husband. Minnie and Fred had married at eighteen and raised eight children—seven boys and a girl. Fred worked as a maintenance man at a Catholic school, but mostly he looked after Freddie Jr. "My son loved animals. There was a thrift shop where the money went to an animal shelter, and every day he'd go there and buy some little item," Minnie told me. "One time, Junior and his dad came home with five dogs. We found homes for most of them. But there was one that was blind and nobody wanted her, so we ended up with her for years." The marriage did not last, and after the kids were grown, Minnie moved to Ohio, while Fred stayed in Clarksburg with Junior. Year by year, the homes on their route deteriorated. Fewer and fewer people subscribed to the paper. Minnie worried about them out there, but the Swiger boys kept walking. "Rain, shine, snow, whatever," she said. "They lived together and they died together." Their bodies fell, askew on the asphalt of Locust Avenue. In the crime-scene photos, Junior still held a copy of *The Exponent Telegram* in his right hand.

———

By dawn, Muller was under arrest. He confessed to arguing with Body and Amos, to scrambling for the gun, to shooting both of them. He didn't know if they had survived, he said, and he had no idea who he had shot in the street. "Aimed as low as I could," he told the police. "Just, 'Hey, back the fuck up. Get the fuck away from me.'"

Prosecutors charged Muller with four counts of first-degree murder. His lawyer, Sam Harrold, did not deny the facts. "He did it. There's no way of getting around that," Harrold told me later, but Harrold, a Navy veteran, found it impossible to separate Muller's crimes from his combat experiences. "He was attempting to get some treatment," he said. "He just needed help with what was going on in his personal life. And the system failed him."

In August 2015, Muller pleaded guilty. The judge, Thomas Bedell, who had been on the bench in Clarksburg for a quarter century, called it the "most difficult case I've presided over." He added, "I don't know that our county's ever suffered such loss." As part of the sentencing, the probation office produced a detailed portrait of Muller's life—his parents, his criminal history, his education, his problems with drugs and alcohol, his experiences in Afghanistan. Among their assessments, the authors concluded that the murderer had no "procriminal attitude." In other words, they explained, he "wished it didn't happen and if he could change the circumstances he would have." The judge sentenced Muller to life in prison; he would be eligible for parole after twenty-five years.

Reading the report at my desk one afternoon, I turned it over in my mind for a long time, considering the sheer waste of it all—the lives Muller took, the families he ruined, the hole he tore in the town. Muller was obviously responsible for his crimes, but is that the end of the story? How should a society account for the fuel that fed that fire? What happened to the promise made by the secretary of defense on the visit to Sangin: "If there's anything you need at all, anything I can do to help you, don't hesitate to ask." When Muller needed help, he received prescriptions and a check, which was more than many veterans of earlier wars received. But then he was returned to a life as hollow of meaning and dignity as the slogan of its time: *Thank you for your service.*

When I spoke to Muller's friend Herman Lubbe about the murders, he said he sometimes felt guilty about them. He wished he had stayed in better touch. When the details of the case became clear, he saw the chain of events as a grotesque cascade that nobody stepped in to arrest. By contrast, Lubbe's life after Afghanistan had been a path of recovery. His mother spent months by his side at Walter Reed. More to the point, unlike Muller, he had such vivid wounds that society could not avoid the responsibility to repair them. The surgeons rebuilt his legs and erased enough of the scars on his face that people only occasionally asked what happened. Lubbe found work as a civilian with the Department of Defense. He moved to Germany. He met a woman.

But he never pretended that his experiences in Afghanistan had not altered him. On the phone with me from Germany, he said, "It's early spring here. Then it will be summer. And that's the time that we really started the heavy fighting in Afghanistan. My girlfriend says, 'Herman always gets irritable around now.'" But understanding himself was enough progress for the moment. He could not undo what had happened; he could only be humbled by it. "I can't make it stop," he said.

———

Muller was assigned to the maximum security prison at Mount Olive, a couple of hours south of Clarksburg. He found work as a barber, just as Reese Clark did, and was accepted into a bachelor's degree program, run by a Bible college. Most days, he read for five or six hours. "I'm finally calm. It took years," he said. He had come to believe that his mistake was not joining the Marines but leaving them. "I was good at being a Marine," he said. "When you get out and you don't have a plan, it's like you're moving a hundred miles an hour and then you stop." He thought of his brain as a switch that got stuck in the on position. "You've got to shut it off, but you can't," he said. We spoke about the murders, and he said, "I take responsibility because I did it. But I didn't mean to, if that makes a difference." Over and over, he said the wars "desensitized" him to killing and the risks of dying. "Death was nothing new. Maybe after my first deployment to Fallujah, it might have been something. But after my third deployment, I don't even know how many people we were responsible for killing. A lot, I know that."

Whenever I try to take stock of the full legacy of the wars since September 11, my mind returns to a comment made years ago by Neil Postman, the author of *Amusing Ourselves to Death*. He perceived American history as a sequence of metaphors that, he wrote, "create the content of our culture." Each era had its own: the western frontier, Upton Sinclair's urban slaughterhouse, and eventually the gilded illusions of Las Vegas. Postman died in 2003, but he might have found the central metaphor of contemporary American culture in the era of "twilight" warfare—a description of an American conflict with no clear geography or victory.

In the early years after September 11, when Americans were still shaken by a sudden sense of vulnerability, they had been eager to avoid the divisiveness of the Vietnam era. They wanted to differentiate between objecting to a conflict and to the people who went to fight it. But as the United States prepared to invade Iraq, the urge for solidarity had settled into an undeclared hostility toward some of the rightful questions about America's use of its awesome force. By the eve of the war in Iraq, the author Norman Mailer worried about what he called "a pre-fascistic atmosphere in America." In a speech in early 2003, he suggested, presciently, that democracy was "a condition we will be called upon to defend in the coming years."

As the wars ground on, the language of conflict blended with entertainment and bled back into politics in ways that were distorting and reductive. In 2006, Laura Ingraham, the conservative commentator, cited the TV series *24*, which featured frequent depictions of torture. "The average American out there loves the show *24*," she said. "In my mind, that's as close to a national referendum that it's okay to use tough tactics against high-level Al Qaeda operatives as we're going to get."

At times, the war came home, captured in headlines about a foiled plot or a radicalized "homegrown" terrorist. But for most Americans, it was an abstraction, fought far away from what was now routinely described as the "homeland." In the twilight war, Americans had acquired an enemy that felt invisible but ever present, everywhere and nowhere, threatening enough that any measures felt permissible. More than three years into the Iraq War, a *National Geographic* poll found that fewer than a quarter of Americans with some college education could locate Iraq, Iran, Saudi Arabia, and Israel on a map. In the war novel *Missionaries*, by the Marine veteran Phil Klay, a character described the expanding array of American military ventures as an "extension of the same war, not the endless war on 'terror' but something vaguer, harder to pin down and related to the demands of America's not-quite-empire."

The appetites of its "not-quite-empire" were altering America's sense of its strengths and its weaknesses. As the wars dragged on, unburdened by the political pressures of a draft or a war levy, the United States faced a growing, practical struggle to recruit enough troops. Year by year, it dropped its recruiting thresholds to accept people it had previously marked as low priority; first, it expanded the ranks to those without high school diplomas; then it expanded the recruitment of new immigrants who were eager to trade their service for citizenship. Since the Revolutionary War, the United States had allowed non-Americans to fight on its behalf, and as the federal government grew more desperate, President Bush changed the rules to allow service members to apply for citizenship on their first day, instead of waiting for three years. Before long, more than 40,000 noncitizens were serving in active or reserve duty, and making up 3 percent of America's casualties in Iraq.

But the hunger for more troops collided with another product of September 11: a deep new cleavage in the Republican Party over the scope and merits of immigration. At the same time that the government needed more and more immigrants to fight, a rising wave of xenophobic conservatives were pulling fringe ideas into the mainstream, including denying birthright citizenship to American-born children of illegal immigrants and demanding to build a wall on the southern border. In 2004, more than a decade before Trump entered politics, Tom Tancredo, a right-wing populist congressman from Colorado, warned that undocumented immigrants were "coming here to kill you and to kill me and our families." Tancredo and others used their leverage over federal agencies to make it harder for immigrants in the military to achieve citizenship. In 2005, an Army Reservist in Iraq named Kendell Frederick, who had emigrated from Trinidad, was told he had to submit new fingerprints for his naturalization application because the U.S. Citizenship and Immigration Services was barred from accepting fingerprints he already had on file with the Army. On the way, he was killed by a roadside bomb.

Politicians like Tancredo, it turned out, were not aberrations; they were previews of a politics to come. They had discovered a reservoir of political power in Americans' merging fears of Islam and of demographic change. The country was entering one of the most rapid diversifications in history. In the 1970s, about 5 percent of the people in America had been born abroad; by 2018, that figure was 14 percent, nearly surpassing the record set in 1890, when 15 percent of the population had been born abroad. Moreover, white Americans often felt the change as a generational eclipse, because they were far older than the more diverse cohorts of newer Americans. By 2018, the median age of white Americans would be fifty-eight; for Asian Americans that figure was twenty-nine, and for Latinos it was eleven.

Tancredo seized on those anxieties. During a brief run for president in 2008, he boycotted a debate because it was being broadcast in Spanish; he ran ads referring to "vicious Central American gangs, now on U.S. soil, pushing drugs, raping kids, destroying lives." At a Tea Party convention, he drew links between immigration, Islam, and hatred of Obama, telling the crowd, "People who cannot even spell the word 'vote,' or say it in English, put a committed socialist ideologue in the White House. His name is Barack Hussein Obama." In Congress, Tancredo introduced the Jihad Prevention Act, which required immigrants to pledge that they would not advocate sharia law in the United States.

Tancredo, who left Congress in 2009, eventually faded from prominence, but he had exposed a powerful new combination of American phobias. Jason De León, an anthropologist at UCLA, observed the transformation through the evolution of the government agency Immigration, Customs and Enforcement (ICE). He met border-control agents who had joined in the belief that they would stop terrorists from invading the country, noting that, over time, that image had widened once more, to encompass the full realm of immigration. "The sleight of hand that has happened is that we now conflate terrorism with undocumented migration across the southern border," De León observed.

├──┤

In Clarksburg, Muller's killings seemed to have struck at the very things that once held the place together: the pride of military service, the relief provided by the VA, and a small-town newspaper produced, as the motto had it, "by West Virginians for West Virginians." In all the particulars, the killings were a moment of moral violence that made you question the underlying health of your hometown, as searing as the Ku Klux Klan assembling in front of the courthouse. Only this time, there was no easy way to wave it off as an oddity from the margins. When Muller unraveled, nobody caught him—not his family, his hometown, or his country. It was a conspiracy of failures.

More and more, those kinds of overlapping explanations were the only way to make sense of the crisis enveloping much of West Virginia. The state population had plateaued in 2012 and declined since then. It was 94 percent white, and the oldest and least-educated state in America. More than half the kids qualified for free or reduced-price lunch at school.

In Clarksburg, Crystal Wimer, the official historian of Harrison County, encouraged people to look deeper than the drug epidemic or the end of the glass-manufacturing era in town. "The closing of the factories is only one spindle of a wheel," she told me one afternoon in her office overlooking Main Street. "It's not just because a lot of good-paying manufacturing jobs left. It's a lot of different things. You need to address the generational poverty. You need to address the brain drain. Of my graduating class, there are very few of us left in West Virginia. I've chosen to stick it out as much as I can, because I feel that it's important to keep people here. But, honestly, Walmart is not going to save us."

At *The Exponent Telegram*, the murders were, of course, personal. Every morning, the Swigers had picked up their papers on the loading dock out back. "They were just barely getting by," the editor, John Miller, told me. "Working a paper route. People loved 'em." Miller prided himself on trying to focus on the best parts of his hometown, but this was a moment that exceeded his capacity to find a bright side. As he often did, he hunted for a logic in the statistics.

"When the Industrial Revolution was going on in the 1900s, Clarksburg used to have fifty thousand people in it," he said one day as we talked in his office. "You had so many people coming in on trains, and so much going on. There were six or eight hotels downtown. You had all this business and commerce: glass plants, coal, oil, gas. And then it all went away."

In the big bound archives of the old papers, you could see yellowed pictures of the city at its peak; there was the ticker-tape parade for John W. Davis, getting the Democratic nomination in 1924. And in the background, the Waldo Hotel rose up like a cliffside. "It was just opulent," Miller said. The Waldo symbolized Clarksburg's connection to power. In the 1920s, one of the men who owned it, Guy Goff, served in the U.S. Senate and lived in a suite of rooms on the fourth floor. Later, conservative Republican senators convened at the Waldo to plot an effort to get Goff on the presidential ballot instead of their party's nominee, Herbert Hoover.

But Clarksburg's connections to power had deteriorated as visibly as the old wrecked buildings downtown. Over the years, Miller had ventured into the darkness of the abandoned buildings, with their floors of Italian marble and ornate tin ceilings. If you looked up, you could still make out traces of what had vanished. "You can see the moldings and the high ceilings," he said.

Every few years, usually around a boom in the fossil-fuel business, someone would announce plans to fix up one of the old buildings. Not long ago, it was the Parsons Hotel, which had a classic bar and restaurant and elegant details. The newspaper even threw a celebratory dinner there. But every boom had a bust. "Then it goes away again," Miller said. "It just sits there and deteriorates." He caught himself. "Highs and lows," he said.

His childhood church was barely a hundred yards from the site of the murders. He often drove around and took note of which neighborhoods were doing well and which ones were collapsing. "It amazes me. This section over here's pretty good. That section there's pretty good, but in between it's a freakin' war zone." He paused at the sight of homes that seemed to be inhabited but collapsing around the people inside. "They're not really being torn down. It just looks like they've fallen apart."

He dreamed of big, bold moves, and he ticked off the numbers in his imagination. "They've torn down one hundred to two hundred homes, I would estimate. And there's probably another five hundred to go." He said, "Change obviously is good if it's engineered correctly, but if no one's driving the train and it just decomposes . . ." He trailed off.

In his office upstairs, Miller's boss, the young lawyer Brian Jarvis, who had bought the newspaper to honor his late father, did his best to project calm and composure. When the national news called for a comment on the murders, Jarvis gave the kind of formal statement he figured was appropriate. "They were extremely nice, loyal, and cared very deeply about their customers. Their customers cared very deeply about them."

But, privately, he was shaken. He had owned the paper for barely a year. "I'm still trying to figure out what the newspaper *is*," he told me. "And our carriers are killed. I'm thinking: *What's going on?*"

NINE

BUYING POWER

IN JANUARY 2012, Chip Skowron prepared to report to federal prison in Schuylkill County, Pennsylvania. Before departing his home in Greenwich, he sat his four kids down and told them the truth about his case, his guilty plea, his sentence. He tried to avoid the usual euphemisms about "going away" on "a long trip." At Greenwich Country Day School a few days later, his youngest daughter, who was six, raised her hand and said, "My daddy's going to go to prison."

In the months since his undoing, he had begun to gain a certain clarity about his crimes, his lies and extramarital affairs, and his success on Wall Street. "I never would have left it because the money was too good," he said. "It would not have been a leap at all to leave my wife and children to start a new life. I was a hair's width away from that." And beneath it all, he said, "there was so much emptiness and loneliness in my life."

His professional and social world had collapsed with impressive speed. "All of the things that I had put my hope and trust in were now suddenly blown up. My wealth is gone, my reputation is gone, my business is gone, my wife doesn't even know who I am." One night, in the midst of that period, he had an unusually vivid dream. "And I'm not one of those guys that has lots of dreams," he said. In the dream, a large male figure with a face painted half in blue declared, *You need to read Leviticus!* "And then I woke up," he said. Skowron, who had been a regular but casual church-goer since childhood, climbed out of bed and padded downstairs to scan the shelves for a Bible, left to him by his mother. While his wife slept, he sat in the dressing room off the master bedroom suite and read. "It's not like I got out of that dream and went, 'Oh, Jesus is real to me now.' It was more like awe and fear of something so utterly beyond me."

Skowron started spending more of his time with members of a Christian men's group. He traveled to Virginia to attend a retreat, where he experienced an awakening; when he returned home, he said, "I basically lay on the floor for three weeks and cried. People around me thought I'd lost my mind." He continued, "It was what the monastic tradition refers to as the dark night of the soul. Those tears are what the monks pray for. That closeness with God. I don't know how to describe it other than it's an intimacy with the brokenness of humanity and specifically *my* brokenness."

In the months afterward, he thought about the origins of his sense of impunity. "There were all these little lies that I had begun to treat as truth, once you sprinkled millions of dollars on them. The saying on Wall Street is money doesn't corrupt character; it reveals it. If you believe that performance makes you above the rules, and then you have millions of dollars and you're performing, well, guess what? The rules didn't apply to you." The more someone was able to use their intelligence to succeed, the harder it became to see the moral wreckage they were creating. "Reason is never going to tell you right from wrong," he said. "Reason is only going to allow you to bend the morality."

Skowron, and the Rogues of Round Hill, had been prosecuted in a wave of cases that grew out of the financial crisis. In four years, at least seventy-five people were convicted of insider trading and related crimes, and four multibillion-dollar hedge funds collapsed under the pressures of the investigations. But hardly anyone on Wall Street really saw the prosecutions as a new era of accountability; they were narrow punishments that left the heart of the culture untouched.

As far as Skowron could discern, the boundary between what landed you in prison and what elevated your stature in Greenwich or Washington hinged mostly on who wrote the rules; how they defined concepts like freedom, fairness, and personal responsibility; and, most of all, who had the means or connections to avoid real punishment. After all, was trading money for inside information all that much worse than the culture of favor-trading and political influence peddling that happened every day in Washington? He said, "Most relationships these days *are* transactional. I do something for you. You do something for me." He went on, "I was just more overt about it."

The years of the financial crisis and its fallout laid bare, with impressive clarity, just how thoroughly some Americans were able to engineer advantages for themselves not only financially but also politically. Just as they had developed more refined tools of profit, they had embraced more refined tools of politics—for influencing voters and candidates, and for advancing more orthodox candidates who would prosecute their agendas in Washington. In the years that Greenwich was becoming vastly richer, local Republican donors and activists used some of that extraordinary wealth to hasten an evolution in American public attitudes on taxes, regulation, equality, and, ultimately, the legitimacy of the state itself. It was an evolution that eventually cleared the way for Trump to seize control of the commanding heights of politics, but to understand how it happened, you had to go back in time.

If you'd asked the people of Greenwich, in the fat years of the twentieth century, to vote for the *beau idéal* of local politics, the icon of their image of democracy, there would not have been much of a contest. Prescott Bush cast a dominant shadow, even in a town with an unusually high number of powerful citizens.

Prescott was the father and grandfather of future presidents, an investment banker, the moderator of the Representative Town Meeting (New England's version of the town council), and, from 1952 to 1963, a U.S. senator. He was also the eight-time club champion on the golf course at the Round Hill Club, one of eight country clubs in town, and a staunch believer in standards; he required his sons to wear a jacket and tie for dinner at home. He was tall, restrained, and prone to righteousness; friends called him a "Ten Commandments man." In the locker room at Round Hill, someone once told an off-color joke in front of his fourteen-year-old son, George H. W. Bush, and Prescott stormed out, saying, "I don't ever want to hear that kind of language in here again."

In Washington, Prescott was President Eisenhower's golf partner, and the embodiment of what Ike called "modern Republicanism." Though Eisenhower had campaigned as an ideological conservative, he governed as a moderate. He was so determined to avoid partisanship that he privately discussed the idea of founding a new party called the Middle Way, which might seek common ground between Republicans and Democrats. Similarly, Prescott wanted government lean and efficient, but, like Nelson Rockefeller, the New York governor whose centrism inspired the label "Rockefeller Republican," he was more liberal than his party on civil rights, birth control, and welfare. He denounced his fellow Republican Joseph McCarthy for creating "dangerous divisions among the American people" and for demanding that Congress follow him "blindly, not daring to express any doubts or disagreements." Prescott could be ludicrously aristocratic—his grandsons called him Senator—but he believed, fundamentally, in the duty of government to help people who did not enjoy his considerable advantages. He supported increasing the federal minimum wage and immigration quotas, and he beseeched fellow senators, for the sake of science, education, and defense, to "have the courage to raise the required revenues by approving whatever levels of taxation may be necessary."

Long after Prescott died in 1972, his family stayed central to the community of Greenwich Republicans. His son Prescott Jr., known as Pressy, served as the chairman of the Republican Town Committee; alumni of the Bush administrations still live around town decades later. Each year, the highest honor bestowed by the Connecticut Republican Party is the Prescott Bush Award.

But the moderate Republican consensus that Prescott embodied was always shakier than it looked, and by the mid-1960s it was disintegrating. In 1955, William F. Buckley Jr. had established his magazine *National Review* on the principle that government exists only "to protect its citizens' lives, liberty and property. All other activities of government tend to diminish freedom and hamper progress." It was the opening shot of the modern conservative movement, though, on the whole, liberal intellectuals did not regard it as a serious challenge. In 1963, John Kenneth Galbraith, the liberal economist and adviser to the Kennedys, mocked the modern conservative for being engaged in "one of man's oldest, best financed, most applauded, and, on the whole, least successful exercises in moral philosophy. That is, the search for a truly superior moral justification for selfishness."

In Greenwich, however, some people were seized by the new conservatism. J. William Middendorf II was a Harvard-educated investment banker who had served on the town council with Prescott, his friend and neighbor. "I sold him a piece of land at the foot of my property," Middendorf told me. When he retired to his porch in the evening, he could hear the Bushes singing Yale songs in their backyard. But beneath the similarities, Middendorf had adopted a strikingly different ideology; he had become, in his words, a "disciple" of the libertarian movement, enthralled by Friedrich Hayek and Joseph Schumpeter. He condemned Eisenhower's moderates for regarding government as "a working tool that should be used to shape society." Instead, he wrote, "I believe that society is shaped by individuals."

Middendorf wanted to push libertarianism into mainstream politics, and he found a vehicle in Barry Goldwater, the fiery Arizona senator. Goldwater, the heir to a department-store fortune in Phoenix, ran for president in 1964, fueled by what he described as his "resentment against the New Deal." When Goldwater looked at Roosevelt's signature achievement, he did not see the benefits of Social Security, rural electrification, and the GI Bill of Rights. Goldwater's campaign was a backlash against liberalism—civil rights, welfare, and the expanding scope of government programs—but also against moderate Republicans. Nelson Rockefeller was a "cardboard candidate," Middendorf told me. "He could speak for an hour, but I honestly could not remember a single word he ever said." Middendorf became Goldwater's campaign treasurer, raising money from other well-to-do dissidents of the East Coast establishment. "He was obviously out of the mainstream, and we had an uphill battle," he said.

They prevailed that summer at the Republican National Convention in San Francisco. Rockefeller made a desperate last attempt for relevance: from the lectern, he denounced the advent of a "radical" rightwing element within the party, in the hope that the moderates would rise up and resist. Instead, the hall erupted in boos. Jackie Robinson, the Black baseball star and an avatar of integration among Republicans, heard the catcalls and felt, as he said later, like "a Jew in Hitler's Germany." Middendorf, who was also in attendance, received Rockefeller's denunciation as an affirmation. "He was talking about me and my friends," he wrote in *Potomac Fever*, his political memoir.

In the general election, Goldwater lost—spectacularly—to Lyndon Johnson. But his brand of libertarian, antitax absolutism found in the coming years a fervent audience among American executives who were confronting a troubling shift: after a quarter century of relentless growth, American profits were declining. Japan and Western Europe, finally rebuilt after World War II, were formidable new competitors; the Arab oil shock of 1973 triggered the longest recession since the 1930s. Moreover, the environmental and consumer-protection movements had hastened new regulations on products ranging from flammable fabrics to cigarettes and bank loans.

Executives felt besieged. "They decided regulation was mostly to blame," the historian Rick Perlstein wrote in his book *Reaganland*. In Perlstein's telling, "The denizens of America's better boardrooms, who had once comported themselves with such ideological gentility, began behaving like the legendary Jacobins of the French Revolution. They declared war without compromise."

Conservative business interests mobilized to reshape American politics around a pro-business, low-tax agenda. In a strategy memo for the U.S. Chamber of Commerce, the lawyer Lewis Powell, who later joined the Supreme Court, warned that the "American economic system is under broad attack." In defense, they would need public relations, think tanks, the media, and armies of lobbyists. "Strength lies in organization," Powell wrote.

In 1971, fewer than 200 companies had lobbyists in Washington; by 1982, nearly 2,500 did. By the late 1980s, corporate PACs had increased their spending in congressional races nearly fivefold in a decade, swamping the contributions from union PACs. The benefits came fast: they thwarted the creation of a new Office of Consumer Representation, and in 1981 the Federal Trade Commission suspended a program that collected data on industry profits and concentration, which had been used to identify the risks of emerging monopolies. The flood of campaign money also affected the outcome of presidential races by delivering an average of 3 percent of votes during elections in the 1970s and almost 7 percent in the 1980s, according to analysis by the political scientist Larry Bartels.

In the competition for corporate money, Democrats grew desperate to keep pace, by supporting pro-market public policies. As unions lost power, they lost the ability to turn out votes, and Democrats voiced a growing suspicion of taxes and regulation. In 1978, it was a Democratic Congress and President Jimmy Carter who reduced capital gains taxes from 48 percent to 28 percent. Later, it was Clinton who signed some of the most pivotal changes that contributed to the financial crisis—the repeal of Glass-Steagall, the ban on regulation of derivatives. The logic of deregulation had taken on a momentum that crossed party lines.

Back home in Greenwich, Middendorf—who went on to work in the Nixon, Ford, and Reagan administrations—gloried in having vanquished the moderates. He wrote, "We created the conditions that put conservative Republicans back in power after more than thirty years of domination by the liberal eastern establishment—the so-called 'Country Club' Republicans."

├────────┤

As the legacy of Prescott Bush faded, the generations that followed him in the Greenwich Republican Party were less interested in the "Middle Way." They had new priorities.

A short drive from the Round Hill Club, in a Georgian manor overlooking a lake, Lee and Allie Hanley were early converts to the conservative movement. Lee had graduated from St. Paul's and from Yale, where he played polo, squash, and soccer, and he had taken over Hanley Co., his family's bricks-and-oil business. He was a bon vivant with a fondness for salmon-colored slacks and a ready checkbook for political ventures. "Very warm and engaging," a Greenwich friend said. "A collector of curiosities, a Renaissance man at sort of a superficial level. More of a gut player who wanted to be in the game."

Allie was a devout Christian with a keen interest in politics. The 1980 Republican primary was shaping up to be a contest between the old Republican Party and the new—George H. W. Bush, a Washington insider known around town as Poppy, versus Ronald Reagan, the conservative governor of California who hailed what he called the "magic of the marketplace." On that question, the Hanleys broke with their neighbors in Greenwich. "For us, it was never Bush country," Allie told me. "It was always Reagan country."

Roger Stone, the right-wing adviser who was Reagan's campaign director for the northeastern states, recalled that most people in Greenwich recoiled from his candidate: "They thought, Reagan, oh, my God, he's another Goldwater. He has no chance in the general election. He's a cowboy-movie actor," Stone told me. "Hanley was the only high WASP we had. All the 'right' people were for Poppy."

The Hanleys, hoping to spread their enthusiasm in Greenwich, agreed to host a reception at their home. But when they met Reagan to discuss the plans, over lunch at the Pierre Hotel, Allie saw a problem. "He had on a brown tie, and it was ghastly," she told me. "When you go to a different part of the country, the most important thing you need to do is dress like they do. They feel more comfortable talking to you. So I ran to Bloomingdale's, and I bought four ties." When the Reagans turned up for the party, Allie said, "Here's a gift for you! Go upstairs and freshen up." Reagan came back down a few minutes later, and the offending tie had been replaced by her gift. "He wore it on all the posters after that," she said.

Stone and Lee Hanley adopted an approach that uncannily prefigured Trump's electoral strategy decades later: they built a coalition of conservative elites and the white working class. Hanley introduced Stone to small-business owners in Greenwich, many of them Italian American—"mining for Catholic votes," as Stone called it. "Lee was very well connected with the merchants in town—the grocer, the butcher," Stone said. "He could talk to anybody. He was not stuffy like some WASPs." Hanley told Stone before one visit, "We're going to have to drink some espresso, but we can get them." The strategy worked; in the Connecticut primary, Reagan beat Bush in the Bush-family stronghold of the southern panhandle. In 1984, Reagan rewarded Hanley by nominating him to the board of the Corporation for Public Broadcasting. Two years later, he became the chairman.

In the next three decades, Hanley and other wealthy conservatives—Richard Scaife, Robert Mercer, the Koch brothers—helped train a generation of Republicans in Congress to adhere to ideological orthodoxy. Hanley made a string of historic political investments. He saved Regnery, America's most prominent conservative book publisher, with a crucial infusion of cash. He helped found the Yankee Institute for Public Policy, the Connecticut affiliate of a network of think tanks that advocate for low taxes and small government. He became the principal backer of a political consulting firm formed by Stone and two other young Reaganites, Charlie Black and Paul Manafort. "We had the credentials and the potential business and all that, but we didn't have any money," Black told me. "Lee was a good friend, so we approached him." Black, Manafort & Stone, as they called themselves, became pioneering lobbyists, known for their brazen use of what Manafort described as "influence peddling." Clients included Rupert Murdoch's News Corp. and a young real-estate developer named Donald Trump.

By the end of the century, the courtly politics of Prescott Bush were gone, a change accelerated by the decisions of his son George H. W. Bush. George had inherited his father's restraint—at school in Greenwich, he was nicknamed Have-Half, for his willingness to share—and also the family tradition of public service. But, running for president in 1988, George H. W. Bush unleashed his brawling campaign manager Lee Atwater on the governor of Massachusetts, Michael Dukakis. Atwater vowed to "strip the bark off the little bastard." In the most searing moment of the campaign, a political action committee linked to the Bush campaign paid for a television ad blaming Dukakis for the case of Willie Horton, a convict who had committed rape during a furlough from a Massachusetts prison. The ad crudely exploited white fears, showing pictures of Horton, who was African American, while a narrator spoke of kidnapping, rape, and murder. Atwater denied any involvement in the ad, but Bush recognized the power of the rhetoric, and took to mentioning Horton almost daily on the stump. Atwater boasted that he would make Horton "Dukakis's running mate."

Not long before Atwater died, in 1991, he apologized to Dukakis for the "naked cruelty" of that campaign. But the Willie Horton strategy was the forerunner of a more savage era in American politics—of Swift Boat attacks on a war hero; of the racist birther fiction against America's first Black president—and it pushed candidates to avoid looking weak by advancing tough-on-crime policies that both parties now see as devastating for low-income and minority Americans.

In the end, Bush was "a gentleman, but he was a politician, too," his biographer Jon Meacham wrote. For all Bush's decency, he had decided early on that, in order to serve, he needed to win. In a tape-recorded diary entry near the end of the 1988 campaign, Bush told himself, "The country gets over these things fast. I have no apologies, no regrets, and if I had let the press keep defining me as a wimp, a loser, I wouldn't be where I am today."

———

Bush gained the White House, of course, but his party was moving away from him, toward a most absolutist posture. Two years after he was elected, Bush agreed to raise taxes, breaking his own promise—and losing the ascendant anti-government conservatives, precursors to the Tea Party that arrived a generation later. After the Tea Party peaked in 2010, Republicans achieved greater gains than in any congressional election in six decades. Even in Greenwich, where people were not quick to hoist placards, Tea Party activists protested in front of Town Hall, and the first selectman Peter Tesei, the town's top elected official, joined in. "Liberty has contracted today because the role of government has expanded," he told the crowd.

The sentiment was a familiar one—even the Romans resented their taxes—but Greenwich was not traditionally known for absolutism on the subject. In the 1980s, Lowell Weicker, a Greenwich Republican who had served as first selectman and gone on to the U.S. Senate, became known in Washington for blocking Reagan's attempts to cut spending on health and education. In 1991, after Weicker became governor, he imposed Connecticut's personal income tax, which was so unpopular that protesters cursed and spat at him. In a speech that fall, he said, "Respect—if not reelection—comes from speaking the truth."

But, to Greenwich's new concentration of libertarians, a fiercer resistance to taxes and to government was a matter of moral principle. Cliff Asness, of AQR Capital Management, was among the most vocal. When Governor Andrew Cuomo, of New York, discussed raising taxes on hedge funds, Asness tweeted that he was a "flat out lying demagogue" who was trying to run a "gulag not a state." Around town, the expectation that a person of substantial means might pay substantial taxes no longer held sway. That became especially clear in 2013, when Thomas Foley, a Greenwich private-equity investor, ran for governor. He owned a yacht, a number of vintage cars, two British fighter jets, and a house that *Greenwich Time* likened to "the Hogwarts castle." But on tax returns that he showed reporters he had claimed so many investment losses and alimony payments that his federal taxes amounted to $673 that year. (Foley lost the race.)

Charles Rossotti, a Republican businessman who served as the commissioner of the IRS from 1997 to 2002, has estimated that sophisticated tax ploys and shelters cause ordinary citizens to pay an extra 15 percent in taxes each year. According to a comprehensive study, tax havens were costing the U.S. government about $90 billion each year, in tax avoidance and evasion, as companies and wealthy individuals moved their money abroad. Brooke Harrington, an economic sociologist at Dartmouth, told me, "Some of that shortfall just never gets made up. Those are roads that don't get improved, public transport that doesn't get built, schools that don't get fixed." Connecticut has the richest 1 percent of any state, but, according to several studies of crumbling infrastructure, its roads are among the worst in the country.

People often defended their avoidance of even reasonable taxes by saying they were just doing what the law allowed. But it was an explanation that plainly ignored how the law came to be what it was—the

efforts and fortune expended to write it for their own maximal benefit. It reminded me of Steven Stoll's description of "seeing without the
past"—a view of the country that saw the ruins but ignored the hurricane. Harrington said, "For an earlier generation, even if your heart
wasn't in it, you'd say, 'I've got to join the local charity board, to project
that I deserve this wealth.'" The current generation, instead of focusing on the local charity board, prefers targeted private philanthropy,
bypassing public decisions on whom to help and how. "The underlying
massive change is that wealth no longer needs to justify itself—it is self-
justifying," Harrington said. "I look back, and I think, that's when we
gave up on being a 'we.'"

In his book *The Tyranny of Merit: What's Become of the Common Good?*
the political philosopher Michael J. Sandel argued that the change owed
partly to the triumph of a malignant form of meritocracy. Since the word
"meritocracy" was coined in 1958—by Michael Young, a left-leaning
British sociologist—Americans, who were already inclined to put their
faith in individuality, had come to see meritocracy as an argument for
equating credentialed success with moral virtue. Treating success—
either economic or political—as its own justification fed a "toxic brew
of hubris and resentment," Sandel wrote. "It flattered the winners and
insulted the losers." Wealth and winning had been liberated from responsibility.

In Greenwich, one of the people who noticed the trend was Ed
Horstmann, the pastor at the Round Hill Community Church. For
fourteen years, he and his wife, Susan, had lived in Hartford, working
with a low-income congregation. When they moved to Round Hill in
2013, it took some adjustment. At lunchtime, Horstmann crossed town
to attend a fundraiser for a nonprofit group that helped low-income
Black and Latino students succeed in private school; he expected a
familiar scene—foam cups, the passing of the hat. Instead, the keynote
speaker was Spike Lee, and the lunch raised $390,000. "The money
that can be raised in this town in two hours is unlike anywhere else,"
Horstmann told me. At the time, the Round Hill community was still
absorbing the recent arrests. "We were suddenly thinking, 'This is an

interesting place we've moved to,'" he said. "All of that just made me think this is going to take a long time to peel back the layers."

Horstmann was in his midfifties but looked a decade younger; he had a tall forehead, pale brown hair, and patient green eyes behind rimless glasses. When he wasn't at the church, he could often be found in his studio, where he painted and worked in charcoal and pastels. His sideline as an artist heightened his awareness of the landscape, and what it reflected of its people. "It took me months to find my way around. You're going through these rabbit warrens of roads, and all of a sudden you come on a gate. You can see the roofline of a house. It's intriguing in that sense, because it gives you glimpses of things, but never the whole thing." He often lingered on the sight of the tall new walls. "It's almost as if we're surrounded by neighbors but we don't have access to each other. People felt compelled to say to me, 'Those gates and walls are a recent phenomenon.' There was a huge longing for community." It reminded him of an old line from Winston Churchill, who said, "We shape our buildings; thereafter they shape us."

Horstmann treaded gingerly on matters of equity and justice. "When I moved to Greenwich, I got some advice that people were very interested in charity—there was a deep human desire to meet the need. But people were less comfortable talking about *justice.*" He discovered it was true. "When a pastor starts talking about 'justice,' it can make people a little uneasy, because all of a sudden it's not about the need—but about changing the system that *created* that need. You can tell that in people's minds, they're asking: 'Are we going to start marching? Are we going to have to take sides?'"

———

In the political ferment brought on by the Tea Party and the resistance to Obama, conservative donors expanded their influence. The Hanleys were joining an informal community of like-minded wealthy families, including the Adelsons, the Kochs, and the Mercers, who were directing their corporate fortunes toward shared objectives. Jane Mayer, a journalist who chronicled their activities in her book *Dark Money*, wrote, "Philanthropy, with its guarantees of anonymity, became their chosen instrument. But their goal was patently political: to undo not just Lyndon Johnson's Great Society and Franklin Roosevelt's New Deal but Teddy Roosevelt's Progressive era, too."

For men who had mastered much of their world, one of the few opponents left to subdue was government itself. Clayton A. Coppin, a researcher at George Mason University who was hired by Koch Industries to write a company history, eventually concluded that the Koch brothers' political objective was larger and more radical than advancing free-market policies. If that was the objective, they had mainstream candidates and organizations to support. On the contrary, Coppin observed of Charles Koch, "He was driven by some deeper urge to smash the one thing left in the world that could discipline him: the government."

The Hanleys became funders of Turning Point USA, a nonprofit founded in 2012 that promotes conservatism in high schools and colleges. More important, Allie Hanley helped its founder, Charlie Kirk, meet other donors. "Hanley opened the entire southern corridor for us," he wrote later. Kirk became a conservative celebrity and the chairman of Students for Trump, a campus political network.

Lee Hanley used his fortune to elevate candidates on the right wing of the Republican Party. In 2014, he donated some $357,000; the money went to stars such as Ted Cruz, but also to provocative outsiders like Chris McDaniel, a Mississippi state lawmaker and former talk-radio host who was trying to unseat the incumbent senator Thad Cochran. On his radio show in the mid-2000s, McDaniel ranted against hip-hop, referred to Mexican "mamacitas," and mocked gay people. As a candidate, McDaniel picked up the trail blazed a decade earlier by the anti-immigration crusader Tom Tancredo, and pledged to block increases in residency permits and work visas.

McDaniel also made coded appeals to white voters; he appeared before the Sons of Confederate Veterans, and, much as segregationists once spoke of defending "our southern way of life," he cultivated a sense of dislocation and loss. "Millions in this country feel like strangers in this land—you recognize that, don't you?" he told an audience of farmers in March 2014. "An older America passes away, a new America rises to take its place. We recoil from that culture. It's foreign to us. It's offensive to us." As spring gave way to summer in 2014, immigration was a constant, fearsome theme on right-ring media. "It literally is an invasion of people crossing into Texas," Laura Ingraham said. Congressman Louie Gohmert, a Texas Republican, said the "invasion" was "twice as big already than D-Day and twice as many again still coming." That fall, McDaniel lost, but his campaign themes were a preview of the anti-immigrant rhetoric to come.

Even if some of those candidates didn't win, Cruz represented a powerful new generation for conservative business interests in Congress, defined by its willingness to bring the work of government to a halt. On many issues, businesses stood to gain the most by slowing the process of reform. After Congress vowed to crack down on Wall Street for abuses that led to the crisis, the financial industry gave more campaign contributions over the course of 2009 than any other sector of the economy. When Congress took up major health-care reforms, drug companies, insurance, and other powerful interests spent half a billion dollars on lobbying against them. If lobbying failed, Mitch McConnell was ready to use the filibuster. In their book *Winner-Take-All Politics*, the political scientists Jacob Hacker and Paul Pierson described it as a "profound if little appreciated asymmetry" between the parties. "To win, the GOP often needed only stalemate. To renew the federal government's commitment to the middle class, Democrats needed to pass multiple pieces of substantial, ambitious legislation."

⊢——⊣

After Mitt Romney, a moderate former governor of Massachusetts, lost to Obama in 2012, Republicans were desperate to find a way forward for the party. The leaders of the Republican establishment issued a report that became known as the "autopsy." It argued that the party needed to move left and win over minorities, a case that implied a bright prospect for presidential hopefuls along the lines of Marco Rubio, a son of Cuban immigrants who praised American diversity while also drawing limits on immigration. Even the increasingly right-wing talker Sean Hannity advocated a pathway to legalization for America's 11 million undocumented immigrants. Ralph Reed, an evangelical leader, promoted immigration in religious terms, telling an audience, "Both David's palace and Solomon's temple were built with skilled artisans from Lebanon and elsewhere."

But alongside the route suggested by the autopsy, a very different path was also becoming visible. At the same time that establishment Republicans were calling for an embrace of immigration, Hanley commissioned a pollster named Patrick Caddell to investigate why conventional Republican candidates were underperforming. Caddell had first made his name advising Jimmy Carter, but over time he had broken with Democrats and begun appearing frequently on Fox News. As he and Hanley discussed the project, both suspected that Romney's loss suggested a deep frustration with the status quo. "I said, 'I think something's happening in the country,'" Caddell recalled. "Lee said, 'You know, I think something may be, too. I want you to go out and just find out.'"

In 2013, Sean Trende, an elections analyst for RealClearPolitics, wrote an essay titled "The Case of the Missing White Voters, Revisited." Trende cited population estimates to argue that Romney's biggest mistake was not failing to attract minorities; on the contrary, he wrote, Romney lost because he failed to generate votes from some 6.5 million unenthusiastic white voters. They stayed home. "The next Republican," he wrote, "would win narrowly if he or she can motivate these 'missing whites.'"

Hanley's project was converging on a pivotal insight. The polls he commissioned from Caddell showed that the "level of discontent in this country was beyond anything measurable." The mainstream pro-business, low-tax mantra was no longer bringing in working-class Republican voters. With yawning inequality and dying industries, it was getting harder and harder to inspire them with hymns to "job creators" and the solemn belief, as Romney put it, that "corporations are people, my friend."

Hanley asked Caddell to show his findings to Steve Bannon, the executive chairman of the conservative Breitbart News, and to another patron, Robert Mercer, a hedge-fund billionaire who was expanding his spending on politics. In 2013, they huddled over the data during a conservative conference in Palm Beach. Caddell called it the Candidate Smith Project—a search for a political savior along the lines of *Mr. Smith Goes to Washington*. The numbers, Caddell told them, indicated a public appetite for a populist challenger unlike any conventional Republican, a figure who could run as an outsider, railing against elites, corruption, and the very notion of government itself.

Only one thing was certain: the money and the message for an outsider candidate could come from Palm Beach and Greenwich, but the crowds would have to come from somewhere else. Hanley, Caddell, and Mercer needed to reach people around the country who were just angry enough to believe them.

TEN

BALL-LESS PECKERHEADS

ONCE OR TWICE A GENERATION, Americans rediscover Appalachia. Sometimes they come to it through caricature—Li'l Abner or Honey Boo Boo or *Buckwild*, a reality show about West Virginia teenagers, which MTV broadcast with subtitles. Occasionally, the encounter is more compassionate. In 1962, the social critic Michael Harrington published *The Other America*, which called attention to what he described as a "vicious circle of poverty" that "twists and deforms the spirit."

Around the turn of this century, hedge funds in Greenwich, Manhattan, and elsewhere took a growing interest in coal mines. Coal never had huge appeal to Wall Street investors; mines were dirty, old-fashioned, and bound up by union contracts that made them difficult to buy and sell. But in the late 1990s, the growing economies of Asia became ravenous consumers of energy, which investors predicted would drive up demand halfway around the world, in Appalachia. In 1997, the Hobet Mine, a twenty-five-year-old operation a couple of hours south of Clarksburg, was acquired for the first time by a public company, Arch Coal. It was led by a CEO whose pay depended heavily on the stock price, and he embarked on a major expansion, dynamiting mountaintops and dumping the debris into rivers and streams. As the Hobet Mine grew, it consumed the ridges and communities around it. Seen from the air, the mine came to resemble a giant gray amoeba—twenty-two miles from end to end—eating its way across the mountains.

Up close, the effects were far more intimate. When Wall Street came to coal country, it triggered a cascade of repercussions largely invisible to the outside world but of existential importance to people nearby. Down a hillside from the Hobet Mine, the Caudill family had lived and hunted and farmed for a century. Their homeplace, as they called it, was seventy-five acres of woods and water. The Caudills were hardly critics of mining; many were miners themselves. John Caudill was an explosives expert until one day in the 1930s, when a blast went off early and left him blind. His mining days were over, but his land was abundant, and John and his wife went on to have ten children. They grew potatoes, corn, lettuce, tomatoes, beets, and beans; they hunted game in the forests and foraged for berries and ginseng. Behind the house, a hill was dense with hemlocks, ferns, and peach trees.

John Caudill's eyes could still make out shapes, so his wife staked out the land with white sheets to help him navigate. "He would take a sickle and cut the grass right up to where the sheet was flapping," his grandson Jerry Thompson told me. He would send the kids to weed the gardens. "If you missed one weed in a whole acre, somehow he'd find it," Thompson said. They had little money, but as far as they were concerned, they lived in a world of plenty. The root cellar was "always full from floor to ceiling," Thompson said.

One by one, the Caudill kids grew up and left for school and work. They settled into the surrounding towns but stayed close enough to return to the homeplace on weekends. Jerry grew up a half hour down a dirt road. "I could probably count on one hand the number of Sundays I missed," he said. His grandmother's menu never changed: fried chicken, mashed potatoes, green beans, corn, and cake. "You'd just wander the property for hours. I would have a lot of cousins there, and we would ramble through the barns and climb up the mountains and wade in the creek and hunt for crawdads."

Before long, the Hobet Mine encircled the land on three sides, and Arch Coal wanted to buy them out. Some of the Caudills were eager to sell. "We're not wealthy people, and some of us are better off than others," Jerry said. One cousin told him, "I've got two boys I got to put through college. I can't pass this up because I'll never see fifty thousand dollars again." He thought, "He's right; it was a good decision for him."

In the end, nine family members agreed to sell, but six refused, and Jerry was one of them. Arch sued the lot of them, arguing that storing coal-mine debris constituted, in legal terms, "the highest and best use of the property." The case reached the West Virginia Supreme Court, where a justice asked, skeptically, "The highest and best use of the land is dumping?"

Phil Melick, a lawyer for the company, replied, "It has become that." He added, "The use of land changes over time. The value of land changes over time."

Surely, the justice said, the family's value of the property was not simply economic? It was, Melick maintained. "It has to be measured economically," he said, "or it can't be measured at all."

———

To their surprise, the Caudills won their case, after a fashion. They could keep twenty-five acres—but the victory was fleeting. Beneath their feet, the land was becoming unrecognizable. Chemicals produced by the mountaintop mine were redrawing the landscape in a bizarre tableau. In streams, the leaves and sticks developed a thick copper crust from the buildup of carbonate, and rocks turned an inky black from deposits of manganese. In the Mud River, which ran beside the Caudills' property, a U.S. Forest Service biologist collected fish larvae with two eyes on one side of the head. He traced the deformities to selenium, a by-product of mining, and warned, in a report, of an ecosystem "on the brink of a major toxic event." (In 2010, the journal *Science* published a study of seventy-eight West Virginia streams near mountaintop-removal mines that found nearly all of them had elevated levels of selenium.)

This was more than just the usual trade-off between profit and pollution, another turn in the cycle of industry and cleanup. As my editor Bill Sedivy had predicted years earlier in his warnings in *The Exponent Telegram*, mountaintop removal was, fundamentally, a more destructive realm of technology. It had barely existed until the 1990s, and it took some time before scientists could measure the effects on the land and the people. For ecologists, the southern Appalachians was a singular domain—one of the most productive, diverse temperate hardwood forests on the planet. For eons, the hills had contained more species of salamander than anywhere else, and a lush canopy that attracted neotropical migratory birds across thousands of miles to hatch their next generation. But a mountaintop mine altered the land from top to bottom: after blasting off the peaks—which miners call the "overburden"—bulldozers pushed the debris down the hillsides, where it blanketed the streams and rivers. Rainwater filtered down through a strange man-made stew of metal, pyrite, sulfur, silica, salts, and coal, exposed to the air for the first time. The rain mingled with the chemicals and percolated down the hills, funneling into the brooks and streams and, finally, into the rivers on the valley floor, which sustained the people of southern West Virginia.

Emily Bernhardt, a Duke University biologist who spent years tracking the effects of the Hobet Mine, told me, "The aquatic insects coming out of these streams are loaded with selenium, and then the spiders that are eating them become loaded with selenium, and it causes deformities in fish and birds. The Mud River, downstream of the Hobet, has one of the highest rates of bluegill deformities ever measured in a natural water body." She said, "Eighty percent of the landscape has been converted to this thing that's chemically distinct. You're getting a totally different landscape." The effects distorted the food chain. Normally, tiny insects that hatched in the water would fly into the woods, sustaining toads, turtles, and birds. But downstream, scientists discovered that some species had been replaced by flies usually found in wastewater treatment plants. There were holes in an ancient web of life that signaled a new biological poverty. By 2009, the damage was impossible to ignore. In a typical study, biologists tracking a migratory bird called the cerulean warbler found that its population had fallen by 82 percent in forty years. In 2010, in *Science*, a team of scientists concluded that the impacts of mountaintop-removal mining on water, biodiversity, and forest productivity were "pervasive and irreversible." Mountaintop mines had buried

more than a thousand miles of streams across Appalachia, and, according to the EPA, altered 2,200 square miles of land—an area nearly the
size of Delaware.

Before long, scientists discovered impacts on the people, too. Each
explosion at the top of a mountain released elements usually kept
underground—lead, arsenic, selenium, manganese. The dust floated
down onto the drinking water and the backyard furniture, and through
the open windows. Researchers led by Michael Hendryx, a professor
of public health at West Virginia University, published startling links
between mountaintop mines and health problems of those in proximity
to them, including cancer, cardiovascular disease, and birth defects. Between 1979 and 2005, the seventy Appalachian counties that relied most
on mining had recorded, on average, more than two thousand excess
deaths each year. Viewed one way, those deaths were the cost of progress,
the price of prosperity that coal could bring. But Hendryx also debunked
that argument: the deaths cost $41 billion a year in expenses and lost
income, which was $18 billion more than coal had earned the counties
in salaries, tax revenue, and other economic benefits. Even in the pure
economic terms that the companies used, Hendryx observed, mountaintop mining had been a terrible deal for the people who lived there.

———

One afternoon, I hiked up through the woods behind the Caudills'
house to see the changes in the land. By law, mines are required to
"remediate" their terrain, returning it to an approximation of its former
condition. But far from the public eye, the standards can be comically
lax. After climbing through the trees for a while, I emerged into a sun-
drenched bowl of stone and dirt the size of a small stadium. In the
center was a man-made pond, ringed in rubber tubing, full of water that
was murky and still. Above the pond, a gravel driveway connected it to
a mesa left behind after a peak had been blasted away. Technically, the
driveway was a "stream." For most of human history, the area had been a
dense forest. Now it was a strangely lunar place that reminded me of the
canyons in Greenwich where the new mansions were going up.

Down the road, I stopped at another mesa that had once been a peak. Under the law, mining companies have to spread fertilizer and fast-growing plants, so tall grasses and broomsedge waved in the wind. It looked less like an Appalachian mountain than a grassland in Mongolia. I mentioned that analogy to Bernhardt, and she said the likeness was more than just aesthetic. "You have these new flat Appalachian 'plains' that are covered in Asian grasses and Russian olive trees. The rock itself is so alkaline, there's not many Appalachian species that can grow in it." And they had begun to be populated by alien species—birds of the Great Plains that had moved into the remnants of old coal mines. "You create these unique and weird habitats," she said.

The consequences of big-money mining were percolating through families and the broader culture, too, in ways that the country was only beginning to calculate. Jerry Thompson became a vice president at a manufacturer of home-construction materials. "I'm a business guy. I understand profits, and I understand margins," he told me. "But the destruction has been amazing to me. It has been so disruptive to so many people. Not just our family. There were families and there were homes and there were kids and there were lives being made. And it's just all gone." Thompson was well acquainted with the free-market arguments for expanding the mine; after all, nobody had physically coerced his family to sell. But in practice, he wondered, were they really free to make their own economic choices? "Do you want to raise your family in the middle of a mountaintop-removal site? Probably not," Thompson said. "I guess you can say you had a choice. But did you?"

A generation after the mountaintop mine started devouring the Caudill family homeplace, the long-run effect was a hollowing out, an extraction of the place and experience that had once bound them together. The court case had been divisive, and there wasn't much to come back to on a Sunday. Thompson's cousin Ronda Harper told me bluntly, "After that, the family just kind of fell apart." Once a summer, they still had a reunion, but the family was never the same again.

When I spoke to the Caudills, I finally understood what Judy Bonds, the coal miner's daughter who became a West Virginia environmentalist, had meant when she told me years earlier: the "mountains are in our soul." You could visit the land, Harper said, but it wasn't the same: "You feel lost when you look at it. The wildlife has been buried, the streams and creatures, the wildflowers, trillium, and so many beautiful flowers that you would see when you walked up behind the house." The way she talked about the land reminded me of the line from Emerson: "We see the world piece by piece, as the sun, the moon, the animal, the tree; but the whole, of which these are shining parts, is the soul."

Over the years, Vivian Stockman, a local environmentalist, worked on scores of cases like the Caudills', in which people lost their land to mines and pollution. "You hear all the time, 'We grew up poor, but we didn't know it,'" she told me. Poverty can be as much about power as it is about possessions; they hadn't felt poor until someone came along and showed them how little power they really had.

⊢──────┤

The growth of mountaintop mining could not disguise the larger fact that coal was in decline. Old mines were running empty; new competition was rising from natural gas and other sources of energy. Jobs were dwindling, because the industry relied more and more on machines. But in the 2010s, Wall Street investors glimpsed another new opportunity to enlist the coal industry in a profitable bet.

Financial speculators believed that China's appetite for metallurgical coal, which is used to make steel, would continue to rise, and they thought American companies could grow and be ready for that demand. Bankers helped coal companies borrow billions of dollars for expansion and shed unprofitable mines and obligations, and earned a percentage on every deal.

As a cost-saving maneuver, in 2007, Peabody Energy, the world's largest coal company, spun off some of its least productive elements, including ten unionized mines in West Virginia and Kentucky, and $557 million in health-care obligations to retirees. The new company, named Patriot Coal, was born at a disadvantage: it contained 40 percent of Peabody's health-care liabilities and only 13 percent of its productive coal reserves. The executives who offloaded those costs did not hide their delight. In a call with investors, Peabody's CFO, Rick Navarre, said, "Our legacy liabilities, expenses and cash flows will be nearly cut in half."

Patriot Coal, the spin-off, acquired some new operations—the Hobet Mine, next to the Caudill homeplace, was one of them—but within a few years, Patriot was ailing. Wall Street's bet on Asia had been wrong. China's economic growth was slowing, the American companies faced unexpected competition from Australia, and in five years a glut of metallurgical coal had dropped the price by half. Appalachian coal companies, saddled by billions in debt, started to collapse. Patriot Coal had nearly three times as many retirees as active employees, and in the first half of 2012, its losses totaled $430 million. By 2016, six of the biggest coal companies had declared bankruptcy, wiping out not only 33,500 jobs in Appalachia but also billions in tax revenue that would have gone to schools, hospitals, roads, and other infrastructure.

Patriot Coal filed for bankruptcy. In response, the miners' union sued Peabody Energy, accusing it of setting up Patriot as a financial ploy to escape pension and health-care commitments—a ploy that miners call a "liability dump." (Peabody denied it.) The union urged miners and their families to write letters to the court, to make the case for upholding their benefits. More than a thousand letters arrived. Most were handwritten; some contained family pictures, or lists of ailments and medications. I found them all tucked away in court files, among the legal documents. Read today, the letters feel, in retrospect, like a premonition of America's rising discontent—testimonies of humiliation and injustice and desperation. Dona J. Becchelli, the wife of a retired Patriot miner in Kincaid, Illinois, wrote, "Please, please do not let another large company turn our history back in time. Our great country cannot continue to allow the corporate world to see only the money. We are here; we are people who have built this country on our broken backs and deaths. We only ask for what we have always worked for and were legally given."

As the bankruptcies accumulated, some Wall Street investors glimpsed one more opportunity: with enough money and the right maneuvers in bankruptcy court, they could pick off prime morsels from dying companies, shed expenses, and pocket the proceeds. On Wall Street, some of the specialists in "distressed" investments were known as "vultures," a term that conveyed a mixed reputation. A Bloomberg profile of Mark Brodsky, a prominent vulture investor nicknamed "The Terminator," reported that his critics called him a "bully," an "extortionist," and a "suppository."

Brodsky's firm, Aurelius Capital Management, invested in Patriot Coal, as did another vulture firm: Knighthead Capital Management, which was cofounded by a veteran investor named Ara D. Cohen. Like many of his peers, Cohen lived a long way from Appalachia—in the Golden Triangle, the most prosperous sliver of Greenwich. Like the Hanleys, he owned a Georgian manor of 17,000 square feet and twenty-seven rooms, with two pools (indoor and outdoor), a home theater, a billiards room, an elevator, and a life-size chess set.

Knighthead provided an infusion of cash, ostensibly to keep Patriot afloat, but effectively to gain more control of it. Kevin Barrett, a lawyer who represented West Virginia in negotiations over the cost of environmental cleanup, told me, "They did exactly what hedge funds do: they stepped in and went to the board meetings and controlled the management." Vulture investors have a reliable playbook. One explained, "You can try to strong-arm management and get them to sell assets and do shit. Try to settle with the government at some discounted value on the reclamation claims."

In February 2013, Patriot asked the bankruptcy court for permission to pay more than $7 million in retention bonuses to managers so they wouldn't flee during bankruptcy. It was awkward timing; barely a month later, the company announced an unusually audacious effort to cut costs: it asked the bankruptcy court for permission to abandon a union contract that provided health insurance for 23,000 retired miners and dependents, which could save the company at least $1.3 billion. The court agreed. To coal miners and retirees, it was a distressing precedent; in the past, coal companies had dropped pension and health-care benefits when they went out of business, but now Patriot was seeking to escape those obligations and stay in business.

Cecil Roberts, the longtime president of the United Mine Workers of America, told me, "The bankruptcy judge simply hits the gavel and says, 'You don't have health care anymore.' I'm sure many people on Wall Street and across this country say, 'That's probably a good thing. Now the balance sheet gets cleaned up. It's more inviting to investors.' But that one-point-three billion dollars was supposed to go for people I grew up with and I've been around all my life, people up and down Cabin Creek, and Paint Creek, and over in Boone County, and Allegheny County, Mingo County, all through Indiana and Illinois. And they're faced with huge medical bills."

Roberts is a war horse of the labor movement, with three decades of experience in strikes and standoffs. But none of that equipped him for the language and strategies of Wall Street. "I'm thinking, 'What the heck is a debtor-in-possession loan? And first liens?' and all those things," he told me. "Folks like Knighthead ride in here, and they're calling the shots and say, 'Get rid of the company! Sell it all, or sell it in pieces, and we can get our money back.'" He went on, "Average people can't do these things, but when you're a huge corporation, you can. That's just not right. The bigger you are, the more rights you have? . . . Some of these entities couldn't find Boone County, West Virginia, on the map, but they're making money off the people who live there. The question really is: What kind of country are we that this can happen?"

Roberts had the job of relaying the events in court to the miners who would be affected. "These are real people we're talking about here who had earned these benefits, after thirty or forty years of work," he said. "They lost their health care because a company they never worked a day in their lives for has gone into bankruptcy."

———

Larry Knisell had worked underground for Peabody since 1975, much of it at the big Federal No. 2 Mine, an hour north of Clarksburg. By mining standards, it was a prestige assignment. He still remembered when Elizabeth Dole, the secretary of labor during the administration of George H. W. Bush, paid a visit in 1989. "I've got a picture of us sitting together, eating a bologna sandwich." When Knissel learned about the spin-off of Patriot coal, it sounded like a "sham," he said. "You take three tires off a car and try to push it down the road? It ain't going to work." He was especially embittered by the $7 million in retention bonuses for executives. "Bean counters," he said.

Knissel traveled to St. Louis to join a union protest in front of Peabody's corporate headquarters. He saw that the company had posted armed guards. "I looked across there and I said, 'Do you guys realize we are American citizens?' It pissed me off so much." Three months later, he drove all the way to Gillette, Wyoming, to attend a Peabody shareholders' meeting. Seated in the back of the room, he watched an executive report on the company's progress in cutting costs. "He starts raving about 'I saved twenty-six million dollars.' And, man, he couldn't have stuck a dagger in my heart and have it hurt any worse. I thought, 'You son of a bitch. If they've got a chance for me to talk, I'm going to light you up.'"

When it was time for questions, Knissel was ready: "I want to let you know something," he said. "The guys in this back row are the people that are responsible for you making all these millions that you brag about. The guys right here were the backbone of your coal company. You should be ashamed by the way you treated these people. That twenty-six million dollars you saved was the money you took from the pensions." Knissel was braced for a rebuttal—some kind of defense, maybe even an attempt to cut his microphone. But nothing happened. In fact, the executives barely responded. They didn't have to. Knissel wasn't an influential shareholder or a hedge-fund manager or an activist investor. As far as they were concerned, he was just a crank. His comments hung in the air, unacknowledged. It was as if they didn't even hear him. And that only made him angrier. He told me, "Not one of those ball-less peckerheads turned around and challenged me in any way."

Eventually, he stormed out of the room. "They had one of those canopies that went clear down to the parking lot, and I could hear someone behind me. So I turned around, and there's a security guard. I say, 'We're here in peace. We're just begging for what's due us.'"

The steady loss of status—what scholars called the "hidden injuries of class"—lay in plain sight around Appalachia. In her book *White Working Class*, Joan C. Williams identified an arc of diminishing respect, reflected in pop culture. In the 1930s, working-class men were depicted in heroic poses on post office murals put up by the Works Progress Administration and exalted by John Steinbeck in *The Grapes of Wrath*. By the '70s, they were showing up in the aggrieved laments of Archie Bunker, a whingeing racist left behind by progress; and, by the '90s, the archetype had devolved into Homer Simpson, an incompetent alcoholic who dozes on his job at a nuclear power plant and whose mistakes are mended by the quiet ministrations of his wife and daughter.

Williams, a professor at the Hastings College of Law, noted that at the very moment that "wealthy white Americans have learned to sympathetically imagine the lives of the poor, people of color, and LGBTQ people, the white working class has been insulted or ignored during precisely the period when their economic fortunes tanked." Sarah Smarsh, a journalist and author raised in Kansas, couldn't help but notice that American pop culture had retired crudely racist and sexist jokes but "blatant classism generally goes unchecked." A popular blog called *People of Walmart* showcased unflattering photos of shoppers around the country. To Smarsh, it was, she wrote, a portrait of "contemporary U.S. poverty: the elastic waistbands and jutting stomachs of diabetic obesity, the wheelchairs and oxygen tanks of gout and emphysema."

In this century, American elites became aware of studies proving systemic hiring discrimination against women and people of color—often on the basis of their names alone. But elites were slower to acknowledge discrimination based on class. In a 2016 study in the *American Sociological Review*, fictional applications to 316 law firms found that men who listed upper-class hobbies such as sailing and classical music were twelve times more likely to get called back than those who expressed a fondness for country music.

In the Patriot case files, some of the most memorable letters were from miners who described what the loss of health benefits would mean for their families. David Efaw, a retiree an hour north of Clarksburg, typed out a plea to the judge. "I am writing this letter, not for myself so much, but mainly because of my wife, Ruth Ann. We have been married for over 33 years and she has been a real blessing to me." At fifty-three, Ruth Ann was diagnosed with rheumatoid arthritis and fibromyalgia, a neurologic syndrome that causes pain throughout the body. She relied on regular injections "and we cannot afford them without our insurance," David wrote. "Without these shots, her doctor has told her that she could become very crippled and unable to perform most of her normal activities because of the pain and the damage."

David and Ruth Ann Efaw lived in a nineteenth-century farmhouse along a serpentine road, at a bend so tight that Ruth Ann called it a "kiss-your-butt turn." When she gave me directions, she said, "We're the house on the hill, around the barn that's in need of paint." When I stopped by, David was trussed up in splints and bandages, marooned on a recliner in the living room. "My nineteenth surgery," he said, and gave a weak smile. Rotator cuff, in this case, but after a life underground, one thing or another always seemed to be giving out.

David Efaw grew up in West Virginia, did three tours as a medic in Vietnam, studied math and engineering on the GI Bill, and then worked thirty-five years as an electrician in the mines. He never paid much attention to corporate maneuverings, though he had met the president of Peabody Coal during a visit. Efaw has a blunt, precise way of talking about technical problems, and the president sensed it could be useful for him. "Every time he'd come, he'd look me up and we'd go talk," Efaw said. The executive told him, "You sit next to the phone, so I can get ahold of you if anything ever happens to me or this company." Efaw had no illusions that they were friends. But he sensed they both stood to gain if the company succeeded. "You're one part of it and I'm another part of it," Efaw said. Things were never cozy with management—they had bitter strikes and standoffs—but Efaw said, "Those people respected you because of who you are. That's not that many years ago, but it was a whole different feeling."

He said, "They're getting million-dollar bonuses and I'm fighting for a few hundred dollars' pension. That ain't the same family. That's a greedy bureaucrat. You've got your CEOs pulling four hundred or five hundred times what the American man does. Is there any man worth four hundred or five hundred other men? I've never met one. Have you?" Efaw went on, "They've got the power, and they abuse the power, but how do you stop it? It's getting worse every day."

For a time, Patriot Coal recovered from bankruptcy and limped along. But in 2015 it went belly up again, and this time executives and investors such as Knighthead were not looking for a way to survive. They made plans to recover whatever money they could by auctioning off the mines and equipment. Nobody, it seemed, would ever pay for the "remediation" at Hobet and scores of other places spoiled by mining.

In the fall of 2015, Barrett, the lawyer representing the state, filed a scathing criticism of Knighthead and other investors for threatening, as he put it, to "expose the people of the State of West Virginia to the serious public health and safety risks associated with unreclaimed land and untreated water." Selling the most valuable assets for "hundreds of millions of dollars," would leave "not one dime" for the "mess left behind," he wrote. "Instead, the banks and the hedge funds backing Patriot's plan will walk off with all of that value and consideration, leaving a carcass."

Weeks later, the case generated one final flurry of unflattering attention. Court filings revealed that executives were seeking to divert $18 million from health-care funds in order to pay bankruptcy lawyers, creditors, accountants, and other costs. According to an investigation by ProPublica, the funds had been earmarked for 208 retirees, wives, and widows in Indiana, until executives took steps to steer it to the law firm Kirkland & Ellis and the consultancy Alvarez & Marsal. By that point, the presidential election was gathering steam, and Hillary Clinton made a point to say the move was "outrageous and must be stopped."

Patriot abandoned the idea, but it was only a brief reprieve. On October 28, 2015, Patriot Coal closed down for the last time. The mines had been sold off to a range of buyers around Appalachia. For a while, the health benefits kept going, but eventually that fund ran dry. In

October 2016, the union sent a letter to 12,500 retirees, informing them that their health-care coverage was ending in ninety days. The cause: a "critical financial shortfall."

In the years that followed, the dismantling of Patriot Coal became known as a precedent. "It was the test case," Phil Smith, a union spokesman, told me. Hedge funds went on to play powerful roles in the bankruptcies of other major coal companies, including Alpha Natural Resources, Walter Energy, and Westmoreland Coal. In every case, Smith said, the funds asked bankruptcy courts to drop their obligations for pension and health-care costs. "They would buy up properties nobody else wanted for pennies on the dollar or an assumption of debt." The Patriot case had "created a road map" for extracting value from bankruptcies in Appalachia. (In 2017, Congress, under pressure from miners and unions, established a fund to protect the health care for 22,000 miners and dependents.)

As an old adage in the coal industry put it, "The company gets the profits; the miners get the shaft." But, to the men and women affected, Patriot and the cases that followed its pattern were the perfect illustration of a growing crisis: the laws and values of modern capitalism had been honed by lobbyists and political donors to advantage those with the most power already—to ensure that the winners kept winning. The looting of Patriot Coal was not illegal; the scandal, as the saying went, was that it was legal.

For coal miners in Appalachia, Wall Street's efforts to profit from their decline was an especially acute humiliation. Coal country had steadily lost its one true asset—the land itself—without ever securing the payoff that it expected. The drama reached back to the nineteenth century, when West Virginia officials predicted that the question of the future would be whether "vast wealth shall belong to persons who live here" or to those who "care nothing for our state except to pocket the treasures which lie buried in our hills."

The harvesting of the state's dwindling assets by remote funds and financiers was a humiliating coda on a century of declining status, self-reliance, and power. The miners had once prided themselves on fighting, literally, for a greater share of the pie. At the Battle of Blair Mountain, in 1921, more than ten thousand miners in southern West Virginia confronted police and federal troops backed by machine guns and biplanes—the largest insurrection since the Civil War. It contributed to Franklin Roosevelt's efforts, more than a decade later, to protect collective bargaining. By the 1930s, the United Mine Workers of America had grown to 800,000 members, and it won job protections, such as an eight-hour workday and bans on child labor. In 1946, after a nationwide strike, President Harry Truman made a landmark deal with John L. Lewis, president of the union, which established lifetime health benefits for miners after retirement.

As recently as the 1970s, there were 170,000 union miners in America. "If you lost your job in the coal industry you'd just drive down the road and get another one," Cecil Roberts said. "You could be in the middle class. Then, in the blink of an eye, you have a series of events: steel bankruptcies that shut down many of the metallurgical coal mines in this country, most of them in Appalachia. The Clean Air Act, and revisions dealing with acid rain. Then, climate change."

It was a steady, taunting erosion of the mantra "You have a right to feel proud." If the soul of West Virginia really was in the mountains, that soul had been carted away, one mine at a time, for the benefit of those far away. And when the mines were finally empty, the "bean counters" sold the equipment and sent the proceeds somewhere else. It felt so relentless, Roberts said, that people got angry. "Now that it's evaporated, they're blaming lots of folks for that," he said.

Much of the blame was cast on Obama. During his second term, more than half of West Virginia's 160 underground coal mines closed. As the 2016 election approached, just 68 mines remained. The decline of coal was producing a political cascade that reminded me of the biological cascade you saw deep in the hills, where the water was running over the strange new chemistry upturned by the mines. In politics, an upturned landscape of ideas about regulation, business, taxes, and responsibility was altering what flowed downstream, rendering it increasingly unrecognizable. The analogy applied in the other direction, as well: ideas that were bubbling up from frustrated towns across rural America—fears about race, immigration, and loss of status—were climbing through the political food chain and producing an array of deformities.

By 2013, West Virginia had fewer miners than nurses; nationwide, the union had lost 97 percent of its membership from its peak. Instead of jobs in steel mills and coal mines, West Virginians looked for work in restaurants, call centers, elder care, and home health services—all of which paid below the national average. The change felt especially acute because, a generation earlier, coal-mining counties had been the very places where miners could walk across the street and find a new job; now they were among the poorest communities in the region, racked by opioid addiction and unemployment. In Boone County, where part of the Hobet Mine was located, 58 percent of the jobs vanished in just four years. Fathers and grandfathers were competing for jobs against teenagers.

The land, the body, and the economy—all were broken. Coal companies had always come and gone, but the esoteric power of modern finance allowed investors and executives to prosper even when the business was failing. "Our union has spent enormous sums of money trying to fight with these folks who have more money than you can ever imagine," Roberts said. "People who go into bankruptcy court as lawyers, accountants, investors always make money. But if you're a coal miner, and you work forty-five years for this company, you're the last person in line."

In a broad sense, Wall Street and Washington had come to practice a shared approach to the experience of Americans far away. The content of business and politics—the practical effect of a policy or a transaction— mattered less than the sheer facts of winning and advancing. A member of a vulture firm told me the decision to direct their power toward the coal industry was not a grand strategic decision to find value even in hard times; it was barely a decision at all. It was a few numbers on the page. "They were invested in coal because that's what was distressed at the time," he said.

Kevin Barrett, the attorney who represented West Virginia, had a view into both sides of the transaction: he had grown up near Huntington, the grandson of a miner, and left for New York, where he became a high-ranking corporate lawyer. Eventually, he started taking on cases in his home state, dividing his time between Charleston and a comfortable home in Westchester County, just over the border from Greenwich. He was sometimes struck by how little his two worlds understood the experiences and motives of each other. "It never makes it out of the hills down here and never makes it outside of Greenwich and Manhattan up there," he said. "I don't know how much these hedge funds really care about what goes on in West Virginia, not for bad reasons, but just because they look at the world through their own perspective, which is dollars and cents and money movement. The effect on people just doesn't enter into their calculus."

Like so much about America's agonies in these years, the clearest accounting of history was inscribed on the land itself. In Greenwich, Ara Cohen, the cofounder of Knighthead Capital Management, eventually sold his Georgian manor in the Golden Triangle, in order to move to Florida. For the house, he received $17.5 million—less than he had hoped but enough to be the most expensive home sale in town that year. Six hundred miles away, the Hobet Mine was eventually abandoned. Nobody was going to pay the millions required for environmental remediation. There was talk of building a Walmart up on the strange plateau, with its Asian grasses and Russian trees. But by then, almost all of the potential customers, like the Caudills, were long gone. The Walmart plan never happened.

Finally, the state settled on a very different use—a plan rich with unintended symbolism. In 2017, West Virginia announced that the mine would become a training ground for the Army National Guard. The strange, barren landscape would be a classroom for teaching local soldiers how to parachute into foreign lands and survive in hostile environments.

ELEVEN

I SMELL FREEDOM

JUST AS HEDGE FUNDS were discovering West Virginia, political entrepreneurs were dawning to its potential, too. Decades after the Kennedys and FDR Jr. passed through, people still reminisced about West Virginia's moment at the center of political attention. Long after the Stonewall Jackson Hotel had closed down, *The Exponent Telegram* now and then republished glamorous photos of Kennedy's visit. To the end of the twentieth century, Democrats in West Virginia maintained an advantage of nearly twice as many registered voters as Republicans, and Democrats had a lock on the state's seats in Congress.

But in 1999, Karl Rove, George W. Bush's campaign strategist, made an audacious bet: he put West Virginia on a list of long-shot states that he suspected Republicans might be able to snatch away. In Rove's view, West Virginia's loyalty to the Democrats was an antique ready to shatter. His strategy rested on the prospect of pulling the state into the nationalization of politics. The culture wars and the Christian Coalition had been steadily drawing most of rural America into Republican hands, but West Virginia was an exception; the Democratic Party's historical attention to the problems of Appalachia had made the state unnaturally resistant to the national trends. "Many Democratic voters were pro-life, pro-prayer, and pro-gun, even if they had voted

Democratic for decades, and it seemed Bush would be a better fit than
the elitist Al Gore," Rove later recalled in his memoir, titled *Courage
and Consequence*. In particular, the progressive environmental policies
of the Clinton administration had vexed coal miners, and nobody was
more associated with efforts to raise attention on climate change than
the Democratic nominee for president.

The Bush-Cheney campaign opened eighteen offices across West
Virginia. It barraged the state's tiny media market with ads, funded
most importantly by a coal tycoon named James H. Harless. Better
known by his nickname, "Buck," Harless had looked at Gore's agenda
and decided, as he put it, "I needed to fight much harder than I ever
had." The coal industry tripled its campaign donations from four years
earlier. To project the right image, the campaign enlisted Charles Kim-
bler, an unemployed official from the miners' union, to wear his miner's
helmet and introduce Bush at rallies with the line "The Democrat administration shut my mine down, and I lost my job." In November 2000,
Bush became the first nonincumbent Republican presidential candidate
to win the state since Herbert Hoover, in 1928. (If Al Gore had carried
West Virginia, he would have won the presidency.)

Bush's victory was a gateway to a new era in West Virginia politics.
Conservatives realized that if they could turn West Virginia in a presidential contest, they could also enlist it in the larger libertarian project
funded by the Kochs and Hanleys and other wealthy donors: the organized resistance to business regulation and taxes. For years, the state
had greeted visitors with billboards that said "Wild Wonderful West
Virginia." In 2006, it adopted a new slogan: "Open for Business." Conservatives in West Virginia presented the regulation of heavy industry as
a threat to the state's cultural and existential survival. In an email to supporters, local Republicans warned that Democratic Party "foot soldiers
seek to destroy our very way of life for the sake of an agenda that guts
our economy." John Alexander Williams, the Appalachian historian,
told me, "There is an irony that at the one hundred and fiftieth anniversary of its birth, West Virginia has joined the confederacy—the melding
of the South and the Midwest into the attitude that being pro-business
is patriotic."

The Republican awakening in West Virginia reflected a larger transformation under way—a change in how some of America's most vulnerable citizens perceived the legitimacy of their government. The change took hold, most vividly, in state capitals across the country. State politics had always had its share of graft and influence peddling, but those forces were being supercharged by new technologies of political engineering, in the realms of campaign finance, public relations, and misinformation. The full extent was often opaque to the general public, except at rare moments when the effects became visible. One of those moments erupted on a frigid morning in 2014, when the people of Charleston, West Virginia, awoke to a strange tang in the air off the Elk River.

It smelled like licorice. The occasional odor is part of life in Charleston, the state capital, which lies in an industrial area nicknamed Chemical Valley. In the nineteenth century, natural brine springs made the region one of America's largest producers of salt. The saltworks gave rise to an industry that manufactured gunpowder, antifreeze, Agent Orange, and other "chemical magic," as *The Saturday Evening Post* put it in 1943. When John Gunther visited the valley in 1945, he was struck by how much industrial might it contained—"one factory on the Kanawha sits immediately adjacent to the next," he marveled.

In recent years, the industry has boomed because cheap natural gas lowered the cost of the power needed to run the chemical factories. But not much of the profits have filtered down to ordinary people in West Virginia. Most of their gains amount to a flinty, fragile pride in the area's industrial reputation. The Chemical Valley Roller Girls still compete in Roller Derby events with a logo of a woman in fishnet stockings and a gas mask.

On this particular day—January 9, 2014—the smell was not just in the water. At 8:16 a.m., a Charleston resident called the state Department of Environmental Protection and said that something in the air was, in the operator's words, "coating his wife's throat." Downtown, the mayor, Danny Jones, smelled it and thought, Well, it's just a chemical in the air. It'll move. A few minutes passed. "I stuck my mouth up to a water fountain and took a big drink," he told me. "And I thought, We're in trouble."

├─────┤

People were calling 911, and the state sent out two inspectors to begin tracing the source of the smell. After a while, it led them to a chemical-storage facility, a rickety business with an august name: Freedom Industries. It consisted of seventeen white metal pillbox-shaped containers, a "tank farm" as it was known, on a bluff above the Elk River.

The staff at Freedom Industries initially said that there was nothing out of the ordinary, but when the inspectors asked to look around, a company executive, Dennis Farrell, conceded that he had a problem at Tank No. 396, a 48,000-gallon container of industrial material. At the foot of the tank, the inspectors found a shallow open-air lake of an oily substance, gurgling like a mountain spring. When hazardous-material crews arrived, they followed the trail of liquid under a concrete wall, into the bushes, and down a slope, where it disappeared beneath the broad pale ice on the surface of the river.

By law, Freedom Industries had to report its own spill to a state hot line. The operator, who identified herself as Laverne, asked what was leaking; the caller, a staff member named Bob Reynolds, said, "Uh, MCHM."

"MCHM?" Laverne asked.

"Right," he said, and offered the scientific name.

Laverne paused and said, "Say again?"

MCHM—4-methylcyclohexane methanol—is part of a chemical bath that the mining industry uses to wash clay and rock from coal before it is burned. There are more than 80,000 chemicals available for use in America, but unless they are expected to be consumed, their effects on humans are not often tested. MCHM was largely a mystery to the officials who now confronted the task of containing it. But they knew that the site posed an immediate problem: it was barely a mile upriver from the largest water-treatment plant in West Virginia. The plant served 16 percent of the state's population, some 300,000 people.

This was West Virginia's fifth major industrial accident in eight years. Most of the others unfolded deep in the mountains, far from public attention, but in this case the spill hit the state's largest city with extraordinary timing: it was the second day of the annual legislative session; hundreds of state lawmakers were in Charleston, convening at the state capitol, a handsome limestone edifice with a gilded dome.

Like many states, West Virginia has a part-time legislative body. Members of the Senate and the House of Delegates meet at the beginning of each year for sixty days, before returning to regular life. With sparse funding, the state legislature has always been vulnerable to the forces of outside influence. Until 1993, committees had no permanent legal staff, so they had to bring in lawyers as consultants, many of whom represented local industries. Even afterward, West Virginia's public salaries remained among the lowest in the country. Lobbyists were often quick to offer expertise. In a typical instance, a legislator who introduced a rule change in a hearing on water pollution spoke from a script written by lobbyists, which read, in part, "We must be sure that our standards are protective of our streams without being overly protective."

At times, the political manipulation was ludicrously brazen. In the 1980s, coal companies converted part of a hotel near the capitol into a lounge known as the Coal Suite, where lawmakers could enjoy an open bar, a buffet, card tables, and private areas. The investment more than paid off: for decades, lawmakers effectively forced taxpayers to subsidize coal companies by absorbing the costs to the environment and public health. In the most acute example, a dam holding up millions of gallons of liquid coal waste gave way in 1972, sending a tsunami as tall as a house roaring down the hollow known as Buffalo Creek. The disaster killed 125 people and destroyed $300 million worth of property. The owner, Pittston Coal, blamed it on "water God poured" into the dam— even though the federal dam regulators had banned that design three years earlier. West Virginia had to spend millions to clean up the disaster, but the governor, Arch Moore, settled with Pittston for all of $1 million. (Moore later went to prison for extortion and other corruption.)

In 1989, after two successive presidents of the state senate were charged with taking money from lobbyists, the state passed the Governmental Ethics Act, which limits gifts and forces legislators to report on their finances. But coal companies still found ways to achieve their ends. In 2004, Massey Energy, one of the country's largest mining companies, appealed a $50 million judgment for fraud and contract interference. Shortly before the state supreme court took up the case, Don Blankenship, the company chairman, spent more than $3 million to help elect a judicial candidate who became the first Republican on the court in decades. The money went mostly to ads accusing his opponent of being soft on child molestation and drugs. Blankenship's candidate delivered the decisive vote that overturned the judgment against Blankenship's company. (Later, the U.S. Supreme Court tossed out the ruling, saying the judge should have recused himself from the case.)

Eventually, the Coal Suite was gone, but companies were scarcely more constrained from doling out favors. Unlike in most states, West Virginia industry groups and their clients don't have to report anything about how much they spend. In 2010, the Pacific Research Institute compared state laws on transparency in politics—the requirement, for instance, that a lobbyist disclose its spending on behalf of a client. West Virginia tied with Nevada as the least transparent in America.

Over the decades, the combined effects of pressure, incentives, and sheer corruption formed a West Virginia political culture in which virtually any attempt to protect lives or land was reduced to a false choice: jobs or health. The very day before the chemical spill in the Elk River, the governor, Earl Ray Tomblin, delivered his State of the State address, criticizing federal environmental regulators and vowing, "I will never back down from the EPA, because of its misguided policies on coal." Tomblin, a conservative Democrat elected in 2011, cut corporate taxes and denounced the federal government for overstepping its authority. To balance the budget, he tapped other government funds and called for broad cuts, including reducing agency spending by $70 million. For the second consecutive year, West Virginia's Department of Environmental Protection would take a 7.5 percent cut in state funds, dropping to its lowest level since 2008.

When word began to spread of the chemicals on the Elk River, Freedom Industries offered a reassuring estimate that the leak was likely no more than 2,500 gallons, about sixty barrels. But within days, the estimate had tripled. Eventually, the company raised it to 10,000 gallons and reported that a second chemical, known as PPH, had leaked as well. Governor Tomblin, just days after crowing about his cuts to the environmental-protection budget, appeared on television and issued a warning unprecedented in Chemical Valley: he told 300,000 people that their tap water was not safe for "drinking, cooking, washing, or bathing." It was one of the most serious incidents of chemical contamination of drinking water in American history. By the time he went on television, people had been drinking the water all day.

———

In the first three days after the chemical spill, more than two hundred people showed up at emergency rooms with rashes, nausea, and other complaints. A dozen were admitted; none were seriously ill. Meanwhile, the contaminated water from Charleston had emptied into the Ohio River. The Greater Cincinnati Water Works, which served more than a million people, closed its intakes and shifted to emergency reserves until the chemicals had passed.

Around Charleston, schools, restaurants, and businesses shut down. The National Guard arrived with bottled water, but it had to focus on hospitals and nursing homes. Candi Shriver, a mother of two who worked as an emergency medical technician and sold Avon products, tried to stock up and was demoralized by the scenes. "I shouldn't be surprised, but I was surprised, or outraged, by the people who were fighting in the stores. People were getting in knock-down drag-outs over the last case of water."

Candi's husband, Josh, improvised. He was an IT consultant who could take apart his Harley and put it back together again. They'd met on Plenty of Fish, the dating website, and had much in common, although Candi had voted for Barack Obama and Josh had switched his registration from Democrat to Republican in 2008. When the water ban went into effect, Josh drove his truck eighty miles south, to Williamson. At a Big Lots superstore, he asked for a pallet of bottled water. "The whole thing?" the clerk inquired. Shriver paid a dollar a gallon for 275 gallons and hauled it home for his family and his neighbors. As the water ban continued, it revealed harsh differences of class: affluent residents were able to rent apartments in unaffected towns nearby in order to bathe their kids and wash their clothes. The less fortunate put out buckets and hoped for rain.

As the crisis developed, I drove to Charleston and paid a call to John Unger, a pastor and former Rhodes scholar who was serving as the majority leader for Democrats in the state senate. I asked Unger how the pressures of political influence affected the work of the legislature. He let out a bark of a laugh and then ticked off what he considered the three undeniable steps by which lobbyists won the loyalty of his peers in the legislature. "First, they try to wine and dine you. Then they try to set you up. And then they try to threaten you."

Set you up? I asked.

"Set you up in the sense of getting something on you so that you become beholden to them," he said. "Back when I was a freshman, I stayed at the Marriott during the legislative session. And they would send people up to your room and knock on the door." He grew accustomed to looking through the peephole and seeing a woman waiting nervously in the half-light of the hallway outside his door. "I'd call down to security and say, 'Someone's lost, they're knocking on my door.' Then I moved out."

In his midforties, Unger had a round face and an impish humor that disguised his moral intensity. He recalled the first time that a lobbyist for a chemical company asked him to vote on a bill. "I said, 'I don't sign on to anything until I read it.' And he said, 'Well, that's not the way it works around here.' I said, 'Well, I don't know how it works down here, but that's the way I work.' And he said, 'Well, if you don't learn to get along, when it comes to your reelection, we'll stick a fork in you.' And I looked at him and said, 'Sir, with no due disrespect to you, but you weren't for me when I got elected, and I got elected!'"

For those who were uncooperative, the payback could be swift. In 2012, a coal-industry lobbyist asked Larry Barker, then chair of the House Energy, Industry, and Labor Committee, to advance an industry-backed bill out of his committee. Barker declined, and the meeting adjourned. Afterward, Barker told me later, a lobbyist "walks over and crowded me with his shoulder, kind of back to the corner, where there was nobody there but me and him. And I'm looking up at him, and I said, 'What is it?' And he said, 'What's it going to take for you to run our bill?' And I said, 'I want to look it over. I want to let the attorney look at it, I want the union to look it over.' He said, 'This is the last meeting. You can call a special meeting and put this bill on there.' And I said, 'Well, now, why do you think I would do that?' He said, 'Because we want it.' We, meaning the coal industry. 'We want it. Period.' I said, 'Well, we've reached a deadline. If I'm still here next year in this same position, if this is a good bill, I promise you I'll run it in the first meeting next year.' He looked me in the eye and he said, 'That will be too late for you.' And he turned and walked out, and I never heard from anybody else in the coal companies after that." That fall, a first-time candidate backed by the coal industry challenged Barker and defeated him.

———

When coal mining began to lose its economic power, it took a lesson from the tobacco industry. Ushered toward oblivion by natural gas, climate change, and the profiteering of the hedge funds, the coal industry expanded from backroom lobbying to a sustained attempt to undermine public confidence in the science that threatened their business. They cast Democrats and environmental groups as whining elites and worriers, indifferent to the economic pain caused by regulation. In 2013, the industry encouraged members of the West Virginia legislature to form a Coal Caucus. When I arranged an interview with one of the Coal Caucus's most dedicated members, the delegate Rupert Phillips Jr. of Logan County, he arrived accompanied by Chris Hamilton, a coal-industry lobbyist. They asked to do the interview as a team. Hamilton, in pinstripes and tasseled loafers, was a constant presence in the state capitol, where he saw himself as an "educator" for lawmakers who couldn't be faulted for not knowing "the difference between a dragline and a drag queen."

Phillips makes his living selling mining equipment to coal operators, and after he was elected, in 2010, he ordered license plates for his SUV that say "COALDEL"—for "coal delegate." I asked him if he expected the chemical spill to lead to stricter regulation. "The environmentalists want to blame the coal industry," he said, but he believed that the dangers posed by MCHM had been overstated. When he had handled it in the past, he said, "I've rinsed my hands off and go eat a sandwich!" He suggested I look at a study of the chemical's effects on aquatic life. "I was told that they used some type of little microorganism, or whatever they test. Supposedly, they put an extra amount of this chemical in there, and it never killed the deal . . . A live fish in a tank, and it's still living! But they don't release all that, the environmentalists. They don't want the truth. It's fiction."

Hamilton exuded patient, prosperous calm, the satisfaction of a man who did not worry about unflattering questions from an out-of-towner. He told me it was a common misconception that his industry could "run roughshod over environmental concerns, and its general citizenry." On the contrary, he said, "I think you will find the most credible, upstanding people running our regulatory programs, who truly care, who want to see business, at the end of the day, compete in domestic and world markets, but have the utmost respect and sensitivities to personal safety, environmental quality."

Hamilton praised elected officials for staying loyal to coal. He called it a "growing maturity within those elected to public office." He said, "We have a strong core of conservative Democrats, with some very knowledgeable and seasoned members of the Republican Party as well. And I think there's a realization that coal *always* has been, and hopefully will continue to be, a major industry in the state."

To ensure the spread of that view, the coal industry created a propaganda campaign that rivaled anything I saw in China: Friends of Coal was a nonprofit public advocacy group intended to "educate West Virginia citizens about the coal industry and its vital role in the state's future." It ran television and radio ads, and for several years it sponsored a Friends of Coal Bowl, to appeal to college football fans. It signed up the former head coaches of the state's favorite athletic teams, Marshall University and West Virginia University, to serve as spokesmen. For children, the Friends of Coal Ladies Auxiliary started a program called

Coal in the Classroom and produced a workbook titled "Let's Learn About Coal." For a lesson on economics, the book featured a cartoon character of a smiling lump of coal with arms and legs, holding open the door to a bank. (Little wonder that by 2018, a national survey by Yale researchers found that just 59 percent of West Virginians believed in global warming, the lowest of any state.)

Because West Virginia has a population of only 1.8 million—less than the city of Houston—an investment in influence goes far. Before long, the prospect of reshaping the state's political culture was attracting attention from big national donors. The conservative fossil-fuel magnates Charles and David Koch, through their charitable foundations, devoted particular attention to the state. The Investigative Reporting Workshop, at American University, found that, between 2007 and 2011, the Kochs gave $30.5 million to 221 universities; West Virginia University received $965,000, the third-highest amount, behind George Mason and Florida State.

The Kochs also helped fund research at the Public Policy Foundation of West Virginia, a think tank that, in 2007, published *Unleashing Capitalism: Why Prosperity Stops at the West Virginia Border and How to Fix It*, edited by a West Virginia University economics professor named Russell Sobel. The book argued against mine-safety regulations, on the ground that "improved safety conditions result in lower money wages for workers," and asked, "Are workers really better off being safer but making less income?" It also called for relaxing rules on water usage. "Although they are intended to benefit citizens, water use regulations will only hamper prosperity by impeding the state's ability to retain and attract businesses and to generate new employment opportunities." The governor at the time, Joe Manchin, invited Sobel to brief his cabinet, as well as a joint session of the Senate and the House Finance Committees. The state Republican Party chairman said, "Unleashing capitalism will be our party platform."

In February 2014, Americans for Prosperity, the political advocacy group funded heavily by the Koch brothers, established a chapter in West Virginia. A state Republican consultant told me, "You can do things here incredibly, incredibly cheaply. For instance, AFP, the Koch brothers, went and did North Carolina last time. Well, a legislative seat here is about one fourth the size of a legislative seat in North Carolina. So there's bang for your buck." In any given district, he said, "You can go in for twenty grand, and probably fix a problem." He also noted, "People are just showing up with pockets full of money, saying, 'We want to help you out.'"

———

On the third day without water, left-leaning activists organized a public town-hall meeting in a church in Charleston, and two hundred people showed up. Katey Lauer, a community organizer in her twenties with short, dark hair, climbed onto a chair and said, "I want to welcome everyone who hasn't had a shower in three days." One by one, people stood to ask questions or express frustration. A young mother said, "I bathed my daughter, and now I don't know if she's sick." She tried to keep her composure as tears fell. "I don't know what to do," she said.

Lauer, the organizer, was part of a younger generation of activists in West Virginia who had come of age amid the clear, inescapable evidence of climate change and had come to view the overwhelming influence of the mining industry as a sign of a political crisis. She had attended a small college in Ohio where refugees from Hurricane Katrina arrived on campus, in 2005, as part of a resettlement program. "The climate crisis felt like it was at our doorstep," she told me. "I was feeling a lot of urgency as a young person saying, wait—how many years do we have to solve this crisis?"

In the years after college, she became head of the Alliance for Appalachia, a network of groups opposed to strip mining. But the chemical spill was heightening her sense that their efforts were hopelessly outmatched. "The political odds are so stacked against us," she told me.

Dr. Rahul Gupta, the head of the Kanawha-Charleston Health Department, was tracking the spill's effects from his office. At forty-three, Gupta had a boyish face and a trace of silver in his hair. The son of an Indian diplomat, he grew up partly in Maryland and graduated from the University of Delhi before returning to America. He moved to Charleston with his wife and children in 2009. He approached the job with an entrepreneurial bent: to fight obesity and diabetes, he had created a mobile app that plotted restaurants by GPS and allowed users to compare menus and calorie counts.

As the water ban dragged on, public officials pressured Gupta to permit restaurants and other facilities to reopen. But he was hesitant. "I have to be honest and transparent with the public," he said. "I didn't know enough about the chemical. I wanted more data." The loss to businesses was estimated to be $19 million a day, but before shops could reopen, Gupta needed to send in inspectors. "I had officials come to me and say, 'Use the honor system.'" That struck Gupta as profoundly misguided. "The honor system is *bad*—it's why a local health department exists," he said. "I had to put my foot down."

On January 12, the fourth day without water, Governor Tomblin held a press conference to say that the "numbers look good" and "we're seeing light at the end of the tunnel." Though the water in many homes still smelled of licorice, state officials told the public that it posed no obvious health risk. But, during the next four days, Gupta recorded a rising number of emergency room and doctor's visits for skin rashes, eye irritation, nausea, vomiting, anxiety, and migraines. He said, "As a scientist, I can't prove cause and effect, but it was a matter of fact: whether it was introducing a new chemical into the water, and people were having a hypersensitive-type reaction, or it was the odor triggering nausea, migraines, and asthma attacks, it was very clear that something was going on." Tomblin's haste to end the water ban was catastrophic; it undermined public trust in official statements. "People who followed every guideline to the T were still ending up with rashes or eye irritation, and that made them mad."

On January 15, two days after Tomblin began lifting the ban, the CDC, "out of an abundance of caution," issued an advisory to pregnant women to avoid the water. The public recoiled. If the water wasn't safe for pregnant women, why was it safe for infants or toddlers? Day by day, schools that had been declared safe were running into problems. Plumbing systems differed, so one school could be free of MCHM while another still had traces. Governor Tomblin stopped urging people to drink the water and adopted a legalistic position: "I'm not going to say absolutely, one hundred percent, that everything is safe. But what I can say is, if you do not feel comfortable don't use it." He added, "It's your decision." On February 5, two schools shut down after teachers and kids complained of dizziness and nausea. "The following day, we had three more schools close," Gupta said, "and we had up to fourteen schools that complained, but the day ran out, so the kids were let go." At the end of February, he told me, "We're getting complaints from schools almost every day."

For West Virginians, the battle to obtain some of the basic elements of government service—potable water, safe schools, public health advice—was disorienting. Josh Shriver said, "They didn't know exactly what it was, they didn't know how much of it had leaked, and they didn't know how long it had been leaking." At one point, Candi Shriver, hauling water from outside to flush the toilet, said to her husband, "It's like we're living in a Third World country."

———

Once the water ban was lifted, attention shifted to determining what had happened, who was responsible, and how to prevent it from happening again. Freedom Industries, unsurprisingly, was a legal mess; the cofounder had once pleaded guilty to selling cocaine and later served time for tax evasion and other charges. More disturbing, however, was how many red flags had slipped through an enforcement system that had been steadily enfeebled by politics and disinvestment.

The responsibility for regulating Freedom Industries had fallen to the state's Department of Environmental Protection, an agency so degraded by budget cuts and political misdirection that it was known, among public health advocates, as the "Department of Everything Permitted." Decades of lax enforcement had taken an inescapable toll. In 2008, *The Charleston Gazette* had discovered that in a nearly five-year period coal companies had self-reported around 25,000 violations of the Clean Water Act, but the DEP had not reviewed the reports or issued a single fine. In 2009, four environmental organizations petitioned the federal government to take over enforcement of parts of the Clean Water Act in West Virginia; they described the state's regulatory system as approaching a "nearly complete breakdown." Nothing came of the request.

Pam Nixon, who had retired after fifteen years as a senior department official, told me the agency faced ever-rising pressure to reduce enforcement of basic environmental protections. "It's not subtle," she said. She recalled a staff meeting in which Joe Manchin, the conservative Democrat who was governor from 2005 to 2010, "said that when the industries see the DEP coming onto their property he wanted them to feel comfortable." Manchin had prospered as a middleman who helped coal mines sell to power plants and other users. Once in office, he repeatedly advised the department to shift its emphasis from enforcement to "compliance assistance." By that, Nixon said, "He didn't want us to come down heavy-handedly."

In 2010, Manchin left the governor's mansion and ran for the U.S. Senate. He promised to protect the state from environmentalists' "attempts to destroy our coal industry and way of life in West Virginia." The American Chemistry Council, the leading industry group, spent $225,000 on advertisements praising Manchin as the "Senator for Our Future." He won. On his Senate financial disclosures, he reported income of more than $3 million between 2009 and 2012 from Enersystems, a coal brokerage that he owned. (It was later run by his son.)

Evan Hansen, an environmental consultant who testified about the leak before the West Virginia legislature, told me, "In the past ten or fifteen years, they've systematically weakened virtually all the major water-quality standards that apply to the coal industry. One by one, there's been a steady effort to undermine the implementation of environmental laws, to the point that it's become a part of everyday normal life here."

But the inescapable threat to public health from Freedom Industries seemed to break that public tolerance. Governor Tomblin announced that his office would propose legislation—a "spill bill," as it was known—to govern tanks of the kind that leaked. To understand who had a hand in creating the bill, Ken Ward Jr. of the *Gazette* filed a Freedom of Information Act request for communications between the governor's office and lobbyists and lawyers connected to the chemical and coal industries. He received 158 pages of emails and documents. They revealed that the governor's office had arranged a closed-door meeting for what it called "the stakeholders," which included the Chamber of Commerce, the Oil and Gas Association, and the Coal Association. No citizens' groups or environmental organizations were invited.

Six weeks after the Freedom Industries spill, the National Guard and the news trucks were gone. In Charleston, people resented the fact that their ordeal had received less national coverage than a recent headline about a routine virus on a cruise liner. "If this were three hundred thousand people in northern Virginia, I think the president would've been here," Ken Ward told me. "Or at least Biden." In a stab at levity, the radio station Electric 102.7 was playing a country song about what it called the "Aquapocalypse": "I smell freedom in my shower. I smell freedom in my sink. I will shower in my freedom, but my freedom I won't drink."

———

Six weeks after the leak, Josh and Candi Shriver were down to a quarter of their pallet of bottled water. They were using tap water to bathe, but it was giving Freddie, age three, a rash. At thirty, Candi was slender, with red hair and delicate features; her eyes were rimmed red from exhaustion. The house was carefully decorated—wine corks in a shadow box, inspirational quotes on small wooden plaques—but it was cluttered with jugs of water and other detritus of life after the spill. In February, the Shrivers decided to test their pipes, and Andrea Varrato, an environmental scientist for a consultancy called Downstream Strategies, arrived at the front door with a set of amber glass bottles to collect samples. The test covered cold water, but Candi wanted to test the hot as well. She asked, "It would be six hundred and some dollars per test?"

Varrato nodded.

"Holy smokes," Candi said.

Josh looked at her and said, "It's up to you."

She thought for a moment and said, "I just don't know that we can do twelve hundred dollars." The experience was making her angry. "I don't think that my three-year-old should have to worry about coming in contact with water," she said.

While Varrato collected samples from a pipe in the garage, I asked the Shrivers if they thought that the spill should lead to stricter regulation. Josh had misgivings. "If you regulate it more, and it cuts into coal, then it's ultimately going to force the coal companies to shut down, or they'd have to shut down because they can't compete with the rest of the country's prices," he said. "So regulating it might create benefits up front, but in the end it's going to cause harm."

West Virginia's coal industry had succeeded in recasting an economic and health question as a cultural debate: a yes-or-no question, all or nothing. Viewed in that light, a vote for the industry was a vote for yourself, your identity, your survival. The coal industry had created the illusion of vitality. At the Shrivers' house, I asked Josh what percentage of the state's workforce is directly employed by coal. He guessed 15 percent. That night, I looked it up; the answer was 3 percent.

Candi had begun to imagine a dark future. She wondered if leukemia and other cancers might increase. I asked if they'd considered moving away. Josh said, "I have a number of people that have put their houses up for sale in an attempt to see if anybody'll actually buy. But one of them said, 'Nobody's going to want to buy here now.'"

Candi said, "I would love to move out of this area, to Tucker County. There are no plants up there. If we had the money just to pick up and move . . ." She trailed off. They had too many ties to family and work to imagine leaving. Like people hundreds of miles away in Chicago, they were stuck in place.

As I crisscrossed the state that month, it became clear that the water crisis had exposed a vast, mounting frustration among the public. One morning in late February, Senator Manchin was in Fayetteville, an hour from Charleston, for an event called Coffee and Common Sense at a café in a converted church. Manchin, who stands six feet three inches and went to West Virginia University on a football scholarship, is an affable, drawling figure in his sixties with a thick brush of gray hair. He was a proud son of the state, and in Washington he kept a boat named

Almost Heaven, in homage to the opening words of John Denver's classic song about West Virginia.

The café was packed. When it was time for questions, Alan Jennings, the operations manager at a wilderness outfitter, said that many people in town were worried about a local plant that held wastewater from a natural-gas drilling operation. "It makes you feel like you're not going to know you're in danger until you die," Jennings said. "They have a holding pond there that's not safe." Later, a man who was younger and brawnier than others in the room stood and unfolded a piece of paper. He was in his early forties and worked on a gas rig in Pennsylvania. I expected to hear a voice on behalf of the industry. Instead, he said, "Senator Manchin, if you are truly interested in stopping the environmental and human disaster occurring in West Virginia, you will help craft legislation that will hold accountable those in charge." He went on, "The West Virginia DEP simply has no teeth. If state troopers walked out and arrested the CEO of Freedom Industries, their friends would surely decide to take better care of their facilities." Reading from his statement, his voice grew into a shout. "We're small folks and we'll never attend black-tie, thousand-dollar-a-plate fundraising galas in Manhattan, but we demand justice. *We, the people, demand justice!*" The room broke into applause. The man sat down and did not speak again.

After everyone went home, I asked Manchin if the spill had led him to adjust his sense of the balance between environmental protection and business promotion. "My balance is always in the same place," he said, and smiled. When I pointed out that citizens did not seem impressed by the state's enforcement, he sounded defensive. "If someone is saying that someone has sold out to business over enforcing government, that is so false. I have never seen that." In Congress, Manchin is the only Democrat among the top twenty recipients of campaign money from the mining industry. Three of his top five donors are energy companies. I asked him if his personal income and his campaign donations made it difficult for him to render an unbiased opinion. "It does not affect my decision-making to do the right thing," he said. "I haven't brokered coal for a long time. We do a lot of different things. But the bottom line is this: I still believe wholeheartedly you can do it"—coal mining—"and do it right."

⊢————⊣

Later that spring, the legislature passed the spill bill despite objections from industries. The pastor John Unger was the lead sponsor, and that fall he was bracing for an effort to unseat him in the state senate. "I have an opponent that jumped into the race after I started coming forward on water issues," he said. "I'm sure he'll be well funded in the fall. I know I'm targeted. I see the red dot on me."

The last time I saw Unger that spring, he expressed his worry that the water crisis would be ignored by the rest of the country, which did not perceive its larger implications. "Martin Luther King said that injustice anywhere is a threat to justice everywhere," he said. "Why should anybody care about what goes on in West Virginia? Because it's the canary in the mine shaft. If you ignore it in West Virginia, it's coming, it's going to continue to build, and the issue is: Should our country have the debate about our rights to the very basic infrastructure that sustains us? Or should we continue to ignore it?"

To Dr. Gupta, the head of the health department, the 2014 water crisis in West Virginia exposed a rot beneath the surface of American democracy—a broad corrosion. It was hardly unique to Appalachia; less than three months later, a water crisis erupted in Flint, Michigan, where more than 100,000 residents, overwhelmingly African American, were exposed to elevated levels of lead. Drawing on his own biography, Gupta saw something deeper in those cases. He had left a country defined in part by profound divides and hierarchy in human development, and he thought he understood the fundamentality of America's belief in the basic provision of elements for a thriving life—ingredients as essential as safe drinking water. "Do we understand the path we're taking here, by defining two different classes of water, for two different groups of population?" he asked me. "Do we really want to go down that path? In the history of this nation, it doesn't end well when we go down this path."

TWELVE

OUT OF THEIR SLUMBER

THE UNITED STATES THAT Donald John Trump saw from his apartment in Manhattan was a nation at perennial risk of victimhood. In 1987, in his first public flirtation with the presidency, the forty-one-year-old real-estate developer voyaged north, to New Hampshire, to tell an audience that America was getting "kicked around" by Japan, Saudi Arabia, and other allies. "I'm tired of nice people already in Washington," he said.

He delivered again on Larry King's show—"Behind our backs, they laugh at us." And, for Oprah Winfrey, he combined the victimhood routine with a dash of prosperity gospel, declaring that, if he became president, Americans "would make one hell of a lot of money from those people that for twenty-five years have taken advantage." That year, his presidential flirtation was brief, but, for years afterward, he revived the patter every now and then; it was a reliable marketing opportunity.

By the spring of 2011, however, he was taking the routine further toward an actual candidacy. Trump publicly embraced the crackpot theory that Obama was not a U.S. citizen, declaring, "I want him to show his birth certificate." (Never mind that it had already been publicly available for more than three years.) Most of the Republican establishment was dismissive; Karl Rove said Trump's embrace of birtherism consigned him to "the nutty right." But Roger Ailes at Fox News recognized the potential for profit, and, less than a month into Trump's birther campaign, he awarded him a regular Monday appearance on its morning show, ensuring he would appear in millions of Republican homes every week.

Ultimately, Trump did not run in 2012—he reupped with *The Apprentice* instead—but birtherism paid incalculable dividends; Trump's political adviser Roger Stone said that the decision to become a birther was "a brilliant base-building move." Less than a week after Mitt Romney lost the 2012 election, Donald Trump trademarked the phrase "Make America Great Again." On his trademark application, he specified that it was for "fundraising in the field of politics."

Trump, much like Stone's friend the benefactor Lee Hanley of Greenwich, sensed that voters were craving an alternative to Ted Cruz, Marco Rubio, and the other insiders bubbling up from Washington. He represented another step along an ideological path from the Tea Party's mantra of "Take It Back" and Limbaugh's laments about whites as "the new oppressed minority." On the eve of the 2012 election, Bill O'Reilly, America's top-rated cable news anchor, emphasized the sense of a zero-sum contest for resources, values, and power. He told his audience, "It's a changing country; the demographics are changing. It's not a traditional America anymore. And there are fifty percent of the voting public who want stuff, they want things. And who is going to give them things? President Obama."

Trump was mastering other features of his emerging political life. In February 2013, he typed out a tweet for the first time. (It was a thank-you note for a flattering remark about him on television.) Until then, his staff had used his account for bland corporate tweets, but Trump started thumbing out messages directly, on his Android phone. It was a turning point that his social-media director, Justin McConney, later compared to "the moment in *Jurassic Park* when Dr. Grant realized that velociraptors could open doors."

Over the next two years, Trump's following soared from 300,000 followers to 4.3 million. In 2014, Stone introduced Trump to Sam Nunberg, a young operative who was hired to spend thousands of hours monitoring talk radio and right-wing media. Nunberg summarized the themes for Trump, and his briefings highlighted an array of popular post–September 11 sensibilities—xenophobia, conspiracy, racism, anti-government fervor, and religious fundamentalism. Ted Cruz was touting the idea that Muslims who fled persecution in Syria should be resettled in "majority Muslim countries," not the United States. Jan Brewer, the Arizona governor, was blaming undocumented immigrants for beheadings. Billy Graham's son Franklin was praising Russia for "protecting children" from the "homosexual agenda."

Trump digested those ideas into a platform. His approach hinged on finding those coveted "missing white voters," the cohort that Romney, the establishmentarian, never reached. "His core positions on all these issues had been advanced by other candidates. Trump, however, was an outsider untarnished," Sam Popkin, a veteran pollster, observed. "He knew far less than any of them, but saw one big thing that mattered: some of the party's base were hurting economically, and extremely negative about Obama . . . They were virulently anti-government mostly when the money was going to people they viewed as lazy and undeserving—which is how they viewed minorities."

Trump's developing political persona was a pastiche of proven elements: he would be the workingman's billionaire, an opponent of immigrants, taxes, globalization, and elites. He would run against a phantasmagorical image of marauding people of color, and an entitled, self-satisfied "swamp" that ignored people's fears. "The whole aim of practical politics," H. L. Mencken had written a century ago, is to "keep the populace alarmed (and hence clamorous to be led to safety) by menacing it with an endless series of hobgoblins, all of them imaginary." Trump was a capable student of Roger Stone's philosophy: "Politics is not about uniting people. It's about dividing people. And getting your fifty-one percent."

For all the planning, even Trump could not know, in advance, how well his message would match the mood. On June 16, 2015, he entered the presidential race. The staging was fine enough; his campaign had dedicated $12,000 to a talent agency, Extra Mile Casting, for actors to applaud; they were paid $50 each, "to wear T-shirts and carry signs and help cheer," as the casting call put it. But it was his speech that altered the prospects of his stunt. As written, Trump's script contained no more than two sentences about immigration. But, in the event, he ad-libbed extra lines about Mexicans: "They're bringing drugs. They're bringing crime. They're rapists. And some, I assume, are good people."

Three of the statements had no basis in fact—the crime rate among first-generation immigrants was lower than that for native-born Americans—but it was all bunting around his central idea, to build a two-thousand-mile-long wall to stop Mexico from "sending people that have lots of problems." The Republican establishment was withering. Senator Lindsey Graham, of South Carolina, dismissed Trump as a "race-baiting, xenophobic bigot" who can "go to hell." Around Washington, Republicans placed bets on how long it would take for the campaign to implode.

And yet to many conservatives, who had wondered if Trump was even truly a Republican, his expression of naked contempt was refreshing; Ann Coulter called it "the Mexican rapist speech that won my heart."

———

Trump's campaign announcement was mocked and condemned—and utterly successful. His favorability among Republicans leaped from 16 to 57 percent, a greater spike than that of any other candidate's debut. If Trump's prior careers had taught him anything, he knew how to engineer an emotional impact for an audience. When the establishment denounced him, that only solidified his sense that he had found an issue that would endear him to the very people he needed—Americans who detested the establishment and felt slighted by mainstream arbiters of taste.

"They gave it to me," he said later of the media's outrage at his immigration rhetoric. As Trump trooped to larger and larger events—in Phoenix, Jacksonville, Oklahoma City—he heightened his warnings that immigrants brought crime and death. Onstage, he called up Jamiel Shaw Sr., whose seventeen-year-old son was killed in 2008 by a man who was in the country illegally. Trump stepped aside and looked on while Shaw told the crowd how his son was shot. "Donald Trump has changed the entire debate on immigration," Limbaugh told his listeners that month, which was not exactly true. Immigration had already been cultivated as a neuralgic issue; he had just found powerful new ways to deliver it.

Not long after Trump entered the race, my editors at *The New Yorker* asked me to write a piece about his campaign. In New York, he was a familiar, often-ignored piece of mental furniture, and we figured I could set aside a few weeks, at most, to write up his encounter with America, however long that would last. I flew down to Texas to see him on the stump. It was July 23, and I watched his red-white-and-navy-blue Boeing 757 touch down in the border town of Laredo, where the temperature was climbing to 104 degrees.

In the weeks since Trump had become a presidential front-runner, he had encountered a delicate staging issue: now that he was being filmed getting off and on planes so much, a rogue wind off the tarmac could render his comb-over fully erect in front of the campaign paparazzi. So in Laredo, Trump emerged from his plane for the first time wearing a protective innovation: a baseball hat stamped with his slogan "Make America Great Again." In my notes, I jotted down the presence of the headwear, which had the rigid facade of a cruise-ship giveaway. It added an expeditionary element to the day's outfit, of blazer, pale slacks, golf shoes—well suited for a mission that he was describing as one of great personal risk. "I may never see you again, but we're going to do it," he told Fox News on the eve of the Texas visit.

Before departing for Laredo, Trump said, "I've been invited by border patrols, and they want to honor me, actually, thousands and thousands of them, because I'm speaking up." Though Trump said "border patrols," the invitation had in fact come from a local branch of the border-patrol union, and the local, after consulting with headquarters, withdrew the invitation a few hours before Trump arrived, on the ground that it would not endorse political candidates. Descending the airplane stairs, Trump looked thrilled to be arriving amid a controversy. In his television phase, he had cultivated a lordly persona and a squint that combined Clint Eastwood on the high plains and Derek Zoolander on the runway. In the small airport terminal, he waded into a crowd of reporters and described the change of plans as the handiwork of unspecified enemies. "They invited me, and then, all of a sudden, they were told, silencio! They want silence." Asked why he felt unsafe in Laredo, which has a lower crime rate than New York City or Washington, D.C., he invoked another "they": "Well, they say it's a great danger, but I have to do it. I love the country. There's nothing more important than what I'm doing."

Trump was now going to meet with city officials instead of with the union. He disappeared into one of seven SUVs, escorted by a dozen police vehicles—a larger motorcade than Mitt Romney merited as the Republican nominee. He passed shopping malls, churches, and ranch houses with satellite dishes in the front yard. Some drivers waved; others stared. A car had been positioned along the route with a sign across the windshield: "MR. TRUMP, FUCK U."

He reached the World Trade Bridge, a trucking link to Mexico, where he stepped inside an air-conditioned building for a half-hour briefing. He emerged to talk to reporters, and, after pausing to let the cameras set up, resumed his event. He was asked, "You keep saying that there's a danger, but crime along the border is down. What danger are you talking about?"

Trump gave a tight, concerned nod. "There's great danger with the illegals, and we were just discussing that. But we have a tremendous danger along the border, with the illegals coming in."

On the way back to the airport, Trump stopped at the Paseo Real Reception Hall, where his supporters had assembled a small rally; guests were vetted at the door to keep out protesters. I sat beside a Latino family and asked the father what had attracted him to the event. He said that a friend involved in the Border Patrol had called him and asked him "to take up the spaces." He'd brought five relatives. Trump told the group, "I don't think that people understand the danger that you're under and the talent that you have. But I understand it." When he opened the floor to questions, Jose Diaz-Balart, an anchor for Telemundo and MSNBC, said, "Many feel that what you said, when you said that people that cross the border are rapists and murderers—"

Trump cut him off: "No, no, no! We're talking about illegal immigration, and everybody understands that. And you know what? That's a typical case of the press with misinterpretation." His supporters jeered at the reporter, and Trump shouted over the jeers: "Telemundo should be ashamed!"

Diaz-Balart said, "Can I finish?"

"No, no. You're finished," Trump said. He did his thank-yous, flashed thumbs-up signs, and headed for his airplane.

———

My requests for interviews went nowhere. Trump resented *The New Yorker*, which had covered him off and on for years, sometimes in terms that he did not find to his liking. In truth, I didn't try all that hard to speak to him, because I sensed that plumbing Trump's psyche was often as productive as asking American Pharoah, the winner of the Triple Crown, why he ran. The point was what happened when he did.

To inhabit Trump's landscape for a while, to chase his jet or stay behind with his fans in a half-dozen states, was to encounter a confederacy of the frustrated—less a constituency than a loose alliance of citizens who were breaking faith with the institutions of American politics and economics. They described themselves as victims of one distant force or another—of ball-less peckerheads (or words to that effect) who traded and sacrificed companies like pawns in a life-size chess set; of a mortgage boom that had rewarded the "Friends of Angelo" while harming millions of others; of fourteen years of deployments to the Middle East, with no relief in sight for the trauma and dislocation they left behind. They reserved some of their greatest fury for fellow Republicans, the creatures of permanent Washington who devoted themselves, above all, to courting the likes of Sheldon Adelson and Lee Hanley, primed to "Ask for $1m now."

A few weeks after the trip to Laredo, I visited relatives in New Hampshire, a state where voters pride themselves on being unimpressed. But Trump's recent visits had generated a frisson of Yankee excitement. Fred Rice, a Republican state representative, had arrived at a Trump rally in the beach town of Hampton and found people waiting patiently in a two-hour line that stretched a quarter of a mile down the street. "Never seen that at a political event before," he said. Other Republicans offered "canned bullshit," Rice went on. "People have got so terribly annoyed and disenchanted and disenfranchised, really, by candidates who get up there, and all their stump speeches promise everything to everyone." By the night's end, Rice was sold. "I heard echoes of Ronald Reagan," he told me, adding, "If I had to vote today, I would vote for Trump."

Trump's constant talk of his money, his peering down on the 1 percent (not to mention the 99), was helping him. "I love the fact that he wouldn't be owing anybody," Nancy Merz, a fifty-two-year-old Republican in Hampton, told me. She worked at a furniture company, she said. Her husband, Charlie, used to build household electricity meters at a General Electric plant. After the job moved to Mexico, he took to parking cars at a hospital. Trump, in his speech, had promised to stop companies from sending jobs abroad, and the Merzes became Trump Republicans. They were churchgoers, but they didn't expect Trump to become one, and they forgave his unpriestly comments about women. "There are so many other things going on in this country that we've got to be concerned about," Nancy said. "I've seen a lot of our friends lose their houses."

Unlike most of his competitors, Trump understood the true targets of that rage. "The hedge-fund guys didn't build this country," he said that summer. "These are guys that shift paper around and they get lucky." He vowed to raise their taxes. "These guys are getting away with murder. I want to lower the rates for the middle class." Trump's fans projected onto him a vast range of imaginings—about toughness, business acumen, and even honesty. In partisan terms, his ideas were riven by contradiction—he called for mass deportations but opposed cuts to Medicare and Social Security; he vowed to expand the military but criticized free trade—and yet that was a reflection of voters' often incoherent sets of convictions. Most of all, he had rekindled the intensity of the Tea Party. Barely a month into his race, his favorability among Tea Partiers had nearly tripled, to 56 percent, opening a lead over other favorites, such as Cruz of Texas, that they could never close.

One afternoon, as I waited for a rally to begin in Oskaloosa, Iowa, I chatted with Stephanie DeVolder, an elegant fifty-something with blond hair and bright green eyes, a Jewish mother of two who had worked as a sales rep for Dice, a job-search site. She was glad that Trump had "brought up the horrific treatment of the veterans" and that "he is a foremost believer in the military," and she admired his work on television. "I bought the videos of *The Apprentice*, and watched the whole thing," she said. "He is a phenomenal judge of character, and he actually does have a heart. He is absolutely amazing." Moreover, DeVolder was eager to see someone beat Hillary Clinton, whom she considered a prime example of Washington's entitlement and disregard. "I will never forget what she said when asked about wiping her server," DeVolder told me. (When a reporter had asked Clinton if she had wiped her server, she replied, "Like with a cloth or something?" and laughed.) DeVolder said, "It's so obvious that she is dirty."

Onstage that afternoon in Oskaloosa, Trump deployed, as he always did, a powerful set piece about Mexican criminals who are allowed to "roam around, shooting people and killing people." He described that as a hidden scourge: "Such a big problem, and nobody wants to talk about it." He reminded the crowd of his trip to Laredo: "I told the pilots, I said, 'Fly a little bit away from the border, please. Fly a little bit inland.' It's a whole scary thing." He said that when he returned to New York his wife had greeted him in tears. "You made it safely from the border!" she cried. As always, he described a case of a man killed by an undocumented immigrant ("an animal that shouldn't have been in this country"), and he urged Iowans to be afraid, even if they didn't perceive a threat in their own lives. "When you're afraid to walk into your own country, it's pretty bad," he said. "Hard to believe. You don't have that problem in Iowa, in all fairness. But it's pretty rough out there."

Hearing Trump's constant invocation of the border reminded me of the Border Patrol brochure I had picked up two years earlier at the airport, landing home in the United States. "Welcome to the United States," it said over images of the Washington Monument and cherry trees in bloom. That border was a symbol of relief, of welcoming.

In Trump's telling, the "border" served a different function; it was a threshold between chaos and security, between "them" and "us." When I spoke to DeVolder about immigration, she said Trump's fame had led her to his discussions of immigration, and she had concluded he was "absolutely right about border security."

Outside the auditorium, I met Ron James, a construction worker who was wearing a T-shirt that said "Every-Juan Illegal Go Home." I told him I didn't expect that message in Iowa, because we were a long way from Mexico. He said the "invasion of illegals" was eroding American culture: "We're getting flushed down the toilet." Inland America was proving to be optimal territory for Trump's talk, especially places that were overwhelmingly white but experiencing a steady rise in Latino immigration. Iowa, for instance, remained 90 percent white, but its Latino population had more than quintupled since 1990, as immigrants came for jobs at dairy farms, meat-packing plants, and factories. (Northwestern Iowa was represented by Steve King, the most stridently anti-immigrant member of Congress.) Since the beginning of this century, more than half of the American counties with the largest rise in diversity were in midwestern states—Iowa, Indiana, Wisconsin, Illinois, and Minnesota, according to *The Wall Street Journal*. In fact, people who lived less than 350 miles from the border were the *least* likely to support a wall, according to the Pew Research Center.

Like other right-wing populists, Trump had found that a sizable share of Americans were reacting to greater diversity with unease, fear, or resistance. In their imagination, they saw changes as even more drastic than they were; in a survey conducted by the Center for American Progress and other groups, Americans were asked to estimate what share of the country was nonwhite; the median answer was 49 percent; in reality, the number was 37 percent.

The phenomenon was not new; more than a decade earlier, a study of forty communities by Robert Putnam, of Harvard, an advocate for greater immigration, found that, in the early stages of diversification, the change appeared to "bring out the turtle in all of us." The resistance to change was strongest among white people who felt economically precarious; changing demographics heightened the fear of falling from their place a few rungs up from the bottom of the ladder, a phenomenon that social scientists described as "last place aversion."

In 1999, Leonard Zeskind, a researcher of the American far right, warned that in the decades to come "race will once again divide Americans. And this time white people will lose the prerogatives of majority status." Demographic projections held that non-Hispanic whites would become a minority around 2045. Zeskind suspected that, as that transition approached, white Americans would mobilize to retain their political and economic influence. "If the past is prologue, a bitter conflict will begin mid-century and continue a full generation," Zeskind wrote. When I called him to talk about Trump's campaign, Zeskind said, "Well, that part has snuck up on us quicker than I thought."

———

When the Trump storm broke that summer, I happened to be midway through researching a piece on far-right racist groups, and I observed at first hand their reactions to his candidacy. Trump was advancing a dire portrait of immigration that partly overlapped with their own. On June 28, twelve days after Trump's announcement, *The Daily Stormer*, America's most popular neo-Nazi news site, endorsed him for president: "Trump is willing to say what most Americans think: it's time to deport these people." *The Daily Stormer* urged white men to "vote for the first time in our lives for the one man who actually represents our interests."

Ever since the Tea Party's peak, in 2010, and its fade, citizens on the American far right—patriot militias, border vigilantes, white supremacists—had searched for a standard-bearer, and now they'd found him. In the past, "white nationalists," as they called themselves, had described Trump as a "Jew-lover," but the new tone of his campaign was a revelation. Richard Spencer was a self-described "identitarian" who lived in Whitefish, Montana, and promoted "white racial consciousness." Spencer had degrees from the University of Virginia and the University of Chicago. He served as president and director of the National Policy Institute, a think tank cofounded by William Regnery, a member of the conservative publishing family, that was "dedicated to the heritage, identity, and future of European people in the United States and around the world." The Southern Poverty Law Center called Spencer "a suit-and-tie version of the white supremacists of old."

Spencer told me that he had expected the presidential campaign to be an "amusing freak show," but that Trump was "refreshing." He went on, "Trump, on a gut level, kind of senses that this is about demographics, ultimately. We're moving into a new America." He said, "I don't think Trump is a white nationalist," but he did believe that Trump reflected "an unconscious vision that white people have—that their grandchildren might be a hated minority in their own country. I think that scares us. They probably aren't able to articulate it. I think it's there. I think that, to a great degree, explains the Trump phenomenon. I think he is the one person who can tap into it."

Jared Taylor, the editor of *American Renaissance*, a white-nationalist magazine and website based in Oakton, Virginia, told me, in regard to Trump, "I'm sure he would repudiate any association with people like me, but his support comes from people who are more like me than he might like to admit." Matthew Heimbach, a twenty-four-year-old white-nationalist activist in Cincinnati, told me that Trump had energized disaffected young men like him. "He is bringing people back out of their slumber," he said.

In generating his portrait of the country, Trump talked obsessively about Chicago; the city became his preferred dystopia, a vision of moral dysfunction and Democratic failure. He recycled racist tropes that had been used for decades to inspire fear in suburban white voters, and had gained prominence during the Obama years on Breitbart News and other right-wing media. On Fox, Bill O'Reilly talked about "death and destruction" and asked if Chicago was more lawless than Afghanistan. As a candidate, Trump retweeted bogus crime statistics about people "KILLED BY BLACKS." If elected, he told a crowd in Akron, Ohio, "we'll get rid of the crime. You'll be able to walk down the street without getting shot. Now, you walk down the street, you get shot." In the emerging vocabulary of the Trump era, the violence in Chicago did not call forth an effort to address generational poverty, segregation, or mistrust of police; it was an argument only for unmerciful force.

Trump, of course, was not the first aspiring president to carry a strain of racism. Thomas Jefferson, in *Notes on the State of Virginia*, wrote that Black people had a "very strong and disagreeable odor." Ronald Reagan, in a phone call with Nixon, referred to African diplomats as "monkeys" who were "still uncomfortable wearing shoes." But what set Trump apart was that he made rank prejudice a central pillar of his public appeals, and like-minded people recognized that. Ordinarily, white-nationalist websites mocked Republicans as Zionist stooges and corporate puppets who had opened the borders in order to keep wages low. But, on July 9, VDARE, an opinion site founded to "push back the plans of pro-Amnesty/Immigration Surge politicians, ethnic activists and corrupt Big Business," hailed Trump as "the first figure with the financial, cultural, and economic resources to openly defy elite consensus. If he can mobilize Republicans behind him and make a credible run for the Presidency, he can create a whole new media environment for patriots to openly speak their mind without fear of losing their jobs." The piece was headlined "WE ARE ALL DONALD TRUMP NOW."

———

Trump's admirers heard in his words multiple appeals. Michael Hill headed the Alabama-based League of the South, a secessionist group that envisioned an independent southern republic with an "Anglo-Celtic" leadership. In 1981, Hill began teaching history at Stillman College, a historically Black college in Tuscaloosa. He applied for jobs at other schools and was turned down, which he attributed to affirmative action. In 1994, he cofounded the League, which put him at odds, he said, with "civil-rights-age, older Black faculty and administrators, looking down their nose at this uppity white boy coming out here, talking about the Confederate flag and all that kind of stuff." In 1999, he left Stillman. He told me, "If academia is not for me, because of who I am—a white southern male, Christian, straight, whatever—then I'm going to find something that is. I'm going to fight this battle for my people."

Hill was moved by Trump's frequent references to Kathryn Steinle, a thirty-two-year-old woman who was walking with her father on a pier in San Francisco, in 2015, when she was fatally wounded in what police described as a random shooting. When police arrested Juan Francisco Lopez-Sanchez, a repeat felon who had been deported from the United States five times, Trump adopted the story of "that beautiful woman" as "another example of why we must secure our border immediately." Hill told me, "That struck such a nerve with people, because a lot of this political stuff is abstract, but, as a father, I've got a daughter as well, and I could just see myself holding my daughter, and her looking up at me and saying, 'Help me, Daddy.'" Hill, who condemned immigration and interracial marriage and warned of the influence of "Jewry," said, "I love to see somebody like Donald Trump come along. Not that I believe anything that he says. But he is stirring up chaos in the GOP, and for us that is good."

I joined Hill at a League of the South meeting one afternoon in July at its newly built headquarters on a couple of verdant acres outside Montgomery, Alabama. It was the League's annual conference, and there were about a hundred men and women; the older men were in suits or jackets, and the younger set favored jeans, with handguns holstered in the waistband. The vendors' tables had books (*The True Selma Story*, *Authentic History of the Ku Klux Klan*), stickers ("The Federal Empire Is Killing the American Dream"), and raffle tickets. The prize: a .45-caliber SIG Sauer pistol.

After years of decline, the League had recently acquired a number of younger members, including Brad Griffin, a thirty-four-year-old who wrote an influential blog under the name Hunter Wallace. He wore Top-Siders, khaki shorts, and a polo shirt. As we talked, Griffin's eyes wandered to his two-year-old son, who was roaming nearby. Griffin told me that he embraced white nationalism after reading Patrick Buchanan's *The Death of the West*, which was published in the wake of September 11. The book mixed Buchanan's despair over contraception with his warnings of an "immigrant invasion" and a "Third World America." It left Griffin convinced, as he put it, that "all of the European peoples were dying out, their birthrates were low, and you had mass immigration and multiculturalism." Griffin once had high hopes for the Tea Party. "They channeled all that rage into electing an impressive number of Republicans in the South, but then all they did was try to cut rich Republicans' taxes and make life easier for billionaires!" he said. "It was all hijacked, and a classic example of how these right-wing movements emerge, and they're misdirected into supporting the status quo."

Griffin had recently told his readers that his opinion of Donald Trump was "soaring." He saw Trump's surge as a "hostile takeover of the Republican Party. He's blowing up their stage-managed dog-and-pony show." Griffin was repelled by the big-money politics engineered in Greenwich, Palm Beach, and similar precincts, so I asked why his suspicions did not extend to Trump. "He's a billionaire, but all of these other little candidates are owned by their own little billionaires." He mentioned Sheldon Adelson and the Koch brothers. "So I think Trump is independent."

The longer I stayed, the more I sensed that my fellow attendees occupied a parallel universe in which white Americans faced imminent demise and the South was preparing to secede from the United States. When Hill took the stage, he spoke gravely of a recent effort to lower the Confederate flag. A few weeks earlier, a gunman had killed nine Black parishioners while they prayed at a church in Charleston, South Carolina, and the massacre had inspired a broad effort to remove the Confederate flag from the state capitol and from the shelves of Amazon, Walmart, and a host of other retail stores. Hill told his compatriots that the movement against the flag was just the beginning. Soon, he warned, the unspecified "they" will come for the "monuments, battlefields, parks, cemeteries, street names, even the dead themselves." The crowd was on its feet, cheering him on. "This, my friends, is cultural genocide," he said, adding, "Often, as history has shown, cultural genocide is merely a prelude to physical genocide."

———

"Why are whites supposed to be happy about being reduced to a minority?" Jared Taylor, of *American Renaissance*, asked me. "It's clear why Hispanics celebrate diversity: 'More of us! More Spanish! More cucaracha!'"

Taylor, who called himself a "racial dissident," was slim and decorous in gray trousers and a button-down when we met. For years, he and others had sensed an opportunity on the horizon to expand their ranks. The Klan, weakened by lawsuits and infighting, barely existed anymore, but the Internet drew in young racists like the gunman in South Carolina. In response to the campaign against the Confederate flag, America's far right organized more than a hundred rallies around the South, seizing on the moment as a chance to strike back against the Obama era, political correctness, Black Lives Matter, and multiculturalism.

A group calling itself the Conservative Response Team placed robocalls to South Carolina residents, framing the flag issue as a matter of survival: "Just like ISIS, Obama's haters want our monuments down, graves dug up and schools, roads, towns and counties renamed. They've even taken *Dukes of Hazzard* off TV. What's next?" Griffin, the blogger, told me that the removal of the flag had crystallized "fears that people have about what happens when we become a minority. What happens when we have no control over things? You're seeing it play out right now."

Over sandwiches in the dining room of Taylor's brick Colonial, with views of a spacious backyard, a half hour from downtown Washington, D.C., five of his readers and friends shared their views on race and politics. They were white men, in white-collar jobs, and each had a story of radicalization: Chris, who wore a pink oxford shirt and a tie and introduced himself as an employee of "Conservatism, Inc.," the Republican establishment, said that he had graduated from a public high school where there were frequent shootings, but he felt he was supposed to "ignore the fact that we were not safe on a day-to-day basis because of all of these Blacks and the other immigrants in our schools."

Jason, a muscle-bound commercial-real-estate broker in a polo shirt, said, "I've had personnel—in strict, frightened confidence—just tell me, 'Hey, look, we're just hiring minorities, so don't appeal, don't come back.'" This sense of "persecution," as he called it, was widely held. In a study published in 2011, Michael Norton, a professor at Harvard Business School, and Samuel Sommers, a professor of psychology at Tufts, found that more than half of white Americans believed that whites had replaced Blacks as "the primary victims of discrimination," even though, as Norton and Sommers wrote, "by nearly any metric—from employment to police treatment, loan rates to education—statistics continue to indicate drastically poorer outcomes for Black than White Americans."

The men around the table, unlike previous generations of white nationalists, were inspired not by nostalgia for slavery but by their dread of a time when non-Hispanic whites will no longer be the largest demographic group in America. They nursed a private chronology of insults, some well known, others obscure. They brought up the 2006 Duke lacrosse case, in which three white athletes were falsely accused of assaulting a Black woman; they seethed over Obama's criticism of police for acting "stupidly" in the arrest of Henry Louis Gates; they even pointed to the moment, in 2009, when Kanye West interrupted Taylor Swift at the MTV Video Awards to say that the award should have gone to Beyoncé. As with Trump's visions of Chicago, they shared a conception of America that was haunted by their fears of physical violence. Erick, who wore a Captain America T-shirt, invoked one of Trump's signature phrases. "The American dream is dead, and the American nightmare is just beginning," Erick said. "I believe it's that way. I think that whites don't know the terror that's upon us."

All the men wanted to roll back anti-discrimination laws in order to restore restrictive covenants and allow them to carve out all-white enclaves. Henry, a twenty-six-year-old with cropped blond hair, said, "We all see some hope in Donald Trump, because it's conceivable that he could benefit the country in a way that we feel would be helpful."

├────┤

In early August, the Republican candidates convened in Cleveland for their first debate. I watched it on television with Matthew Heimbach, the young white nationalist in Cincinnati, and some of his friends. Heimbach, whom anti-racist activists call "the Little Führer" for his tirades against "rampant multiculturalism," founded the Traditionalist Youth Network, a far-right group that caters to high school and college students and pushes for the separation of Blacks and whites. Stocky and bearded, Heimbach was ambitious. He graduated in 2013 from Towson University, in Maryland, where he attracted controversy for forming a "white student union." He had met with European fascists, including members of the Golden Dawn, in Greece.

Heimbach rented part of a house on a placid side street and worked as a landscaper. He and his wife had a baby named Nicholas. When I asked Heimbach how he got involved with fascist politics, he laughed. "I was not raised like this," he said. "I was raised to be a normal small-town Republican." The son of teachers in Poolesville, Maryland, an hour from Washington, he, like Brad Griffin, credited Buchanan's book *The Death of the West* for seeding his conception of a desolate future. "Even if you play the game, even if you do everything right, then the future, when it comes to your income, when it comes to benefits, when it comes to everything, we are going to be the first generation in American history to be living worse than our parents." He went on, "My own parents tell me, 'Well, you should just shut up, you should go get a normal job, and get a two-car garage, and then you'll be happy.'"

Heimbach was consumed by grievance. During a half century of change in the American labor market—the rise of technology and trade, the decline of manual labor—low-skilled, poorly educated men had fared badly. Between 1979 and 2013, pay for men without a college degree fell by 21 percent in real terms; for women with similar credentials, pay rose by 3 percent, thanks partly to job opportunities in health care and education. Heimbach had consoled himself with a vision of racist revival—a weaponized version of the "missing white voters" thesis. "We need to get the white community to actually start speaking for the white community," he said, "instead of letting a bunch of Republicans that hate us anyway, and don't speak for our values, be the unofficial spokespeople." Trump had made him believe the Republican Party might be able to speak for him.

During the debate, Mike Huckabee was asked how he might attract enough support from independents and Democrats to get elected, and Heimbach shouted at the TV, "You don't need to! All you need to do is get the Republican base to get out and vote."

On a couch across from the television, Tony Hovater, who used to be a drummer in a band and was working as a welder, said that, from what he had heard from Trump, he suspected that Trump shared his fears about immigration but couldn't say so openly. Hovater told me, "I think he's, like, dog-whistling," adding, "He's saying we should probably favor more European immigration, or maybe more of just a meritocracy sort of system, but he's not coming out and saying it, because people will literally stamp him: 'Oh, you just hate Mexicans.'" Hovater hoped that Trump would find a way to be more forthright: "Why not just say it?"

As the debate wound down, Trump, in his final statement, recited his mantra of despair. "Our country is in serious trouble. We don't win anymore," he said. Matthew Parrott, a Web developer who was sipping coffee from a cup adorned with a swastika, was pleased with Trump's performance. "He was sassy without being comical. He struck exactly the tone he needed to give the people supporting him exactly what they want more of." He went on, "The political system hasn't been providing an outlet for social-conservative populism. You had this Ron Paul revolution, and all the stuff about cutting taxes, small government, and that's just not the electrifying issue that they were expecting it to be. Simple folks, they want the border secure. They want what Donald Trump is mirroring at them. I think he's an intelligent businessman who identified what the people want to hear."

Trump emerged from the debate on a wrathful tear. When Megyn Kelly, the Fox News host, asked him to explain why he called some women "fat pigs, dogs, slobs, and disgusting animals," Trump replied, "What I say is what I say." In an interview the next day, he said that Kelly had "blood coming out of her eyes, blood coming out of her wherever." In the attendant uproar, Trump played dumb, declaring that only a "deviant" would think he was referring to menstruation, when he was thinking only of her nose. The Republican commentariat celebrated what finally seemed to be Trump's immolation.

A couple of days after the debate, Stephanie DeVolder, in Iowa, emailed me to say that Trump had lost her. "I am not offended by his comments (as much as I am embarrassed for him and his family)." She had soured on his "bullying," and his "total disregard for manners." The polls did not follow suit, though. Trump not only remained the front-runner, but broadened his lead. Two weeks after the debate, DeVolder changed her mind on Trump again. "I forgave him, as his message/platform continues to resonate above all else," she wrote to me.

I was getting accustomed to that kind of hedging from his supporters. As Trump's candidacy grew, his rants against elites and bankers were almost perfectly engineered to resonate with coal miners in West Virginia, left raw by the bankruptcies of Patriot Coal and other companies. When I asked Efaw, the mine electrician, what he made of Trump, he told me, "He says things I don't like, and does things I don't like, but you've got to admit, he was a man running a business. He's pretty much approaching this like he would that, and people don't like it. If he doesn't like you, he says, 'I don't like you, get out!' He's used to doing that. He's got the guts to say it, and he's got the guts to do it." He went on, "Most of our politicians come from, I guess you would say, a higher class of society. We're just excess baggage to a lot of them." He put Hillary Clinton in that category. Trump, in his judgment, was "the lesser of two evils."

———

As Trump consolidated his lead in the Republican Party, I wondered how his success was reverberating through bastions of Republican leadership such as my hometown. He was hardly a natural heir to the Greenwich Republican tradition. In the 1980s, he had owned a mansion on the town's waterfront, but he never took to the spirit of the place—"courage and thrift"—and locals were embarrassed by his house's gilded décor. After he and his wife Ivana divorced, she sold it. When the Greenwich son George H. W. Bush called for a "kinder, gentler nation," Trump responded, "If this country gets any kinder or gentler, it's literally going to cease to exist."

So when Trump emerged on the scene, much of the political and financial world dismissed him. Jeffrey Sonnenfeld, a professor at the Yale School of Management, attended a salon that summer at the Connecticut home of Larry Kudlow, the business commentator who later headed Trump's National Economic Council. "It was a lot of very deep-pocketed Republicans from Greenwich and New York," Sonnenfeld told me. "Not one person had a pleasant thing to say about Trump." Sonnenfeld urged them to take Trump's chances seriously, but a fellow guest, who worked for a super PAC supporting Ted Cruz in the primaries, disagreed. "She said, 'I'm a lifelong expert on the psychographics of women voters' behavior, and I can tell you that Donald Trump will never get two percent of Republican women voters," Sonnenfeld told me. "She got wild applause. That was Kellyanne Conway." (Conway, who later became one of Trump's most loyal mouthpieces, called that recollection a "specious, self-serving claim.")

In early 2016, Trump was denounced in the pages of *Greenwich Time* by Leora Levy, a prominent local fundraiser. "He is vulgar, ill-mannered and disparages those whom he cannot intimidate," she wrote. "His modus operandi is to try to intimidate people then call them names and calumniate about them and then if those tactics do not work, to sue them. That is how he has run his businesses and that is how he is running his campaign." Levy, who later won the Prescott Bush award, was lending her support to Prescott's grandson Jeb, the former governor of Florida.

But it soon became clear that not everyone in Greenwich was excited about Jeb. Jim Campbell was the chairman of the Republican Town Committee. The Campbells, like the Bushes, had deep roots in town. Jim prepped at Exeter and graduated from Harvard and Harvard Law School before working in Europe and returning home as a real-estate executive. On a fall evening, Campbell attended a reception for Jeb Bush at the Belle Haven Club, a private tennis-and-boating club overlooking Long Island Sound. Jeb was expansive and mild, which struck Campbell as precisely wrong for the political moment: "He gave a whole talk about a woman named Juanita in South Florida, and how 'immigration is love,' and I just looked at the people I came with and said, 'Does he think he's already the nominee? He's running in a tough Republican primary, and just because we're at the Belle Haven Club doesn't mean we're all voting for him.'"

Watching television at home one night in the fall of 2015, Campbell happened on a Trump rally in Iowa. "I'm not a hard-core conservative— I'm a Republican from Greenwich," Campbell said. "But I listened, and he had that line that he would use: 'Folks, we either have a country or we don't.' And I felt the chill—like Chris Matthews with the little Obama zing up the leg. I'm, like, 'Oh, my God, this is a really good line.'" To Campbell, Trump was describing immigration in ways that resonated: "Could somebody finally say that we're allowed to enforce the law at the border without being called a racist? I lived in Switzerland for ten years. Do you think I was allowed to go around without a passport?"

Campbell tapped out a text message to a friend: "Trump live—can't turn the channel. Unbelievable. I don't think any R can beat him." Campbell watched the rally for forty-five minutes. "He was mesmerizing," he said. Not long afterward, he saw a Republican debate in which Trump described the invasion of Iraq as a mistake. For Campbell, the acknowledgment came as a catharsis. "Of course it was a big, fat mistake," he told himself. He recalled a conversation with an early Trump supporter, who told him, "He says everything I think."

In early 2016, Campbell attended a dinner for Republicans at the Delamar Greenwich Harbor, a Mediterranean-themed boutique hotel that is popular with local finance executives. After a dinner speaker mocked the notion of building a wall and imposing tariffs, Campbell raised his hand: "I said, 'With all due respect, why is it that we're not allowed to support a candidate who supports the things that you just ticked off?'" Campbell knew that his question would cause a stir, but he had decided that it was time "to let everybody know who I was supporting." When the event was over, he discovered that he was not alone: "I had four guys make a beeline for me, Wall Streeters, all saying, 'What can we do? Can I sign up? Are you organizing?'"

In February 2016, with Jeb still vying for the nomination, Campbell endorsed Trump. The news generated a flurry of uneasy attention in Greenwich. Campbell was undeterred. He told me, "I just think there's a lot of people supporting Donald and don't want to say so."

THIRTEEN

UNMAKING THE MACHINES

FOR HIS FIRST FORAY into politics, Trump benefited from uncanny timing. The institutions that might have thwarted him at other moments in history—the mainstream press, the church, the Republican National Committee—were beset by declines in trust and resources. By 2016, the Republican leadership had a smaller payroll than the Koch brothers' private political network. Fortunately for Trump, he had also caught the Democratic Party at a perilous moment. As usual, after eight years in the White House, the party in power was the focus of discontent and malaise; as the campaign progressed, that diminished enthusiasm started shaping who voted for whom, where, and why.

Across the country, the Democratic Party was struggling to generate excitement for political grandees who had presided over politics for a generation. In Illinois, Michael Madigan was the longest-serving leader of any state or federal legislature in U.S. history, having been Speaker of the House for all but two years since 1983. In the city of Chicago, new blood was almost as scarce; for forty-three of the past fifty-five years, the city had been run by one of the Daleys, father or son. When the son retired in 2011, he left a lot of deferred political maintenance: the budget deficit totaled $637 million, low-income neighborhoods were plagued by violence, and relations between Chicago police and the public were unraveling.

One measure of the city's health was not encouraging: the population of the area was falling. Those who moved away voiced various reasons—taxes, corruption, traffic among them—but researchers paid particular attention to an exodus in the Black community. Since 1980, Chicago had lost at least a quarter of its Black population; between 2000 and 2010, 181,000 Black residents left Chicago. Initially, they headed to the suburbs, but more and more they were going farther—to Indiana, Iowa, the Sun Belt, and the South. Some felt priced out of the city—"strategic gentrification," as it became known—while others cited violence and the languishing economy on the South and West sides. Whatever form it took, the message was the same: they felt powerless to make the city pay attention.

"We feel like the forgotten people," Tenesha Barner told me. At her church, a nondenominational parish called New Beginnings on the edge of Parkway Gardens, the pastor had become so desperate that he took a drastic step. The Reverend Corey Brooks marched across the street to a vacant motel that attracted drug-dealing and prostitution. He climbed up to the roof, took a seat, and refused to come down until he had raised enough money to demolish the building. It was the middle of a frigid Chicago winter, but Brooks stayed up there for months, sleeping in a tent with electric heaters on extension cords, while Barner and the rest of the parish watched his sermons on a digital feed across the street. As time wore on, the stunt attracted a parade of bigwigs; the governor of Illinois climbed up to take a look, as did the Reverend Jesse Jackson and the Reverend Al Sharpton. In the political class, everyone snickered that Brooks was a shameless publicity hound—which was precisely the point. And it worked. After three months on the roof, Brooks had raised more than $450,000. He climbed down, and the building was demolished.

Over the years, Barner had kept one eye on politics, but it had begun to feel absurdly estranged from her life. "I watch the debates and stuff like that, and I'm sitting there like, 'Who can you really trust? Who do you really believe? Who's really for us?' And when I say 'us,' I'm not talking about being Black. I'm talking about 'us'—the *United States*. Like, who cares about us?"

Despite her bluff exterior, Barner was a worrier. She saw a therapist for her anxiety, especially about her kids. Her daughter, Mekaela, was in high school and getting by. Her son, Antwan, was a good student, but he had edged close to serious trouble. In 2014, when he was twenty, he got into an argument with a police officer and was charged with battery. Antwan had no criminal history and was released on probation. He had grown up around police, including Officer Thomas and a great-uncle who taught at the police academy. But tensions between police and young men in the neighborhood were getting more acute all the time. Barner told her son, "They're afraid as well. You cannot be the aggressor."

From her window on the third floor, Barner watched her neighborhood slip further into economic desolation. In 2015, the McDonald's closed; Walgreens closed soon after—and each disappearance seemed to remove another tiny pin that held the community together. "We have no food, no pharmacy, no medical facilities," she said. I mentioned that it was a food desert, but Barner corrected me: "It's an everything desert," she said.

At the heart of Chicago's troubles was a failure of political courage: for half a century, the public finances of Chicago and Illinois had been deteriorating like a roof caving in, because nobody in government was willing to risk the political harm of raising taxes to pay for what they had promised. By 2015, the state's finances had sunk into paralysis. Leaders couldn't pass a budget, and paying interest on its debt was consuming $31 of every $100 from taxpayers. The state resorted to harsh cuts in services, mostly for people who lacked the power to resist, including relief for the homeless and funding for domestic-violence shelters. At Northeastern Illinois University, where close to half the student body was Black or Latino, administrators had to freeze spending and drain most of the school's bank accounts.

The declining Black population, the growing violence, and the state's financial mess felt intertwined, and in the final weeks of 2015, the tensions in Chicago ignited, sparked by the death of a teenager named Laquan McDonald, who received more attention in death than he ever did in life.

The life of Laquan McDonald was short and cruel. His mother, who was fourteen when she became pregnant, had a boyfriend who abused him. By the time he was five, McDonald was punching himself in the face at day care. In his teens, he was arrested repeatedly for drug possession. On the last night of this life, he had PCP in his system. It was a few weeks after he turned seventeen, and he was confronted by police, who were responding to suspected car break-ins. He had a knife in his hand. In the police account of what followed, McDonald raised his knife and lunged at an officer, a white man named Jason Van Dyke, who opened fire. McDonald died that night; the report of his death barely registered in the headlines.

Soon, though, activists and political circles were hearing that it was a volcanic case. For months, the administration of Mayor Rahm Emanuel fought, in court, to prevent the release of a police dashcam video. City attorneys maintained that the release of the video would taint an investigation before it was complete, even as critics accused Emanuel of burying it to protect his reelection. In an unmistakable sign that the city recognized the volatility, it agreed to pay $5 million to McDonald's family, even though they hadn't filed a lawsuit. When I read that, it reminded me of the old refrain that ran through so many lives in the city, the old combination of race, money, and violence.

In November 2015, a Cook County judge ordered the release of the tape; the public discovered that it flatly contradicted the police's account of the shooting. In the nighttime footage, McDonald was walking away from police, with a knife in his hand, when the officer, Van Dyke, started shooting. McDonald collapsed, but Van Dyke kept shooting—sixteen shots in all—each round producing a puff of smoke from the body on the ground.

Hours before the video's release, prosecutors filed first-degree-murder charges against Van Dyke, the first such charge against an on-duty police officer in Chicago in more than three decades. The timing backfired; activists saw it as a classic political attempt to short-circuit a broader public outcry. When the video emerged, it ignited a fury in Chicago. Even for a city accustomed to death, the grief was profound—not only for McDonald but also for layers of overlapping failure and political self-protection that had smothered his death in silence. Protesters shut down Michigan Avenue's high-end shopping district on Black Friday. Protests continued for weeks afterward, with marchers shouting "Sixteen shots and a cover-up" and demanding that Emanuel resign.

For people of color in Chicago, the video of McDonald's killing was a revelation of truth even larger than the killing itself. The unblinking eye of a police camera had pierced a skein of fictions and abuses of power that reached back generations, a genealogy of poisoned encounters with law enforcement: Old Man Daley's "shoot to kill" order during the riots after the assassination of Martin Luther King Jr.; the killing of the Black Panther Fred Hampton in 1969; the years of torture conducted by the police commander Jon Burge, a former Army police officer, who had served in Korea and Vietnam. Burge's legacy—he was accused of torturing more than a hundred men, to force confessions, between 1972 and 1991—was such an enduring offense on Chicago's history that the city council had issued reparations to many of his victims and added the Burge story to the public-school curriculum.

But the death of Laquan McDonald was also a preview of a national reckoning, not only with crime and punishment, forgiveness and victimhood, but also with the most elemental divide between those who have and those who have not, an inequity in the most basic rights of citizenship: the freedom from state violence, the presumption of innocence. He was killed about two months after the police shooting of a Black teenager in Ferguson, Missouri, which gave new prominence to the Black Lives Matter movement that had taken root in 2013. Protests were growing into a national reexamination of police tactics.

In Chicago, Black Lives Matter carried special resonance: between 2007 and 2014, Chicago police shot nearly four hundred people, and, in all but two cases, the city had ruled that the shootings were justified. In McDonald's case, moments after the shooting, a dispatcher on the police radio asked officers at the scene about the medical condition of the teenager who had been shot. The dispatcher called him the "victim," but an officer interjected. "Offender," he said. And the dispatcher agreed. "That's what I meant," she said.

McDonald's killing symbolized far deeper problems, including the police department's indifference to citizen complaints, its rare punishment of problematic officers, and city hall's tacit cooperation. Since 2004, Chicago had quietly approved more than $500 million in settlements for police misconduct. As complaints gained public momentum, Rahm Emanuel's approval rating dropped to 27 percent. He was nicknamed "Mayor 1 Percent." Protesters picketed his house.

In private, the Reverend Michael Pfleger, an activist Catholic priest who had taken part in some of the marches, confronted Emanuel about the case. I asked Pfleger about the encounter, and he said, "He told me to my face, 'Mike, I did nothing illegal. I swear to God. Nothing, Mike.' 'It's okay, I believe that,' I said." Emanuel maintained that he was following city hall procedure by keeping the video a secret, but Pfleger considered that to be a failing. "I said, 'You knew the process was fucked up, so you hid behind the process.'"

⊢―――⊣

Not long after the tape came out, I made an appointment to see Emanuel. His office asked me to come at noon on a Saturday to one of his preferred restaurants, a pleasant nouveau-comfort-food place in the West Loop that was popular with middle-class families. On a cold, slushy morning, it was warm and lively inside. Emanuel ordered oatmeal and blueberries. Settling into a booth, he winced and rubbed his right leg. "I stretched something in the hip. I probably should rest, but I'm going to yoga right after this."

At fifty-six, Emanuel was still coiled like a spring, just as he had been twenty-five years earlier, when he came to national attention as an ambitious, acerbic aide on Bill Clinton's campaign. From the first, he was known as a ruthless tactician, impatient with idealists and the weak of will. He was the fiercest of the Clinton circle's warriors: profane, abrupt, and, at his best, effective. As a member of the House, and then as President Obama's chief of staff, he used much the same approach. More than most politicians, he embraced his stereotype—the pugilism, the thin skin, the vocabulary. During our interview, I asked if he was conducting any internal polling about the crisis. He said no, adding, "Now you know that all the assumptions you have about me are fucking wrong." It was echt Emanuel, quick to put his interlocutor on guard and off balance.

I brought up the video of the killing. Everyone was still wondering if Emanuel was telling the truth when he said that he knew nothing about the case before his reelection. Many in Chicago found it hard to imagine that the mayor of a city with historic police problems, at a moment when law-enforcement conduct was a national political issue—a mayor who cultivated an image of attention to small details—would not have wanted more information. He said, "I was reassured that four entities were crawling all over this thing: one, the state's attorney; one, the U.S. attorney in the name of the Justice Department; the Federal Bureau of Investigation; and IPRA"—the Independent Police Review Authority, the civilian board that investigates the most serious cases. Dismissing claims that he helped prevent the release of the video, he defined his mistake narrowly: "I don't think I ever thought that it still would take until December, a year later," for local prosecutors to finish their investigation.

In an effort to regain the city's trust, Emanuel had fired the police superintendent, Garry McCarthy, and had delivered an unusually emotional apology in front of the city council. "If we're going to begin the healing process," he said, choking up, "the first step in that journey is my step, and I'm sorry." He promised to remake the Chicago Police Department, though in practice that was colossally complicated. He had to find a way to reform it without so demoralizing it that it abandoned him. And he was starting at a disadvantage. Unlike Richard Daley, who was reared among cops in the Irish American neighborhood of Bridgeport, Emanuel grew up in suburban Wilmette, the son of an Israeli immigrant. His father was a pediatrician, his mother a civil rights activist. He turned down a scholarship at the Joffrey Ballet and graduated from Sarah Lawrence College. (Among themselves, the cops called him Tiny Dancer.) I asked him if his relative distance from the police department makes it easier for him to impose tough reforms—or harder for him to get a sense of what's going on.

"I don't know what the question is asking," he said. "Why do you assume it's harder?"

If Emanuel didn't realize that he had a gap to close with his police department, that would be an answer in itself. He changed tack: "Let me say this. There are benefits to it, and there are vulnerabilities to it, and that's the truth." For years, Emanuel had reminded reporters and voters that his mother's brother, Les, retired as a police sergeant. "Look," he said. "What your questions assume, which is true, is that the police department is somewhat a reflection of our city." He went on, "I run into officers every day who say, 'Oh, I served with Uncle Les, how's Uncle Les?' So there's benefits to that. Being a foot inside but being an outsider, I can push certain changes that an insider could not." "Outsider" was not a term I usually associated with Rahm Emanuel, but it captured the reality—Chicago politics was so entrenched along narrow pathways that even lifelong politicians felt captive to it. It reminded me of how much of the town felt "stuck in place." It was Mud City all over again.

Even before McDonald's death, Emanuel had a tense relationship with Black residents of Chicago. Since taking office, he had muscled through one of his signature education goals—lengthening the school day—and distressed many public-school parents by closing fifty schools. Nearly all of the shuttered schools were in predominantly Black or Latino communities. In his reelection in 2015, support for Emanuel declined by the largest margins among African Americans affected by the school closures, according to an analysis by Sally Nuamah, a political scientist at Northwestern University. Against that history, Emanuel's apologia in the city council did not produce reconciliation. A week after the speech, he visited Urban Prep, a prominent, predominantly Black charter school for boys, and students chanted, "Sixteen shots!"

A few days before Emanuel and I met, some Black pastors had boycotted a breakfast hosted by the mayor to commemorate Martin Luther King Jr.'s birthday. Protesters had interrupted the event, shouting, "Shame on you!" When we spoke, he dismissed the protests as people "relitigating" the elections, but he registered something larger under way—an emerging national trend. "I found out from my colleagues:

the mayor of Minneapolis was booed off the stage; she didn't finish her speech. The mayor of Denver couldn't get his MLK event off the ground." He said, "I'm not the only person getting protests across the country."

He ticked off projects that he hoped would begin to restore public support: "GE Healthcare Worldwide is coming to Chicago—an eighteen-billion-dollar company," he said. The following day, he planned to announce $1.3 billion in funds for overhauling O'Hare Airport.

But in communities of color, people tended to see the benefits of those deals and investments accruing to the city's most fortunate. Between 2011 and 2016, Chicago spent $650 million on new school construction, but 73 percent of the money went to schools where white students made up more than double their average level in the city. I asked Emanuel if reducing segregation was on his agenda, and he said that it was reflected in his investment in the Red Line, the rapid-transit system that serves the South Side. "If you want to end segregation not only in housing but in the workplace, you've got to have a public-transportation system that works." He added, "I didn't do the Red Line north in Lincoln Park and Lakeview"—two prosperous neighborhoods. "I took a lot of shit for this," he said.

I sensed that our interview had run its course. I thanked Emanuel and slipped out of the booth, leaving him to a line of voters who had spotted him across the restaurant and gathered to talk to him. Walking back through the snow, I tried to make sense of his defiance. Understandably, he wanted to see the protests as post-election griping, and any politician would downplay the disconnection between himself and the public. But I suspected that, for all his savvy, he did not fully grasp the sheer span of the gulf widening between his realm of existence—the world of secure, advantaged, well-hedged lives—and the world of urgent, accumulating, radicalizing insecurity. That was the world that dominated parts of the city where a teenager became an "offender" in the instant after the gunshot, a lethal verdict that would have gone unchallenged if not for the truth unearthed from a buried video. Emanuel might not have acknowledged it to me, or to himself, but I sensed that his political antennae were picking up a small, growing reality that his moment in Chicago politics was closing. The system he had mastered—the era he represented—was losing credibility. But it was not at all clear what was going to replace it.

———

I stopped by to see Natalie Moore, a journalist and author who grew up in Chatham, a historic Black neighborhood on the South Side. She worked out of a storefront bureau beside a bakery, on Seventy-fifth Street, reporting for the local public-radio station WBEZ. Her most recent book was *The South Side*, a history of race and inequity. Moore told me she sensed a growing impatience not only with the city's white leadership but also with the old-line, established Black leaders.

"Chicago is kind of like Rome, the city-state," she said. "The transition from King Richard to Emperor Emanuel has not been an easy one, and I think people have felt more empowered to do something now," to demand more from city hall. The activists, not the politicians, were ascendant, she said. "I don't think anyone really feels like elected leadership has moved the mayor on the Laquan McDonald case. The activism is all from outside."

Chicago's storied political machine had been an engine of clannish insider politics, fueled by patronage jobs and vote-counting, a system that built on the idea, as the old line had it, that "we don't want nobody that nobody sent." But the machine had been weakening for decades, and now the establishment was being challenged by a new generation of activists. Ja'mal Green was one of them. He had been raised by a single mother who worked as a mail carrier for the postal service. The demands of her work had often left Green isolated. "It was long hours; you get off work, come home tired, go to sleep. And then I'm back at school, and she's back at work. It's the same cycle."

His mother found mentors to provide what she could not. "Great men in the neighborhood," Green said; one was a school principal, another was a film producer. Green was kicked out of nine schools before he found a sense of purpose in the world of entertainment; he became an R&B performer and an actor. When Green was fifteen, Emanuel's administration hired him for a campaign it called "Put the Guns Down!" Green was an ambassador, paid to visit schools and events, handing out posters and appealing for peace—until, that is, he saw the McDonald video. "That was about the moment that I was just like, 'I know what side I want to be on,'" Green said. He has lingered on the sight of smoke rising from the body. "That's where the emotions really struck me—that smoke," he said.

When Green and I met for dinner on the South Side, he wore a thin mustache and browline glasses in the style of Malcolm X. He had a natural sense of culture and the Internet. He had popularized the slogan "Sixteen Shots and a Cover-up," and during a protest outside Emanuel's house, Green wore a T-shirt with the message "Rahm Failed Us." But Green's criticism did not stop with Emanuel. He ticked off the names of Black icons in Chicago politics: "Bobby Rush is a sellout," he said of the congressman who had beaten Obama in the race years earlier. "You got all these people that've been in office that've been selling us out and working with the system." He was critical of older activists, too. "A lot of the last generation has dropped the ball," he said. But he acknowledged the support he received from some, such as Jesse Jackson. "We're kind of now calling the shots," he said. "They have stood behind us, not in front of us. They understand that it's our time, and they need to step back."

To Green and others, the declining population of the Black community was a sign of a place going to pieces. In 2015, murders in Chicago had increased by 58 percent, and the number of nonfatal shootings grew by 43 percent, according to the University of Chicago Crime Lab. The more violent it was, the more people left if they could, which only added fuel to the fire by removing the kinds of mentors who had changed his life. "There are no judges, no doctors. Anybody with money don't want to live in a neighborhood like this. So you're growing up with nobody to look up to," he said. "Most likely, your parents are traveling far to their job, to try to feed you, so they're out of the house most of the time. So you're really raising yourself to an extent." He paused. "There is no village," he said.

As we wrapped up, I asked Green what he made of presidential politics. He had recently attended a Bernie Sanders rally. He wasn't ready to commit his vote, he said, but added, "I like Bernie a lot. Actually, his campaign just called me a little while ago." Like other young Black activists, Green saw Sanders as a break from a generation of Democratic Party ideas, especially about drugs and incarceration. "He understands that marijuana should not be the reason why everybody has Xs on their backs," he said. Most of all, though, he was unwilling to accept the status quo. "He understands exactly what we're going through, and he wants to change it," Green said.

In ways that were, so far, only barely visible, Clinton's campaign was generating a tepid reaction from Black voters. Obama, who remained popular to the end of his term, had all but endorsed her, and had signaled his belief that she represented his natural successor. In private, Obama had gently urged his vice president, Joe Biden, to avoid a race that might split the party; Obama also worried that Biden risked an embarrassing loss as the final act of a dignified career.

In national polls Clinton was handily leading Sanders among Black voters, three to one. But that margin vanished among younger, more progressive Black voters. Sanders had picked up influential supporters, including the author Ta-Nehisi Coates, the actor and activist Harry Belafonte, and Professor Cornel West. Among other arguments, they faulted Clinton for cozy ties to Wall Street and for echoing the myth, in 1996, that some young men were "superpredators," remorseless criminals who required harsher punishment. "Obviously she's preferable to Donald Trump, and I don't blame Black folks who vote for her or support her. I get it," Coates told an interviewer in the summer of 2016. "But I just don't know. When I see her husband defending her use of the 'superpredator,' come on." Coates, who was born in 1975, had come of age when that rhetoric was applied to young men around him in Baltimore. "Talking about how the crime bill actually cut crime, come on," he said. "Defending welfare reform at this hour? Here's the thing that's most damning for me: How do you take six hundred thousand dollars from Goldman Sachs for speeches, knowing you're going to run for president? Somebody says, 'What were you doing?' and you say, 'Well, that's what they offered.' It's a disturbing lack of personal judgment."

In Cornell West's view, Clinton had never fully acknowledged the costs of her support for the 1994 crime bill (though the measure was supported, at the time, by the Black political establishment and by then-congressman Sanders). Moreover, West said, Sanders supported a range of policies that would help the Black community, including a fifteen-dollar minimum wage, an expansive federal jobs program, free college tuition, and single-payer health care. Nobody expected Clinton to achieve the level of support among Black voters that Obama had inspired, but as the primary season progressed, the distinct lack of enthusiasm was becoming clearer, even if the press and her advisers paid little heed. Black voters were splitting sharply along generational lines; over thirty, the majority backed Clinton. Under thirty, they were lining up for Sanders.

Green, the young Chicago activist, became a campaign surrogate and one of the most outspoken Sanders advocates in Chicago. In March, when Green saw that Trump was coming to the University of Illinois at Chicago, he posted to Facebook, "Everyone, get your tickets to this. We're all going in!!!! #SHUTITDOWN." His appeal spread rapidly. On the night of the rally, protesters—mostly students of color, from local public universities—flooded onto the floor of the rally to disrupt the proceedings, while thousands more marched outside. As the scale of the protest became visible, Trump's organizers called off the rally. The protesters rejoiced, but in a sign of things to come, they did not proclaim themselves to be supporters of the Democratic front-runner. In Chicago that night, the protesters were chanting, "Ber-nie, Ber-nie!"

⊢——⊣

A white democratic socialist in his eighth decade was not an obvious favorite for Black and Latino young people on the South Side of Chicago. But Sanders had tapped into a fury in America about corruption, fairness, and political paralysis—the very culture of "thoughts and prayers." His refusal to accept the status quo was not just resonating with progressives in big cities; support for Sanders also found its audience in Appalachia. In the West Virginia Democratic primary in May, Sanders beat Hillary Clinton in every county, a startling victory because Clinton had easily won the state in 2008. Separate polls suggested that in a one-on-one contest in West Virginia, Sanders could beat Trump there, too. "West Virginia is a working-class state," Sanders said, matter-of-factly, after the news broke, and invoked his constant mantra: "We need an economy that works for all of us, not just the one percent."

Sanders's win in West Virginia went almost unnoticed at the time—Clinton already had an insurmountable lead—but it was a blaring siren about the breadth of dissatisfaction at the Democratic establishment. The party had once dictated politics in West Virginia with nearly as much machine-like control as it exercised in Chicago. But Katey Lauer, the environmental activist, was among the West Virginia voters who favored Sanders over Clinton. "That was an anti-establishment vote," she told me. "It's a vote that says, 'The people that have been in control of our state for so long, it's not working—and we reject that political class.'" She said, "For eighty years, Democrats have been in power in our state, and people's lives have gotten worse, and we can argue about if that's entirely the Democratic Party's fault or not, but I don't think it's illogical or irrational for people to reject the Democratic Party."

She hated the way Democratic Party leaders talked about places like West Virginia. "When people are told by, quite frankly, wealthy people in cities that haven't been to the state, that 'You're voting against your own interests, or you're dumb, or you're something,' then, hell yeah, there's going to be resentment about that. Neither party, quite frankly, has been curious about what people need to actually improve their lives. They're curious about how do they maintain their power."

In West Virginia, people prided themselves on a self-narrative of grit and independence, even though it had become the most dependent state in America; nearly 29 percent of all personal income came from federal payments, the highest rate of any state. Work was no guarantee of escaping poverty; many who had jobs reported that they could not afford three meals a day or an adequate place to live. Over lunch one day in Clarksburg, a former state lawmaker named Mike Queen told me, "We've been turned into a poverty-ridden, federal-program-dependent state with no hope."

Queen's family had played a prominent role in local Democratic politics. His father, aunt, and uncle had all held public office, and, in 1988, when Queen was twenty-five, he was elected to the lower house of the state legislature as its youngest member. (He served one term before he was outflanked by a more progressive candidate.) Since 2006, Queen had been on the school board, and the issues that came before him revealed a broad social crisis that undermined his faith in politics-as-usual. He said, "Our state has the highest teenage pregnancy rate in the country. We have one in eight kids in Harrison County living with a grandparent, because of the number of thirty- and forty-year-olds who have drug issues, and we don't have facilities to treat them properly. We have one of the highest misdemeanor incarceration rates, if not the highest, for illegal prescription drug use in the country. We're having to build more prisons for our own people—in a state with only one-point-eight million people!"

Queen had given up on the Democratic Party—but he wasn't throwing his support to Bernie Sanders. He was becoming a Republican. Many others were, too. West Virginia was passing a series of milestones in its partisan transformation; after Senator Rockefeller retired in 2015, he was succeeded by Shelley Moore Capito, the first Republican senator from West Virginia since 1956. Republicans had also gained control of the House of Delegates for the first time in eighty-three years. The state had moved so sharply to the right that, in 2012, President Obama lost all fifty-five counties, a first for a presidential candidate of either major party. In the Democratic presidential primary that year, a challenger had won 41 percent of the vote—impressive in part because the candidate, Keith Judd, was serving seventeen and a half years in a federal prison for extortion.

The larger fact was that, year by year, the West Virginia public was losing faith in politics at all. In 1960, more than 75 percent of eligible voters had cast ballots—almost 14 percent more than the national average. By 2012, West Virginia's turnout had sunk to 46.3 percent, the second-lowest level in America. Over the decades, the compounding effects of political cynicism and influence had broken public faith in government. Half a century after Harrington called Appalachian poverty the "other" America, the historian Ronald Eller, of the University of Kentucky, concluded, "Appalachia was not different from the rest of America; it was in fact a mirror of what the nation was becoming." Another historian, John Alexander Williams, reached a similar conclusion. "In some ways, West Virginia no longer lags the nation; it is leading it," he told me. "Nationally, the rate of voter participation has declined as well, and the question is why?" The answer, he suspected, lay in the broad apparatus of democratic distortion.

After changing parties, Queen told me, "I'm not saying the Democrats encouraged" the state's distress. "But the Democrats have allowed it to happen, with no planning for how we're going to get out of this hole." Year by year, people in West Virginia were only more dependent on federal relief; the number of West Virginians receiving Medicaid had *grown* by more than half. It clashed with their image of self-reliance. Even as West Virginians like Mike Queen gravitated to the Republican Party, they had their misgivings, but they liked the mantras of self-reliance. "I don't think people believe that the Republican Party is going to save them," Queen said. "West Virginians want to save ourselves."

It was a dignifying analysis—a framing that made support for Trump into a matter of heroic independence. But Jim Griffin, the former head of the NAACP in Clarksburg, offered me a blunter description. "It comes down to three things: abortion, guns, and immigrants." Trump, in that sense, had mastered the national iconography of politics and divorced it from the actual conditions on the ground. Jim recalled a conversation with a neighbor who complained of Democrats, "They're bringing all these immigrants here." He went on, "And I said, 'Let me ask you, sir, how many immigrants on a daily basis do you run into here in West Virginia?'" They represented just 2 percent of the state population—one of the lowest levels in America. "I said, 'Probably the only time you run into an immigrant is when you go to the doctor.' And the doctors live in a ritzy area so the everyday person doesn't even socialize with them. He said, 'Well, they're coming here, taking my job.' And I said, 'What jobs do they take?'"

When Jim's friends and neighbors took to praising Trump, Jim liked to challenge them: "I'd like to see you go up to Trump Tower as a coal miner and see if you can get in there. See if he respects you." But Jim underestimated his neighbors' hunger for a cause. "He makes people think that they could be something that they aren't," he said. It was an enchanting form of escape, he realized. Among his civic commitments, Jim made frequent trips across West Virginia, recruiting people for community college. But more and more he found that Trump's dream palace of a future built on whiteness and coal was thrilling people. "I encourage them to go to community college and get a skill, but they don't want to have anything to do with it. They're set on going back into the coal mines," he said. "They said, 'Trump is going to turn this around and give us all an equal chance.'"

———

As I traveled between Clarksburg and Chicago in that year of election, I was sometimes struck that, for all their differences, Black Chicagoans and white Appalachians had come to share a sensation that was calcifying in America's political culture—a feeling of being trapped by an undertow of economics and history, of being ill-served by institutions, of being estranged from a political machinery that was refined, above all, to serve itself.

If Americans needed any further evidence that politics seemed increasingly detached from real life, the Supreme Court provided it: in June, the court overturned the conviction of the former Virginia governor, Robert McDonnell, who had hoovered up the gifts of the patron who had asked for the governor's help. Chief Justice John Roberts wrote that the gifts—a Rolex, ball gowns, tens of thousands of dollars in cash—were merely "distasteful"; they did not produce what the law narrowly defines as "official acts." The McDonnell verdict, which was widely criticized by activists for ethics in government, represented a moment of liberation for other corrupt politicians as well. The former congressman William J. Jefferson, a Democrat from Louisiana, who was best known for having stashed $90,000 in bribes in his freezer, walked out of prison.

In Clarksburg, my mind often returned to Trump's nostalgic mantra, "Make America Great Again." The word "nostalgia" is derived from
the Greek for "home" and for "pain," and for years West Virginia had
been steadily losing a sense of home, while gaining a sense of pain. City
records showed that nobody in Clarksburg had embarked on the construction of a new building in five years. More than half a century after
Kennedy had considered Clarksburg important enough to stop there on
his campaign for president, the sidewalks and storefronts during this
election were silent. Nobody was coming. Banners hung from lampposts with the slogan "Proud past. Unlimited future," but it was hard to
conjure any image of that future except for a hollow promise of reviving
the past.

Once you started to see metaphors for the failing machinery of politics, it was impossible to ignore them. One morning in June, most of
the headlines were focused on national and foreign dramas—in particular, the United Kingdom was voting on the once-implausible idea of
exiting the European Union—but in West Virginia, the news was all
about rain: a warm, hard rain that had started to fall just after dawn and
wouldn't stop.

The rain poured down the hills and pooled in the valleys. Then it
surged out of the creeks and formed roiling brown rivers that tumbled
down the main streets of towns and cities. Inside their homes, people
grabbed family photos and laptops and cash and waded into the rising
waters, trying to stay connected to one another by makeshift ropes made
of bedsheets and extension cords.

By the time the water hit the houses in towns like White Sulphur
Springs, it was moving at sixty miles an hour; it punched through
windows and enveloped the people inside with a force so strong it felt
supernatural—"the hand of God pushing down on you," as one survivor
put it. The floodwaters swept homes and bridges from their foundations,
and heaved cars into the woods.

By the end, twenty-three people were dead and some of them were
swept so far from home that it took rescuers eight weeks to locate the
last body. It was one of the worst floods in West Virginia's long history
of calamity. People called it a "thousand-year" flood, but that expression

no longer held true. As the waters receded, FEMA warned the people of West Virginia that, in a warming world, floods of that scale would hit them "more frequently than previously thought." In response, the state's Republican leadership moved to squelch any suggestion that the disaster was related to a warming planet or the burning of coal. State senator Chandler Swope, the Republican cochair of a joint flood committee, informed a local reporter that climate change had been "happening for millions of years" and "you just have to deal with it."

In the barest gesture toward the future, the state established a "Resiliency Office." But when reporters checked on it a few years later, it had one employee. Survivors went on with their lives, but many of them never shook the physical sensation of the moment it began—an instant they could not see but could feel, when the ground turned to liquid, and the foundations beneath their lives started to fall away.

FOURTEEN

THE COMBAT MINDSET

IT WAS MAY 2016—six months to Election Day—and 70,000 members of the National Rifle Association were visiting Louisville, Kentucky, for an experience that combined qualities of a political convention, a trade show, and Comic-Con. A giant banner promised "11 Acres of Guns and Gear." For kids, there were .22-caliber handguns designed to look like military-issue sidearms. In a gun review for the magazine *Junior Shooters*, a thirteen-year-old raved that his weapon "looks cool and feels like a Beretta, which I think is awesome." For adults, much of the business revolved around the AR-15, a semiautomatic rifle known in the industry as the "Barbie doll of guns," because it was designed to keep buyers coming back for new grips, sights, and other mix-and-match accessories.

In the world of guns, as in the world of Trump, it was sometimes difficult to separate politics from profit. Inside the doorway, I encountered a lumbering figure in a giant bird costume—the mascot of the NRA's Eddie Eagle GunSafe program, which teaches children up to fourth grade not to touch guns. After fourth grade, the industry hoped they would become avid consumers. Attracting younger members was a consuming priority for an industry beset by a rapidly graying customer base. A report by its trade association urged recruitment programs "aimed at middle school level, or earlier." *Shooting Sports Retailer*, a trade publication, was warning bluntly that "the problem with failing to recruit and grow is that numbers equate to political power."

Since entering politics, Trump had fashioned himself into the most fervently pro-gun nominee in presidential history; he was calling for a national right to carry concealed firearms, among other changes to loosen gun laws. His enthusiasm was rewarded. At gun shows that year, vendors were selling olive-green T-shirts marked "Trump's Army." Elements of his platform were well suited to the prevailing ethic. After Trump promised to resume the use of waterboarding, vendors added shirts in lifeguard-style red and white, marked "Waterboarding Instructor."

In recent years, the NRA had found ways to draw on the rising resentment in American politics. In the years since the Tea Party and Occupy emerged as mirror images of disillusionment, the new populism had presented opportunities. Though the gun lobby thrived on its intimate dealings with political leaders, it crafted a public message that portrayed powerful Americans as seeking to disarm and endanger less-privileged citizens. As Trump prepared to take the stage, the crowd watched a video about "political elites and billionaires." "The thought of average people owning firearms makes them uncomfortable," the narrator said. "They don't like how the men and women who build their office buildings, vacation homes, and luxury cars, who mop their floors, clean their clothes, and serve their dinner, have access to the same level of protection as their armed security guards."

Trump emerged to raucous applause, and he brought up the news of a recent massacre of fourteen people in San Bernardino, California. "If we had guns on the other side, it wouldn't have been that way," he said. He made a gun out of his thumb and forefinger, and said, "I would have—boom!" The crowd erupted. Trump called on Hillary Clinton to give up her Secret Service protection. "They should immediately disarm," he said. "And let's see how good they do." He promised his audience a vast, encompassing relief from their worries about the future of America. "We're going to bring it back to a real place, where we don't have to be so frightened."

In her book *The Monarchy of Fear*, the philosopher and classicist Martha Nussbaum called it a "necessary precondition for anger." As early as the fourth century BCE, Aristotle had already discerned the formula by which political speakers could whip audiences into a wrathful frenzy: frame a matter of life or death; portray the event as imminent; declare an emergency so grave that it was beyond the listener's ability to defend himself alone. Richard Nixon knew it. "People react to fear, not love," he said, according to his aide William Safire. "They don't teach that in Sunday school, but it's true."

Fear, in the right hands, was a powerful tool of profit. Cambridge Analytica, a firm that extracted data from Facebook and other sites, specialized in exploiting the underlying emotional opportunities specific to each user. "You didn't know that was a fear until you saw something that just evoked that reaction from you," an executive named Mark Turnbull explained to an undercover reporter. The firm, as he put it, sought "to drop the bucket further down the well than anybody else, to understand what are those really deep-seated underlying fears." As Alexander Nix, the CEO, admitted, "It sounds a dreadful thing to say, but these are things that don't necessarily need to be true as long as they're believed."

——

Nothing in American culture or commerce brought Nixon's principle to life more vividly than the role of guns, which had come to resonate on the level of cosmology. Around the world, there was only one developed country regularly beset by mass shootings—and only one country where it was legal and easy to amass a personal arsenal. Americans had accumulated 310 million firearms, roughly one per person, the highest rate of civilian gun ownership in the world. (The second-highest was Yemen, which had barely half the rate.)

Americans and foreigners often assumed that America's singular gun culture was an outgrowth of the frontier history, back to the Old West, but that was false; it only dated to the 1970s. For most of U.S. history, gun owners mocked the idea of walking around with guns. In 1934, the president of the National Rifle Association, Karl Frederick, testified to Congress, "I do not believe in the promiscuous toting of guns. I think it should be sharply restricted and only under licenses." In 1967, after a public protest by armed Black Panthers in Sacramento, Governor Ronald Reagan told reporters that he saw "no reason why on the street today a citizen should be carrying loaded weapons."

But the politics around fear, race, and warfare were changing. In 1972, Jeff Cooper, a firearms instructor and Marine veteran who had fought in World War II and Korea, published *Principles of Personal Defense*, which became a classic among gun-rights activists. His book captured a generation's anxieties: "Before World War II, one could stroll in the parks and streets of the city after dark with hardly any risk," he wrote. But in "today's world of permissive atrocity" it was time to reexamine one's interactions with fellow citizens. Adapting a concept from the Marines, he urged civilian gun owners to assume a state of alertness that he called "The Combat Mindset." He wrote, "The one who fights back retains his dignity and his self-respect."

Despite Cooper's success, by the late 1970s American gun manufacturers were in business trouble because of a basic problem: a gun made out of steel or plastic remained usable for decades. If companies wanted to remain profitable, they needed new customers or, short of that, novel ways to sell more guns to old customers. This was not a new problem—it was Samuel Colt who was said to have coined the phrase "new and improved"—but it was worsening because hunting was in decline. Rural America was emptying out; in 1977, a third of all adults lived in a house with at least one hunter; by 2014, that statistic had been cut in half. Mike Weisser, who entered the gun business in 1965 and worked as a wholesaler, retailer, instructor, and writer, told me, "The gun industry, which had been able to ride on an American cultural motif of the West, and of hunting, is realizing that's gone."

They found their solution in politics. In 1977, at the NRA's annual meeting, conservative activists led by Harlon Carter, a former chief of the U.S. Border Patrol, wrested control from leaders who had been focused on rifle training and recreation rather than on politics, and created the modern gun-rights movement. In 1987, the NRA successfully lobbied lawmakers in Florida to relax the rules that required concealed-carry applicants to demonstrate "good cause" for a permit, such as a job transporting large quantities of cash. Under the new rules, almost anyone was eligible, and two dozen other states later followed suit.

In the decades that followed, the industry learned to exploit moments that could kick-start sales. In 1992, in an indelible moment in America's torturous relationship to race, a Los Angeles jury acquitted four police officers of using excessive force in the beating of Rodney King, and the city erupted in riots. "It was the first time that you could see a live riot on video while it was going on," Weisser said. "They had a helicopter floating around when a white guy pulled up to the intersection. These Black guys pull him out of the truck and are beating the shit out of him right below that helicopter." The new market for self-defense guns was born. Weisser said, "That was the moment, and if you talked about 'crime' everybody knew what you meant."

But the boost in sales from riots was temporary. The gun industry was facing the bleak fact that America was becoming, by any measure, a *less* dangerous place. Violent crime peaked in 1991, during the crack-cocaine era, and dropped by almost half in the two decades that followed. Victimization rates of rape or sexual assault fell 60 percent from their historic highs. For the gun business, another moment of salvation arrived in the form of the September 11 attacks. Richard Feldman, a former NRA lobbyist, told me, "The threat is no different on 9/12 than it was on 9/10, but the perception of it changed dramatically." Survivalist fantasies about the breakdown of society "crossed over from being the lunatic fringe to more serious after September eleventh," Feldman said. "It's not about the government coming after you. It's about terrorists taking out the electrical grid."

The industry had discovered a marketing opportunity that was as fruitful for gun sales as it was for political opportunists like Tom Tancredo, the congressman who took to warning that undocumented immigrants were "coming here to kill you and to kill me and our families." Since September 11, a trend under way since the 1980s had accelerated; police forces expanded the ranks of SWAT teams and adopted more lethal hardware. In practice, local SWAT teams rarely had anything to do with terrorism—statistics showed that most of their work was serving warrants on drug offenses—but their expansion helped popularize the new military aesthetic.

The archetypal American warrior was no longer a nameless GI with a buzz cut and an M-16, humping through the jungle. The new icons were wreathed in heroic individualism, figures like the Navy SEAL Chris Kyle, who served four tours in Iraq and published a memoir, *American Sniper: The Autobiography of the Most Lethal Sniper in U.S. Military History*. It led to a Hollywood blockbuster about a bearded, brooding iconoclast with a ball cap and a tricked-out sniper's rifle. As in life, the film ended when Kyle was killed at a shooting range in Texas in 2013 by a fellow veteran with post-traumatic stress disorder. Sidney Muller, on his Facebook page, posted an image of a bearded member of the Army Special Forces who had returned to Afghanistan even after his leg was amputated. "This dude is a badass," Muller wrote.

In the gun world, the industry became so focused on promoting "tactical" gear, suitable for making war, that some hunters felt ignored. David E. Petzal, a columnist for *Field & Stream*, mocked the "SEAL wannabes" and wrote that "you have to look fairly hard for something designed to kill animals instead of people." The contempt was mutual; some concealed-carry activists call hunters "Fudds," as in Elmer.

In the Obama era, guns sales set new records. The demand to use guns anywhere was an essential part of modern white-identity politics. In 2008, Rick Wilson, a Florida-based Republican ad maker, produced ads attacking Obama by showing the most provocative statements of his former pastor, Jeremiah Wright. Wilson said later, "I wanted to scare the living shit out of white people in Pennsylvania and Ohio."

The NRA embraced the maxim "The only thing that stops a bad guy with a gun is a good guy with a gun." It hardly mattered that it was plainly false: a study by the FBI found that, in 160 "active shooter" incidents from 2000 to 2013, armed citizens who were not security guards stopped the "bad guy" on one occasion (when a patron shot an attacker at the Players Bar and Grill, in Winnemucca, Nevada, in 2008). By any accounting, the proliferation of guns was a lethal fact of life. More American civilians died by gunfire in the decade leading up to Trump's visit to the NRA than all the Americans who were killed in combat in

World War II. Though high-profile massacres attracted the most attention, shootings in America were often impulsive, up close, or accidental.

In an average year, more American children under the age of five died from gunshots than police officers in the line of duty. In the decades since the Columbine shooting in 1999, which we had covered in Clarksburg's *Exponent Telegram* as an aberration, gun violence had hit another 249 American schools. In a kindergarten classroom in the Boston suburbs, a poster taught the children a nursery rhyme to be sung to the tune of "Twinkle, Twinkle, Little Star":

> *Lockdown, lockdown, lock the door*
> *Shut the lights off, say no more*
> *Go behind the desk and hide*
> *Wait until it's safe inside*
> *Lockdown, lockdown, it's all done*
> *Now it's time to have some fun!*

———

Buried in the statistics on gun ownership was a profound fact: guns were consolidating into fewer and fewer hands. In 1977, more than half of all households in America had a gun in the house. But by 2014, it was less than a third. And yet the number of guns sold in America continued to climb. The result: each American gun owner had accumulated an average of eight guns. The boundary between the tribe of armed citizens and everyone else was stark. "Gun control" was such a poisonous term in some communities that, in a survey on American fears in 2016, more Americans reported that they were afraid of "gun control" than they were of "loved ones dying."

Very often, when I spoke to people about guns, they framed it as a matter of local culture; if people had always been free to hunt in these hills, what difference did it make to people hundreds of miles away? But in twenty-first-century America, very little stayed local very long anymore. In 2016, an analysis of data from the Bureau of Alcohol, Tobacco, Firearms, and Explosives found that more guns from West Virginia were trafficked to other states and used in crimes than from any other state. West Virginia's guns were showing up in places such as Philadelphia, Albany, and Chicago at a rate more than twice the national average. Federal agents named it the "iron pipeline."

For all of the nostalgic talk of hunting and tradition, modern gun culture was fed, overwhelmingly, by more contemporary features of American culture—especially marketing, partisanship, and other tools that were honed to manipulate perception. Though crime rates were dropping, almost 70 percent of Americans believed that crime had *risen* in the previous year, a 2015 study showed. By some analyses, the misperceptions grew partly out of changes in lifestyle: as people drove more and receded into the world of "bowling alone," they had less contact with neighbors, and they reported a greater fear of crime. Other studies focused on the news media's tendency to overplay low-probability threats. An analysis of Los Angeles television stations in 2009 found that local broadcasts often started with crimes that were not even in Los Angeles, leaving viewers with the impression that the biggest thing happening most days was something awful. That pattern only intensified after Fox fixated on Chicago's "death and destruction," as Bill O'Reilly had it. On national television, people could also see endless repetition of the falling Twin Towers, even though, in the first decade of the twenty-first century, the odds of an American dying by terrorism were less than one eighth as large as the chance of death by falling off a ladder.

By the summer of 2016, the fear business was thriving. Studies of the effect of terrorism on American attitudes found a distinct difference between the effects of September 11 and of previous terror attacks. After the terrorist bombing of the federal building in Oklahoma City in 1995, Americans reported an elevated fear of falling victim to terrorism, but the effect subsided after about eighteen months. By contrast, the fear of terrorism remained elevated more than a decade after September 11—and it surged, especially, following the rise of ISIS in 2014. Trump encouraged that sensation in his campaign patter; he would reject Syrian refugees, he said, because "they could be ISIS."

At the NRA convention, I wandered around after Trump's speech and came upon a large, busy exhibit for the U.S. Concealed Carry Association. It was a company based in Wisconsin that sold training materials and merchandise, as well as a startling product called "self-defense insurance"; for a fee, they would subsidize your legal fees, and help manage your legal defense, in the event that you shot someone with your gun. Members received daily emails urging them to buy additional training and insurance in case, as a typical email put it, "God forbid, the unthinkable should happen to you, and you're forced by some scumbag in a drug fueled rage to pull the trigger." For the right price, the association even promised to help people gain an advantage in court: "Should you face charges, we'll provide and pay for expert witnesses to testify on your behalf."

Tim Schmidt, the founder, told me, "When I had kids, I went through what I call my 'self-defense awakening.'" He had launched the magazine *Concealed Carry*, which encouraged people to see themselves as part of a community. "This lifestyle is complete with its own peer groups, activities, and even language," the editor, Kevin Michalowski, wrote. Later, when I looked Schmidt up online, I discovered that he had a sideline in packaging his sales approach, which he called "tribal marketing." It was based on generating revenue by emphasizing the boundaries of a community. "We all have the NEED to BELONG," he wrote in a presentation titled "How to Turn One of Mankind's Deepest Needs Into Cold, Hard CASH." In a section called "How Do You Create Belief & Belonging?" he explained, "You can't have a yin without a yang. Must have an enemy."

For years afterward, I received emails from the NRA that mingled the promise of guns and wealth. A typical message began with the subject line "Evan—Win Guns & Gold," and opened to reveal a mountain of gold coins and firearms—an AR-15, a .45 revolver, a pair of hunting rifles. The NRA was running its own lottery, with the appeal: "Strike it RICH In our BIGGEST Sweepstakes EVER! Hundreds of Winners Guaranteed."

In two days at the convention, talking to members of the rank and file, I was struck by how many people described their experience of armed citizenship as a form of belonging. Sid O'Nan, a genial father of two teenagers who worked as an IT specialist for the Department of Agriculture, told me that he never had much relationship to guns, but in recent years he had seen more and more of them around. "As I would invite buddies over, they would always have handguns," he said. He had taken to carrying a Glock 17. "I just see all the garbage that's going on, and I thought, You know what? I couldn't live with myself if I couldn't be there to protect my family," he said. "I don't know firearms. I don't know ballistics. I don't know holsters. I'm just trying to glean from a friend what he says. I've asked him, 'Should I go for the head if somebody has full-body armor?' He says, 'No, just center mass. Your nine-millimeter will knock them to the ground, and you can get the heck out of there.'"

For many of the people I met, carrying a gun, much like joining the Trump movement, carried a meaning larger than itself. At the airport on the way out of town, I watched a dad hauling an infant car seat upholstered in the colors of hunting camouflage. When I saw that, I paused to absorb the full symbolism of it. It seemed to set a new water-mark for "tribal marketing"; nobody was driving that baby around the woods hunting deer, but a camo car seat was an announcement of whom you wanted to associate with, and whom you did not. As Trump put it to an audience that spring, "The only important thing is the unification of the people—because the other people don't mean anything."

———

In West Virginia, which had the fourth-highest rate of gun ownership in the country, Joe Manchin played a pioneering role in expanding the stagecraft around guns in political advertising. In his campaign for the Senate in 2010, he developed a television ad that began normally enough. Manchin strode through a rolling country field in autumn. He offered a few lines of campaign boilerplate—"I'll take on Washington and this administration"—and then he lifted a rifle to his shoulder. "I'll cut federal spending," he continued, "and I'll repeal the bad parts of Obamacare. I sued the EPA and I'll take dead aim at the cap-and-trade bill, because it's bad for West Virginia." Then he fired a bullet through a copy of climate-change legislation, which was pinned to a target down-range. The camera zoomed in on the entry point, the center mass of the bill, a few inches below the introductory text, which began, "In the Senate of the United States."

For decades, politicians had been photographed with guns, but this was the first time anyone had assassinated a piece of proposed legislation on film. In Washington, Manchin's ad touched off an arms race, of sorts, in political advertising. Other candidates took to shooting legislation in their ads, and by 2014, the symbolism had escalated to the point that a Republican candidate in Arizona upped the stakes by showing himself shooting a copy of the Obamacare bill with a handgun, a rifle, and a semiautomatic before, finally, running it through a wood chipper.

Manchin's advertising had helped make the combat mindset more explicit in Appalachian politics. Trump made use of that evolution because otherwise he had little in common with that part of the country. Long before he ran for president, he told *Playboy* in a tone of amused disbelief, "The coal miner gets black-lung disease, his son gets it, then *his* son. If *I* had been the son of a coal miner, I would have left the damn mines. But most people don't have the imagination—or whatever—to leave their mine. They don't have 'it.'"

But on the campaign, he adopted so much of the culture of Appalachia that it was easy to overlook that his message contained little more than an economic promise. At a rally in Charleston, West Virginia, he put on a coal miner's helmet. "We're going to put those miners back to work. We're going to get those mines open," he said. "You're going to be working your asses off." The crowd went nuts.

The lawyer Kevin Barrett, the West Virginia native who challenged the hedge funds' attempts to drop health-care benefits, told me, "It's all complete and total B.S., but people said, 'Yeah, we know it is, but what is anyone else promising?' You just have to understand that nobody else is talking *to* them." In Barrett's view, Trump's popularity was the consummate result of a legacy of economic decisions to extract profits from Appalachia, no matter the human, ecological, and political costs. "Those kinds of decisions helped create this environment in which the state of

West Virginia—which used to be a union state—turned ridiculously red, and red in a Trump kind of way," he said.

The contrast with Clinton was stark and easy to exaggerate. In a moment that Clinton later said she regretted more than any other on the campaign, she told a West Virginia audience, "We're going to put a lot of coal miners and coal companies out of business." Her line, ripped from context, played endlessly in Republican attack ads, cut off from her compassionate sentences afterward: "We're going to make it clear that we don't want to forget those people," she said. "Now we've got to move away from coal and all the other fossil fuels, but I don't want to move away from the people who did the best they could to produce energy that we relied on."

The truth was, even if coal-country propagandists had not edited out Clinton's fuller comments, Democrats had all but lost Appalachia, because they were too slow to recognize the full scale of its despair. As the coal industry imploded, the Obama administration developed plans to create jobs and direct federal investments into struggling towns. But as Ken Ward Jr., the award-winning investigative reporter in West Virginia, put it, Democrats were "too little and too late" and too quiet about it. "How often did any West Virginia Democrats talk about the black-lung crisis?" he wrote.

Trump's promises of help were vague and inflated, but to his fans, his combat with the professional class was a gratifying twist on the usual class identities. He was decoupling money from credentialed status. He was a billionaire who indulged his appetites for Big Macs and porn stars and casinos. "Brashly wealthy celebrities epitomize the fantasy of being wildly rich while losing none of your working-class cred," Joan Williams wrote. For most people, America's billionaires were far away—a source of abstract entertainment on *The Apprentice* or *Shark Tank* or *Lifestyles of the Rich and Famous*. But, as Williams put it, working people encountered "class affronts from professionals every day: the doctor who unthinkingly patronizes the medical technician, the harried office worker who treats the security guard as invisible, the overbooked business traveler who snaps at the TSA agent."

Over time, Trump's mantra of proud victimhood furnished a combat mindset for politics. It popularized an irredentist claim on a culture. Julie Cryser, the city editor of *The Exponent Telegram* during the campaign against the Ku Klux Klan, sensed that Trump's constant talk of threats was producing an effect beyond the ranks of the far right. "He says, 'Everybody's trying to take their guns, everybody's trying to take away their rights, everybody's trying to bring them down.' And then it's filtered into that somewhat moderate group where they're like, 'Yeah! We *are* getting a raw deal. And why *can't* we have 'locker room' conversations?'" Trump made people more comfortable going public with ideas they had hidden. Cryser went on, "If you go back to the KKK rally, even if you had improper thoughts, you weren't going to be seen at a KKK rally. Now you have carte blanche to go to that KKK rally and you're 'okay,' because you're just showing that 'this is who you are,' and these are 'your rights as an American citizen' to go do this. It's disappointing to find out that there are so many people who now feel empowered. Your neighbor who you thought was just down the middle was really, really over the top."

In the end, Trump dominated West Virginia by 42 points, a margin surpassed only by a bleaker measure: 43 percent of West Virginia adults did not vote at all.

———

Trump's embrace of the NRA's warnings to "political elites and billionaires" made him an awkward fit for political elites and billionaires. The seacoast of Fairfield County had always been one of America's most affluent places, but by 2016 it was the wealthiest metropolitan area in the United States, outstripping the oil country of Midland, Texas, and the technology hub of San Francisco. Even though a string of tycoons had fled Connecticut in search of lower taxes, the latest *Forbes* rankings of the world's billionaires listed fifteen of them in the "Greater Greenwich Area."

But as Trump's lead proved durable, a certain calculation took hold among some of the elite Republicans who scorned him. Leora Levy, who had denounced Trump as "vulgar" and "ill-mannered" in *Greenwich*

Time, changed her view. She gave $50,000 to his campaign and the party, and explained to a local reporter, "I am a very enthusiastic supporter of Donald Trump today because the proof is in the numbers, and the numbers are terrific."

Thomas Peterffy, a billionaire who owned the largest estate in Greenwich, donated to Trump but told me he did not admire him. "When the choice is between two ideologies, then it's a luxury to dwell on the personalities of the candidates," Peterffy said. "It's a luxury that we cannot afford." Having made his fortune as a pioneer in digital trading, he told me that the choice between Trump and Clinton was between "a high degree of government regulation or a diminished amount of government regulation, because, basically, that's how the U.S. will get to socialism—increasing government regulation."

From outside, it was easy to misread the broader politics of Greenwich: like much of America's coasts, the Gold Coast had swung left, culturally and politically, since the days of Prescott Bush. The largest share of voters in Greenwich was unaffiliated; though Republicans still held an edge over Democrats, the margin was fewer than four thousand registered voters. Thirty-eight percent of its public-school students were minorities, mostly Latino; in some elementary schools, at least half the students qualified for free or reduced-price lunch. Many of their parents worked in local service jobs, bearing high rents and expenses in order to access some of the country's best public schools. Frank Farricker, a real-estate developer and a Democratic activist, said, "I tell everybody that Greenwich only discriminates on the basis of one color: green."

But that portrait—of liberal cosmopolitans appalled by Trump—obscured a potent element of American politics: the executive class of the Republican Party. Its members were wealthier, more conservative, and more politically active than their forebears, in ways that were helping Trump edge closer to the White House. Understanding how he was attracting the overwhelming support of Republicans required an accounting of not only what he promised Americans at the bottom but also what he provided Americans at the top.

The story of Trump's rise was often told as a hostile takeover. In truth, it was something closer to a joint venture, in which members of

America's elite accepted the terms of Trumpism as the price of power. Long before anyone imagined that Trump might become president, a generation of unwitting patrons had paved the way for him. From Greenwich and places like it, they launched a set of financial, philanthropic, and political projects that changed American ideas about government, taxes, and the legitimacy of the liberal state. In every element of his commercial and political persona, Trump was a consummation of that project. He stood for a liberation from restraint and a willingness to go to war for that liberation. He was contemptuous of political correctness, dismissive of climate change, and scornful of sacrifice; he lampooned prisoners of war. Most of all, of course, he stood for a belief in unbridled self-enrichment, and on that basis some of his more genteel supporters were willing to overlook the rest. As Mitch McConnell had said of himself, they wanted to win.

Even as the full implications of Trump's politics were becoming impossible to explain away, David Duke, the former grand wizard of the Ku Klux Klan, called Trump a "great opportunity," telling listeners of his radio show, "He's certainly somebody that we should get behind." Two brothers from South Boston attacked a homeless Hispanic man, breaking his nose and urinating on his face. They told police, "Donald Trump was right—all these illegals need to be deported." Trump continued to up the rhetoric against immigrants; he called for a ban on Muslim immigration, a religious prohibition that was unlike anything in American history. In every respect, Trump was ushering a spirit of bigotry onto the main stage of American politics more overtly than any figure in decades.

As Connecticut Republicans prepared to vote in their primary, political observers predicted that John Kasich, the moderate governor of Ohio, would prevail in towns and cities from Greenwich to Fairfield. Instead, Trump largely dominated the region.

America's country-club Republicans didn't have much in common with the clichéd image of Trump's admirers: anxious about losing status to minorities, resentful of imperious elites, and marooned in places where life expectancy had fallen. But the full picture has never been that simple. As early as May 2016, exit polls and other data showed that

Trump supporters earned an average of $72,000 a year, while supporters of Hillary Clinton averaged $11,000 less. Two thirds of Trump's supporters had incomes higher than the national median—sometimes, as in Greenwich, much higher.

Lee Hanley, the patron who had commissioned Pat Caddell to find a path to Republican victory, concluded that Trump was the closest thing they would find to a Candidate Smith. Trump had none of Reagan's optimism, but he had name recognition, money, and a preternatural sense of how a billionaire could surf the emotions kicked up by the financial crisis. Their conviction persuaded Robert Mercer to invest in Trump, and other wealthy donors followed. As Election Day approached, Charlie Glazer, a Greenwich money manager who had served as George W. Bush's ambassador to El Salvador, began talking to friends, "rationalizing why we should all vote for Trump," one recalls.

After a certain point, no revelation seemed to hurt him—not his mockery of war heroes or his voice captured on the *Access Hollywood* tape, boasting about sexually assaulting women. One by one, Republicans threw themselves behind him. Kellyanne Conway became his campaign manager. Hope Hicks, who had once captained the Greenwich high school lacrosse team, served as his spokeswoman. Linda McMahon, a Greenwich resident and former professional-wrestling executive, became a favorite for a presidential appointment. (She later headed the Small Business Administration.)

In Greenwich, Edward Dadakis, a corporate insurance broker who had been involved with Republican politics for fifty years, told me that many of his friends remained "below the radar screen." He went on, "In a sense, I'm one of them. I'm out there in the public domain, so people know where I stand, but in 2016, for the first election ever, I did not put a bumper sticker on my car." He worried how strangers would react. He said, "I still have two 'Make America Great Again' hats at home, wrapped in plastic."

As expected, Clinton beat Trump in Greenwich's overall count—57 to 39 percent. But the results contained a startling fact: Trump's greatest support in Greenwich was not in the middle-class sections of downtown. It was in two of the wealthiest precincts—the Tenth and Eleventh

Districts, which sprawl across the lush northern backcountry, encompassing the Round Hill Club, where Prescott Bush once reigned, and the estate of Steve Cohen, the investor with the nine-foot wall. Cohen, whose hedge fund had pleaded guilty to insider trading, donated $1 million to support the inauguration. Thomas Peterffy chipped in $150,000. Charlie Glazer joined the transition. In all, just 158 American families had donated half of all the money to candidates on the ballot. "That's a banana republic democracy," Lawrence Lessig, the campaign-finance activist, observed. "That's not an American democracy."

Lee Hanley didn't live to see it. He died in Greenwich, four days before the 2016 election. Bannon wished that more people knew about Hanley's discreet contribution to the movement. "Lee Hanley is like, when you read the history of the American Revolution or the Civil War—all these great events—you find out about these individuals in back that never won any credit, but, if it was not for them, the victory would not be achieved," he told a conservative audience in 2017. "He had a real love of the hobbits, of the deplorables, and he put his money where his mouth was."

———

So much attention centered on the surge in white votes for Trump that many people overlooked prescient signals about African American voters. Across the country, the Black voter turnout rate in a presidential election declined for the first time in twenty years, falling seven points from 2012. At the very moment that white turnout was rising, the share of Black votes fell farthest in crucial battleground states, such as Michigan and Wisconsin, where the election was decided by less than one point.

The result partly reflected the effects of voter suppression: since 2012, Republican leaders in numerous states had passed laws that raised the threshold for voter identification, reduced the window for early voting, and eliminated same-day voter registration—each of which was shown to reduce the number of Black voters. The Trump campaign, by its own admission, also used social-media ads emphasizing Clinton's reference to "superpredators" to discourage Black turnout. A senior campaign official told Bloomberg, "We have three major voter suppression operations under way"—targeting idealistic white liberals, young women, and African Americans.

As Americans later discovered, the potentially pivotal power of Black voters also attracted the involvement of Russian agents of disinformation. A month before Election Day, a Russian-controlled Instagram account called "Woke Blacks" told followers that "we'd surely be better off without voting AT ALL." A little less than a week before the election, Russian agents purchased Instagram ads to promote an account called "Blacktivist," which declared: "Choose peace and vote for Jill Stein [the Green Party nominee]. Trust me, it's not a wasted vote."

Beyond the manipulation, Clinton never generated enough enthusiasm. In all, she won 88 percent of the Black vote, the same percentage that John Kerry won in 2004, which was not sufficient to overcome Trump's insurgent effect on white voters. The results were dramatic. A study by the Center for American Progress found that if Clinton had achieved the level of Black turnout that Obama received in 2012, she would have won Pennsylvania, Wisconsin, Michigan, Florida, and North Carolina—which would have tipped the results in the Electoral College. Even though Trump received one of the lowest levels of support from Black voters of any Republican in decades, he told a crowd in Pennsylvania, "They didn't come out to vote for Hillary. They didn't come out. And that was a big—so thank you to the African American community." The crowd applauded.

In one Chicago neighborhood, the scene on Election Day offered a fitting finale to a campaign punctuated by the killing of Laquan McDonald and defined, above all, by Trump's combat mindset. Three decades after Reese Clark was bused through protesters to his school in Mount Greenwood, the neighborhood that had been nicknamed "Chicago's Little Rock" was once again the site of a bitter racist clash.

A few days before the election, cars in a funeral procession, consisting mostly of African Americans, had been winding through the neighborhood. The procession irritated some locals, who complained that it was noisy and disruptive. Mount Greenwood remained 86.5

percent white and fiercely conservative. A melee erupted on the edges, and videos showed Joshua Beal, a twenty-five-year-old member of the procession, brandishing a gun. Confronted by police, Beal was shot to death. (After an investigation, officers were cleared of wrongdoing. The editorial board of the *Chicago Sun-Times*, which was often critical of police conduct, wrote that Beal shared blame for "all around stupidity" for pulling a gun, adding, though, that the fracas was fueled by "good ol' Chicago racism.")

On Election Night, three days after Beal's killing, dozens of activists representing Black Lives Matter returned to the neighborhood to protest; for many, it was an extension of the protests that had been unfolding for months, ever since the video of McDonald was released. But in Mount Greenwood, they were met by throngs of hundreds of residents. Tensions erupted right away. "Try to stop the police!" a white supporter shouted. "Fuck the police!" a protester shouted back. The activists knelt and sang the national anthem, and the crowd booed. Each side claimed to represent the country at its core: the protesters carried an American flag; so did the neighborhood crowd, which tried to drown out the protesters with chants of "USA! USA!"

As the sun set over a warm, cloudless evening, the standoff in Mount Greenwood was an exhibit of America's fracturing coherence. Protesters had timed their visit to Election Night, calculating that a Clinton victory would serve as a repudiation of what one called a "mob of white thugs." But, like so many Americans, they were wrong about the results of that evening. When the votes were counted, Chicago's Little Rock stood out for a new distinction: it was the only neighborhood in the city of Chicago that Trump won.

———

When Trump leaped to the head of the Republican Party, he brought a moral vision once confined to the fevered fringe, elevating furies and fantasies from social media to the center stage of political life. In doing so, he guided the United States into a current that was coursing through other Western democracies—Britain, France, Spain, Greece,

Scandinavia—where xenophobic, nationalist parties had emerged since the 2008 economic crisis to besiege middle-ground politicians. In country after country, voters beset by inequality and scarcity had reached past the sober promises of the center left and the center right to the specter of a transcendent solution, no matter how cruel. "The more complicated the problem, the simpler the demands become," Samuel Popkin, a political scientist at the University of California in San Diego, told me. "When people get frustrated and irritated, they want to cut the Gordian knot."

Trump had succeeded in unleashing an old gene in American politics—the crude tribalism that the historian Richard Hofstadter named "the paranoid style," and, over the course of the campaign, it replicated like a runaway mutation. Democracy, as political scientists put it, depended on the "consent of the losers." But throughout history, that consent had tended to erode when Americans confronted the reshuffling of status and influence—the Great Migration, the end of Jim Crow, the end of a white majority. In those moments, we succumbed to the politics of absolutism, to the "conflict between absolute good and absolute evil," in which, Hofstadter wrote, "the quality needed is not a willingness to compromise but the will to fight things out to a finish. Nothing but complete victory will do."

Trump was born to the part in this existential war. "I'll do nearly anything within legal bounds to win," he had written years earlier in *The Art of the Deal*. In a moment that was easy to forget, during one of his feuds on the campaign, he publicly released Lindsey Graham's cell-phone number. Graham tried to play it off—he made a show of smashing his phone in public—but that moment in Trump's emerging approach lingered with me. It was impressively malign, an action conceived in the knowledge that, with a single utterance, Trump could subject an enemy to that most savage weapon of all: us.

FIFTEEN

RADICAL SELF-RELIANCE

EVERY YEAR SINCE 1947, the *Bulletin of the Atomic Scientists*, a magazine founded by members of the Manhattan Project, gathers a group of Nobel laureates and other luminaries to update the Doomsday Clock, a symbolic gauge of our distance from wrecking civilization. In January 2017, less than a week after Trump's inauguration, the panel announced that it had moved the clock to two minutes and thirty seconds—the closest to Doomsday since the first U.S. hydrogen bomb test, in 1952. "Never before has the *Bulletin* decided to advance the clock largely because of the statements of a single person," the organizers explained. "But when that person is the new president of the United States, his words matter."

Even before Trump won the White House, the sheer fact of his candidacy had raised an awareness of catastrophic potential. Americans who had adequate resources embarked on steps to protect themselves. Steve Huffman, the cofounder and CEO of Reddit, which was valued at $600 million, had been nearsighted until November 2015, when he arranged to have laser eye surgery. He underwent the procedure not for the sake of convenience or appearance but, rather, for a reason he didn't usually talk much about: he hoped that it would improve his odds of surviving a disaster, whether natural or man-made. "If the world ends—and not even if the world ends, but if we have trouble—getting contacts or glasses is going to be a huge pain in the ass," he told me. "Without them, I'm fucked."

Huffman, who lived in San Francisco, said he was less concerned with any specific threat—a pandemic, a dirty bomb, a coup—than he was with the potential aftermath, "the temporary collapse of our government and structures," as he put it. That was the scenario that survivalist blogs call WROL, "without rule of law." At Burning Man, the annual clothing-optional festival in the Nevada desert, he had embraced one of its core principles, "radical self-reliance," which he took to mean "happy to help others, but not wanting to require others." (Among survivalists, or "preppers," FEMA, the Federal Emergency Management Agency, stood for "Foolishly Expecting Meaningful Aid.") In addition to his eye surgery, Huffman said, "I own a couple of motorcycles. I have a bunch of guns and ammo. Food. I figure that, with that, I can hole up in my house for some amount of time."

He had come to believe that contemporary life rested on a fragile consensus. "I think, to some degree, we all collectively take it on faith that our country works, that our currency is valuable, the peaceful transfer of power—that all of these things that we hold dear work because we believe they work. While I do believe they're quite resilient, and we've been through a lot, certainly we're going to go through a lot more."

The sense that America's long, clattering experiment with democracy might be heading toward chaos was not entirely new. In 1923, D. H. Lawrence diagnosed a specific strain of dread in America's brief history. "Doom!" he wrote. "Something seems to whisper it in the very dark trees of America." The urge to hedge against disaster fluctuated over the decades, but it started to grow steadily among conservatives after the oil shock of the 1970s, especially in the years that President Reagan sanctified a pioneer's spirit of self-reliance. In one of his favorite laugh lines, he said, "The nine most terrifying words in the English language are: 'I'm from the government, and I'm here to help.'"

The survivalist spirit had surged again since September 11, including, quietly, in affluent quarters of the United States, where people accustomed to control of their lives confronted a realm of vulnerability they had not foreseen. Robert A. Johnson, a former managing director at the hedge fund Soros Fund Management who had lived in Greenwich, listened to neighbors debate various strategies of escape in the event of other assaults. "More and more were saying, 'You've got to have a private plane,'" he told me. "You have to assure that the pilot's family will be taken care of, too. They have to be on the plane.'"

In the years since September 11, wealthy survivalists had joined private Facebook groups and meet-ups where they took the concept of the combat mindset and honed it to maximum advantage; they swapped tips on cryptocurrencies, foreign passports, and locations safe from the effects of climate change. One member, the head of an investment firm, told me, "I keep a helicopter gassed up all the time, and I have an underground bunker with an air-filtration system." He said that his preparations probably put him at the "extreme" end among his peers. But he added, "A lot of my friends do the guns and the motorcycles and the gold coins. That's not too rare anymore."

The discussion was especially lively in finance and technology circles, where people were trained to detect, and capitalize on, emerging trends in society and the economy. During the financial crisis, Huffman had picked up precursors of the coming catastrophe from users' comments on Reddit: "People were starting to whisper about mortgages. They were worried about student debt. They were worried about debt in general. There was a lot of, 'This is too good to be true. This doesn't smell right.'" He knew that social media could magnify public fear and suspicion. "It's easier for people to panic when they're together," but it also alerted people to emerging risks. He said, "There's probably some false positives in there as well, but, in general, I think we're a pretty good gauge of public sentiment. When we're talking about a faith-based collapse, you're going to start to see the chips in the foundation on social media first."

How many wealthy Americans were taking steps to survive a catastrophe? That was hard to know exactly; a lot of people didn't like to talk about it. ("Anonymity is priceless," one hedge-fund manager told me, declining an interview.) Reid Hoffman, the cofounder of LinkedIn and a prominent investor, called it "apocalypse insurance." He told me, "Saying you're 'buying a house in New Zealand' is kind of a wink, wink, say no more. Once you've done the Masonic handshake, they'll be, like, 'Oh, you know, I have a broker who sells old ICBM silos, and they're nuclear-hardened, and they kind of look like they would be interesting to live in.'"

I asked Hoffman to estimate what share of fellow Silicon Valley billionaires had acquired some level of "apocalypse insurance" in the form of a hideaway in the United States or abroad. "I would guess fifty-plus percent," he said, "but that's parallel with the decision to buy a vacation home. Human motivation is complex, and I think people can say, 'I now have a safety blanket for this thing that scares me.'" The fears varied, but many worried that, as artificial intelligence took away a growing share of jobs, there would be a backlash against Silicon Valley, America's second-highest concentration of wealth. (The Gold Coast of Connecticut was first.) "I've heard this theme from a bunch of people," Hoffman said. "Is the country going to turn against the wealthy? Is it going to turn against technological innovation? Is it going to turn into civil disorder?"

Trump's election had sent elite anxieties into a new phase, one that cut across political lines. Robert H. Dugger, a former partner in the Greenwich hedge fund Tudor Investment Corporation, told me that even some financiers who supported Trump for president, hoping that he would cut taxes and regulations, were unnerved at the ways his campaign had hastened a collapse of respect for established institutions. Dugger said, "The media is under attack now. They wonder, is the court system next?" He went on, "Do we go from 'fake news' to 'fake evidence'? For people whose existence depends on enforceable contracts, this is life or death."

One measure of the rise in survivalist thinking was that some people were starting to speak out against it. Max Levchin, a founder of PayPal and of Affirm, a lending startup, told me, "It's one of the few things about Silicon Valley that I actively dislike—the sense that we are superior giants who move the needle and, even if it's our own failure, must be spared."

In that view, elite survivalism was not a step toward prevention; it was an act of withdrawal. Philanthropy in the United States was still three times as large, as a share of GDP, as philanthropy in the next closest country (the United Kingdom), but it was accompanied by a deeper disinvestment from some of America's most successful and powerful people. Faced with evidence of frailty in the American project, in the institutions and norms from which they had benefited, some were permitting themselves to imagine failure, so long as the winners would find a way to keep winning.

To Levchin, prepping for survival was a moral miscalculation; he preferred to "shut down party conversations" on the topic. "I typically ask people, 'So you're worried about the pitchforks. How much money have you donated to your local homeless shelter?' This connects the most, in my mind, to the realities of the income gap. All the other forms of fear that people bring up are artificial." In his view, this is the time to invest in solutions, not escape. "At the moment, we're actually at a relatively benign point of the economy. When the economy heads south, you will have a bunch of people that are in really bad shape. What do we expect then?"

———

In Washington, the Trump presidency introduced its own version of radical self-reliance. Steve Bannon, the campaign chief, called it the "deconstruction of the administrative state"—the undoing of institutions, regulations, and taxes that he believed constrained American power in the name of a false promise of communitarian good. It was a goal that reached back decades, from Goldwater and Ayn Rand to Reagan, Limbaugh, Santelli, the Kochs, and the Hanleys. The new administration regarded the federal system not as a machine that could implement its vision but as a vanquished foe—a defeated empire in need of occupation.

The administration embarked on a wholesale reduction in federal function. Nancy McEldowney, who retired not long into Trump's term after thirty years in the Foreign Service, told me that she recognized the process from her years abroad. "In the anatomy of a hostile takeover and occupation, there are textbook elements—you decapitate the leadership, you compartmentalize the power centers, you engender fear and suspicion," she said. "They did all those things."

Since the Great Depression, the government had expanded the ranks of civil servants to administer growing programs on health, welfare, science, the environment, and financial regulation. Advocates of limited government mocked the civil service as a "snivel service" of Ivy Leaguers, "a bureaucracy of short-haired women and long-haired men, bent on replacing the traditional American family," as the historian Landon R. Y. Storrs put it. In 1951, *Washington Confidential*, a bestseller by two journalists working for the conservative press mogul William Randolph Hearst, presented the federal workforce as a domain of "mediocrity and virtual anonymity" in a city of "economic parasites." The modern conservative movement aspired to slash away at what it considered a bloated, meddling civil service, and privatize the management of social and political problems.

Richard Nixon's aides produced an eighty-page manual on the removal of "undesirable" careerists, which proffered a system for grading civil servants on political "dependability," ranging from "L" (for "Let's watch this fellow") to "O" (for "Out"). To marginalize the troublesome ones, it suggested a "New Activity Technique": create an "apparently meaningful, but essentially meaningless, new activity to which they are all transferred." Such an activity, Nixon's aides wrote, could serve as "a single barrel into which you can dump a large number of widely located bad apples." After the manual became public, during the Watergate hearings, Congress passed a law to prohibit discrimination against federal workers for "political affiliation, race, color, religion, national origin, sex, marital status, age, or handicapping condition."

But presidents retained broad latitude to reshuffle civil servants without breaking the law in obvious ways. That would prove indispensable for the Trump administration as it set out to "deconstruct the administrative state." Trump left no illusion that he privileged loyalty over expertise. At a campaign rally in 2016, he mocked the notion of independent expertise. "Oh, we need an *expert*," he said, and the crowd tittered. "They say, 'Donald Trump needs a foreign-policy adviser.' Supposing I *didn't* have one?"

In office, Trump made a point to challenge the integrity of government agencies that were known for independence, including the FBI ("reputation is in tatters") and the Department of Justice ("embarrassment to our country"). His relationship with the State Department was especially vexed. In January 2017, when he issued an executive order that barred travelers from seven Muslim countries, more than a thousand U.S. diplomats criticized it in an official dissent cable. In response, Sean Spicer, the press secretary, said that public servants should "either get with the program or they can go."

Every president expects devotion. (Lyndon Johnson wished for an aide who would "kiss my ass in Macy's window at high noon and tell me it smells like roses." He said, "I want his pecker in my pocket.") Trump liked his advisers to demonstrate their fealty in public. As cameras rolled at his first cabinet meeting, a beaming Sonny Perdue, the secretary of agriculture, told Trump and other department heads, "I just got back from Mississippi. They love you there." Kellyanne Conway, one of the president's most abject attendants, took to referring reverently to the "October 8th coalition," the stalwarts who remained at Trump's side even after the world listened to the recording of him boasting about grabbing women by the genitals.

Trump refused to consider Democrats, or even Republicans who had signed letters against him as a candidate, so the White House turned to an array of novices. As an assistant to the secretary of energy, the administration installed Sid Bowdidge, whose recent employment had included managing a Meineke Car Care branch in Seabrook, New Hampshire. (Bowdidge departed after it emerged that he had called Muslims "maggots.") Matthew Spencer Petersen, a nominee to the federal bench, became a brief online sensation when Senator John Kennedy, a Republican from Louisiana, asked him a series of basic law-school questions, and his answers revealed that Petersen had never argued a motion, tried a case, or taken a deposition by himself.

Over time, a culture of fealty compounds itself; conformists thrive, and dissenters depart or refuse to join. The president's advisers competed to be the most explicitly quiescent. Peter Navarro, the head of the White House National Trade Council, told an interviewer, "My function, really, as an economist is to try to provide the underlying analytics that confirm his intuition. And his intuition is always right in these matters." After scarcely more than a year, Trump was on his sixth communications director and his third national security advisor, John Bolton, whom Trump knew so slightly that he sometimes referred to him as "Mike Bolton."

The White House left hundreds of critical jobs unfilled. That was deliberate. As a candidate, Trump had promised to "cut so much your head will spin." In addition, large numbers of employees were opting to leave the government rather than serve it. In Trump's first nine months, more than 79,000 full-time workers quit or retired—a 42 percent increase over that period in Obama's presidency. "We've never seen vacancies at this scale," said Max Stier, the president and CEO of the Partnership for Public Service, a nonpartisan group that works to make the government more effective. "Not anything close."

After nearly two years of attacking his own government, Trump took his campaign to hobble the federal government a step further: he forced it to shut down unless he received $5.7 billion in federal funds for his border wall. Three days before Christmas, more than three quarters of a million employees across the country were furloughed or forced to work for free. Some were unable to meet rent and buy groceries, so they resorted to waiting on line at food banks. Wilbur Ross, the commerce secretary with a net worth of $2.9 billion, was puzzled. "There's no real reason why they shouldn't be able to get a loan," he said. The president's daughter-in-law Lara Trump called it "a little bit of pain." In January 2019, when FBI agents arrested Trump's longtime associate Roger Stone, who once oversaw the Reagan campaign in Greenwich, the agents were working without pay.

Eventually, with air traffic controllers so scarce that planes were being grounded in New York, Trump abandoned the shutdown, empty-handed. It had lasted thirty-five days, the longest in history, costing the American economy at least $11 billion. The next month, he instead declared a national emergency so that he could use military funds to build the wall.

In physical terms, Trump took to operating as if he were facing hostile terrain. In Washington, only 4 percent of residents voted for him, and, to avoid unwelcome protests, the president hewed to a narrow patch of trusted terrain: he rarely ventured beyond his home, his hotel, his golf course, and his plane, taking Air Force One to Mar-a-Lago and to occasional appearances before devoted supporters. He never attended a performance at the Kennedy Center or dined in a restaurant that was not on his own property.

The more the administration retreated into the comfort of its own mythology, the more it reminded me of another experience in regime change I'd observed. As a reporter, I arrived in Baghdad in April 2003, and covered Iraq off and on for two years. At the time, the U.S. occupation was led from the Green Zone, a fortified enclave where Americans lived and worked in a sanctum of swimming pools and black-market scotch. The Green Zone—officially the home of the Coalition Provisional Authority—functioned as an extension of George W. Bush's White House, led by political appointees, staffed by civil servants, and attended by waiters in bow ties and paper hats. Before long, the Green Zone had acquired another connotation, as a byword for dysfunction: the failure to stop looters or to restore Iraq's electricity, the decision to disband the Iraqi Army, the blindness to a growing resistance to the occupation. As problems accumulated, the Bush administration turned, more than ever, to loyalists. The rebuilding of the stock market was entrusted to a twenty-four-year-old. A cohort of recent college grads, recruited because they had applied for jobs at the Heritage Foundation, were put in charge of Iraq's national budget. Inside the Green Zone, rhetoric prevailed over reality ("Mission Accomplished!"), and appearances became a stand-in for facts. Those who recognized the self-delusion and incompetence began referring to the Green Zone as the Emerald City.

Trump's White House was becoming his Emerald City: isolated, fortified against nonbelievers, entranced by its mythmaker, and constantly vulnerable to the risks of reality.

———

In the war on Washington, one of Trump's most ardent lieutenants was Ryan Zinke. He gloried in the role. Six foot two, with broad shoulders and a cleft chin, Zinke was a fifth-generation Montanan who was recruited as a linebacker at the University of Oregon and spent twenty-three years in the Navy SEALs. In 2008, he entered politics, in the Montana state senate. After one term in Congress, he was appointed secretary of the interior, and arrived for his first day of work on horseback, riding down C Street in a ten-gallon hat and jeans. After that, Zinke attracted attention mostly for his zealous promotion of Trump's energy agenda. He opened up America's coasts to offshore oil and gas drilling; overturned a moratorium on new leases for coal mines on public land; and recommended shrinking national monuments in Utah by two million acres, the largest reduction of protected lands in American history.

Within the department, Zinke adopted the president's approach to expertise, loyalty, and dissent. Early in his term, Zinke received a briefing from a scientist named Joel Clement, the director of the department's Office of Policy Analysis. Clement noticed that Zinke had redecorated the office with a grizzly bear, mounted on its hind legs, and a collection of knives. Zinke had no professional experience in geology, but he described himself as a "geologist" because he majored in geology in college. Clement told me, "He comes over and sits down, and he says, 'Okay, what are we here for?'" To keep Zinke's attention, staff hewed to subjects related to his personal experience. "I briefed him on invasive species," Clement said. "It was one issue where it looked like we might actually get a little traction, because in Montana they had just discovered mussels that could really screw up the agricultural economy." The strategy failed. "He didn't understand what we were talking about. He started talking about other species—ravens and coyotes. He was filling the intellectual vacuum with nonsense. It's amazing that he has such confidence, given his level of ignorance."

A couple of months later, Zinke ordered the involuntary reassignment of dozens of the department's most senior civil servants. In Washington, the tactic of marooning civil servants in obscure assignments is known as sending them to the "turkey farm." (An Asia specialist assigned to the turkey farm explained the experience as akin to a Japanese tradition in which unwanted workers are relegated to a "banishment room," to encourage them to resign out of boredom and shame.) Clement, who had been his agency's public face on issues related to climate change, was assigned to the accounting office that handles royalty checks for oil and gas and coal extraction. His new job had no duties and appeared on no organizational chart. He quit. "I really didn't feel like I had a choice," he told me. "I wanted to keep my voice more than I wanted to keep the job."

Like his commander in chief, Zinke made no secret of his distrust. "I got thirty percent of the crew that's not loyal to the flag," he said in late 2017 to an advisory board dominated by oil and gas executives. He likened his leadership of the department to capturing a ship at sea, and vowed to prevail over resistant employees. Zinke's comment drew a rebuke from fifteen former Interior appointees, in Republican and Democratic administrations, who appealed to him to let public servants "do their jobs without fear of retaliation on political grounds." In a private mutiny, some of his staff printed T-shirts that read "30% DISLOYAL" and took to calling themselves "the disloyals."

Zinke eventually left the administration in 2018, under pressure from more than a dozen investigations into his conduct, including scrutiny of a land deal involving a foundation he led. But the administration's commitment to fossil-fuel companies was undimmed. At the Department of Energy, appointees adopted a vocabulary of nearly divine faith in natural gas, which they called "freedom gas." The department hired, as a special adviser, Douglas Matheney, who had worked for the National Mining Association and the Koch brothers' political organization. Matheney promptly headed to West Virginia for a coal-industry conference and told the crowd, "I went to Washington, D.C., for one purpose, and that was to help create coal jobs in the United States. That's my total purpose for being there. I'm not a researcher. I'm not a scientist. I'm an advocate for the coal industry." With a smile, he nodded to Reagan's famous quip and said: "The good news is I'm with the federal government, and I'm here to help."

The administration was not just gutting the federal government; it was empowering it in the name of private interests. In West Virginia, it accelerated a boom in the natural gas industry that had begun under Obama; employers needed people for construction, driving, warehouses, oil fields, and laying pipelines. In Trump's first three years, West Virginia recorded the fastest per capita labor-force growth of any state. At the hotels on the edge of Clarksburg, parking lots filled up with workers coming in. David Efaw, the coal miner who had cast a wary vote for Trump, was impressed. "I'll have to admit, Trump has done a better job than I thought he would, honestly," he told me. Since at least 1950, when the first records were kept, West Virginia had the lowest labor-force participation rate in America, but by 2020 it had surpassed Mississippi and was approaching several other states. After years of frustration, people without college degrees were getting hired for wages of up to $30 an hour. State unemployment fell to some of its lowest levels in decades.

But the gas boom was also underscoring the underlying frailties in West Virginia's political culture—widening the gap in power between the state's corporate elite and everyone else. In 2018, Evan Hansen, the environmental consultant I traveled with during the water crisis, won a seat in the state House of Delegates. He started making the drive back and forth from his home in Morgantown, in the north of the state, to the legislature in Charleston. After years of pressing the government from the outside, he was startled to discover the full scope of ways that powerful energy companies shaped politics on the inside. In one case, the House Energy Committee debated a bill to expedite permits for fracking. "Then the next word out of the chairman's mouth was, 'Don't forget that lunch is provided tomorrow by Dominion'"—one of the energy companies that stood to gain from the bill. "Without any sense of irony or impropriety or anything," he said. "It was just so *normal*."

Signs of political capture were everywhere. When Hansen met some staff attorneys who drafted the technical language of legislation, they apologized about a new rule. "They were like, 'I'm really sorry, but we can no longer accept bills from lobbyists without your signature to say that you want to cosponsor the bill.' I'm like, 'You're *apologizing* to me that an elected representative needs to sign a bill to indicate they're cosponsoring it?" He told me, "Lobbyists used to be able to hand them a bill, and say, 'This delegate and this one told me they're on it.' It's just the way it's been done for decades."

But nothing frustrated Hansen more than observing the extent to which coal companies used their clout to hedge against their own economic doomsday. "We've known for *decades* that the coal industry was going to steeply decline. There was a report that my company put out in 2010 that laid it all out." They were losing the competition to cheap natural gas, and by the end of 2018, five more U.S. coal companies had declared bankruptcy in three years. As they failed, they asked the state to prop them up. To survive, the industry lobbied successfully for a tax cut that would save it $60 million a year. In an unsubtle political move, Murray Energy, a coal company, bused in miners to fill seats in the legislature's gallery. "The economists said it might create a hundred jobs. So it's costing us six hundred thousand dollars a job," Hansen said. "And that's what it *might* do. It's probably not going to create any." When the coal industry succeeded in winning a tax cut, other industries lined up—including natural gas, limestone, and sandstone.

To Hansen, the giveaways represented a delusional faith in the dismantling of the administrative state. More deeply, it marked a failure of democracy's basic function: to deliberate over the shared problems of a people and to convert their public assets into the public goods they need in order to flourish. He said, "At a time when we really need to be investing in roads, and teachers, and things that will actually bring people here, we're dumping the money into places that are not going to be productive over the long term." He said, "It's going to line their pockets, and it's going to go out of the state."

At its core, the campaign to subdue the administrative state could not succeed without a major assault on taxes. Trump had campaigned on the promise of a colossal tax cut, and in a moment of candor, Congressman Chris Collins, a New York Republican, told reporters, "My donors are basically saying: 'Get it done or don't ever call me again.'"

In the end, the donors were well served. Three days before Christmas 2017, Trump signed a $1.5 trillion tax cut, one of the largest in the nation's history. He called it a gift to "the folks who work in the mail rooms and the machine shops of America." That was impressively false, according to the Institute on Taxation and Economic Policy, a nonpartisan think tank. On average, a household in the bottom 20 percent of American income received a cut of $120; a household in the top 1 percent received $48,000. The new rules cut the corporate tax rate by 14 percentage points and made it easier to avoid the estate tax; they also introduced a range of new tax breaks, including some specifically for the commercial-real-estate industry and for wealthy heirs.

At opposite ends of America's income ladder, the tax cuts, and the resulting cuts to government service, played out as near mirror images—as if they represented alternative definitions of a government "here to help." In Chicago, the Illinois Policy Institute, a conservative think tank, hailed Trump's corporate tax cut as an instrument to "attract global headquarters and high-paying corporate jobs." But for people who would not get high-paying corporate jobs, the benefits were scarce. Some employers, such as Home Depot, announced bonuses "up to $1,000," but bonuses, unlike raises, are one-off payments, and many companies simply moved up bonuses they would have given later.

The administration proposed its sharpest cuts to social agencies such as the Department of Housing and Urban Development, which primarily serves the poor. Trump's 2018 budget aimed to slash $6.2 billion from HUD's budget—more than a fifth of its funding—and the effects would trickle down across the country. Cook County, home to Chicago, prepared to cut spending on sheltering homeless people and cut off rental assistance to 800 households, which the director of the program called a "doomsday scenario" for people who depended on it. (Another 6,000 households were on a waiting list.) When the director of HUD,

Ben Carson, visited Chicago in January 2018, he was shouted down by protesters. A woman yelled, "You're taking homes from people like me!" (Faced with a growing outcry, Congress intervened to prevent the cuts.)

But by then, Chicago had become almost entirely symbolic for Trump. Since activists shut down his rally, he had not set foot in the city again. And yet it only continued to grow as a symbol in his imagery of lawlessness and violence. "Seven people shot and killed yesterday in Chicago," Trump tweeted in early 2017. "What is going on there - totally out of control. Chicago needs help!" The help he envisioned was not to generate jobs or repair schools or expand public transit. He suggested sending the National Guard. He told Bill O'Reilly that Chicago police should get "very much tougher," and he invoked a conversation with an unnamed cop, a "top police officer," Trump called him, who said he could stop the violence in "one week" if he was given a freer hand.

———

Every town in America had its story of what changed after Trump came to power. In Greenwich, his era had begun almost instantly. A few weeks after the election, a town employee reported to police that Christopher von Keyserling, a well-known member of the Representative Town Meeting—the town council—had touched her groin after saying, "I love this new world. I no longer have to be politically correct." Lynn Mason, the accuser, warned von Keyserling not to touch her again, to which he allegedly replied, "It would be your word against mine, and nobody will believe you." After the town government contacted von Keyserling about the complaint, he said that Mason had overreacted to a "little pinch," according to court records. He was charged with misdemeanor sexual assault. He pleaded not guilty and awaited trial.

The combination of Trump and the von Keyserling incident caused an immediate reaction in local politics: women signed up to run for office, and in the fall of 2017 more than fifty won seats on the town council. "A lot of us just woke up," Joanna Swomley, a retired lawyer who entered the race, said. "We were horrified." Democrats also won control of the town finance board for the first time in recorded history, and the following year, they picked up seats in the state legislature that no Democrat had occupied since Herbert Hoover was in the White House.

But the local blue wave subsided. In 2019, Republicans reclaimed control of the finance board and elected as first selectman (the equivalent of mayor) a local businessman and state lawmaker who had voted for Trump. On election day, Swomley had sensed a change in the atmosphere. "I was holding a Democrat's sign, and a Republican yelled out, 'Oh, hell no!' It was not the embarrassment, the quietness that you saw in 2017. It was 'I am going to own this. I like this.'"

Claire Tisne Haft, a *Greenwich Time* columnist who lived in town with her husband and three kids, was appalled by Trump, and she initially assumed that her neighbors were, too. She got her first indication to the contrary at a dance recital for her daughter, when another mother told her how excited she was to "see what Trump can do." Not long afterward, Tisne Haft and her husband had dinner with friends, and the conversation turned to politics. "We realized halfway through the meal that we had to adjust our tone," she told me.

The moderate Republicans who once defined the local political culture were increasingly out of favor. Christopher Shays had been elected eleven times to represent Greenwich and the Gold Coast in Congress, from 1987 to 2009. When he appeared in the press now and then, in the Trump years, conservatives mocked him as a RINO—a Republican in name only. "When Sean Hannity calls someone like me a RINO, I want to punch him in the nose," Shays told me. "I got elected as a Republican for thirty-four effing years, and Hannity has never gotten elected for anything." When Shays talked to former staff and constituents in Connecticut, he came to recognize the delicate language of accommodation: "I was talking to a guy I know well, after some pathetic thing that Trump did, and his response was 'Yes, but he's selecting the right Supreme Court justices.' I started to laugh at him, because I know for a fact that's a minor issue for him." Shays believed that many Americans quietly shared Trump's desire to reduce immigration and cut social-welfare programs for the poor. "He's saying what people think, and they appreciate that," Shays said. "But not many are going to admit that's why they support him."

Trump signs remained scarce in Greenwich, but his supporters were easy to find. In addition to the first selectman and local residents who had joined the administration, there was the chairman of the Greenwich finance board, as well as an ardent backer who served in the state House of Representatives. Leora Levy, who had called him vulgar in the local paper, took to applauding his "leadership" and quoting him on Twitter, where she adopted some of his rhetorical style. "AMERICA WILL NEVER BE A SOCIALIST COUNTRY!!!" she posted. "WE ARE BORN FREE AND WILL STAY FREE!!!" Eventually, Trump nominated her to be the U.S. ambassador to Chile.

But the fuller impact of Trump's era ran far deeper than just the jockeying for proximity to power. The more Trump conducted the presidency around the combat mindset, the more it seemed to seep into the national groundwater—into the ways people perceived their connections to one another. In early 2019, a powerful Greenwich attorney named Gordon Caplan, cochairman of the law firm Willkie Farr & Gallagher, was indicted for paying $75,000 for a test proctor to fix his daughter's ACT exam. Caplan was one of fifty-three defendants in the college admissions scandal, a list dotted with addresses in Atherton and Bel Air. In phone calls recorded by the FBI, Rick Singer, the consultant behind the scam, had explained to Caplan that his daughter would never know that her family had cheated on her behalf: "She will think that she's really super smart and she got lucky on a test." Caplan uttered one of the scandal's indelible expressions: "To be honest, I'm not worried about the moral issue here." Caplan pleaded guilty and served a month in prison.

After the scandal broke, Tisne Haft, at *Greenwich Time*, wrote that the case brought up "a whole lot of uncomfortable in a town like Greenwich." It exposed how far some of America's most powerful, educated, and prosperous people were going to give their families an advantage in a life already full of them. She sensed that some people in town had become so cynical about the workings of power that they had lost their moral footing. "A friend said, 'You know those kids whose parents gave libraries to their colleges? How is that so different than pushing the boundaries of the truth about your kid?'" she told me. "I just had to look at this person and say, 'Hang on. Someone photoshopped a kid's *head* onto a *picture*.' I feel like we jumped off a cliff there somewhere and didn't notice."

The Americans who broke the law to get their kids into better schools had provided unwitting testimony on the full scale of America's crisis of inequality; the gap between elites and the rest had grown so large that parents panicked at the prospect that their offspring might land on the wrong side of the divide. Their reasoning reminded me of the rationale I kept hearing for looking past Trump's behavior toward women, minorities, immigrants, war heroes, democracy, and the truth: a conviction that, ultimately, nothing mattered more than cutting taxes and regulations and slowing immigration. Places like Greenwich took pride in their commitment to civility and decency, but Caplan's indifference to the "moral issue," as he put it, bespoke the kind of quiet compromises that a person makes in the privacy of a phone call, or a voting booth.

For years, Americans who could invest in hedging against catastrophe had imagined a range of scenarios that might subject them to a world "without rule of law." But they could have dispensed with the science fiction. Rule of law, it turned out, could founder anytime, if enough people used their power to escape it.

SIXTEEN

THE BODY OF FACT

ON A BALMY THURSDAY NIGHT in Huntington, West Virginia, several thousand Trump fans lined up early outside the Big Sandy Superstore Arena. Some had traveled hundreds of miles; when a summer squall off the Ohio River drenched them in a downpour, nobody budged. It was August 2017, nearly nine months after Trump had won the White House, but the rallies continued. They had long since evolved past the point of drumming up votes; they had become something closer to a sacrament—a ritual that established what should be believed and what should not.

For both the crowd and the performer, the evening promised a moment of escape. The city of Huntington was a place of faded glory; since the 1960s, the population had sunk by more than a third, to 49,000 people—smaller than Greenwich—and it made news, in most cases, for its distinction as a hot spot in the opioid crisis. Trump, for his part, was having a difficult week: in recent days, Republicans had finally acknowledged that they had been falsely promising their supporters that they could overturn Obamacare; moreover, his communications director had resigned after lambasting his colleagues in vivid profanity; and Trump himself had been roundly condemned for telling a crowd of police officers "please don't be too nice" to people under arrest.

But inside the arena, all of that seemed far away. The president, in a dark suit, white shirt, and striped blue tie, luxuriated in the usual chants—"Trump! Trump! Trump!" and "Lock her up!" He did his classic bits about "the swamp," the "fake news," and the second coming of "beautiful, clean coal." He claimed, falsely, to have brought back "hundreds of thousands" of manufacturing jobs, and repeated a list of bogus talking points about the economy, immigration, and Hillary Clinton. For a demonstration of fealty, Trump invited up Jim Justice, the richest man in West Virginia, who was also the governor. Justice, a Democrat, announced that he was becoming a Republican. He offered Trump fulsome praise: "He cares about us in West Virginia. And most importantly of all, you know what, he has made us, as common everyday Americans, feel good and be proud of who we are."

But all of that was preamble to Trump's main purpose of the night—to remind his people not to trust what they heard from the press, the Justice Department, or Congress. He taunted the special counsel Robert Mueller, who was investigating Russia's involvement in the election. "Have you seen any *Russians* in West Virginia or Ohio or Pennsylvania?" he asked the crowd. "Are there any Russians *here* tonight?" Then, so subtly that it was easy to miss, the president eased from playful to conspiratorial. "They're trying to cheat you out of the leadership that you want," he declared, "with a fake story that is demeaning to all of us—and most importantly demeaning to our country and demeaning to our constitution."

Trump's mode of deception had been so essential to his politics from the beginning that it was easy to lose sight of the accumulating effects it had on his audiences. To outsiders, it was tempting to write it off as nothing but a circus. But that was a mistake. Since the ancient Greeks, effective politics had combined spectacle and substance, and Trump had discovered that with the right spectacle, people would follow him almost anywhere on the substance. Did any of his words really matter? What were they giving people? Where would it lead? To understand the pressures that were building inside American political culture, I looked further into the past, to another uncertain and incendiary moment.

In the summer of 1858, the American experiment was careening toward war, and two foes—Abraham Lincoln and Stephen A. Douglas—met in northern Illinois for the first in a series of debates on the future of slavery. Lincoln, who was challenging Douglas for his seat in the Senate, loomed a foot taller than his opponent, a squat, tenacious debater celebrated as the Little Giant. The men embodied both sides of America's fatal divide: Douglas, who warned that Lincoln would make the prairie as "black as night," advocated "popular sovereignty," which would hasten the spread of slavery into the western territories—a prospect that Lincoln could not abide.

By the standards of politics today, the debates—seven in all—were an exhibit of unrecognizable democratic rigor. In each one, either Lincoln or Douglas spoke first for an hour; then the other responded for an hour and a half; finally, the first spoke for another half hour. (In a previous encounter, they had held forth for seven hours straight.)

Lincoln-Douglas was "the best circus in town," as a reporter on the scene described it. Before the speakers began, bands played and liquor flowed. But if the debates were social occasions, they were not trivial ones. Thousands of people crowded around to listen, without the comfort of chairs or shade or electric amplification. Politics was mostly reserved for white, wealthy males, but on the edges of the crowd were women, European immigrants, and semiliterate frontiersmen. Attendees were so desperate to hear the debaters that they climbed onto a wooden platform, which collapsed under their weight. They shouted encouragement ("Hit him again!") and hung banners with taunting nicknames ("Douglas the Dead Dog—Lincoln the Living Lion").

Week after week, the debaters traversed Illinois. Lincoln, short on cash, traveled by coach and ferry, while Douglas, a wealthy man whose wife owned slaves, journeyed on a private train, announcing his arrival by firing a cannon marked "Popular Sovereignty." At times, the discourse onstage neared combustion. When Douglas falsely accused Lincoln of a conspiracy to abolish slavery, Lincoln leaped from his seat and advanced on his opponent until a colleague pulled him back. But the event stayed in the realm of persuasion. As Lincoln had put it, "Reason—cold, calculating, unimpassioned reason—must furnish all materials for our future support and defense."

For Lincoln, the debates became the venue for the full expression of his humanism. He sought to be progressive but electable, "radical without sounding too damned radical," in the words of his biographer David S. Reynolds. Lincoln's boldest comments came in the final encounter, when he made a stark distinction between "one class that looks upon the institution of slavery as a wrong, and another class that does not look upon it as a wrong." Framing the issue in clear moral terms, he said, "It is the eternal struggle between these two principles—right and wrong—throughout the world. They are the two principles that have stood face to face from the beginning of time."

Lincoln lost his race for the Senate, but his performance in the debates made him famous. In the presidential contest of 1860, he won the North, which included all the states in which Black men could vote and also the six states in which the Lincoln-Douglas debates had been published. The Lincoln-Douglas debates came to be regarded as a preeminent example of American political discourse in the nineteenth century—a fierce clash of ideas, sustained by the close attention of the public.

But they also came to represent a darker lesson: for all their eloquence, they could not avert the Civil War or protect Lincoln from assassination. American political culture was bounded by a contest between reason and violence—a seesawing battle that continues to this day, between the aspiration to persuade fellow citizens to accept your views and the raw instinct to force them to comply.

———

In its most idealized form, the original ambition of the United States was to fashion a system that improved on "what kings and popes had decreed," the Stanford historian Caroline Winterer wrote in her book *American Enlightenments*. "Wielding the gleaming razor of human reason, sharpened by empirical evidence, common sense, and withering sarcasm, they would slash away at traditions that rested on nothing but the dust of convention and privilege," she observed.

Early Americans formed literary salons, subscription libraries, and scientific societies, animated by the spirit of the Enlightenment. Benjamin Franklin gathered what he called "ingenious Acquaintances" into a "Club for mutual Improvement." Known as the Junto, it was devoted to rigor, training, and the spread of the printed word, an ethic that the club called "Reason's eye."

By the mid-nineteenth century, the country was in the midst of a vibrant literary outpouring. In Washington, orators such as Henry Clay and Daniel Webster gained influence through speeches that drew huge crowds. "Eloquence, in this empire, is power," a journalist observed. A generation of thinkers and politicians—Margaret Fuller, Elizabeth Peabody, Frederick Douglass, Walt Whitman—produced impassioned writings and speeches that they hoped would reform the young republic, giving rise to what the scholar James Perrin Warren later called a "culture of eloquence." They traveled from town to town on the lyceum circuit, an adult-education campaign offering lectures on everything from physical exercise to the moral crisis of slavery. Alfred Bunn, an Englishman visiting in 1853, said that it was "a matter of wonderment" to see "the over-tired artisan, the worn-out factory girl" rush from work to "the hot atmosphere of a crowded lecture room." Even as the country slid toward the Civil War, the lectures continued, rooted in the belief in what Warren called "the word as a means toward reform."

At the same time, however, America was embarking on a surge of political violence, much of it directed at Black people, immigrants, Native Americans, and abolitionists. Between the 1830s and the outbreak of war, there were at least thirty-five major riots in the Northeast. One of them began in June 1857, when three nativist gangs—the Chunkers, the Rip-Raps, and the Plug Uglies—attacked Catholic immigrants in Washington, D.C., as they tried to cast ballots.

But the most ominous sign for the republic was the growing brutality among some of the country's most powerful people: members of Congress. In *The Field of Blood*, the Yale history professor Joanne B. Freeman examined scores of previously unstudied attacks and melees, often initiated by southern lawmakers who regarded opposition to slavery as a threat to their property and their power. In the 1840s, Representative John Dawson of Louisiana threatened to cut a colleague's throat "from ear to ear," and was stopped from shooting another only by the intervention of other congressmen. Freeman described a legislature guided by the ethics of professional wrestling: "Punching. Pistols. Bowie knives. Congressmen brawling in bunches while colleagues stood on chairs to get a good look." The fighting escalated to the point that a southern lawmaker threatened to lead an assault on the Capitol, and British diplomats came to regard the House floor as too dangerous to visit. Benjamin Brown French, a genial New Englander who served as clerk of the House of Representatives, stopped socializing with southerners and ultimately took to carrying a pistol.

When I asked Freeman how violence and the cult of reason could coexist, she said that they sprang from a shared motive: "How did you prove that you were a leader in that period, to a vast audience? How did you earn support? Maybe through aggressive oratory. Maybe by making, and keeping, promises for your constituents, state, and section of the Union. And, for a time, maybe by displaying your domination of the political playing field with bullying and aggression."

Freeman's history of congressional violence is an account of how some of the most privileged members of a society began to see their counterparts as enemies, and eventually as existential threats. Once political leaders lost trust in one another, the public was doomed to follow. "Unable to turn to the government for resolution, Americans North and South turned on one another," she wrote.

The enduring tension between violence and politics attracted the attention of Richard Hofstadter, the historian best known for his work on what he called the "arena for uncommonly angry minds," including anti-intellectualism and "the paranoid style." In 1970, near the end of his life, Hofstadter became fascinated by the juncture of democracy and force. It had swept through American society in recent years, producing assassinations and riots. Working with a coauthor, Michael Wallace, who collected two thousand cases of violence—massacres, rebellions, vigilantism—he hoped to address what he called the American paradox: "There is far more violence in our national heritage than our proud, sometimes smug, national self-image admits of."

Hofstadter noted that in America, unlike the rest of the world, political violence rarely involved poor citizens rising up against a powerful state; more often, citizens attacked one another, and, usually, the attackers were established Americans—white Protestants, in many cases—turning on minorities, immigrants, "Catholics, radicals, workers and labor organizers." Hofstadter made note of "verbal and ideological violence" that laid the foundation for actual harm. He also fretted about a "rising mystique of violence on the left." By 1969, the Student Nonviolent Coordinating Committee, a civil rights group cofounded by John Lewis a decade earlier, had elected new leadership and dropped "Nonviolent" from its name. The usually staid *New York Review of Books* had featured an instructional diagram for making a Molotov cocktail. In the age of television, Hofstadter sensed, practitioners had figured out that what played well on TV was often the language and the imagery of force. On both the left and the right, he wrote, politics was giving way to a culture of self-expression in which the "distinction between politics and theatre has been deliberately blurred."

That blurring of distinction, between politics and theater, was a remarkably fitting preamble to the observations, in the decade that followed, by Neil Postman in *Amusing Ourselves to Death.* He watched the 1984 presidential debates, between Ronald Reagan and Walter Mondale, and lamented the hollow dodges, casual deceptions, and abbreviated answers. With a level of concern that now looks quaint, he bemoaned Reagan's easy laugh lines and wrote, "The men were less concerned with giving arguments than with 'giving off' impressions, which is what television does best." It would be three decades before the host of a reality show entered a bid for the presidency. But Postman had already sensed that "the demarcation line between what is show business and what is not becomes harder to see with each passing day."

———

For as long as Americans had strained to cultivate "reason's eye," they had fretted about the perennial perils of ignorance. Less than a generation after the founding of the country, Thomas Jefferson wrote, "If a nation expects to be ignorant and free, in a state of civilization, it expects what never was and never will be." But by the early years of the twenty-first century, Americans were no longer surprised by annual reports that showed our students falling behind other countries'. In a 2005 survey, two thirds of Americans could not name the three branches of government. Scarcely a third of high school seniors read at or above the level of proficiency.

Every turn in technology carried potential for not only liberation but also deceit and degradation. In a radio address in 1931, the philosopher and educator John Dewey warned of a growing vulnerability in the very medium he was using. "Democracy will be a farce," Dewey said, "unless individuals are trained to think for themselves, to judge independently, to be critical, to be able to detect subtle propaganda and the motives which inspire it."

Human beings, as Dewey knew, were better at absorbing new information than at defending against lies. In a classic study, people shown a list of novel pieces of information were warned that some of it was bogus; but, quizzed later, they tended to remember the information and forget which pieces were false. Advertisers have known for decades that people are not good at resisting even naked efforts to distort their decision-making. In a study by the marketing professors Gavan Fitzsimons, of Duke, and Baba Shiv, of Stanford, a group of subjects were told simply that cake "may have some major health benefits." As vague as that was, when they were later offered a choice of cake or fruit, those subjects were nearly twice as likely to choose the cake as other people were. (In follow-up interviews, the cake eaters roundly denied that their behavior had been affected by the suggestions.)

Manipulation is an ancient feature of politics, but in the modern age it has acquired new effectiveness, not only because the technologies of influence have been refined but also because the economic stakes have grown. In the late 1960s, at the same time that libertarians such as Bill Middendorf in Greenwich were growing concerned about the environmental and consumer-protection movements, executives were embarking on a creative campaign to defend their industries. In 1969, as the cigarette industry faced stricter regulations, a memo circulated among executives at Brown & Williamson tobacco. "Doubt is our product," it explained, "since it is the best means of competing with the 'body of fact' that exists in the minds of the general public. It is also the means of establishing a controversy."

That strategy—the mass production of doubt, to compete against "the body of fact"—was a quiet revolution. The tools for generating the political theater of skepticism—think tanks, campaign finance, dubious science—would eventually be deployed against a broad range of political targets. On one front, Republican lawmakers promoted a campaign against "voter fraud," calling for stricter ID laws that tended to reduce turnout among Democratic-leaning voters—mainly minorities, students, and the poor. Researchers found that, of one billion votes cast in all American elections between 2000 and 2014, election officials detected a total of thirty-one possible cases of impersonation fraud. But the controversy was the point. In a candid email in 2011, collected during a campaign-finance investigation, a Republican lobbyist in Wisconsin wrote to colleagues even before votes had been counted: "Do we need to start messaging 'widespread reports of election fraud' so we are positively set up for the recount regardless of the final number?" (By the fall of 2020, polls showed that nearly half of registered American voters believed in the existence of widespread voter fraud.)

Over time, contempt for facts came to be an ideology. In 2004, an aide to George W. Bush (widely identified as Karl Rove, though he denied it) dismissed the "reality-based community," by which he meant people who insist on inconvenient facts. "We're an empire now," the aide told the journalist Ron Suskind, "and when we act, we create our own reality."

Magical thinking was taking its place on the main stage of politics. Bill Moyers, in a speech on end-times rhetoric in evangelical politics, lamented, "One of the biggest changes in politics in my lifetime is that the delusional is no longer marginal." In the 2008 book *The Age of American Unreason*, Susan Jacoby declared, "America is now ill with a powerful mutant strain of intertwined ignorance, anti-rationalism and anti-intellectualism." Fact-checking, as a mode of thinking, became suspect. In 2012, after the Obama campaign said Romney's claims about welfare were "blatantly false," Romney's pollster, Neil Newhouse, memorably responded, "We're not going to let our campaign be dictated by fact checkers."

Even as industries were getting bolder in their manipulations of the public sphere, the die-off of traditional sources of information was accelerating. In February 2018, the *Charleston Gazette-Mail*, West Virginia's most powerful newspaper, filed for bankruptcy. In August, in a milestone for the decline of local news, the *Pittsburgh Post-Gazette* announced that it would no longer print on Tuesdays and Saturdays—making Pittsburgh, a straight shot up the highway from Clarksburg, the largest city in America without a daily paper.

⊢——⊣

In Clarksburg, *The Exponent Telegram* was scrambling to survive. In 2018, the local Kmart closed, followed by Sears—and they had been two of the biggest advertisers in town. Brian Jarvis, the young lawyer who had gone into the newspaper business, told me, "All of a sudden, they're gone. We lost more than half of what we had in 2012."

He landed on an idea: he bought some other tiny papers—the *Garrett Republican*, the *Weston News*—and combined their back offices. He adopted the language of new media. The old office in Clarksburg became, in Jarvis's words, a "creative hub." At his cluttered desk in the creative hub, he told me, "We've got ninety-seven employees, thirty-eight content generators, and close to three hundred stories a week." He smiled. "I'm only thirty-six, so I'm just going to keep going until somebody tells me to stop, or the good Lord does."

It was up to John Miller, the editor, to figure out how to generate those stories. He prodded his reporters to meet a formidable threshold: each was expected to write ten stories a week. He knew how difficult that was, but, as usual, he found a noble spin for it. "If you want to be a writer, you've got to practice the trade," he told them.

The blunt fact was that, as the business shrank, the paper could hardly afford to be as bold as it was in the days when the old editor, Bill Sedivy, was railing on the editorial page against mountaintop mines. "When everyone else is closing, it's difficult for small newspapers to do things that are very controversial," Julie Cryser, the former city editor, told me. "Newspapers are less likely to go across the line and really push the envelope, and to ask questions and look deeper." Cryser worried that the disappearance of strong local papers was forcing people toward television and dubious sources on the Web. "There's this big void where nobody is getting alternative opinions or ideas," she told me. "There's nothing that combats the concepts you have about the way the world works." She brought up the KKK rally that came to town in 1999. "If, twenty years later, the KKK would come to Clarksburg today, I don't know that it would have been the same as it was. People would be charged up by whatever they read on their iPhones or their Samsungs, and it would have been a lot more divisive and explosive than what it was."

Not far up the highway from Clarksburg, David Efaw, the miner who used to work for Patriot Coal, had received two newspapers at his house for years. "My mother-in-law preferred one, and I preferred the other, and then we'd swap," he said. Even if he didn't like it, he enjoyed seeing what the other had to say. For a time, even after his mother-in-law died, he kept reading them both. But eventually, they got so thin that he got more and more of his news from his computer's homepage—which was set, out of habit, to MSN.com, a remnant from Microsoft's heyday, which aggregated news stories from around the Web. "I used to read a lot more newsmagazines than I do now," he added. But many of them—*Newsweek*, *U.S. News*—scarcely existed anymore.

Most of all, Efaw said, he didn't know what sources to believe anymore. He flicked back and forth between CNN and Fox but remained chronically unsatisfied. "So much of it is politically biased," he said. It was exhausting to be so alert to deception. "You've got to look around you and think, Are they telling you the truth or not?"

———

Of all the sentiments I heard as I ventured from place to place in those years, that was the most frequent—a constant, defensive anxiety that people felt unsure whom to believe. Once, in an unintended fashion, I found myself at the receiving end of that paranoia.

At home on a Sunday in 2019, I went looking for the iPad that we used for watching movies—and for distracting kids on car trips. Ollie, who was three, loved the iPad, no surprise, and whenever he got ahold of it, he entered random numbers into the passcode screen to try to unlock it. When I found it that afternoon, Ollie had made an especially diligent run at it. It wasn't clear how many codes he had tried, but by the time he gave up, the screen said "iPad is disabled, try again in 25,536,442 minutes." That worked out to about forty-eight years. I took a picture of it with my phone, wrote a tweet asking if anyone knew how to fix it, and went downstairs to dinner.

I didn't think much about the iPad again until the next morning, when I received an email from the news division of CTV, a Canadian television network, asking for information about "the locked iPad." Three minutes later, another email arrived, this time from the *Daily Mail* Online, in London. I ignored them. Soon I was hearing from CNN and *USA Today*. A British friend sent a text of condolences on the locked iPad and a screenshot of another article headlined "LOCK SHOCK: Baffled dad locked out of iPad for 25 million minutes after son, 3, tried to guess password." (It was featured beside pregnancy photos of Meghan Markle.)

When I went online, I discovered that the tweet had taken flight and generated thousands of reactions. Some people were scolding: "I wonder why a 3yo is in reach of an iPad. Deserved this tbh." Others were heartfelt: "Obviously, your offspring has the dogged, unfailing persistence required for a future career in a research field." But I was intrigued, above all, by a subset of readers who had scoured the photo like the Zapruder film and pronounced it a conspiracy or a fraud: "Its display is not Retina and the wallpaper is from the first iOS series," someone wrote. "Great work of deceiving people!"

I contacted the guy who wrote that—a Pakistani teacher named Khalid Syed—and he was happy to chat. "Sorry for my terrible English," he said. He and friends had seen the story about my iPad on CNN and suspected it was corporate dark arts by rivals of Apple. Or maybe, he suspected, "you want to be popular on Twitter." He said, "People are so after money. And can do anything to get money. I have seen it."

The emails and tweets kept arriving for several more days. The more I read, the more they reminded me of what Hannah Arendt called a "peculiar kind of cynicism" that settles into societies that allow the "consistent and total substitution of lies for factual truth." To get through the day, she wrote, people eventually embrace "the absolute refusal to believe the truth of anything." I had first jotted that line down a few years earlier, to make sense of my life in China. I had not expected it would be relevant once I came home.

Often, when I talked to Reese Clark, he had a theory that he wanted to test out on me. The theories varied in reliability. At the most exotic end, he suspected the government was planning to impose martial law, beginning in Black neighborhoods. He pointed out the pattern of traffic circles that were common in residential enclaves on the South Side. Those, he said, were not intended to prevent cars from speeding; they were "checkpoints" in the event that the military ever moved into the neighborhoods. "And they made the expressway wide as hell—for the tanks," he said.

Most of the time, though, his anxieties seemed to reflect an effort to find a logic in the cruelties and frustrations around him. He suspected the federal government funneled guns into the Black community in order to keep people fighting one another. "We've got military-grade bullets. How did we get *them*?" He had a memory from his drug-dealing days when an older white addict beckoned him into a garage to look inside a wooden crate. "It had hay in it, and it had damn AK-47s. Military shit. And, I said, 'Hell no, I'm gone. I don't want no part of it.'"

He had come to believe that politicians and police allowed Black neighborhoods to deteriorate on purpose; if people left, he figured, it would be easier to gentrify and profit from the real estate. "They're trying to get Blacks out," he said. "How do you get 'em out? You close down stores." He added, "It's not about being Black or white no more. It's the haves and the have-nots."

Most of all, he said, he was convinced that Donald Trump had only won in 2016 by cheating. "The voting was rigged," he told me. "I was watching the vote. They had the map of the United States, and they showed the blue parts, how much the Democrats won. Then they went to commercial, and when they came back, more of the states were red, and they said Trump won the motherfucking White House!"

├────────┤

At its core, Trump's project transcended simply dismissing the "reality-based community." His administration was undermining the notion of verifiable reality itself. After less than twenty-four hours in office, his spokesman Sean Spicer accused the media of deliberately underestimating the size of the crowd for Trump's inauguration. He called it the "largest audience to ever witness an inauguration—period—both in person and around the globe." When Spicer was mocked and condemned, Kellyanne Conway went on television and serenely defended Spicer's rant as an example of "alternative facts." Her term produced a chorus of ridicule, but she was undeterred; in a radio interview, she framed the criticism as a condescending hang-up of the liberal elite. "Americans are their own fact checkers," she said. "People know, they have their own facts and figures, in terms of meaning which facts and figures are important to them."

Within a month, Trump had declared the press the "enemy of the people," and that attack became a standard piece of his presentations. By the time Trump was performing before the crowd in Huntington that summer, his supporters had already been conditioned to expect that he rejected the facts that others told them to believe. The following year, he made it explicit. In a moment that could pass as mock-Orwell, he told a crowd, "Just remember: what you're seeing and what you're reading is not what's happening." (By the end of his term, he had made 30,573 false or misleading claims, according to *The Washington Post*.)

But the effect of his deceptions was not just an assault on knowledge. In ways that were only becoming visible over time, he was dismantling not only the concept of a common truth but also the notion of a truly shared world. He was rejecting the very notion of an empirical commons—the idea that anything could be free from the abuses and cynicism of politics. For a population already atomized and disillusioned by false promises, subjected to relentless reminders that government was not "here to help," it was its own call to arms. Trump was giving them not only permission to ignore the facts that seemed to be hoarded and treasured by the meritocratic elite; he was offering them an exhilarating antidote to loneliness—a new sense of solidarity defined, above all, by doubt.

To govern, he relied on the manufacturing of doubt, titillation, and seductive fictions—a politics by peek-a-boo. In its clearest formulation, Steve Bannon, the former head of Breitbart News and chief strategist for Trump, told the writer Michael Lewis, "We got elected on Drain the Swamp, Lock Her Up, Build a Wall." He said, "This was pure anger. Anger and fear is what gets people to the polls." Bannon added, "The Democrats don't matter. The real opposition is the media. And the way to deal with them is to flood the zone with shit."

The forces arrayed on the side of truth were ludicrously outmatched. In March 2018, Google pledged $300 million over three years to "help journalism thrive in the digital age." The company planned to train journalists in artificial intelligence and other technologies, and to help publishers enhance their digital products. It was a worthy initiative, though the impact was slight; the investment equated to less than the company earned in profits in a week.

At the same time that Americans were becoming less mobile— socially and geographically—they were being liberated from the old boundaries of information. Ideas—at their best and worst—were becoming only *more* mobile, racing around the country without the friction once imposed by gatekeepers such as John Miller in Clarksburg. The arbiters who used to weigh what was verified and important enough to merit attention, and what deserved to be shunted to the margins, had lost their mandate. Americans were voting in smaller and smaller numbers for mayors and county commissioners while adopting fiercer and more strident positions on issues thousands of miles away, from transgender bathrooms in North Carolina to gas pipelines in North Dakota.

The extraordinary political and economic changes of the last half century had exerted stresses on what people believed. In 1968, Peter Drucker, the American management consultant, predicted an "age of discontinuity" as globalization and technology made some jobs extinct and created new surges of wealth. In 1992, the political scientist Francis Fukuyama—who was often too quickly cast by critics as a triumphalist—warned that, after the Cold War, people in the West might well "struggle for the sake of struggle. They will struggle, in other words, out of a certain boredom: for they cannot imagine living in a world without struggle," he wrote. "And if the greater part of the world in which they live is characterized by peaceful and prosperous liberal democracy, then they will struggle against that peace and prosperity, and against democracy."

There was a prescient truth in it. Trump, the Tea Party, the NRA—they all made use of that rising unease of Americans who could not quite put a name to the anxieties they felt about the disordering of their world, about the puncturing of American invincibility, the browning of America, the vanishing of jobs to automation, the stagnation of their incomes. The language of force gained ground. Sarah Palin, in her appearances at Tea Party rallies and online, made frequent use of metaphors from the Revolutionary War and the world of guns. "Don't retreat, reload," she liked to say.

By the end of the Obama years, Americans were ideologically restless. Socialism was growing on the left, especially among young people who had been disillusioned by the Democratic Party. They had watched bankers escape punishment after the financial crisis, even as their own prospects for wealth and safety and opportunity declined. "You can make it if you try," Obama liked to say, but it was becoming ever harder to see that as a fact. On the right, meanwhile, nativism was growing. For those who were already stewing in economic or racial resentment, it had to do less with ideology than with a rootlessness of the mind—a loss of purpose, inspiration, and community. For people who felt excluded from the commanding heights of American life, it was tempting to hunt for explanations in conspiracies and superstitions, even when they bordered on the supernatural.

By November 2016, the demonization of Clinton and her advisers was so intense that even the most outlandish allegations about pedophilia, murder, and the occult found an audience. On Reddit, 4chan, and other forums, people hunted through emails leaked from the account of her campaign chairman, John Podesta. In their search for anything sinister, self-styled sleuths conjured up the suggestion of code words and hidden meanings: "pizza" could be code for child pornography; "pasta" meant little boy; "sauce" was an orgy. The delusions gained attention when they were amplified, on Twitter, by prominent figures such as retired general Michael Flynn, Trump's designated national security advisor. An especially deranged thread on Reddit tied it together into a theory that Podesta was a pedophile running a child sex-trafficking ring with Clinton from the basement of a pizzeria in Washington called Comet Ping Pong. (Never mind that the building had no basement.) An anonymous poster wrote, "Everyone associated with the business is making semi-overt, semi-tongue-in-cheek, and semi-sarcastic inferences towards sex with minors."

"Pizzagate," as it became known, seemed to crest on a Sunday afternoon a month after the election, when an armed twenty-eight-year-old believer who had binge-watched YouTube videos about Pizzagate, walked into Comet Ping Pong on a mission to save children. As people fled the building, he fired several rounds from his AR-15 rifle into a closet full of office equipment, hunting for a child-sex dungeon. After he surrendered to police, he told them he had come from his home in rural North Carolina to "self-investigate."

Over the next two years, the Pizzagate delusion continued to morph and spread like a pathogen, feeding into new conspiracy theories that fed even larger communities of belief. The most popular was QAnon, which emerged around a set of anonymous Web posts purported to be the work of a Trump loyalist, a U.S. government official with a high-level, or "Q-level," security clearance. The QAnon posts drew people in by unspooling gnomic clues suggesting the existence of a hidden cabal of Satan-worshipping, cannibalistic pedophiles plotting against Trump. It spread from fringe message boards to mainstream platforms, and Facebook eventually found millions of followers across thousands of groups and pages. Trump encouraged the fantasy—retweeting messages about it and praising its believers as "people who love our country."

Anne Applebaum, an American author and journalist who lived in Poland, had watched a wave of delusions sweep through Polish politics, and she came to recognize that each delusion "offered a new reason to distrust the politicians, businesspeople, and intellectuals," an explanation for hatred of the elites, she wrote. "It explains away complex phenomena, accounts for chance and accidents, offers the believer the satisfying sense of having special, privileged access to the truth."

Often, it didn't matter how acquainted with the real world of politics you were; the satisfactions of the fantasy were powerful. In 2018, Kelly Johnston, a former secretary of the Senate who had helped oversee the day-to-day work of the chamber, adopted the fantasy that George Soros's Open Society Foundations was secretly organizing the caravans of migrants that Trump had put at the center of his fearmongering. Johnston, who had become the vice president of government affairs for the Campbell Soup Company, tweeted photos of migrants in Mexico, which he appended with his imaginings about Soros: "See those vans on the right? What you don't see are the troop carriers and the rail cars taking them north." (Campbell Soup disavowed his comments, and he exited the company.)

———

The more Trump struggled to control the government, the more he leaned on the register of force. He stoked racial hostility, white identity politics, and fantastical fears of marauding immigrants.

Technology, of course, was linking right-wing populist believers together across vast distances. In economically struggling parts of the country, people were using technology not only to amplify their discontent but also to forge a sense of solidarity, to see validation in one another—a sign that they are not suffering alone. It allowed them to feel a sense of shared passion and fears and culture in ways that the nation's founders had not predicted. In *Federalist* No. 10, James Madison had argued that the scale of the United States would make it difficult for any faction to dominate all others. Earlier movements had made use of technology as well. After World War II, the civil rights movement that germinated in the rural South achieved broad national impact through the print and broadcast media, which attracted northern activists and eventually pressured politicians to respond. Later, the conservative move-ment used its own media networks, in newsletters, talk radio, and cable television. For Trump, the movement was growing on yet another genera-tion of technology—Twitter, Facebook, 4chan, Reddit.

Watching people slip deeper into Trump's fantasies and conspir-acy theories, I was struck by how much it reminded me of my years in China—where people were sometimes desperate to find causes that inspired them. Once when I wrote about a surge of toxic nationalism there, an observant young writer and translator named Lu Han told me, "Growing up in China, there are very few chances for you to feel like that—to be lifted spiritually, to be working on something bigger than yourself, more important than your immediate, ordinary life circle." Now I was seeing it around me in America.

Boredom, in Fukuyama's sense, was not a lack of stimulation; it was a grasping for meaning and recognition. In 2019, a team of political scientists who study the flow of information online discovered that an obscure segment of the American electorate was rapidly gaining influ-ence through their use of social media. The scholars—Michael Bang Petersen, Kevin Arceneaux, and Mathias Osmundsen—called those us-ers "marginalized status-seekers"; typically, they were male, languish-ing in jobs that they considered beneath them, and acutely sensitive to slights or condescension from elites and political celebrities. With few other ways to have an impact, they adopted what the researchers called a "strategy of last resort"—amplifying the most outrageous and incen-diary information they could find: "conspiracy theories, fake news, dis-cussions of political scandals and negative campaigns."

They had no ideology to advance; they were not sharing rumors because they actively believed them; it was, the authors wrote, "simply a tool to create havoc." They were the superspreaders behind the madness of the birther faction, of Pizzagate, of Alex Jones's delusions that the Sandy Hook Elementary School shooting was staged to promote gun control. In surveys, they asked people if they agreed with apocalyptic statements such as "When I think about our political and social in-stitutions, I cannot help thinking 'just let them all burn.'" They were startled to find that 40 percent of their respondents agreed. For the moment, the authors interpreted these "chaotic motivations" not as a sign that Americans were preparing for "actual fights with the police or to commit other forms of political violence." Instead, they wrote, it was a window into the "thoughts and behaviors that people are motivated to entertain when they sit alone (and lonely) in front of the computer, answering surveys or surfing social media platforms."

Part of America's predicament was that its political parties magnified the intensity of factions, rather than serving to negotiate their differences toward a compromise. Ideally, parties pull people into blocs that help bridge their racial, religious, and professional differences; they provide an alternative collective identity. But America's parties were doing precisely the opposite: they compounded and amplified the differences. In the five years since McConnell had used the bumper sticker "COAL. GUNS. FREEDOM," the identities had become even more distinct. The latest popular T-shirt on sale at rallies declared: "I support Donald Trump. I love freedom. I drink beer. I turn wrenches. I protect my family. I eat meat & I own guns. If you don't like it, MOVE."

At the Fund for Peace, a think tank in Washington, researchers ranked the political "cohesion" of various countries between 2008 and 2018; they measured the entrenchment of factions, trust in the security forces, and the level of popular discontent. The United States recorded the largest drop in cohesion among any of the countries studied, including Libya, Mali, and Bahrain. In a paper presented in 2018, the political scientists Nathan Kalmoe and Lilliana Mason found that 15 percent of Republicans and 20 percent of Democrats believed that the United States would be better off if large numbers of the opposing party "just died."

The culture of political warfare was about more than guns or fringe conspiracy theories. It was a mutant version of a mainstream ethos: a survival mindset derived from a sense of zero-sum contests, in which only one side can prevail. The weaker the public felt, the more they grasped for gestures of force; as in Freeman's portrait of antebellum violence, Americans were coming to believe that they could no longer afford to abide by the old norms. Freeman told me that violence was filling a void left by America's eroded democracy: "The current moment has reams of people who feel unheard and unrepresented amidst multiple crises, people who have been stewing in that gripe for years. They sense that the tides of demographics and culture are turning against them." She continued, "Cloak that in the rhetoric of democracy, and it has a real appeal."

On the left, the sense of an existential showdown was finding its own acute form. In the years since Trump entered politics, far-left vigilantes, operating under the loose label of Antifa, for "anti-fascist," adopted confrontational tactics inspired by the European anarchist tradition. The term originated in the 1930s, when German leftists brawled with Nazis in the streets; in the 1980s, members of the British punk scene tried to purge racism and hypernationalism from their ranks, sometimes with street-level violence. In America, Antifa protesters, often wearing black clothing and bandannas or masks over their faces, became visible on the edges of protests against Trump and white nationalism. Some employed violence in the belief that it was "preemptive" self-defense. Antifa gained wider public attention on Trump's inauguration day, when the white nationalist Richard Spencer was giving a television interview on a street corner and a masked protester, dressed in black, punched him in the head. Republicans and commentators took to condemning Antifa as a symbol of leftist excess and chaos, and a justification for tougher police tactics.

By the fall of 2018, the tempo of political violence was at a turning point. On both coasts, members of the Proud Boys, a self-described violent "Western chauvinist" group, fought in the streets with activists who identified with Antifa or Black Lives Matter. In Portland and New York City, police broke up melees, and some of Trump's allies expanded their preoccupation with violence in Chicago to blame it on their political opponents. Jeff Sessions, the attorney general, said, "If you want more shootings, more death, then listen to the ACLU, Antifa, Black Lives Matter, and groups who do not know the reality of policing."

The language of mortal confrontation was permeating politics so thoroughly that it no longer attracted notice. More than a year after white supremacists in Charlottesville chanted "You will not replace us," that message had been taken up by mainstream conservative commentators. In December 2018, Tucker Carlson told his audience, "It's like, shut up, you're dying. We're going to replace you." On Fox, Ann Coulter said, "You can't shoot Americans. You can shoot invaders." On August 3, 2019, on 8chan, a far-right forum, a commentator named Patrick Crusius combined those ideas and committed himself to "defending my country from cultural and ethnic replacement brought on by an invasion." Several minutes later, he walked into a Walmart in El Paso and killed twenty-three people.

In a single week in October 2018: A gunman in Louisville killed two Black senior citizens in a grocery store, telling a bystander "whites don't shoot whites." A gunman in Pittsburgh killed eleven people at a synagogue, the deadliest attack on Jews in American history. And, in Florida, a man who lived in a van plastered with Trump signs sent pipe bombs to a dozen people, including Soros and two former presidents. (Reporters later discovered that his house had been foreclosed in 2009 by a bank whose principal owner and chairman was Trump's treasury secretary, Steven Mnuchin.)

At the end of that bloody seven-day span, even Trump seemed to sense that he had unleashed forces that could, in an instant, burn beyond his control. At a nighttime rally in Murphysboro, Illinois, a small city in the rural southern reaches of the state, he said, "If you don't mind, I'm going to tone it down—just a little." But it was too late. The crowd roared back with a resounding "No!"

SEVENTEEN

THE ANTIBODIES

"I'M DONE APPEALING to power from outside," Katey Lauer, the West Virginia activist, told me. "We have to be the people that are governing ourselves."

Four years after the chemical spill that revealed a government in disrepair, a proudly radical movement was gathering in West Virginia. The state was an unlikely laboratory for progressive politics, but a "revolutionary spirit" was in the air, as local activists put it. On February 22, 2018, more than 22,000 West Virginia teachers, school-bus drivers, and staff walked off the job, the first statewide school strike in nearly thirty years. West Virginia teachers were among the most poorly paid in America—forty-eighth in the nation—and they had gone without a raise for four years. Many lived from paycheck to paycheck, and worked second jobs when they weren't in the classroom.

Accompanied by spouses and children, thousands of chanting teachers filed into the doors beneath the golden dome of the state capitol. They wore red bandannas, a symbol of labor battles going back to 1877, when West Virginia railroad workers sparked the first national strike in U.S. history. The workers with red bandannas went on to wage some of America's most iconic labor fights, becoming known as the "rednecks," a term that only later became a byword for poor white prejudice. Over the decades, the spirit of the red bandannas faded in West Virginia as the share of unionized workers sank from 38 percent in 1978 to 13 percent by 2018, but the teachers' strike marked the opening of a different era. It lasted nine days and succeeded in winning a 5 percent pay raise—and inspired similar strikes in other Republican-led states, including Arizona, Kentucky, and Oklahoma. Other industries followed, and by year's end the United States had recorded more workers on strike in 2018 than in any year since Ronald Reagan was in office.

But the revolutionary spirit of 2018 extended far beyond the world of organized labor. In ways only beginning to become clear, the moral calculus of Trump's presidency was stirring a full-scale resistance to the established order, a movement against racism, misogyny, and economic exploitation across a broad spectrum of American life. Since the fall of 2017, when dozens of women had accused the film producer Harvey Weinstein of rape and sexual abuse, the #MeToo movement had catalyzed accusations against powerful men around the globe. The fury was fueled not only by decades of dismissal and silence but also by Trump's ongoing escape from accountability for his own transgressions, despite his own voice on tape and accusations of misconduct from twenty-six women.

By the spring of 2018, the number of women signing up to run for the House of Representatives had broken records, but an even starker measure emerged from Emily's List, a super PAC focused on electing pro-choice female candidates. The group tracked the number of women who contacted it for help in running for office even if most, ultimately, did not run. In 2016, a total of 920 women contacted Emily's List that year for assistance. In 2018, the number was 34,000.

The backlash to Trump was not only a rebuttal to the politics of exclusion and fear and dominance; it was also a war on the dogma of starving a government to the point of dysfunction; it was a declaration of hope that a well-run government could be a unifying force. That rebuttal, from across American life, felt analogous to a biological process—antibodies converging on an illness in the body politic, a battle to suppress the culture of "thoughts and prayers," white supremacy, the corruption of democracy, and the sheer force of cynicism.

Instead of looking at issues separately—as matters of economics or politics or safety or the environment—people demanded to acknowledge how the connections among them were a barrier to progress. In West Virginia, the protests carried the imprint of activism far away—of Occupy Wall Street and of the Sanders campaign. Teachers carried banners that declared, "Public Employee Healthcare—NOT Corporate Welfare." They were rising up against economic and political imbalances that had become increasingly untenable. Recently, the Walmart in McDowell County had closed, which had not only eliminated 140 scarce local jobs; it had also eliminated the supplier to a local food pantry that fed 11,000 people.

<hr />

To Katey and other progressive activists, the teachers' strike was the glimpse of an opportunity: "Evidence that something like what we were imagining could be possible," she told me. After years of issue-based campaigns—gathering signatures, pressing lawmakers—Katey had grown demoralized. The levers of representative democracy were out of reach to those without money. In the fight over water quality, for instance, the chief regulatory agency, the Public Service Commission, was stocked with former industry executives. "They are buddies with the very companies that they're supposed to be regulating," she said. "It was a wake-up call for me," she added. "We're done knocking at the door of the capitol. We want to occupy it."

Even as the strike was under way, Katey started roughing out a political plan with another up-and-coming activist, Stephen Smith, who was considering a run for governor in 2020. At thirty-eight, Stephen was a West Virginia native who had graduated from Harvard and returned home to work on poverty alleviation. He was tall, telegenic, and a passionate speaker, which invited comparisons to Beto O'Rourke, the Democratic congressman who was challenging Ted Cruz for a Senate seat in Texas. Stephen was running a nonprofit that had succeeded in pressing legislators to raise the minimum wage and expand school-breakfast programs. But, like Katey, he was increasingly frustrated by the depth of corruption and propaganda embedded in West Virginia politics. "When your government doesn't do right by you, you have to pick up the slack," he told me. "The solutions will not come from any company or political party, or politician. They will come from regular people, like they always have."

In West Virginia, the incumbent governor, Jim Justice, was an especially attractive target for activists on the left. Justice was a billionaire who had inherited a coal-mining business from his father and expanded it into an empire that encompassed real estate and hotels. Since he had defected to Trump's party, critics had unearthed other similarities between them: according to the *Charleston Gazette-Mail*, "Justice's coal operations have been cited for pollution and safety violations, and his companies have millions in unpaid back taxes."

In November 2018, Stephen entered the race; Katey was his campaign manager. But their campaign against the governor was only the most visible piece of their projects. Their ultimate goal was to recruit a broad slate of candidates they called "West Virginia Can't Wait," to run for offices up and down the ballot. In homage to the rednecks, they wore red bandannas as they traveled the state, signing up people who wanted to become members of city councils, magistrate judges, and county commissioners—all in hopes of creating what they called a "people's government." Wherever they went, they held public town halls—eventually surpassing two hundred—and collected thousands of voter surveys, which formed their platform. At the town halls, one of their most effective bits was a riff on musical chairs: Stephen asked for six volunteers; then he picked two who were permitted to spread out over two chairs each. While the other four jostled for the two remaining chairs, they rarely stopped to question why the first volunteers had received twice their fair share. So it was in America today, Stephen said. The game reminded me of a comment by one of Trump's friends, Carl Icahn, the corporate raider: "I don't believe in the word 'fair,'" he told a biographer. "It's a human concept that became conventional wisdom."

The activists behind West Virginia Can't Wait embraced progressive aims—single-payer health care, free college, an end to homelessness—but they avoided the term "progressive," because rural voters greeted it warily. A generation of conservative attacks on a government "here to help" had left a deep imprint. Instead, the activists created their own label; they declared themselves the opponents of the "good old boys" system, a political culture of cronyism that allowed companies and investors to extract value from the land and the people without a fair return. In policy terms, their proposals included a tax on the state's forestland, which had been owned for more than a century by national railways without generating revenue for citizens.

As they trooped from one county to the next, holding town halls and meetings with local bigwigs, they never knew how their caravan of young, left-leaning activists would be received. In the small southern city of Hinton (population 2,676), while they waited to meet with a local police officer, a receptionist eyed them warily. In the meeting, Stephen started with the question he often opened with: "What's the first thing you would do if you were governor?" The cop's eyes widened. Then he unloaded on the problems of political corruption and corporate influence in politics. "How come these lobbyists are controlling everything?" he asked. For an hour they talked about the levers of influence and the imbalances of power that had drawn Stephen and Katey into the race.

Katey had no illusions that she and a local cop in Hinton would see eye-to-eye on everything. "There are a thousand other things on our platform that we would not have agreed about," she told me. But she was struck by the possibility of assembling a more diverse coalition than people assumed, organized around frustration with the failures of democracy. "It's not as simple as 'This guy is with us on everything—or he's not!'" she said. "I think the left imagines that in order for us to make progress, everyone has to agree about everything. I don't think that's true. I think in order to make progress, we have to build alignment around things that we want to advance, and let there be complexity— and move forward, anyhow."

As months passed, they found their audience. They recruited a slate of rookie candidates, including more than a dozen teachers and other school workers who had been radicalized by the strike. To join their slate, candidates had to promise not to accept corporate donations, or avoid a debate, or cross a picket line. "We thought if we could find twenty or twenty-five of these people to run, that would be a miracle. A year later, there are ninety-three of us," Stephen said.

Their movement stood out in West Virginia for one more reason: in one of the country's most rapidly aging states, they were young. "More than half of us are forty years of age or younger," Stephen said. For millennials, the diverse generation of Americans born between 1981 and 1996, the call for justice and fairness reflected deep frustration with the basic economic framework of American life. The 2008 financial crisis, and the recession that followed, had altered the course of their lives; they were approaching middle age in poorer financial shape than every living generation before them—with less wealth, less property, lower rates of marriage, and fewer children. In 2016, for instance, a typical millennial household had an average net worth of about $92,000, which was nearly 40 percent less than Gen X households in 2001, adjusted for inflation.

Stephen's campaign eventually broke the state record for individual contributions in a governor's race; when they uploaded the donor roll to the secretary of state's office, the website crashed from the load. In one of America's most politically demoralized places, they had attracted 2,449 small donors; Justice, the incumbent, had 13.

———

Far from Washington, each new drama of the Trump era reverberated through American life in ways both public and private. In the fall of 2018, Trump nominated Judge Brett Kavanaugh to the Supreme Court; a psychology professor named Christine Blasey Ford accused him of sexually assaulting her thirty-six years earlier, which Kavanaugh denied. Ford was inundated with death threats, but she testified anyway before the Senate Judiciary Committee: "I am here today not because I want to be. I am terrified." Ford's testimony became an inspiration to women around the world. Members of the public called in to C-SPAN to reveal their own decades-old stories of rape and harassment, and to speak out against their oppressors and for themselves. On social media, women from Ghana to France to Hong Kong posted their admiration for Ford after watching the hearings.

In Charleston, West Virginia, Jamie Miller, an artist and mother of four, heard Ford tell her story and reached a decision: Miller called her grown children and told them that she had been sexually assaulted in her teens. The assault had left her pregnant, and she had an abortion. "It was something I never talked about," Miller said later. Even though Kavanaugh was confirmed, Ford's testimony, she said, "woke me up."

Miller decided to become a volunteer at the Women's Health Center of West Virginia, the state's sole abortion provider. It was harrowing work; she escorted patients through a gauntlet of protesters, including the most persistent among them, an aspiring politician named Derrick Evans. He implied that he was carrying a gun; if his First Amendment rights were taken away, he told a reporter, he still had his Second Amendment rights. He specialized in livestreaming his confrontations on Facebook, where he accumulated a following of more than 40,000 viewers. In one video, he shouted at a patient, "You're still going to be a mother when you come out of there, just the mother to a dead baby!" Evans took a special interest in hectoring Miller, the volunteer, posting videos of himself calling her a "witch" and a "baby killer." On Facebook, one of Evans's supporters wrote, "If you murder her, can we call it abortion!!"

Eventually, inspired by Christine Blasey Ford, Miller took Evans to court. She won an order of protection that barred him from protesting at the clinic for eighteen months. And yet, among his supporters, Evans had succeeded in raising his profile, and in June 2019 he announced plans to run for the state legislature. He was endorsed by powerful political action committees, including the State Troopers Association. Miller wrote to the group, citing the order of protection as evidence that Evans was unfit for its endorsement. "No one would listen to me," Miller recalled. Evans won his election in November 2020.

In the Trump era, Americans were reexamining features of life that had been all but taken for granted. In the summer of 2018, people took to swapping news clips that matched a recurring pattern—purportedly heartwarming stories of persistence or generosity that were, on closer inspection, camouflaged evidence of broken politics. There was the case of Angela Hughes, a mother in Kansas City who gave birth to a premature baby; her coworkers donated their vacation days to her because her job did not provide paid maternity leave. The story circulated on Twitter, and a British journalist wrote, "As an outsider, this is bizarre to me. Here in the UK, 28 days of paid leave per year is considered the baseline, and maternity pay is a statutory right." There was a story of Ian Christensen, a six-year-old boy with Type 1 diabetes who was selling pumpkins in Michigan so that he might afford a dog that can detect dangerous fluctuations in blood sugar. Adam H. Johnson, a journalist, called it "completely batshit this story is framed in a positive light and not a horrifying indictment of our healthcare system." Another commenter wrote, dryly, "You too can make it through hard work and perseverance, and obtain the basics of life!"

⊢———⊣

In November 2018, the gathering forms of backlash to the Trump era converged in a stark political change: Democrats seized control of the House of Representatives, winning forty seats in the largest blue wave since 1974. In Congress, the new arrivals included influential progressives who put immediate pressure not only on Republicans but also on establishment Democrats. Alexandria Ocasio-Cortez of New York, a Democratic Socialist born less than a month after the fall of the Berlin Wall, became the youngest woman ever elected to Congress. Days after her victory, she joined the Sunrise Movement, a youth-led activist group against climate change, in a sit-in outside the office of Nancy Pelosi, the incoming Speaker of the House of Representatives.

Young progressives represented a generation that had come to doubt the central story of how America perceived itself; in their view, it was a system that had failed to stem inequality, climate change, oligarchy, and political capture. They introduced a slate of progressive ideas—debt-free college, Medicare for all, a Green New Deal—and Ocasio-Cortez called for a marginal tax rate of 70 percent on incomes above $10 million.

Within weeks, the 2020 presidential campaign was under way, and progressive candidates seized on Trump's support for the wealthy as an argument for transformational change. Announcing her campaign, Senator Elizabeth Warren of Massachusetts said Trump was "not the cause of what's broken, he's just the latest, and most extreme, symptom of what's gone wrong in America." Among other changes, Warren was promoting a bill that would allow workers to elect 40 percent of the members of corporate boards; she also called for an annual tax of 2 percent on the wealth of Americans with a net worth over $50 million. Sanders, running again for president, called for restoring the inheritance tax to its level in the 1970s, including 45 percent on estates above $3.5 million, and up to 77 percent for billionaires.

The Trump presidency, in its flamboyant embrace of plutocracy and old-school masculine white dominance, had hastened an acute showdown in U.S. politics over inequality. In other moments, Americans had tended to regard the country's largest fortunes as a kind of national spectacle and, for some, a source of inspiration. But that mood no longer prevailed. Polls routinely confirmed a survey by NBC News and *The Wall Street Journal*, in which 70 percent of Americans described themselves as angry "because our political system seems to only be working for the insiders with money and power."

Activists staged a bus tour of Greenwich called "Lifestyles of the Rich and Shameless," which stopped outside the homes (or, more often, the walls) of local financiers. They left giant "tax bills," charging the owners for what the tour's organizers called "the havoc they've wreaked on our economy." At the time, Connecticut was considering cutting 4,000 state jobs, to relieve a $1.7 billion budget deficit. The activists' final stop was at the office of Cliff Asness, the libertarian hedge-fund manager who had observed that children in town debated the finer points of hedge-fund strategies. Outside his office, the demonstrators erected a giant inflatable pig chomping on a cigar.

⊢——⊣

Amid that populist outrage, some prominent citizens of Greenwich joined the ranks of business leaders who argued that capitalism needed to change in order to survive. Ray Dalio, who had founded the hedge fund Bridgewater and accumulated a fortune estimated at $18 billion, which made him the town's richest resident, called income inequality a "national emergency." I stopped by his office, in a modern complex tucked into a secluded estate akin to a state park. We sat beside a wall of glass overlooking a pond where birds swooped in and out of the reeds.

In his late sixties, Dalio was tall and thin, with longish pale hair and a face of expressive intensity. He acknowledged that the full depth of inequality remained largely unseen by many of his friends and neighbors. "That's true for most Americans who are blind to how poverty and bad conditions are," he said. "We don't have direct contact with it. I live in Greenwich, which is a short drive from pockets of poverty in cities like Bridgeport, but the populations are divided by canyons in income and experience." He was awoken to it, he said, not by protesters or by Trump's plutocracy, but by his wife, Barbara, who had been a volunteer and a donor in low-income Connecticut public schools. "If it wasn't for my wife's close contact with those in Bridgeport, we wouldn't have any contact with it either, because who from Greenwich goes and hangs out in Bridgeport?" he said.

No surprise, Dalio didn't agree with what he called "billionaires-are-bad" political rhetoric. "It's bad to demonize any group of people," he said. "Most billionaires are good, hardworking people who made their money by coming up with something that paid a lot. Most aren't evil bloodsuckers. They play by rules that our legislatures made. If you don't like what they're doing, speak with those who wrote the laws. I think that those who write the laws should tax the rich and companies more in order to get resources to help those who are unfairly starved, but that's just what I think."

The longer we talked, the more I sensed that Dalio was mindful not to sound like a scold. Even among Greenwich billionaires who had awakened to the full implications of inequality, many avoided dwelling on the details of how the finance industry had contributed to the problem—how investors had extracted the last value from ailing industries, or "strip-mined" local news, or used the bankruptcy courts to abandon pension and health-care commitments. At a convention in

Greenwich, the hedge-fund manager Paul Tudor Jones urged the audience to recognize that workers had been shortchanged, but he hastened to reassure attendees: "It wasn't because good people did bad things. It was unfortunately just a natural, unchecked movement." Alan Barry, the town's commissioner of human services, told me that he applauded the concern but disagreed with the notion that inequality was unforeseeable. "Stated policies combined to create this," he said. "Now you're turning around and saying, 'Whoa, we've got runaway capitalism.'"

On the whole, the targets of broad American antipathy tended not to look inward for its source. "It's all this rapid technological change that results in income inequality," Peterffy, who had owned the town's largest estate, told me. "It suddenly increases productivity, and we need fewer workers to produce the same amount of goods and services." One remedy, he said, is direct payments to citizens, and he has become an advocate for replacing all government benefits with a universal basic income: "It is much, much cheaper to give the people money and not restrict business in any way." I asked Peterffy, who built a fortune worth an estimated $14 billion, if he thought America could have avoided radical inequality by not permitting people like him to amass so much money. "Well, it would have decreased my incentive to work as hard as I did," he said. "The number of times I nearly went bankrupt, if I would have had an easier way out, I probably would've chosen that." Not long before we spoke, he sold his Greenwich estate and moved to Florida, which had no state income tax.

But, as Sanders, Warren, and others gained attention, some prominent investors sensed that the country was approaching a turning point; if their industry did not begin to acknowledge abuses and imbalances of power, it was courting a harsh reckoning. Not long after the midterm elections, Seth Klarman, a low-key but influential investor based in Boston, told me, "I don't think it's too late for business leaders to start doing the right thing for their employees, their clients, and their communities." And if they don't? He said, "Somebody's going to come along and do it for them."

Klarman, the CEO and president of Baupost Group, a hedge fund with $27 billion in assets, was sometimes called the "Oracle of Boston" and compared with Warren Buffett. His book *Margin of Safety* was a cult collectible; old dog-eared copies sold on Amazon for more than a thousand dollars. For many years, he was New England's largest donor to the Republican Party. But, ever since Trump had emerged as the Republican front-runner, Klarman had been outspoken in his conviction that Trump posed a grave threat to democracy. In the 2018 midterms, he had donated heavily to Democratic candidates and to organizations dedicated to shoring up the rule of law. He knew some people derided that as "flip-flopping." But, he said, "I think people who fail to evolve and learn are part of the problem."

It was an unusual acknowledgment. On both the right and the left, Americans often made a curiously similar case that capitalism had always operated by the norms and behaviors that defined it in the early twenty-first century; to many on the left, there had never been a golden age of American capitalism, and pretending there had been was to ignore the sacrifices of those who were silenced; to conservatives, inequality was a perennial outgrowth of creative destruction, a virtue as much as a problem. But Klarman, after decades in the business, was conceding, unabashedly, that standards *had* deteriorated. "I'm convinced, as an investor, that the world I live in every day has gotten more short-term-oriented," he told me. Some investors, he said, had become too quick to demand ephemeral fixes that reverberated through society: "Why aren't you restructuring? Why aren't you doing a spin-off? Why aren't you buying back stock?'"

Klarman told me, "The pressure on the game changed the game." It reminded me of Chip Skowron's plunge into the pressures of the hedge-fund world, where he had to learn fast from those around him at S.A.C. Capital. They had honed their edges, and if he wanted to succeed, he had to compete. In a speech at Harvard Business School, Klarman argued that the business world had tipped too far toward the fixation on shareholder value, preached by Milton Friedman, to the exclusion of other effects. "Does anyone really believe that shareholders are the only constituency that matters: not customers, not employees, not the community or the country or planet Earth?" he asked. He challenged his peers to accept greater responsibility for the consequences of their actions. "It's a choice to do things that 'maximize profits,' to pay people as little as you can, or work them as hard as you can," he said. "It's a choice to maintain pleasant working conditions or, alternatively, particularly harsh ones: to offer good benefits or paltry ones."

Klarman's critiques of Washington and of irresponsible business practices shared a common target: both cultures had come to celebrate winning at all costs. "If we think of free enterprise and democracy as games, a lot of people are breaking the rules and disrespecting the other players and even the game itself. Mitch McConnell is disrespecting the game. Donald Trump doesn't even know what the rules are," he said. "Just because you *can* do something definitely doesn't mean that you should."

⊢———⊣

For all its agonies, the Trump era had a clarifying effect: it exposed the poisonous personal ambition that drove so many in Washington, especially the city's "good Germans" who shuffled behind a president they privately reviled; it punctured the simplistic folklore that decisiveness was more important than expertise, that blindly cutting costs would pare the government down to strength. Most of all, perhaps, it snapped Americans out of the fantasy that apathy on Election Day was a viable option. Trump had unwittingly demonstrated the wisdom of Elihu Root so long ago: "Men must either govern or be governed." In measurable ways, Trump was embarrassing people into action: in 2003, 70 percent of Americans had said they were "extremely proud" to be American, according to Gallup. By 2018, that number had sunk to 47 percent, the first time it had ever dipped below a majority. The Trump era not only generated antibodies; it also shook the politics of Washington with such force that issues that had been frozen for a generation began to thaw—even if the change was forced, in some cases, by horrific pressures.

In February 2018, a former high school student who had professed hatred for Mexicans, Jews, and immigrants, and done target practice while wearing a MAGA hat, opened fire at Marjory Stoneman Douglas High School in Parkland, Florida. He killed seventeen people and injured seventeen others, surpassing the Columbine attack as the deadliest high school shooting in American history. Within hours, it was clear that the attack was sparking a different political effect than so many other shootings. Many of the Parkland students, unlike those who contended with day-to-day violence in Chicago, were relatively prosperous and well-connected. They used social media to force the country to view the horrors they had survived. Hiding in a darkened classroom, one of the students, David Hogg, held up his phone and taped a calm indictment of American politics: "Take a stance for human lives," he said, "for children's lives."

When politicians responded with the usual thoughts and prayers, the students humiliated them. In a televised town hall a few days after the attack, Senator Marco Rubio stood across from survivors and the parents of dead children. Rubio, more than most of his peers in Congress, had a reputation for smoothness. Even in his twenties, as a local official, he had exhibited such innate promise that one of his colleagues took to saying, "When Marco Rubio speaks, young women swoon, old women faint, and toilets flush themselves." But now Rubio was face-to-face with a seventeen-year-old junior named Cameron Kasky, who asked, simply, "Would you refuse to accept donations from the National Rifle Association in the future?" Rubio, who had an A-plus rating from the NRA, evaded the question with a favorite dodge: "I will always accept the help of anyone who agrees with my agenda . . . But they buy into my agenda; I don't buy into theirs." The crowd booed, and Kasky pursued him again, and again. Rubio had no escape; he gave a pained expression and repeated his platitudes.

Watching the scene at home in Washington, I sensed that the exasperation with Rubio was a sign of a larger despair at the falseness of so many rituals of my city: the evasive pivot, the pallid follow-up question. Rubio, that day, was a portrait of cynicism, as if a computer had been tasked with generating a senator out of bromides and tics and half-truths. I remembered a previous moment when Rubio had been asked, in a routine interview: If you could invite anyone, living or dead, for a beer, who would it be? He thought for a second, as if rifling through index cards, and then solemnly replied, "Malala," referring to the young Pakistani activist awarded the Nobel Peace Prize in 2014 for her advocacy of female education. It was an answer steeped in seriousness, marred only by the vision of him handing a beer to a child who was also an observant Muslim.

In a few minutes on television, the students from Parkland had exposed the void at Rubio's core more vividly than any seasoned interviewer had ever done. In the months after the killings, students organized a series of protests that constituted some of the largest youth-led demonstrations since the Vietnam era. At its core, it was a generational confrontation, in which a rising cohort of Americans pointed their fingers at forebears who had failed to mount serious responses to gun violence, just as they had fumbled the rising threat of climate change. The students joined an increasingly adept political movement for gun control—led, in part, by the former New York mayor Michael Bloomberg and the former Arizona congresswoman Gabby Giffords, who had been shot while giving a speech. By the end of 2018, states had enacted more than three times as many gun-control measures as the year before. In the midterm elections, gun-control groups outspent the NRA, and they narrowly defeated at least eight incumbents with A ratings from it.

By early 2019, the politics of guns were transforming to a degree that is easy to miss from afar. The new Democratic majority in the House of Representatives passed a requirement for universal background checks—the first major gun-control bill to clear the chamber in a quarter of a century. Though everyone knew it would not pass the Senate that year, E. J. Dionne, in *The Washington Post*, called it "the beginning of the end of the gun lobby's power." The NRA, meanwhile, was descending into an internal feud over allegations of corruption and mismanagement. Leaked tax records showed that Wayne LaPierre, the top executive, had billed the NRA for $275,000 in purchases from the Zegna luxury boutique in Beverly Hills, as well as another quarter of a million dollars in personal flights and limousine service, to the Bahamas, Florida, Italy, and elsewhere. The details attracted the attention of the New York attorney general, Letitia James, who launched an investigation into the organization's tax-exempt status.

As the pressure on it rose, the NRA made increasingly desperate demands for money. For years, ever since attending the convention, I'd been receiving emails with one solicitation or another: "Evan, We Want

You Back!" a message began. If I reupped my dues for $35, I could choose from a selection of free NRA-branded merchandise, including an assortment of hunting knives or a camouflage duffel bag.

Over the winter, as Democrats gained control of Congress, the messages grew more urgent. In February 2019, I opened a message marked "Save Freedom! . . . Save Money! . . . Terrific Value!" It reported, "Nancy Pelosi and her gun-ban majority in the U.S. House of Representatives are pushing forward on a sweeping agenda to BAN GUNS and REGISTER gun owners. Angry media elites are flooding the airwaves with their demands for GUN CONTROL—blaming you and your freedoms for the acts of violent criminals and madmen."

On they came, week after week. "Last chance!" another message began. "Offer Expires in 72 Hours!" But it was never really the last chance, and the messages continued. In March, after the New York attorney general filed suit, the NRA's appeals in my in-box acquired a clearer, more apocalyptic cast. The group had a new enemy, and it summoned its members to turn their combat mindset on the latest political target:

> Gun-hating state attorney generals are orchestrating a coordinated campaign to bury the NRA under a mountain of frivolous lawsuits . . . and silence your voice . . . I don't have to tell you that these are must-win battles for us. If we don't meet these threats head on, our enemies will destroy the NRA, annihilate the Second Amendment and fundamentally transform America— FOREVER. Now more than ever, it's up to you . . . me . . . and the more than 5 million members of the NRA to man the barricades and fight back with every ounce of strength we can muster.

⊢————⊣

As I crisscrossed the country in those years, guns were a strangely unifying artifact of American experience—a feature of life that could be found no matter how far apart people were in attitude and experience. They generated political identities and private anguish; they were either loved or hated but impossible to ignore. The longer I was back in the United States, the easier it was to lose sight of how truly bizarre the phenomenon of regular American massacres was to the rest of the advanced world. In 2019, after mass shootings in Dayton and El Paso killed thirty-one people in a weekend, Japan alerted travelers, much as the U.S. State Department warns Americans heading abroad. The Japanese consulate in Michigan reminded its citizens that the United States was a "gun society," in which the potential for gunfire was "everywhere."

To many people in Chicago, the reputation for gun violence was exhausting; the basic facts were true, but outsiders seemed too eager to sensationalize it. Jahmal Cole, a community organizer on the South Side, watched a visiting cameraman from a suburban television station survey a block in search of images. The cameraman turned away from a new community garden and a high-performing elementary school, and instead zoomed in on boarded-up houses, piles of trash, and clusters of young men. Cole watched the results that night on television with frustration; the proportions felt reductive and misleading. It was "propaganda created to scare people," he thought, even as he himself spent his days trying to solve some of the very problems shown on-screen.

One afternoon that summer, Cole walked his eight-year-old daughter, Khammur, to a playground. As he often did, he ventured to a neighborhood safer than his own—on this occasion Hyde Park, where his idol, Barack Obama, used to work. As Khammur played on the jungle gym, Cole heard a bang, then another and another. He grabbed his daughter and pulled her to the ground, willing their bodies into the wood chips beneath them. After a moment, it was quiet again. They were unharmed. But moments like that made him crazy, because he knew from experience that memories from that age would linger with Khammur for a long time. He rolled over and tossed some wood chips into the air, trying to persuade her that it had been a joke all along.

Cole was thirty-six. He stood six feet, three inches tall, with broad, ropy shoulders and broad hands. He had been a bench warmer on his college basketball team, by his own description, but remained a determined athlete who rarely went a day without running three miles through neighborhoods that many people avoided crossing on foot.

It was a posture of willful normalcy; Cole was determined to give his daughters, Khammur and Kennedy, more stability than he had known. His father, Leonard, had served in the Navy and then started using drugs, which tipped the family into chaos. Cole's mother, Gloria, was a Jehovah's Witness who took him to church, where he studied the cadence and confidence of the pastors. His father had no interest in church but let him go, "so I wouldn't be scared to talk to white people," Cole told me.

Cole grew up mostly with his father, who was sporadically employed but joyfully immersed in the art and literature of the Black freedom struggle. They cycled through a series of cheap apartments and motels, where Leonard covered the walls with clippings and posters "like it was the Sistine Chapel," Cole recalled. Each week, Leonard gave his son an allowance of thirty dollars, but by the end of the month, he was borrowing it back to buy them dinner.

Cole developed a stubborn resistance to low expectations. When a guidance counselor told him he should aim for trade school or the army, he ripped a random page from a college guidebook and applied to some of the schools. Cole wound up at tiny Wayne State College in Wayne, Nebraska. It was a blessing. He joined the basketball team, and though he rarely made it onto the court, the team gave him a chance to travel and it held him to a tight schedule. "My basketball coach taught me, 'If you're on time, you're already late,'" he said.

After graduation, he worked odd jobs and partied too much, by his own description. But in 2008, Obama's victory shifted something inside him: "I started reading his books," he said. Cole admired the campaign's use of social media, and he was impressed by Obama's ability to cut across lines of race and class. "If Dr. Martin Luther King Jr. was alive today, the Southern Christian Leadership Conference would be a Facebook group," Cole said.

In 2009, Cole found a few days' work carrying boxes and sweeping up in the office of a trading firm, not far from where Santelli delivered his Tea Party rant. He made a point to show up early, which caught the attention of the bosses, who eventually found a permanent job for him in the IT department. Cole felt out of place; the office was almost entirely white, male, and preppy. "They come from all these environments where they sail and play hockey. And then there's me." He was fascinated by the founder of the firm, a low-key Minnesotan named Will Hobert. "He's white. His wife is white. They're really rich, and they live on the North Side. But you wouldn't know it because he dresses worse than me," Cole said. Not long after Cole started, Hobert threw him the keys to his car and asked him to fetch a computer from their home. Nobody had ever demonstrated that kind of trust in Cole, and it thrilled him.

Hobert sent Cole for training as a Microsoft systems administrator. It didn't go well. "I failed," Cole said. "I went back to him. I was embarrassed. I was like, 'Yo, I know it costs a lot of money but I never knew what that shit was before.' He was like, 'Well, could you do better?' And I said, 'I'm going to get some flash cards, and I'm going to work on it with my wife. Put me in school again.' He put in another ten thousand. Boom, I failed again. But I missed it by like five points, so he put me in one more time. I passed."

He spent the next four years at the trading firm as a Microsoft administrator. But by 2013, his attention was elsewhere. On the side, he had started volunteering as a mentor for juvenile offenders in Cook County. He was startled to discover how few of them had ever spent more than a few minutes in downtown Chicago, even though it was only a bus ride from their neighborhoods. "A kid said, 'My block is Twenty-first Street.' Another said, 'My hood is Roseland.' I was like, why don't you all ever say 'my city'? And they said, 'Because there's no Black people downtown.'"

Cole's own biography had persuaded him of the perils of segregation and of the prospects of getting people into worlds outside their own. He conceived of an idea for a community organization. "I wanted to call the program Changing Your Perspective," he said, "but that would look stupid on a T-shirt. So I called it My Block, My Hood, My City." Around town, people started calling it M3 for short. He left his IT job, and his old boss agreed to be his first donor.

├───┤

Cole started calling businesses to ask if he could bring young men and women on field trips, or "explorations," as he called them. Just about anywhere could qualify, as long as it was a new experience. And so they took field trips to a chiropractor's office, a scuba-diving class, and a waste treatment plant. He also took them to volunteer at a homeless shelter so they could see, as he put it, "somebody whose poverty makes them look like the upper middle class."

As his group expanded, he started to think of it as a "mini city hall." He took to arranging field trips of a different kind—tours for Chicago cops in Black neighborhoods, led by local kids. "They'll say, 'Hey, this is where Dr. King lived when he was in North Lawndale. That's where he spoke. And this is the block where I live. And these are the best hoagies in the city,'" he said. "A lot of cops don't know the history of the neighborhoods before they police them, and it also gives the youth an opportunity to speak to a police officer without being arrested. It's a skill that nobody really has." Everything Cole did was designed to develop what he called "the muscle of empathy."

On a hot afternoon in the summer of 2019, Cole and I were in the back of a jouncy yellow school bus with a dozen kids on their way to a condiment factory. He had arranged a visit to Select Brands LLC ("Makers of Mumbo Bar-B-Q Sauce"). In the seats around us, young men and women—earbuds in, expressions of dutiful attendance—were slumped in their seats. One way or another, they had been led to Cole, because they were out of the usual rhythms of school; some had been expelled, some had gotten pregnant, others had given up on school because it felt too unsafe to be there.

We pulled onto the highway and ground to a halt. All we could see was red taillights to the horizon. An accident had shut down the road. They would miss their appointment. Cole changed plans. For today's exploration, they would go to a restaurant instead, and try a food the kids had never tasted. He offered them some options—Indian, Thai, Sushi. They settled on hibachi.

We pulled into a restaurant, and a waiter laid out the choices. "You've got chicken, steak, salmon, or tuna."

To his left, a boy raised his eyebrows and posed a wary question. "It's going to be raw?"

The sushi discussion had made a deep impression. "No, it's cooked," the waiter said. "They'll cook it right in front of you."

Over dinner, Cole told me that he focused most of his work on what researchers called "the disconnected," young men and women who are at risk of falling so far out of education or the workforce that they might never find a way back in. Like gun violence, disconnection was a growing problem in recent years—especially during the economic torpor left behind by the financial crisis. Between 2007 and 2010, the number of disconnected youth grew by 15 percent, to nearly 6 million Americans—one in every seven young people—and rates were far higher among African Americans. In Chicago, nearly a quarter of all Black young people qualified as disconnected, one of the highest levels of any big city. More than half of the young Black men on the West and South Sides were unemployed. "I go into a school and go, 'How can I help? Who is disconnected?'" Instead of expecting to boost college enrollment and graduation rates, he focused on other metrics. "Are we boosting confidence? Boosting trust? Reciprocity? Generosity?" He said, "When I tell these kids I'm going to do something, I show up. That means a lot. They are so used to people coming in and out of their lives."

Cole was in an optimistic mood. As in many parts of the country, Chicago politics was at a moment of change. The shooting of Laquan McDonald had altered the city's political chemistry. The previous fall, shortly before the police officer who killed McDonald was to go on trial, Rahm Emanuel had made a surprise announcement that he was not seeking reelection. He knew politics well enough to sense that his time had come.

In a crowded field of twelve candidates, hardly anyone put a bet on Lori Lightfoot—a corporate lawyer and former federal prosecutor in her first run for office. But as the campaign unfolded, Lightfoot caught the tailwind that was blowing through American politics. She represented a sharp break from the history of white male political insiders presiding over Chicago; she would be the city's first African American woman in the job, and she would also make Chicago the largest American city to elect an openly gay mayor. The sense of a passing era became even clearer in January, when Alderman Ed Burke, the longest-serving member of the city council in Chicago's history, was indicted for attempted extortion. Burke was accused of shaking people down in order to funnel clients to his law firm; on an FBI recording, Burke could be heard saying that a group of developers who balked at his request "can go fuck themselves."

Burke's undoing made the mayor's race a referendum on generations of corruption, white political power, and the crippling imbalances of opportunity and security—what Lightfoot tidily called the "same old, same old." She ran only a small grassroots campaign, with a straight-ahead message: she was a prosecutor in her bones, someone who could cut the "endless cycle of corruption" and "bring in the light" to an old rusted machine.

In April 2019, Lightfoot won in a landslide—a stunning sweep of all fifty Chicago wards. On the victory platform, she stood with her wife and ten-year-old daughter. "A lot of little boys and girls are out there watching us tonight," she said, and smiled, "and they're seeing the beginning of something, well, a little bit different." She acknowledged that people were frustrated, above all, by the sense that life was locked in place. "We can and will make Chicago a place where your zip code doesn't determine your destiny," she said.

But Lightfoot's honeymoon with the city was brief; America's political mood was too explosive to expect a smooth path ahead. That fall, the wave of strikes that had originated with the red bandannas of West Virginia reached the shores of Lake Michigan. Chicago teachers walked out and paraded through the city in red wool hats and coats, playing recordings of Aretha Franklin singing, "Oh, freedom, yeah, freedom!" For eleven days, students stayed home, and parents scrambled to work and care for them, while negotiators fought over class sizes, support services, and salaries. They finally reached a deal on October 31, after the longest teachers' strike Chicago had gone through in more than three decades. Neither side was happy, but parents rejoiced. "It was the worst experience ever," Dominique Dukes, a mother of two kids, told a local reporter. "Hopefully it doesn't happen again."

By year's end, the pace of the American inundation—the sheer avalanche of news and scandal and outrage—had become so impossibly relentless that it deadened the senses. In December, Trump became just the third president in U.S. history to be impeached; he had asked Ukraine to "do us a favor" and dig up dirt on Joe Biden. But the outcome was never in doubt—Senate Republicans raced to acquit him—and Americans greeted the trial with an existential shrug. Trump emerged emboldened, and in a state of nervous acceleration. At the beginning of his presidency, he had tweeted, on average, 63 times a week. By the end of 2019, in a single week he tweeted 250 times. It was the "peek-a-boo world" that Neil Postman had forecast long ago—"sensational, fragmented, impersonal"—in which nothing lingered long enough to receive the attention it deserved.

And so it was, on New Year's Eve, when a brief article passed across newswires around the world: the Municipal Health Commission of Wuhan, China, had detected a growing cluster of unexplained pneumonia. The infection did not yet have a name, but it was spreading.

EIGHTEEN

FACELESS

ON JANUARY 22, 2020, during an interview in Davos, Trump received his first question about the novel coronavirus. He replied with serene confidence. "It's one person coming in from China, and we have it under control," he said. "It's going to be just fine."

In the weeks that followed, as the virus burned through China, Italy, and Iran, the president became increasingly dismissive. "One day, it's like a miracle, it will disappear," he told the press at the White House. He faulted Democrats for criticizing his lack of concern. "This is their new hoax," he said at a rally on February 28, adding, "So far we have lost nobody to coronavirus." The first fatality was announced the next morning, and within a month, more than a thousand Americans were dying every day.

The Emerald City, for all its boasts and miracle cures and incompetence, was utterly unprepared. But the larger surprise was a deeper level of dysfunction far beyond the White House: the pandemic was revealing the full scope of America's institutional disrepair—the cruelties of the economy, the disparities of systemic racism, the skittering, malleable minds of a public trained to doubt the "body of fact." The civil service, weakened by years of ideological assault and defunding, was riddled by vacancies in crucial positions; Trump had turkey-farmed the "disloyals" and replaced them with political eunuchs who ignored a "pandemic playbook" inherited from the Obama administration and improvised instead. The world's richest, most powerful country struggled even to find masks and diagnose its citizens. A test developed in a lab at Harvard was successfully deployed to Nigeria, Sierra Leone, and Senegal before the administration could make it available in the United States.

On March 27, a Silicon Valley engineer named Yaron Oren-Pines, who had no background in medical supplies or government contracting, tweeted at Trump, "We can supply ICU Ventilators, invasive and noninvasive. Have someone call me URGENT." At the urging of the White House, FEMA recommended him to officials in New York State, who signed a contract for 1,450 ventilators at triple the normal price. They paid him $69 million. No ventilators ever arrived.

By then, the economy was in free fall, and some grew impatient. Rick Santelli, the Chicago financial commentator who had helped spark the Tea Party movement, said of the virus, "Maybe we'd be just better off if we gave it to everybody." Speaking on CNBC, surrounded by traders, he continued, "Then, in a month it would be over because the mortality rate of this probably isn't going to be any different." By slowing it down, he said, "We're wreaking havoc on global and domestic economies." Santelli's vision—which would have swamped hospitals and cost the lives of millions before the development of a vaccine—did not go over well. Viewers called for him to be fired, and the next morning, he conceded that his comments had been "stupid."

But inside the White House, the virus collided with decades of ideological grooming. Members of the administration had been hand-selected precisely for their hostility to a government "here to help," for their loyalty to a president who had mocked the very notion of expertise—"Oh, we need an *expert*." For Trump and his aides, the pandemic was not a grave public health crisis; it was a PR problem to be managed. When he assigned Jared Kushner, his son-in-law, to fix the failures in the supply chain, Kushner, who had no experience with medicine or disasters or government procurement, assembled a team in his own image—young, confident amateurs who, as he put it, would bring "an entrepreneurial approach" to the problem. Others nicknamed them the "slim suits."

Over the next month, they succeeded in relieving the shortage of ventilators, but it was a slender victory; they also bought a million tests that proved to be useless from a company that misspelled its own name on the invoice, and they delivered protective equipment at the behest of well-connected allies. Jeanine Pirro, a Trump booster on Fox News, "repeatedly called and emailed until 100,000 masks were sent to a particular hospital she favored," according to a whistleblower. As mass deaths accumulated, Kushner blamed state governors and proclaimed, "The federal government is not designed to solve all our problems."

At its core, America's failure to confront the pandemic was not only a matter of simple incompetence, although it was that, too; it was also a malfunction of elite imagination. Kushner shared the president's "more jaundiced view" of the virus, *The New York Times* reported, and "considers the problem more about public psychology than a health reality." Their shared perspective was a window into a sociological phenomenon. Trump and Kushner hailed from the same narrow slice of American experience: each was the scion of a family fortune; each had been insulated from responsibility for their own shortcomings; neither could remotely understand a life in which the barrier between security and catastrophe is the slenderest margin of happenstance.

It was a cast of mind that I recognized from the most gilded quarters of the United States. As the pandemic expanded in March, flights from San Francisco to New Zealand filled up fast, until that country closed the border to visitors. Instead, Americans who could afford it fled to the rural reaches of Sonoma and Napa, or Connecticut, Long Island, and the Hudson Valley. It reminded me of a line Jahmal Cole often repeated to his students during field trips: "It rains on people that live in the suburbs, too." There was truth in it, but there were also domains of insularity so rarefied that they were beyond his imagination.

⊢———⊣

When the pandemic paralyzed New York City in the spring, the effects echoed through the suburbs; the city of Stamford, Connecticut, reported that a crematory had caught fire after wiring melted from overuse. The virus seemed to confront Americans with the result of a generation's worth of political decisions. In Greenwich, people felt fortunate to be relatively safe from the virus—but they also felt powerless to address it. Ed Horstmann, the pastor, sensed that the pandemic was stirring, among some, a greater awareness of precarity in America: "We feel like we're going to make it through this, but there are so many people who are not okay, and what are we going to do about that?"

Even on the Gold Coast, the virus exposed cracks in the economic foundation; in Greenwich, municipal employees scrambled to provide emergency meal deliveries to some seven hundred families a week. Alan Barry, the town official, told me, "Greenwich represents two Americas. The haves and have-nots are literally separated and do not mix."

The pandemic forced the town's political divide into the open; after years of hardening Republican resistance to even basic tax increases for public services, local Democrats reached a breaking point; what Prescott Bush, in the heyday of moderate Republicanism, had called "the courage to raise the required revenues" was now anathema. In April, Republican town budget officials proposed slashing $3 million from local public schools, and parents recoiled. They mounted a socially distanced protest, driving and honking around town with signs that said "Books Over Budget" and "Education Cuts Never Heal." Joanna Swomley, the progressive organizer, said, "Those arguments are basically a way of saying, 'I'll take care of me. You take care of you. I don't want my taxes going up. I don't want *them* getting any of my money.'"

As in other parts of the country, some people quickly started to resent the requirements for social distancing. After Greenwich closed its beaches and parks, Thomas Byrne, who held Prescott Bush's old job as moderator of the Representative Town Meeting, told the local media that the government's measures were "the greatest assault on our freedom in my lifetime," adding, "Why we don't have a revolution in the streets escapes me."

Not everyone was ready to stand on principle, though. As stock markets sank, the investor Cliff Asness reconsidered his objections to government aid. On Twitter, he made a series of "economic suggestions that kind of hurt me to admit," he wrote. "We need, and I don't think

I've ever said this before, fiscal help. We need fiscal relief for individuals and small (and maybe large) businesses." Anticipating the charge of
hypocrisy, he wrote, "Yes, I'm losing libertarian bonafides here. I'm ok
with that."

When the president eventually signed a relief bill in March, it included a tax deduction, mostly for hedge funds and real-estate businesses, that was worth an average of $1.7 million for each of America's
43,000 wealthiest taxpayers and cost the Treasury about $90 billion in
the first year. Estimates of hedge-fund managers' performance in 2020
showed that as the economy crashed and unemployment reached record
heights, America's top twenty-five managers earned $32 billion, their
best performance in a decade. The top earner, according to *Institutional
Investor*, was Chip Skowron's former boss, Izzy Englander, who took
home an estimated $3.8 billion. "It may not be seemly," the magazine's
editors wrote, "but it remains fact."

Before long, demonstrators were back in Greenwich, but this time
the prop was grimmer than an inflatable pig. A caravan of cars, calling
itself the "Money Bags and Body Bags" demonstration, drove to the
homes of several prominent Greenwich investors and deposited trash
bags rigged to look like body bags. It was organized by the Service Employees International Union, which represents custodians, nursing-home
workers, day-care staff, and others. According to the union, six janitors
and eleven local nursing assistants had died of the virus in Connecticut
already, and the union was calling for more personal protective equipment for workers, expanded health-care coverage, and expedited workers' compensation for burial expenses. Among their targets, they visited
the Greenwich home of Betsy McCaughey, a Fox News columnist who
backed Trump and opposed the Affordable Care Act. A woman passing
by called the demonstrators "socialists," and a police officer stepped in
to keep it civil. Rick Melita, who was the union's executive director in
Connecticut, told *Greenwich Time* that workers were being told to "get
back to work, suck it up, take the punch." He asked, "How many of our
members have to die for the Dow before we get angry?"

The virus seemed to magnify the central issue running through
America's discussions of wealth and fairness: How, exactly, would a

fractured country define its understanding of the public good? Whom were Americans ready to help? And whom were we willing to ignore? And what was the role of a government in addressing those questions?

Few people in Greenwich had more reason to consider these questions than Michael Mason, who served as the chairman of the town finance board, a sterile-sounding job with vast authority over daily life. He presided over discussions on how much to spend on special education, on poverty programs, and on the teaching of English as a second language. Mason was tall, with parted silver hair and an earnest zeal for discussions of budgets and civic minutiae. His father flew a plane in World War II, and his two older brothers fought in Vietnam. Mason grew up in town, worked in the family aviation business, and volunteered as a fireman before owning a branch of Million Air, a company that served the private-jet industry.

He was also perhaps the town's earliest Trump supporter. He had attended the campaign announcement at Trump Tower. "I'm friends with the family," he told me. He met Trump's sons Don Jr. and Eric through a conservation club for hunters in Chappaqua, New York. They invited him to the convention, in case they needed votes to thwart a challenge from within the party. "I'm not going to run south under political pressure," Mason said. Later, he joined them for private celebrations on Election Night and Inauguration Day.

Mason knew that the president's "culture," as he put it, still upset many people in Greenwich. But, he said, "his policies over the last three years have gained more attention and probably more support." He predicted that the trauma of the pandemic would persuade some voters that Trump was right to want to cut immigration and lure back industries from abroad. "He had policies that he wanted to change on our borders, on immigration. I certainly think people in this country now are worried about that."

Eventually, we wound our way to the inevitable question: How do you make your peace with Trump? His behavior toward women and immigrants? His separation of children from parents at the border? The "shithole" countries? Mason listened calmly. "I have no control over that," he said. "What I have control over is what I worry about—the health and safety of my family, financial security of my family." I pressed him, but he didn't budge. "I've been empowered to care about the financial administrative affairs of a municipality with sixty thousand people sleeping at night," he said. "I care about them."

As Americans reckoned with the origins of our political moment—the Trump years, the fraying of a common purpose—we tended to focus on the effects of despair among members of the working class who felt besieged by technology, globalization, immigration, and trade. But that ignored the effects of seclusion among members of the governing class, who helped disfigure our political character by thrusting absolutists into positions of power and then ignoring their violence—all while enfeebling the basic functions of the state. They had secured their control over the levers of democracy but disowned the consequences of its deterioration. They had receded behind gracious walls.

———

As the death toll climbed, Trump's approach cascaded through American politics. After three years of demanding fealty, lower-level officials across the country took his cues on how far to go, or not go, to curb the spread. In the years since Governor Justice had donned a MAGA hat and switched parties, some of Trump's political aides had joined Justice's reelection effort. As other states and localities were shutting down restaurants and bars, Justice said that he would "not yet" take that step. "For crying out loud, go to the grocery stores. If you want to go to Bob Evans and eat, go to Bob Evans and eat." Later that day, Trump altered his advice—he was now urging people to avoid gatherings of more than ten people—and Justice followed suit. He said bars and restaurants would likely close the next day, "following the president's guidelines."

Stephen Smith, who was running against Justice, was meeting voters in the Shenandoah Valley when he first encountered people holding back their handshakes. "Can we just do *this*?" they said, and offered a wave or an elbow bump. By the following evening, Smith said, "There was someone watching the buffet to make sure people used utensils instead of their hands."

West Virginia was facing an even larger disaster than other places. It had an older population and high rates of smoking, heart disease, and diabetes. An estimated 51 percent of the state's adult population were considered at risk from the virus—higher than in any other state, according to a study published by the Kaiser Family Foundation, and 20 percentage points greater than in Washington, D.C.

Campaigning, in any recognizable way, was over. Around the country, candidates abandoned events and states postponed their primaries. Smith and Katey Lauer, his campaign manager, were stymied. Then they realized that the network they had built for West Virginia Can't Wait could be redirected against the virus. While Justice waited for instructions from Trump, they created a website with information on where to get a test and volunteer, how to vote, and who was entitled to a stimulus check. "We're good at crises in West Virginia because we have to be," Smith told me.

Some took gritty pride in that reputation. (A popular T-shirt in the Covid era had the message "West Virginia: Self-isolating since 1863.") But Smith hated the crowing about grit because it distracted from the failure of institutions. Looking back through local history, he said, "There were essentially two responses to the flood. There was a federally funded government response, where they had a hundred and forty-seven million dollars from the feds to spend—and they still haven't spent most of it four years later." Delays in relief and rebuilding had attracted intense criticism for years. "Meanwhile, there was a parallel response, led by local community groups and churches and volunteers. The community response built more homes, and faster."

Whatever the effect on his election prospects, Stephen saw the virus as prime evidence of the issues at the heart of his candidacy—the radically unequal risks facing Americans with varying levels of savings and health-care protection and different capacities for absorbing a shock to the economy. "It's not just inequality of wealth or income; it's also the inequality of pain," he told me. "The people who have the most bear the least, and the people who have the least bear the most."

Justice, like Trump, resented scientific findings that collided with his pronouncements. In June, public health officials reported slightly higher levels of infection in parts of the state than Justice had announced. In frustration, he forced out the state's seasoned public health commissioner, Dr. Cathy Slemp. But she did not go silently; after she was ejected, she warned that budget cuts, disinvestment, and deferred maintenance had weakened the state's public health system. Workers were scrambling to gather lab reports by fax machine and then enter the data by hand into outmoded computers so old that they sometimes timed out midway through the process. "We are driving a great-aunt's Pinto," she told reporters, "when what you need is to be driving a Ferrari."

West Virginia's spending on public health had sunk by 27 percent between 2010 and 2018, according to an analysis by the Associated Press and *Kaiser Health News*. Full-time staff had fallen by 29 percent since 2007, and Slemp said it was even more dire when the virus hit, because another 20 to 25 percent of all health-department jobs were vacant.

Health-care providers pleaded for more personal protective equipment; some were using a single N95 mask for days at a time. Infections of health-care workers continued to climb, and the CEO of the Charleston Area Medical Center suggested that nurses were getting sick because they were lax about wearing masks at home. It was an effort to shift the institutional failure into the language of personal responsibility, to blame individuals instead of failing systems. The staff rebelled; nurses resorted to a public protest. They stood outside the hospital with signs that said, "From Heroes to Zeroes" and "Where Is Our Hazard Pay?"

├────────┤

Almost immediately, the virus expanded America's economic chasms. In the first two months, the employed share of the population dropped to its lowest level since 1975. Latinos and young people suffered the sharpest drop as restaurants, hotels, and entertainment dried up. The bottom quarter of wage earners lost almost 11 million jobs—more than three times the number lost by the top quarter. But the true damage was just beginning. By June, the stock market had surged and the recession had ended, essentially, for high-income individuals. Almost 80 percent of the jobs still missing belonged to the bottom half of American workers.

In West Virginia, the pandemic brought an end to the boom in the natural-gas business. In the first three years of Trump, West Virginia had added 37,000 jobs; over the next six months, they vanished—and then the state lost another 30,000. Unlike some jobs, you couldn't dig a pipeline by Zoom. Three quarters of the drilling rigs that were running in 2019 fell silent in the next twelve months. By the fall of 2020, unemployment had soared to 8.6 percent, approaching its peak during the financial crisis. Fewer than half of the adults in West Virginia were working. Nationwide, labor-force participation among Americans without college degrees had dropped to its lowest point on record, and four out of every five workers in West Virginia lacked a four-year college degree.

The fault lines in America's political coherence, which had been expanding for years, broke wide open. In some places, a mutant definition of freedom fueled a resistance to social distancing. Some religious leaders continued to hold church services in defiance of emergency orders. Unlike past crises, Americans were not being asked to join the military or labor in a factory; they were being asked to stay home, but, to some, any official advisory was suspect. The first two decades of the twenty-first century had shattered public trust. On September 11, 2001, "people in the rural heartland did not see New York as an alien stew of immigrants and liberals that deserved its fate, but as a great American city that had taken a hit for the whole country," George Packer wrote in *The Atlantic*. "Firefighters from Indiana drove 800 miles to help the rescue effort at Ground Zero. Our civic reflex was to mourn and mobilize together."

Not this time. In the intervening decades, American unity had given way to bitter rivalries—and a contempt for leaders and their institutions, who had marched the country into Iraq and the Great Recession. Older workers had been gutted by debt, and younger people would never make up for the years of lost earnings. As Americans hunted for the origins of their pain, they carved themselves into rival tribes—Republicans and Democrats; city-dwellers and country people; white, Black, Latino, and

Asian; Christian, Muslim, and Jewish; and, centrally, those with college degrees and those without—the winners and losers of the meritocratic hustle.

Historically, outbreaks of disease were powerful fuel for hatred. The bubonic plague led to pogroms against Jews in medieval Europe. And in the present case, a virus that originated in China became a fixation for racists and anti-immigration activists. Jared Taylor, the white nationalist who had introduced me to his fellow Trump supporters at his house years earlier, told his YouTube audience, "We actually have sound, instinctive reasons to be xenophobes." He said, "All people everywhere instinctively avoid certain things that could make us sick. Piles of feces. Rotting flesh. People with running sores. Part of this behavioral immune system is an instinctive fear that people who act or look strange could be carrying disease." Over the next year, hate crimes against Asian Americans soared.

Fear, as always, was good for certain kinds of business. On March 20, 2020, two days after Trump declared himself a "wartime president," the gun industry once again marked record sales. Americans were jittery and amenable to grand, comforting explanations, no matter how illogical. In April, a crowd of protesters massed outside the West Virginia state capitol for a rally they called "Re-Open West Virginia." Unlike in other states, it was peaceful, but the message was increasingly desperate. Marshall Wilson, a member of West Virginia's House of Delegates, spoke to the crowd about his resentment of efforts to close restaurants and businesses. Wilson did not dispute the existence of the virus—his wife worked in a hospital—but he resented the governor's restraints. "I'm begging you to please stand up for your liberties," Wilson told the crowd. "It looks like it's time for a little civil disobedience. So go to your churches, go to your businesses, and go back to work."

Around him, in the crowd of signs and flags, there were indicators of a harder core. A man held placards: "End the Plandemic! Your Lies Have Been Exposed!" and "I Prefer Dangerous Liberty Over Peaceful Slavery!" A child in a stars-and-stripes shirt held a sign that said, "Freedom Is Essential." A woman held up a sign with the QAnon slogan, "WWG1WGA," which stood for "Where We Go One, We Go All."

When the crowd caught a glimpse of the governor in the distance, it only irritated them further. A man shouted, "Your experts are experts in communism and control, not medicine." Another yelled, "Your businesses are open, why not ours? Let us go back to work!"

⊢――――⊣

The virus was burning through vulnerable communities, and the details, in some cases, bespoke a deeper rot in modern American life. In Waterloo, Iowa, at the largest U.S. pork plant operated by Tyson Foods, nearly three thousand workers butchered hogs in close quarters. Employees complained that managers were failing to enforce basic safety standards, and within weeks, more than a thousand employees became infected. Like the hospital staff in West Virginia, the meatpackers were accused of failing to protect themselves outside of work. By the time Tyson agreed to shutter the plant, five employees were dead. In a lawsuit, the son of one of them alleged that the plant manager had organized a "cash buy-in, winner-take-all betting pool for supervisors and managers to wager how many employees would test positive for COVID-19." (The company called it "disturbing behavior" and promised to investigate.)

In cities, millions of Americans found themselves suddenly dependent on frontline workers who were largely ignored in the usual daily bustle. Grocery-store clerks, warehouse workers, mail carriers, mechanics, bus drivers, and prison guards—to say nothing of nurses, firefighters, police, teachers, and day-care workers. If they were faceless before, the metaphor became real as they vanished behind masks and face guards, staying on the job in order to prevent the country from caving in.

The virus was almost perfectly engineered to ravage low-income neighborhoods. In recent years, rising rents and stagnant salaries and wages had pushed people into denser quarters. Nearly 4 million American households lived in overcrowded homes where social distancing was difficult—often consisting of multiple generations. Even outside their homes, life was more crowded for the poor—they crowded into emergency rooms where the uninsured sought care, the jails and prisons where they were more likely to be locked up or visiting family. Moreover, economic uncertainty was a corrosive source of stress, and people in poverty were more likely to suffer from diabetes, hypertension, pulmonary disease, and heart disease—all of which made a patient a prime target for the virus.

In the three years before the pandemic, more than 2 million Americans had lost their health insurance, which researchers estimated led to 10,000 "excess deaths." According to a Gallup survey in 2019, one in four Americans reported that they had put off medical care because of the cost—the highest percentage in the three decades that Gallup had been asking the question. To pay for health care, an astonishing number of people had taken to begging online; more than 8 million Americans had turned to GoFundMe and other crowdfunding sites for medical expenses in recent years, even though 90 percent of the medical fundraisers failed to reach their goals. Yet more lost their insurance as employers laid people off during the pandemic, and vaccine researchers warned against "immunity inequality" if wealthy people found ways to access vaccines in larger numbers.

The administration avoided steps that might puncture Trump's illusion that the pandemic was easing. In previous disasters, such as Hurricane Katrina and Superstorm Sandy, presidents authorized FEMA to cover funeral costs for families too poor to bury their loved ones. (They averaged about $2,700 each.) But as the pandemic spread, and at least thirty states and territories requested assistance for funeral expenses, the White House declined to approve it. In desperation, some families turned to GoFundMe. Others walked away. Even months after the surge of infections in New York City, hundreds of bodies remained unclaimed, hidden away in freezer trucks, because survivors lacked the money to dispose of the remains.

Day by day, the contrast between the scale of suffering in America and the behavior in Washington tested the mind's capacity to absorb. In a moment of indelible absurdity, Trump—the man charged with saving American lives—riffed from a White House podium about the potential value of injecting disinfectant into people. "Knocks it out in a minute. One *minute*," he said, searching the faces of horrified reporters and the deadpan members of his staff. "Is there a way we can do something like that, by injection inside or almost a *cleaning*?" A week later, the death toll from Covid surpassed the American loss of life in fourteen years of the Vietnam War.

In the darkest moments, I sometimes found it impossible to keep my eyes trained on the sheer dysfunction of American politics. In the quiet of my office, I sought refuge in books that were as far away from politics as I could find. I lingered in the parts of my research that unfolded in the natural world; I read about the fires and floods and the glaciers that had deposited the ancient stones eventually piled into the walls of Greenwich. I was, I suppose, looking for reminders of the long view, of geological time, of forces larger than ourselves. In my top desk drawer, I kept a few favorite words from Wendell Berry, the American writer and farmer. In the land beneath his feet, he wrote, he found a source of endurance, a memory that will grow:

> *into legend, legend into song,*
> *song into sacrament. The abundance of this place,*
> *the songs of its people and its birds,*
> *will be health and wisdom and indwelling*
> *light. This is no paradisal dream.*
> *Its hardship is its possibility.*

———

The harder things got for the country, the more the presidential race slipped out of the usual octave of politics, into a different register—a language of suffering, connection, and resilience. Joe Biden had entered the race as the fragile front-runner, with high name recognition and conspicuously low excitement, especially among younger Democrats. He was a white man in his eighth decade who had spent nearly half a century in Washington. Underscoring the sense of a man out of time, shortly before he announced his campaign, he acknowledged complaints that his well-known habit for tactile politics—for whispering into people's ears, bumping foreheads with women and men—had made some women "uncomfortable," as he put it. "I'll be much more mindful."

For a time, his candidacy looked doomed; he finished fourth in the Iowa caucuses, and an embarrassing fifth in New Hampshire. But when the campaign reached South Carolina, it entered a different domain, in which his biography became an asset. Black voters made up 60 percent of the Democratic primary electorate in South Carolina, a state in which a white supremacist massacred nine parishioners as they prayed at their church in Charleston. The prospect of another four years of Trump was not a risk they were willing to take. James Clyburn, the highest-ranking African American in Congress and the godfather of South Carolina Democrats, blessed Biden with an unusually emotional endorsement: "I'm fearful for my daughters and their future, and their children, and their children's future." With Biden at his side, he said, "We know Joe. But, most importantly, Joe knows us."

Biden won South Carolina by 29 points, and within days his moderate rivals had exited and endorsed him. On March 3, Super Tuesday, he won ten out of fourteen states, effectively securing the nomination. And then, almost immediately, the presidential campaign of 2020 became unrecognizable: one week after Super Tuesday, as Americans dawned to the emerging horror of the pandemic, Biden canceled his campaign events and took shelter at home in Delaware, where he would spend the next eight months of a nearly virtual campaign.

As Trump plunged deeper into his rages and fantasies, his unglamorous rival benefited from the contrast. When I visited Biden for an interview at his home, fewer than a hundred days before the election, he had opened a lead larger than any challenger in the history of presidential polling—but his mood was grave. We sat in masks, across the room from each other, and I was struck by how often he returned to the subject of Franklin Delano Roosevelt's response to the Great Depression. "I'm kind of in a position that FDR was in," he said before catching himself. "I'm not comparing *myself* to FDR—for real, it's not like, 'Biden says he's like FDR.'" No, the similarity, in his mind, was to the nature of the remedy that the crises required. "It is not requiring an ideological answer. If you think about it, what, in fact, FDR did was not ideological. It was completely practical. How do we keep America from going totally in the tank and staying in the tank?" He continued, "He focused on the things that would create jobs, and include more people, and generate more security. Physical as well as personal security. From social security straight through to what he did relative to World War Two."

He was making a subtle case, which would grow in the months ahead, for more political ambition than his critics often imagined—a presidency that might attack not only the immediate crises but also the underlying inequities, the apparatus of imbalance, an economic system that reserved forgiveness for those with the money and power to demand it. "Corporate America has now been bailed out *twice*," he told me. "We've got to say, 'Hey, guys, let's look at what works.'"

The agonies of 2020 exposed another element of Trump's frailty. Nobody expected him to emerge as a beacon of empathy. (Tales of his indifference were legion; after his mentor Roy Cohn contracted AIDS in the 1980s, Trump cut off contact, and Cohn observed, "Donald pisses ice water." Alan Marcus, a former PR adviser, recalled that after an associate died, Trump was urged to call the family, and he replied, "Why? He's dead.") To Trump's most zealous fans, that coldness was a virtue, and some adorned their homes and boats with flags that carried his name above the slogan "Fuck Your Feelings." And yet nothing in his presidency delineated his emotional chemistry as clearly as his sheer inability to grasp the suffering from the pandemic. "It is what it is," he said of mass deaths.

In politics, the capacity to understand another person's experience delivers more than just the appearance of concern. Helen Nicolay, the daughter of Abraham Lincoln's private secretary John Nicolay, wrote that Lincoln's "crowning gift of political diagnosis was due to his sympathy . . . which gave him the power to forecast with uncanny accuracy what his opponents were likely to do." For Biden, the experience of suffering was braided into his political life; in 1972, he had buried his first wife, Neilia Hunter, and his infant daughter, Naomi, after a car accident; and in 2015, the death of his firstborn son, Beau Biden, of a brain tumor, had nearly driven the father from politics forever. As the blade of the pandemic sank deeper into American life, Biden could speak of its pain. "People are dying, your friends and coworkers are dying, our family members and friends and neighbors are dying," he said at a virtual town hall, "while Trump is having temper tantrums about his authority." He asked, "Have we heard him offer anything that approaches a sincere expression of empathy for the people that are hurting? Have we seen any sign that he grasps just how hard it will be for people to recover from this, not just economically, but physically and emotionally, as well?"

———

Six months into the pandemic, the Covid recession had become the most unequal in modern U.S. history. Job losses overwhelmingly affected low-wage minority workers. Black women, Black men, mothers of school-age children, and people without college degrees were facing the longest periods of unemployment. But others were hurting, too; by fall, the virus was exacting its heaviest toll in Chicago on Latinos. Five zip codes in Latino neighborhoods recorded the largest rise in cases. In surveys of their surviving relatives, 70 percent believed their loved ones had become infected at work or after working relatives brought the virus home.

For Jahmal Cole, the community organizer, the virus was a puzzle. How do you run field trips in a lockdown? He found a solution: he mobilized the kids in his program to put together wellness packages—hand sanitizer, disinfectant, toiletries, food—for the elderly and the disabled. When local stores sold out of sanitizer, he visited a bank downtown that was offering it to customers and staff. He asked them to donate it instead. They agreed, so he tried other places. "I went to the gas station. I went to Office Depot." As word spread, his office started getting calls from elderly people and groups that needed help.

When students could no longer go on field trips, he put them to work making phone calls. "We created a program off the top of my head called Youth-Senior Connect. I talked to Rush Hospital, 'Hey, can you train our students to make wellness calls to seniors?'" The hospital agreed, and Cole employed seventy-five students at $15 an hour, twelve hours a week, calling elderly neighbors, shipping them supplies, and linking them to doctors and social-service providers. "The ones that show promise in the health-care field, they can get internships at Rush Hospital." It caught the attention of Oprah Winfrey, who called him. Cole was starstruck. She donated half a million dollars (and she complimented him on choosing a name that was good for marketing).

On a Saturday in March, he got a call from his grandmother Lucille Myers, who lived in the suburbs. She was feeling under the weather, but making do, and was grateful to have someone to call. "Please bring me a care package for myself, and one for my ninety-one-year-old neighbor," she told her grandson. Cole dropped off the packages that afternoon. They waved and chatted from opposite sides of the room. That night, she died. On her death certificate, doctors listed the cause as pneumonia.

By late spring, Black people in Chicago were dying of Covid at four times the rate of white residents. Part of the explanation was historical and systemic. Due to economic and social disparities, they had entered the pandemic with far higher rates of preexisting conditions: 49 percent higher for hypertension, 66 percent higher for diabetes. And part of the explanation was logistical: they were getting tested at much lower rates. In the early months, Black people made up 37 percent of the Covid deaths in Illinois, but they had received only 13 percent of the state's tests. From Reese Clark's old neighborhood on the South Side, the closest retail testing site was more than twenty miles away. (Similar problems were unfolding across the country. Nationwide, majority Black counties had nearly six times the rate of deaths as majority white counties.)

Beyond that, some in the Black community were wary of official health advisories, with reason. In one of America's most infamous misuses of science, the Tuskegee Syphilis Study, federal health authorities lied to hundreds of Black men in Alabama between 1932 and 1972, promising them free medical care, when in fact they received only placebos and diagnostic tests. Researchers had wanted to observe the effects of syphilis left untreated. The legacy of that abuse, known as "the Tuskegee effect," has endured for decades.

When the virus hit, misinformation spread rapidly among both Black and white Americans. In videos and social media, Diamond and Silk, a pair of pro-Trump Black commentators from North Carolina, spread conspiracy theories, asserting that the disease was "man-made" and wondering if there was a "little deep-state action going on behind the scenes." Like other far-right pundits, they floated the idea that 5G technology was infecting people in order to fill up "empty" hospital beds, and Silk, whose real name is Rochelle Richardson, questioned whether the World Health Organization had a "switch" to "turn this virus on and off."

On March 16, Chicago recorded its first Covid death. It was in Auburn Gresham. Her name was Patricia Frieson; she was a retired nurse, and, like so many in the neighborhood, she had severe asthma. Nine days later, her sister died of Covid, too. Clark called me that afternoon. He was in Peoria, living near his mother.

"We're just trying to stay away from people," he said. Since leaving Chicago, he had found some stability: he worked as a laborer on residential construction sites. "Pennies and crumbs," but "it's keeping me afloat," he said. Truth was, he was glad to be away from the city—and not only because the virus was roaring through densely packed neighborhoods. "I've got my life together. I can't reach the drugs like I used to. I can't get a gun like I used to," he said. Working on construction sites had stirred his imagination that he might save up to buy a house. "One of those slick little fixer-uppers—that's my goal," he said, but he tried to keep his expectations in check. "It's better to have a raggedy house in a good area than a good house in a raggedy area."

When the pandemic hit, Clark even savored an excuse to hunker down. His sons, Jeremiah and Caleb, who lived mostly with their mother in Chicago, came to live with him in Peoria. As a present, Clark bought them a video-game set from a pawnshop. "I filled the refrigerator up with chicken nuggets and all the stuff they like," he said. "We just bonded for a while. I missed them."

As we talked, I could also hear that the stay-at-home orders were playing into his old conspiracy theories about authoritarianism and a plot to take over Black neighborhoods. "They're conditioning us right now," he said. He didn't want to get a Covid test, because he didn't know what the government would do with the information. He worried about the federal government seizing control of the country. "If it's going to kick off, it's going to kick off in Chicago," he said.

By the end of May, Clark's neighborhood was coming out of lockdown. "They just opened up a *restaurant*," he said with mock drama. It was May 29, and he had a lot on his mind. The virus had just knocked out his job. People didn't want construction crews coming in and out of their buildings, so the boss sent him home. Meanwhile, his mother had suffered a minor stroke that landed her in the emergency room. The doctor said her pacemaker was on the fritz. His boys were getting older, and he worried about them getting into trouble. To scare them away from it, he asked if I knew how to get his old mug shot. "I'm going to put it on the wall. Tell them the real deal I went through," he said. "Where I came from to where I'm at now. You don't want to go in there."

While we talked, Clark had the television on in the background. "I'm looking at the news," he said. It was CBS, which was covering a growing wave of demonstrations in Minneapolis. In the past seventy-two hours, a video had started circulating that showed a Minneapolis police officer kneeling on the neck of a Black man named George Floyd. The scene was barbaric: Floyd, who was forty-six years old, begged for his life and cried out for his mother; for nine minutes and twenty-nine seconds, the police officer did not move, his hand resting casually on his thigh (his dark gloves making it seem as if his hand was in his pocket), until Floyd was dead, facedown on the pavement. The image was instantly iconic. Even after all of America's videos of the killing and assault of Black men, the sheer imbalance of force and power and liberty rendered it a singular horror.

While Clark and I talked, I was driving, and as the headlines grew more dramatic, he started narrating the broadcast to me over the phone. "They're charging this cop with murder now," he said. The governor of Minnesota had called up the National Guard, and the Justice Department was embarking on an investigation of Floyd's killing. Clark watched the images on the screen. He was startled by the scale of the protests. "They burned down a police precinct," he said. "It's spreading."

NINETEEN

ARE WE GOING TO JAIL, DAD?

WHEN THE PROTESTS ARRIVED at the White House gates, President Trump fled into an underground bunker—the ultimate in residential segregation—and, when he was mocked for his fear, he responded with the lie that he had ventured underground to conduct an "inspection."

The killing of George Floyd, and the fury that tumbled out in its wake, laid bare just how separately Americans lived in the twenty-first century—how truly alienated they were across lines of race, class, power, and ideology. Though many white Americans recoiled from the sight of Floyd's death, many Black Americans wondered why it had taken so long for their countrymen to believe their pleas. The answer lay somewhere in the fact that even six decades after King's "I Have a Dream" speech, and twelve years after the triumph of America's first Black president, more than three quarters of white Americans still had no close nonwhite friends—and the same patterns applied in the other direction.

But as the protests grew, those distances suddenly narrowed, for better and worse. Not only did millions of white and Black Americans march side by side, but they also came face-to-face, in unusual proximity, with the police they opposed. On the first night of demonstrations in Chicago, Jahmal Cole joined a march toward downtown and ended up so close to a line of Chicago police officers that he was startled to realize he could make out the tattoos on their arms.

When the police fired a cloud of blue smoke to drive back the crowd, Cole stumbled, twisted his knee, and limped away. He watched the crowd surge and withdraw, and the scene struck him as a pantomime of warfare, an encounter primed for violence. "If you're a police officer, how are you supposed to think about acting with restraint when you have riot gear on, and a helmet, and you have the old wooden billy clubs with etchings in them from prior use?" he asked. "And what does that say to young people that are out there? It says, 'This is a confrontation.'"

The confrontation arrived, in earnest, the next day, when people set police cars on fire and looted stores around Chicago, ranging from a Rolex boutique to a Family Dollar. Across the country, looting was a rare feature of the protests; an analysis of reams of data on protests and interactions with law enforcement calculated that roughly 7 percent of the Black Lives Matter protests involved looting and other violence, according to the Armed Conflict Location & Event Data Project (ACLED), a nonprofit data initiative. But the images of burned and ruined stores spread instantly. And in Chicago, they spurred dramatic steps from the city government. By morning, the mayor had pulled up drawbridges to prevent crowds from crossing the Chicago River to the wealthy precincts of the North Side.

The sight of the raised bridges, one after another toward the horizon, was eloquent testimony to the enduring geography of segregation. "We're fed up, man," Cole told me. "We wore a hoodie for Trayvon, we took a knee for Philando, we held our breath for Eric, we walked for Laquan, but we're done. Enough is enough, you know what I mean? We're rightfully pissed off."

The uprisings of 2020 were rooted in the fact that Black Americans, according to a data analysis by *The Washington Post*, were more than twice as likely as white Americans to be killed during interactions with police. But the movement instantly expanded beyond that, into a confrontation with the full spectrum of racism and inequity—disparities in health, housing, education, employment, and wealth, as well as the more abstract assets of American life: security, dignity, opportunity, and the right to a second chance. They extended a tradition of American activism for racial equity that reached back more than a century. "If there is no struggle, there is no progress," Frederick Douglass, who had escaped slavery and become one of America's leading social reformers, warned in 1857. "Those who profess to favor freedom, and yet deprecate agitation, are men who want crops without plowing up the ground, they want rain without thunder and lightning," he said. "They want the ocean without the awful roar of its many waters."

⊢———⊣

In the span of George Floyd's forty-six years, African Americans had made gains that narrowed many gaps between Black and white experience. The difference in life expectancy had shrunk from seven years to three and a half; the Black middle class had grown, and high school graduation rates had converged. But that progress was undermined by deeper gaps that continued to widen for decades. On average, Black households had barely 10 percent of the wealth that white families had, and the gap in homeownership was *wider* than it was a half century ago. Such was the essence of structural racism: the advantages and disadvantages would continue to compound over time, leaving millions of people in concentrated poverty, unless something was done to change it.

For Cole's small community organization on the South Side, the uprising for racial justice brought a sudden surge of attention. After years of begging for donations, he was inundated with queries from panicky executives. "I've had more corporations call me in the last two weeks than I've ever talked to," he told me. "They're like, 'Hey, can you come talk to our executives?'" He had started the year with hopes of raising a million dollars; by year's end, he had raised more than ten million. He was glad to accept their donations, but he was clear-eyed about the calculations behind it. "I don't know if businesses care so much about justice being denied as much as about their business being interrupted. So you never know going into it. But I feel like the time is now for me to challenge them," he said. "Everybody says, 'How can I make a difference?'

Well, you can start by hiring or promoting Black managers, and putting Black people on your board."

But Cole also sensed that even well-meaning executives had no real sense of just how far behind the city's distressed neighborhoods really were. At both the top and the bottom of society, people were blinkered by the very depth of the segregation that he had founded his organization to confront. "All these vice presidents and CEOs of United Airlines and JPMorgan Chase, you name it, they're like, 'Well, can you teach them the soft skills so we can hire them?' I'm like, 'Listen, these are people that have barely been downtown, and have never seen anybody waving for a taxi. They don't know how to work the new kinds of elevators with no buttons in them. They can't use a debit card.'" Cole went on, "Do you know how many kids on our tours have never seen a Tesla? Or have never been to the lake?" He told me, "I can't solve segregation in Chicago, but what I can do is help plant the seeds."

From Cole's perspective, national politics were so confounding that the situation was preventing people from taking smaller, practical steps. "Right now, it's like everybody knows who's in Donald Trump's cabinet, but nobody knows who their neighbor is. It's just a little backwards," he told me. When businesses called him, he asked for finite fixes—like money for his field trips. "It costs twenty-five thousand a school, and we take eighteen kids from that school on ten trips. I've got thirty-six schools on the waiting list.'"

He had not set out to be a political activist, but around his neighborhood he had taken to chiding people about the need to go beyond civil unrest. "I think people need to learn how change actually happens. I ask, 'Do you even know who your local alderman is? Do you know who your local state representative is?' I keep on saying, if you stole some shoes this summer, I hope you're wearing those shoes come November, to vote."

⊢――――⊣

Around the country, the movement for racial justice collided with local sensibilities and careened in directions that were sometimes difficult to predict. The movement reached Clarksburg, after a fashion, on the morning of June 17, during the regular meeting of the Harrison County Commission. In the wood-paneled chambers at the courthouse, the three members of the commission sat on a dais, in padded chairs, behind brass nameplates. The president, Ron Watson, a white-haired police-officer-turned-civil-servant, oversaw the proceedings with his usual decorous formality. Unusual for the commission, a crowd had gathered, both in person and online.

Citizens had come to argue over the town's most prominent landmark: a tall bronze statue of Stonewall Jackson, the Confederate general who was born nearby in 1824 and killed in 1863—"while fighting for a cause he believed to be just," as the inscription on the statue put it. The sight of Jackson, on horseback, had greeted visitors to the courthouse ever since 1953, when *Brown v. Board of Education* was before the Supreme Court. The statue was erected at the behest of the United Daughters of the Confederacy and dedicated in a ceremony that began with the playing of "Dixie."

In the three weeks since Floyd was killed, campaigns to remove Confederate monuments had succeeded in many places in the United States, from Indianapolis—which dismantled a memorial to southern soldiers that had been organized by the KKK—to Decatur, which removed a thirty-foot obelisk from the town square dedicated to the "Lost Cause." In Clarksburg, the commission was taking up the question of whether to return Stonewall to the United Daughters of the Confederacy. To open the discussion, Watson cleared his throat and read aloud from an email contributed by a local citizen who opposed "nationwide meddling" by "left-wing radicals."

So began a series of defenses of the Stonewall statue. "I've admired it a million times," said Larry Starkey, who used to work for the state highway department. "When I was little, my dad used to raise me up to look at that statue when he came in the courthouse to do business." Some speakers made their case based on nuances of history—"He and his wife were *given* slaves," a man said—while others offered a blunt argument about the future. Robert Freshour, a local school-bus driver, compared the movement against the statues to "driving a wedge in a damn log." He said, "Every time you hit that wedge, it opens up a little more." He ended with a warning to his fellow citizens, who, on that day, were all white. "Decent people better wake up," he said. "This is just a picnic compared to what's going to happen if the wrong party gets in."

It took a while before anyone spoke up on the other side. Eventually, Gabe Rhodes, a teacher at the high school, called for relocating the monument to a cemetery a mile away. "Moving the statue," he said, "would move Harrison County forward and give us an opportunity to represent a new Harrison County, a Harrison County that is ready to rebuild and make itself a place for all." Others agreed, but they were clearly in the minority. Of the three dozen or so who spoke that morning, fewer than a third contended that it was time for Stonewall to go.

Finally, the commissioners spoke. David Hinkle, a local lawyer who often dressed for meetings in a brightly colored suit and tie, pulled off his reading glasses and said, "People should not have to come by and look at a representation of a man who did not support freedom for all people." But Hinkle was outvoted two to one. If citizens still wanted to tear down Stonewall, it would take more than a meeting to do it.

├────────┤

One person who was not at the hearing was Jim Griffin, the former head of the local NAACP. Jim had hoped that Clarksburg might move the statue without him having to push it. For years, he had walked by the statue on his way into the courthouse to pay his taxes, and for years he had loathed the sight of it. But he had never sensed an opportunity to do anything about it—until now. When the first vote failed, he saw an opening. "Time to take a stand," he told me. "Timing is everything."

Jim contacted the commission and asked if he could testify. When they met again two weeks later, he took his seat at the witness table. He had thought hard about what he wanted to say and what he would wear while he did it. He settled on a purple T-shirt with a quote from Martin Luther King Jr.: "It's always the right time to do the right thing." Jim was testifying in his capacity as chairman of the West Virginia Black Heritage Festival. Beside him, Anjellica Scott, a younger member of the group, took turns reading from their statement, which began with a Psalm: "Behold how good and how pleasant it is for brethren to dwell together in unity."

With glasses on the end of his nose, Jim spoke bluntly. "Confederate monuments in public spaces glorify white supremacy and memorialize a treasonous government whose founding principle was to perpetuate and expand slavery," he said. He offered a compromise: the statue should be "preserved but relocated"—a local museum had offered to take it—and he ended with a local flourish, a nod to the state motto, *montani semper liberi*, "mountaineers are always free": "If you approve the relocation of the monument you will assure people of color that *montani semper liberi* applies to them," he said.

The commissioners agreed to take the statue question "under advisement." When I talked to Jim two days later, he was buoyant. "Feeling very positive about it," he said. "With the climate of the country today, we think that we have a good chance." On the day he had testified, the government of Richmond, Virginia, the former capital of the Confederacy, had torn down its own bronze statue of Stonewall on horseback. And, unlike the first meeting, during the latest hearing in Clarksburg only one speaker had stepped forward to defend the statue. "He represents what people who have never been to West Virginia *think* of West Virginia—that it's 'backwards,'" Jim said, proudly. "Everybody in the room just kind of looked at him strangely."

In his decades of local activism in Clarksburg, Jim had come to believe that nudging history forward in a place like West Virginia depended less on persuading your sworn opponents than on mobilizing the indifferent, the people he called the "living room liberals." He said, "In Clarksburg, there's a lot of people who feel like it should be relocated, but they only feel that way in their living room. And they're not going to come out publicly and say it." After so many years of hedging and balancing, Jim was quietly elated at the idea he could speak for his silent neighbors—not as an outsider and a scold, but as a fellow West Virginian, appealing to their best image of themselves.

Over the next month, tense controversies over statues gained attention around the country, and Trump seized on the issue as a rallying cry. It was a splendid diversion from the mounting pandemic's death toll—which by then had surpassed 130,000 Americans—but it also allowed Trump, in his speeches, to conjure a fearsome montage of fires and looting and toppled statues. On July 4, addressing the country from Mount Rushmore, Trump warned of "a merciless campaign to wipe out our history, defame our heroes, erase our values, and indoctrinate our children." If Jim Griffin had succeeded in expanding the perimeter of citizenship to include himself, Trump was cinching it closed and adding an apocalyptic coda: "Tonight, before the eyes of our forefathers, Americans declare again, as we did two hundred and forty-four years ago, that we will not be tyrannized—we will not be demeaned, and we will not be intimidated by bad, evil people."

When the Harrison County Commission reconvened on August 5, the mood had changed since Jim's appearance. One after another, ten people got up to speak in defense of the statue; in their comments, one could hear the influence of Trump's lexicon of gloom and victimhood and paranoia. Scott Swagger, a local resident, was suspicious that the issue had even earned a place back on the agenda. "I don't know how that system works, but it sounds fishy to me," he said.

Jim Griffin came forward once more to testify. This time, he appealed to his neighbors' sense of empathy, encouraging them to see the monument through his eyes. "I truly think these statues were placed to send a message to a race of people: '*We're watching you*,'" he said. For the first time, I also heard him speak candidly about the tension he felt in trying to stand between the white and Black worlds of his hometown. "I've even been ridiculed," he said, "by people saying, 'How can you celebrate your heritage under the watchful eye of your slave master.' But I truly believe that I walk not by sight, but by faith." He quoted King: "The time is right to do the right thing," he said.

But the hearing was already descending into a cruel farce. As Jim talked, one of the attendees on Zoom interrupted and drowned out the sound of his voice with a rap song that featured the N-word. Someone else flashed photos of a nude woman. Finally, Commissioner Hinkle called, once more, for a vote on removing the statue. It was time, he said, to become the "all-inclusive community that Clarksburg proudly tries to promote."

But his colleagues were unmoved. "Do I have a second?" Ron Watson said, peering around the tiny room. After a silent moment, he repeated his own question: "Do I have a second?" The room was quiet. "The motion dies for lack of a second," he said. He looked down at his agenda. "All right, moving on."

⊢———⊣

For Jim Griffin, losing the vote on the statue was crushing. "I really thought they would do it," he told me afterward. "They totally fooled me." Jim was grieving for the politics of his home. "The state and the county have gone totally red—I mean, *totally* red. I think it's at a point where they feel like they don't have to change now. They're in control." He was not just disappointed; he was embarrassed by his optimism. He knew that it would fortify the criticism from some younger Black activists who thought the older generation, for all its sacrifices, was too eager to defuse confrontation instead of embracing it as the crucible of progress. In their eyes, Jim's impressive résumé of civic involvement could also be viewed as a record of excess patience, a gentlemanly response to brutality. After all, as one pointed adage had it, wasn't Martin Luther King Jr. wearing a suit and tie when he was assassinated?

"They call me a dinosaur," Jim told me. "They say, 'Your approach is never going to work.'" But Jim had always prided himself on navigating the boundary between the white and Black worlds of West Virginia. He believed in waiting for the moments when progress became possible. "I tell them, it's not as easy as you think. You need to regroup," he said.

Jim and other local activists were waiting for another opening, a changing of the guard, perhaps, on the commission. But his hopes were limited; for a people without much else to hold dear, his neighbors were leaning ever more zealously on their past. "People say, 'My great-great-grandfather was a proud fighter of the Confederacy.' Well, should you be proud of that?" Jim said. In order to give up the statue, people would need to do the hardest of things—come to terms with the moral flaws in people they loved. "Some people *are* really going to their consciences and asking if they were proud of the great-great-grandfather who was a traitor. But I think a lot of people have not looked at it that way," he said.

As we talked, Jim's voice sounded smaller and reedier than usual. I could hear his exhaustion. For decades, he had tacked back and forth between his pride in being a West Virginian and his quiet anger at its racism. "This is my home," he said. "I've been here all my life." Even if people still wanted to write him out of history, he refused. "West Virginia African Americans have contributed a lot to American history," he said. "And a lot of people don't know that. So we try to educate."

His unrelenting sense of purpose impressed me. I asked him if he thought he'd ever leave West Virginia. "No," he said sharply. "I'm not going to give up on it. I've got to stay here." But, he added, his love for his home state had never shed a trace of horrific realism. "I can't stray too far off the interstate here," he said. "If I go into one of these small towns and little places, I'm putting my life in my hands. It's always been that way. And it hasn't gotten any better."

⊢———⊣

As the country barreled toward the election, every day seemed to bring another test of whether American democracy could manage its combustibility. From the moment the protests began, they had become a bonanza for the gun industry. Colion Noir, a pro-gun activist who was the rare Black man in those ranks, tweeted: "Society can collapse overnight. No matter how Noble the catalyst, there are always other people ready to pervert good intentions w/ opportunistic violence and destruction. Stay safe by staying prepared. No one is coming to save you, be ready to save yourself."

In St. Louis, a husband and wife who feared members of a Black Lives Matter protest emerged from their house brandishing guns. The scene could have been drafted by filmmakers: the husband, Mark McCloskey, a white personal-injury lawyer in his early sixties, stood barefoot in khakis and a pink polo shirt, gripping an AR-15 rifle; his wife, Patricia, in capri pants and a T-shirt, fingered the trigger of a silver handgun. On local television the next day, McCloskey did not hide the fear that dominated his state of mind: "I really thought it was storming the Bastille; we'd be dead and the house would be burned, and there was nothing we could do about it." He said, "My wife doesn't know anything about guns, but she knows about being scared. And she grabbed a pistol."

He wanted people to know he represented clients in cases against police. "I'm not some kind of extreme, you know, anti–Black Lives Matter guy," he said. "But I'm apparently the enemy of the terrorists and the Marxists that are running this organization." In the weeks afterward, the McCloskeys became conservative celebrities. On the opening night of the Republican National Convention, they appeared in a defiant video from their house. "Make no mistake," Patricia McCloskey said into the camera. "No matter where you live, your family will not be safe in the radical Democrats' America." (Mark McCloskey later announced a run for the U.S. Senate.)

By coincidence, on the day the video of the McCloskeys' standoff with protesters first circulated, I got a call from Clark, who was at home, a couple of hours north of St. Louis. He was agitated. "Man, I just encountered some racist shit," he said. He had gone to Walmart with his sons that day to buy a television. But they couldn't fit the box into a taxi to get it home. In the parking lot, he spotted a truck marked "Hauling" on the side. He thought he would hire him to bring the television home. "I put my kids on the sidewalk and said, 'Excuse me, sir.' He said, 'Back away from my truck.'" Clark thought he misheard. "I said, 'What?' He said, 'Get away from my truck.' I said, 'Hold up, man. I see you do hauling. I ain't begging for money.' He said, 'Get your Black ass away from my truck.' I'm like, 'What the fuck is wrong with you?' And he called the cops."

The man spotted a police car in the parking lot and drove over to it to register his complaint. Clark had seen the cops on the way in; his kids had waved at them. Now the officers called him over and asked for his name and identification. "Just in case something happens," the cop said.

Clark's son Jeremiah, who was five years old, watched the police take down his father's name. He peered up at his father and asked, "Are we going to jail, Dad?"

Clark tried to sound reassuring. "Going to jail for what? Asking him about the services on his truck?" But Jeremiah was nervous. He asked again if they were going to jail. "I said, 'No. Just because there is one person that calls the police, does not mean you automatically go to jail. There's a court, you got to hold a hearing. They just can't come and lock you up.'"

As they walked away from the police, Clark tried to put his son at ease. "You know, God's got us." But the truth was that Jeremiah's question left him in despair. After he got the kids home and stepped outside to clear his head, he told me, "This is so fucked up. I've got friends—Asian, Black, white, Puerto Rican. I go off of the content of your character, man. But this dude is a piece of shit." Clark couldn't help feel the echoes of national politics in his experience. "It's getting worse. The powers-that-be are encouraging this shit, and this Donald Trump motherfucker, he could kill all that shit. He's the president. We follow him. But he's making it worse. He's stoking the fires."

His voice that day carried a despair I'd never heard from him. In the four years we'd known each other, Clark had spoken plainly about his own mistakes; he had rarely tried to shift the blame for breaking the law or hurting people or undermining his own future. But I was struck, most of all, by how rarely America had offered him the possibility of grace. I couldn't help wonder about the moments of missed intervention in Clark's life—the curve that was never bent. What if there had been bus fare to get him to Morgan Park High School? Or some mental health treatment after prison? Or a jobs program for ex-cons—and maybe even a jobs program that could fix up the public space near his house and give his kids somewhere to go? None of those were remotely original or ambitious ideas. They were depressingly simple.

The arc of Clark's life had been shaped by generational poverty, structural racism, inferior education, and America's ruinous approach to drugs and punishment. He had been raised in a neighborhood dominated by chronic underinvestment and mass incarceration. The luxuries of impunity, and the burdens of guilt, ran like a lance through the center of American politics in the twenty-first century. Trump had built his politics on celebrating his impunity. "I could stand in the middle of Fifth Avenue and shoot somebody," he said most famously, "and I wouldn't lose any voters." Clark, by contrast, had spent nearly a quarter of his life behind bars, and much of the rest of it tattooed by the stigma. In a country that prided itself on the gift of reinvention—on the "power to begin the world over again"—he had received less than his fair share of redemption.

⊢————⊣

Talking to Clark about his life and his family's path through American history often put me in mind of my own family—and, especially, of my great-grandfather who had nearly died on the street in Chicago. Their stories were linked by nothing but geography, of course; they had grown up a couple of miles from each other, at the opposite ends of a century. But in the years since I had visited the archives and held those bullets in my hand, I often wondered what became of the man who held the gun that day. When I went looking for it, in clips and records and interviews, the story contained more resonance with the present than I expected.

William Wojtkowski did his four years at reform school and was released in 1909. But that was not the end of his criminal career; it was the beginning. Five days later, he held up a saloon with two associates, one of whom shot a Civil War veteran during the robbery. In the months afterward, he acquired a reputation in the pulpy news coverage of Chicago crime: a friend under arrest made the mistake of bragging to the *Tribune* that he and William were responsible for "probably 100 Chicago holdups," and William was sent back to prison for another three years. Out again, in 1914, he was eventually blamed for a string of robberies by a group that the police named the "Franklin Park trio" and was returned to Joliet Prison—this time for nine years.

When William got out in 1923, he changed his life. He dropped the surname Wojtkowski and started introducing himself as William

Viete. He told people he was of German extraction; he found work as a draftsman, and, if anyone asked, he said his birth certificate had been destroyed in the Great Chicago Fire. By 1930, he was married, with a daughter and two stepchildren. He and his wife, Pauline, moved frequently—to Cleveland, Sheboygan, Ford City—before settling in Pittsburgh, where he found work as an engineer in the steel mills. The family bought a tidy two-story brick bungalow. In a family photo, he wore a three-piece suit, white shirt, and striped tie; he had a tall, pale forehead, a heavy nose, and a modest curl of a smile. On February 2, 1950, William Viete died of a heart attack at the office.

I always wondered what his family made of his past and his reinvention. One day, I called Viete's granddaughter Leanna Lang Ayoob. She was thrilled to be reminded of him. "We called him Papaw," she said. "He was eloquent—and meticulous. He dressed and spoke like he'd traveled all over." At the dinner table, he nudged the kids to eat like adults and engage in conversation. "He'd pick up the fork and he'd show me how to move it the right way. He had very good manners." But he was studiously vague about his past, she said. "Nobody would tell us anything. We have almost an empty folder."

I told her what I knew. I explained that he'd gone to jail for shooting my great-grandfather, and I sent her the file I'd accumulated over the years, from his prison records and public filings, and the clippings on his crimes. She studied the details, and said, "I just can't get over it. You would have thought that he came from a well-to-do family, the way he behaved."

And then Leanna remembered something—a fragment of a conversation she'd picked up, as kids do, that suggested a darker chapter. An aunt had once mentioned that her grandmother had visited William in prison. In Leanna's mind, she had composed an explanation to make sense of it—an honorable explanation. "I thought that maybe it was only for a year, and he went to jail because he was working as an accountant, and I thought that maybe there was some kind of funny thing going on with the company and he took a jail sentence to protect them," she said. She gave a light laugh. "But obviously that wasn't the reason."

I spoke to other members of William's family, and none of them knew anything of his early years. His family had thrived in the years afterward: his daughter Cecelia was married to the head of the Chamber of Commerce in Columbia, Missouri; William's grandson became a senior official in the U.S. Forest Service; a great-grandson became an aide to Senator Harry Reid and then a Washington lobbyist.

For all his crimes, William Wojtkowski had eventually found his way back to work, which became the centering force of his life—a source of wealth and stability and dignity that Reese Clark never had. In studies of rehabilitation after prison, researchers found that the ability of a former inmate to make a new start rested largely on the ability to find stable housing and work. Clark was denied both of those, even as many privileged people in American life were the beneficiaries of society's second chances.

In the years after the financial crisis, America's biggest banks escaped with less than $300 billion in fines and settlements—much of which was tax-deductible. No top executives went to jail. Not one bank lost its operating license or corporate charter. Moreover, by 2017, nine years after the financial crisis, federal prosecutions of white-collar crimes had dropped to the lowest level in twenty-two years.

When I stopped by to see Chip Skowron at home in Greenwich, we talked about his life after prison. He had been home for three years. "I'm not welcomed back largely into the business world," he said, and he used an expression that Clark had invoked to describe himself as well. Skowron said, "I'm now a felon. It's a scarlet letter." His country club had eased him out, and his son's soccer team wouldn't let him serve as a manager.

But, of course, in many other ways, Skowron was fortunate. Cheryl had welcomed him back to their house on the hill. His kids had come to terms with his imprisonment and had joined him in an urgent new appreciation for the human costs of incarceration. The family had traveled together to Montgomery, Alabama, to attend the opening of the Legacy Museum, which examined the history of slavery, lynching, and discrimination. And, most of all, even after forfeiting tens of millions of dollars in fines and restitution, he was still prosperous enough to get back into the world of investing, and he was doing it with a friend he'd met in prison.

Kareem "Biggs" Burke, the cofounder of Jay-Z's Roc-A-Fella Records, had gone to prison for conspiring to distribute more than 100 kilos of marijuana. When they were incarcerated they had become close, and once they were both out, Chip and Biggs founded a Christian outreach group to prisoners and made a series of investments in health care and fashion. Skowron's professional life was unrecognizable from what it had been; his undoing had awakened him to an awareness of racial injustice. "It allows me to be free of judgment," he said. "There are things that I have learned that help me relate to people in a tender and compassionate way, whatever color, background, whatever they've done, whatever they think."

When I was with Skowron one evening in his study, with walls of bookshelves and heavy chairs beside a fireplace, the phone rang. A visitor was calling from the intercom outside the stone wall, at the end of the driveway. Skowron tried to open the gate from the keypad; he punched some buttons but nothing happened. His son called from the next room: "Dad, did you get it?"

Skowron frowned at the keypad. "I'm trying to," he said.

"It's line four," his son said, with teenage exasperation in his voice.

Skowron studied the keypad again and punched in more numbers. "And I'm the one who decided to put in the system." He gave a weary laugh. The sense of metaphor hung heavily in the air. He was, for that moment, a man trapped in his manor, unable to let the outside world in. The gate was a remnant of the years when he thought the biggest threats to his future lay outside the wall.

———

In Greenwich, some people became vocal supporters of Black Lives Matter. The pastor Ed Horstmann issued public statements and video messages of support. For Ed, it felt like a test. As a child, he lived in rural upstate New York, where his parents had conservative attitudes about race. "My father was not someone who was going to be talking about how great Martin Luther King Jr. was." But Ed was transfixed by the local pastor, Kalman Sulyok, who had come to this country as a refugee from Hungary. "He had gone through hell and he was passionate about social justice." Sulyok's wife, Catherine, who taught Sunday school, designed a progressive curriculum. "I learned all the protest songs of the sixties because that's what we sang in Sunday school." Eventually, the culture clash erupted. Ed's father was a real-estate agent, and when he received an inquiry from a Black family, he discouraged them from moving to town. "I'm sure he thought it was really enlightened, but he said, 'You know, this probably isn't a place where you want to live.' Well, Kalman Sulyok, the pastor, came to our house and had it out with my father." In the middle of the Black Lives Matter protests, Ed told his congregation the story and asked, "Would somebody growing up in the Round Hill Community Church be able to call back to this time, say thirty or sixty years from now, and say, 'That's where I learned about the common objects of our love'?"

Skowron, whose time in prison had alerted him to racial disparities in criminal justice, attended a local demonstration for Black Lives Matter, which attracted about two hundred people. He was chagrined it was not larger; a recent march in the nearby town of New Canaan, with a population less than a third that of Greenwich, had attracted two thousand. In Greenwich, the demonstration wound its way down the main shopping strip in town, and the leaders offered the bullhorn to anyone who wanted to speak. Skowron took a turn. He peeled off his mask and told the crowd that he was there in a spirit of apology. "I have been, in my life, part of the problem—not because I was overtly racist, but because I was ignorant and uninvolved," he said. He told the crowd that he had spent four years in prison "with people who did not look like me, did not talk like me, and were not from my town. *Those* relationships are what saved me from a life of destruction." There was a big round of applause. "I am here to encourage my brothers and sisters who look like me, who are not part of the minority, to wake up," said. "I have oppressed, unknowingly and unwittingly, and I am sorry for those things I have done."

The march continued down Greenwich Avenue, the main shopping street, where people were dining at outdoor cafés in the sun. Some waved in support, some were impassive, and some were hostile. A jogger passed by and yelled, "All lives matter!" Skowron watched another man shout, of George Floyd, "He deserved it!"

Skowron found the reaction depressing. "The veneer is being scraped away, and what we're seeing underneath is not pretty," he said after the march. "You can call it white supremacy, you can call it entitlement, you can call it corporate narcissism. You can call it all of those things. But what it is, is divisive. It says, 'We are this and they are that.' It's 'us and them.'"

The root of that attitude seemed different at a Trump rally than it was for people who heckled an anti-racist march in Greenwich. In Skowron's view, "It's all about money for them," he said. "That's not to say there aren't real racists there, but, more than anything, they just look at people around them and see them as widgets that are either going to help make them personally get rich or not."

As ugly as it was, Skowron was feeling optimistic. "You can't fix what you don't see," he said. He was encouraged by his children's generation's devotion to Black Lives Matter. "They've been built for this. They are reaching for deeper meaning and substance and things that matter and not getting caught up in the trivialities. To say it bluntly, they're braver."

Over time, Skowron had come to use the analogy of "the good Germans," but he meant it differently than Larry Lessig did. Skowron was not talking about ethics in politics; he was talking about white people who blandly assented to the mass incarceration of African Americans. "There were lots of Germans going about their lives in the face of a great atrocity. There is collective culpability. But this nation also has a collective repentance that it needs to embrace."

For Skowron and many others, the protests were a moment of awakening—a coming to terms with the barriers that separated people from acknowledging the suffering of one another. In a remarkable measure, in the first week of June, Google recorded a rise in searches for the word "empathy" to equal the highest point ever in the search engine's history.

And yet, for a great many others, the protests were a cause of distress—and a moment of political and commercial opportunity. In June, Americans bought more guns—an estimated 3.9 million—than in any previous month in American history. As Trump entered the final months of his campaign, he made a telling change in his rhetoric. In 2016 and 2018, he had focused on conjuring images of marauding immigrants and "caravans" invading the southern border. But, after the racial-justice protests of 2020, Trump shifted his emphasis to "law and order," to fighting "mob rule," to rooting out "the agitators, the looters." The enemy, in other words, was now to be found within.

I asked Jim Campbell, who as head of the Greenwich Republican Town Committee had sensed Trump's potential early on, if he thought the rancor of 2020 was dampening Trump's support in the wealthy provinces of the Gold Coast. On the contrary, he said, "I don't know anyone who voted for Donald Trump in 2016 and won't vote for him again. In Greenwich, he'll probably pick up some votes."

TWENTY

THE RAGING FIRE

THERE WAS SO MUCH for Americans to bear in the dog days of 2020 that the rest of the country scarcely noticed when an extraordinary heat wave settled over California. On August 16, thermometers in Death Valley reached 130 degrees, and NASA declared it "possibly the highest temperature ever reliably recorded on Earth." It was both distressing and unsurprising; the summer was already on track to be the hottest ever recorded in the Northern Hemisphere.

In the hours that followed, the damp, heavy remnants of a tropical storm swept out of the eastern Pacific, heading for the hills north of San Francisco. When the moisture collided with the searing edge of the heat, the collision sparked what scientists call a "lightning siege"—a freakish downpour of electricity. In the predawn darkness over the Bay Area, a torrent of lightning bolts produced a haunting glow, and people in the nearest homes described a vibrating energy in the air, akin to the sensation of approaching a Tesla coil.

Deep in the hills, the lightning splintered redwoods and set some houses on fire. By dawn, after an estimated six hundred lightning strikes, the wildland was burning again. Over the next two weeks, fires swept out of remote stretches of the Mendocino National Forest and merged into an unprecedented inferno—the single largest wildfire in California history. The August Complex, as it was known, was more than double the size of the fire ignited by the rancher's hammer two years earlier, and by October more than 3 million acres of California had burned, the most of any year in recorded history. The fires continued to expand as much as twenty-five miles between dusk and dawn. The intensity of the heat and wind produced "fire tornadoes," great whirling eddies of smoke and ash that had only been observed occasionally in American history. By the fall of 2020, they were appearing every week or two. Unusually tall plumes of smoke climbed ten miles high, above the altitude of commercial jets.

Years earlier, when I had arrived from China, I had marveled at the simple pleasure of American air quality. But as the fires raged in the fall of 2020, they pushed four American cities into the list of the top ten cities with the worst air quality in the world. The smoke veiled the West Coast and extended more than a thousand miles over the Pacific. The season of fire became a fitting backdrop to a country steeling itself for an election unlike any in its history.

In his final weeks as a candidate, Trump was bidding a full farewell to reality. He cycled through fantasies and hobgoblins of the right-wing Web. He endorsed a congressional candidate in Georgia, Marjorie Taylor Greene, who proclaimed that the QAnon network had uncovered a "global cabal of Satan-worshipping pedophiles." Trump called her a "future Republican Star" and "a real WINNER!"

He promoted an anti-mask doctor in Texas who preached about sex with "demons" and a belief that the federal government is run by "reptilian" aliens. (Thanks to Trump's attention, her denunciation of masks was watched 13 million times on Facebook before the site removed it.) And yet, day by day, the president was finding it harder to escape the immovable facts of the virus. In a Rose Garden ceremony for his allies to announce the nomination of Amy Coney Barrett to the Supreme Court, most guests did not bother with masks. They mingled, hugged, and kissed on the cheek, a bizarre spectacle for a country that had gone months without embracing loved ones or seeing friends face-to-face.

Less than forty-eight hours later, Trump tested positive for Covid.

Publicly, his doctor reported no "major clinical concern." In fact, his condition was deteriorating so fast that, privately, officials feared he was on the verge of being intubated. He recovered thanks to a crucial intervention unavailable to ordinary Americans: an experimental antibody cocktail. Days later, with the most acute crisis behind him, he sought to project the message that the virus had not interfered with his work. He released photos of himself signing papers. But the papers were blank.

By the end of the week, at least eight attendees from the Rose Garden ceremony had tested positive, including several of the president's advisers and allies. There were more cases of Covid in the White House than in all of New Zealand.

Trump's political future was slipping into the crevasse between his presumptions and reality. Levels of outright hunger were unlike anything seen in America in generations. In Rhode Island, a quarter of the population reported that they couldn't feed themselves or their families, a height not seen since the Great Depression. "We have done an amazing job, and it's rounding the corner," Trump said in October—on the very day that Wisconsin, one of the states pollsters projected he needed to win, recorded a new daily record, of more than four thousand new cases. It had opened a field hospital on the Wisconsin State Fairgrounds, outside Milwaukee. Less than three weeks before the election, a national poll asked Americans for one word to describe the candidates. For Biden, the top answer was "honest." For Trump, it was "incompetent."

⊢————⊣

The more Trump raged against his problems, the more he leaned on the violent style. "You have to dominate," he told state governors in a conference call as protests expanded in the wake of George Floyd's killing. "Most of you are weak."

He railed against "human scum" and "thugs" and "traitors," and adopted the language of the twilight wars—threatening to send a "surge" of federal agents into cities, such as Chicago, that were home to large Black populations. Mark Esper, the secretary of defense, called for dominating the "battlespace," and Trump dispatched paramilitary agents to

Portland, Oregon ("Worse than Afghanistan," he said), who forced protesters into unmarked cars.

Some of Trump's supporters embraced visions of vast Antifa inva-
sions and deep-state coups, and a cabal of Satan-worshipping pedophile
billionaires. Opponents began to look irredeemable, beyond rehabilitation. In August, Colion Noir, the pro-gun activist, posted a video titled
"Why New Gun Owners Should Fear a Joe Biden Presidency." He told
his audience, "They'll be coming for the handguns. These aren't new
tactics—Hitler did the same thing in Germany."

As the election approached, specters of political violence were ubiquitous: the Boogaloo Bois, with their ironic memes and Hawaiian shirts,
were bracing for civil war; gun sales were breaking records again. On
Facebook, right-wing militants openly swapped disinformation, fraud,
and calls for arming up. In August, to counter a rally in Kenosha, Wisconsin, against police shootings, militants called for bringing weapons on
a Facebook page titled "Armed Citizens to Protect our Lives and Property." Facebook received 455 complaints but let the page stand. At the
event on August 25, two people were shot to death. (Afterward, Facebook CEO Mark Zuckerberg called the company's failure to take down
the page "an operational mistake.") An Illinois teenager named Kyle Rittenhouse was charged with killing two people and injuring a third, and
he became a far-right folk hero. After supporters raised $2 million in bail
money, Rittenhouse was released in November to await trial. His fans
continued to sell merchandise emblazoned with the logo "Free Kyle."

In photos of protests and shows of force, Americans came to expect
a curious new aesthetic, a costume of the Trump era—camouflage, body
armor, tactical gloves, earpiece. It was sometimes difficult to tell if you
were looking at a member of a militia, such as the Oath Keepers, or an
unmarked federal agent or an anti-mask protester. Trump openly encouraged his believers to mix a combat mindset with dark imaginings of
conspiracy. In an interview with Laura Ingraham, the Fox host, he said,
"People that you've never heard of" are controlling Biden. "People that
are in the dark shadows."

"What does that mean?" Ingraham asked. "That sounds like conspiracy theory."

"No," Trump answered. "People that you haven't heard of. They're people that are on the streets. They're people that are controlling the streets. We had somebody get on a plane from a certain city this weekend, and in the plane, it was almost completely loaded with thugs wearing these dark uniforms, black uniforms with gear and this and that. They're on a plane."

On August 29, Trump's most devoted media network, OANN, broadcast a segment titled "America Under Siege: The Attempt to Overthrow President Trump," which argued that "this coup attempt is led by a well-funded network of anarchists trying to take down the president."

Republican leaders in Congress clung to him in the hope of enshrining minoritarian rule by a party that was older and whiter than the country at large. They hustled a conservative Supreme Court nominee through confirmation at breakneck speed, filed scores of suits to bar the casting or the counting of ballots, and curtailed a census that would record growing populations in diverse, Democratic-leaning areas. It was a brazen acknowledgment that, without a significant intervention, Trump lacked the public support to remain president. After a caravan of trucks and cars festooned with Trump signs surrounded a Biden campaign bus on a Texas highway, trying to run it off the road, Trump tweeted, "These patriots did nothing wrong." Rubio, ever alert to an opportunity, heaped praise on them as "great patriots," saying at a Trump rally, "We love what they did, but here's the thing they don't know: we do that in Florida every day!"

Larry Diamond, a political scientist at Stanford's Hoover Institution and a former adviser to the Coalition Provisional Authority in Iraq, told me, "There's no other way to say this: the Republican Party, with notably few exceptions, has become a party of semi-loyalty to democracy. If you want to stop this, the answer is very simple. The Republican politicians who know better, in the House, the Senate, and the governorships, have to speak up. If they don't put the preservation of democracy and civility over their own political careers, we're going to keep sliding down this path."

Hardly anyone who studied political violence expected the risk to subside after the election. In a survey conducted in September, a team of prominent political scientists found that a disturbing number of Americans believed that violence "could be justified to advance their parties' political goals." Multiple studies show that the figure was at least one in six, twice what it was three years earlier. "That's a very significant jump," Diamond, who helped conduct the research, told me. "But it's not just the numbers. It's also the context that is so unsettling. The level of armaments that these people have, the stockpiles of military-style weaponry and body armor, the high-volume gun clips—there's no precedent in American history for this, and that's why I think the current era is more dangerous than anything we've seen in decades."

What might actually push people over the threshold from talking about violence to perpetrating it? Over the years, scholars compared examples as diverse as student protests in Germany and Italy, riots outside the 1968 Democratic Convention in Chicago, and democracy protests in Hong Kong. In many cases, they concluded, the point of ignition was the perception of government repression, real or imagined—a moment that inspired bystanders to join fellow citizens in fighting the perceived abuse of authority.

Trump encouraged his followers to see his political opponents as tyrants. On October 8, federal and state authorities charged six men with plotting to kidnap Gretchen Whitmer, the governor of Michigan. She had been one of Trump's most frequent targets of criticism; in the spring, as protesters with guns demonstrated in the Michigan capitol, Trump tweeted out a militia slogan, "LIBERATE MICHIGAN!," and called them "very good people." The plotters had reportedly found one another online and through friends involved with the boogaloo movement. During a pro-gun rally in Lansing on June 18, some of the men talked about attacking the capitol. They met for tactical training and tried to make bombs. Adam Fox, the accused ringleader, told others, "I just wanna make the world glow, dude . . . I don't fuckin' care anymore, I'm just so sick of it."

Diamond, who had studied the workings of democracy in dozens of countries, recognized a disturbing pattern that led to violence: "All of these instances of pressing out the normative boundaries of what's acceptable are the prelude to more daring, outrageous acts of political

violence. Look at the climate in Israel in the months preceding the assassination of Yitzhak Rabin. You see the same rise in inflammatory
rhetoric and the same erosion of the constraints. It's a downward spiral
that gave the signal to this violent right-wing extremist that it actually
could be okay—even morally necessary—to assassinate the Israeli prime
minister."

When Trump, in a debate with Biden, refused to condemn white
supremacists and hate groups, telling the far-right Proud Boys to "stand
back and stand by," the group rejoiced. On Parler, a social media platform, the Proud Boys organizer Joe Biggs proclaimed, "Trump basically
said to go fuck them up!"

———

Election Day was clear and cold in Washington, with thin streaks of
high clouds. Sarabeth and I drove out to Clifton, Virginia, a little town
where we could chat with voters on the way in and out. I was struck, most
of all, by how many of them wanted to talk less about the candidates—
what more was there to say?—than about the breakdown in America's
political culture. To a person, they said they were exhausted by the rancor, the absolutism, the tribalism.

Many lamented what they saw as the distorting effects of social media and the press. One young couple—Ken and Kinley Spenard—had
gone into the voting booths and, in the grand marital tradition, canceled each other's vote: he went for Trump; she voted for Biden. We
talked for a long time, and Ken lingered on the corrosive effect of Internet anonymity. "A friend of mine said, 'You can only be'—excuse
my language—'an asshole so many times in your life before someone
punches you in the face.' That used to happen to us as kids. You'd run
your jaw too much on the schoolyard, and you'd get roughed up. So
you'd learn, 'Okay, probably shouldn't do that.'" Kinley said she and her
husband had informally stopped talking about politics with neighbors
and acquaintances. "Because you don't want to lose friends," she said.
"We've had a lot of people around us starting to get more extreme views,
which is weird, because we're in our early thirties, and we're like, 'It's a

little young to be having such extreme views!' Why is it okay that somebody thinks that it can be all or nothing?"

In the end, the election of 2020 was not particularly close. It took a few days to count the closest states, but eventually it was clear that Biden had won by more than 7 million votes, with a margin of 306 to 232 in the Electoral College. It was nearly a mirror image of the results in 2016, which Trump had hailed as a "landslide."

And yet the results were also sobering: Biden had presented himself as a firebreak, a barrier against the inferno of another four years, but Americans had not delivered a blunt repudiation of Trump and his values; instead, they had shown themselves to be intractably divided. No fewer than 74 million Americans had cast their votes for Trump. After all they had seen of him, the stalwarts remained loyal.

Jim Campbell, who had predicted to me that Trump would pick up votes in Greenwich, was right. Though Democrats once again prevailed in the town's overall count, Trump received more votes there in 2020 than he had in 2016. Nothing in Trump's four years had deterred Campbell and others. "I could list the accomplishments, and they are numerous," he told me from a new home in the nearby town of Westport, where he had moved not long ago. Campbell cataloged his sense of Trump's achievements: "cutting regulation, tax cuts," avoiding military engagements, "standing up for respecting our borders," a host of new conservative judges, and "the right approach, at last, to Iran and the Middle East." But, at bottom, Campbell's affection extended beyond policy; it came down to style. "I have always admired Trump's willingness to lead the fight," Campbell said, "right up to Election Day."

In the end, Trump's strongest support in Greenwich was in the Tenth District, the Golden Triangle where I grew up and where Prescott Bush once held sway. For years, people had explained Trump's win in 2016 as a reflection of Clinton's unpopularity; but the 2020 results debunked that theory. After four years of Trump's presidency, Trump extended his lead in the Golden Triangle; in 2016, he had won the district by two percentage points; in 2020, he won by thirteen.

├────────┤

On the night that Biden was declared the winner, we took our kids down to the streets near the White House to catch a glimpse of the public reaction. We reached the foot of St. John's Church, where police had fired tear gas into a Black Lives Matter crowd just a few months earlier so that Trump could pose with a Bible in a photo-op. On this night, the mood was celebratory; musicians drummed and played trumpets and trombones as people rejoiced in the fact that a white man and a Black woman of Indian descent had won the White House by talking explicitly about their plans to attack structural racism, profound inequality, and the cruelties of the American health-care system.

On the streets, we watched an exhibit of fierce, pent-up emotion, a mix of joy and contempt that had sent more than 150 million Americans to cast ballots—the highest turnout rate in 120 years. That was good news for the health of American democracy, even if it was driven as much by revulsion as it was by love. But the closer one looked at the results of the race, the more grotesque a story they told about America's democratic institutions. Biden's victory by 7 million votes was larger than the entire population of Massachusetts or Indiana—but, under the esoteric rules of the Electoral College, he could have lost if he had shed just 50,000 votes in the wrong states. To the rest of the world, the system looked no more rational than the mystical divinations of a theocracy. The *Financial Times* compared the Electoral College to "a dodgy appendix that hemorrhages a little more bile with each election."

The longer we stayed that night, the more I sensed that the festivity was shot through with anger, too; Trump had come to office as a symptom of America's rage, and he had amplified it, generating an echo of hostility that redounded upon him. Above the crowd, someone hoisted a life-size effigy of Trump's head at the end of a stick, where it bounced and swayed ghoulishly among us. By every measure, we were in a country in pain—a damaged place—and I wondered how long it would take to repair. Ending Trump's presidency would not solve the underlying problems that produced it, leaving Americans to face a haunting question of history: Could a country argue its way back from the abyss?

Activists on the left faced an awkward choice: As exhausted and alienated as they were by support for Trump, could Americans really afford to let desperate rural states remain fertile ground for the next demagogue? Or would the country attack that desperation at its origins? Katey Lauer, the West Virginia activist who had moved from environmentalism to electoral politics, told me, "After the election results, I saw a post that said something like 'I hope everyone at the Cracker Barrel is crying right now.' I just thought: Why? Why do we want *anyone* to be crying? Why is our wish for that?" She went on, "One of the dimensions of the culture war that we're fighting in this country is urban and rural, this idea that we should or should not 'write this place off.' We should or should not talk to these 'kinds of people.' Or this kind of behavior means they're unworthy. I just don't think that's going to get us where we need to go."

The 2020 election yielded mixed results for Lauer and her colleagues in the West Virginia Can't Wait movement. In the gubernatorial primary, Stephen Smith narrowly lost to an established Democrat, a lawyer named Ben Salango, who went on to get trounced by the incumbent, Jim Justice. But Smith and Lauer saw clear signs of promise; along with breaking records in small donations, they had elected eleven candidates to offices ranging from the legislature to the local school board. Within a week, another eighteen candidates announced plans to run two years later under the banner of West Virginia Can't Wait. Though they were miles away from their dream of a "people's government," the young organizers had proved that candidates could reject corporate donations and still compete in a state dominated by the fortunes of the Koch brothers, the "Friends of Coal," and other powerful tools of influence.

In a way I had not appreciated at the outset, Smith and Lauer had found ways to achieve that rarest of things in modern American politics: a chance for Trump voters to join Biden voters in a shared pursuit. By focusing intensely on local problems—hunger, housing shortages, delays in unemployment benefits—they had succeeded in luring some Americans back from the toxic nationalization of politics. When I asked Smith what his members made of the election result, he said, "The most striking thing is, and pardon my language, people don't give a shit." He let out a bark of a laugh. "Of course, there are some who follow it obsessively just like any other place, but the general mood was that the federal government has done so little for me and my family for so long, that they were open to a different conversation." He was not naïve; he knew that Trump had dominated West Virginia even more than four years earlier, but history had proven that Appalachian voters would gravitate to someone who was listening to them. Though Smith had lost his race, he was patient. "It feels like the country is deciding what kind of place it is going to be," Smith said. "That does not happen very often."

———

In the days after he lost, Trump spiraled through emotions like Lear on the heath. He and his lawyers voiced a range of fantastical theories—that Nevada officials deliberately manipulated machines to allow dubious signatures, that Michigan and Pennsylvania counted the votes of dead people in tallies for Biden, that millions of Trump votes were deleted by voting machines engineered in a secret plot involving Venezuelan socialists. In a forty-six-minute speech posted to social media, the president declared, "You can't let another person steal that election from you." He stopped bothering with the business of the White House; he spent much of the day secluded in the residence or on the golf course, tweeting repeatedly, "We won in a LANDSLIDE!" Much of his staff stopped coming to work, even as the pandemic roared past another grim threshold: on December 9, for the first time, the daily death count exceeded the number of people who were killed on 9/11.

One after another, Trump's claims were debunked by the Department of Homeland Security, by his own attorney general, and, in dozens of cases, by the courts; a month after the election, Trump's lawsuits had been turned away by at least eighty-six judges across the political spectrum, including by some he had personally appointed. Nevertheless, in the Oval Office, he continued to meet with charlatans, paranoiacs, and misfit lawyers, a parade that took on the qualities of a Fellini production. In perhaps the most indelible moment, the president's election advisers botched the location of a press conference intended to be at the Four Seasons Hotel in Philadelphia and instead summoned the world's media to Four Seasons Total Landscaping, a small business located between a porn shop and a crematorium. The sense of something melting down became unusually vivid days later, when Trump's lawyer Rudy Giuliani, the eccentric former mayor of New York City, ranted that Hugo Chavez, George Soros, and the Clinton Foundation had stolen the election as a line of black ooze—hair dye or makeup, it wasn't clear—slid down his cheek.

It was all so ludicrous that it was easy to overlook the disturbing fact that, in the background, many of America's most powerful Republicans were endorsing and amplifying Trump's lie. Kevin McCarthy, the party's highest-ranking member of the House, told a television audience on November 6, "President Trump won this election. So everyone who's listening, do not be quiet. Do not be silent about this." Days later, in a speech to a crowd in Washington, Congressman Louie Gohmert of Texas encouraged people to consider "revolution" akin to the Egyptian uprising seven years earlier. "One third of the Egyptian people in 2013 went to the streets, all over Egypt" to oust "Obama's friend the Muslim brother," he said. "If they can do that there, think of what we can do here." Long after Trump's lawsuits had failed in the courts, Mike Pence, the vice president, faced a crowd chanting "FOUR MORE YEARS!" and he embraced the delusion: "I'll make you a promise," he declared. "We're going to keep fighting until every legal vote is counted!"

What had appeared at first like absurdist theater rapidly evolved into a full-scale attempt at subverting the election. On January 2, in an infamous phone call with Georgia's Republican secretary of state, Brad Raffensperger, Trump cajoled and threatened him to "find 11,780 votes." Raffensperger refused. When the call became public the next day, it was the kind of scandal that, in any other moment, would have resulted in bipartisan demands for the president's resignation. But Republicans defended it. "The president has always been concerned about the integrity of the election," McCarthy said.

Across the country, Trump's fictions were permitting a casual embrace of violence; the odes to revolution were becoming blunter. In Oklahoma, the chairman of the Cleveland County Republican Party, Dave Spaulding, mocked the argument that "violence is unacceptable." On Facebook, he wrote, "What the crap do you think the American revolution was? A game of friggin pattycake? Blood was shed and rightfully so!"

If Trump was actually going to upend the results of the election, his last chance would be on January 6, when Pence was scheduled to oversee the final certification of the vote by Congress. As the day approached, Trump returned, at last, to the tool that had served him so reliably ever since his first moments as a candidate, when he released Lindsey Graham's cell-phone number to the public: Trump would subject his enemies to the power of the public. "Big protest in D.C. on January 6th," he tweeted. "Be there, will be wild!"

———

For a brief moment, early on the morning of January 6, Democrats had reasons to celebrate. Overnight, after tense runoff elections for the U.S. Senate, the state of Georgia had made history: Jon Ossoff would be Georgia's first Jewish senator and, at age thirty-three, the youngest member in the chamber. (For young Americans, it was only modest cause for comfort; the Senate still had fewer members born after 1980 than it had members with the first name Chuck.)

The other victor in Georgia was the Reverend Raphael Warnock, the state's first Black senator, the culmination of years of strategy by the voting-rights activist Stacey Abrams and others to ensure that Black citizens were not denied access to polls. Moreover, the Georgia results completed a sweeping rebuke to Trump. He was now the first president since Herbert Hoover to preside over the loss of the White House, the House, and the Senate. But if those victories marked the crest of America's progressive politics, the rest of the day would illuminate, with lethal clarity, the opposition to that future.

The "Save America Rally" began at 10 a.m., south of the White House, just as members of Congress were starting to certify Biden's victory. The crowd was a maskless congregation of the rebellious, the devout, the bored, and the bitter. They erected a wooden gallows with a hanging rope. Early speakers included Roger Stone, who had helped Lee Hanley of Greenwich organize local Republicans and later been pardoned by Trump for lying to Congress, and Mo Brooks, an Alabama Republican who called it a day for patriots to begin "kicking ass." Finally, Trump took to the stage and declared, "If you don't fight like hell, you're not going to have a country anymore." He told them to march to the Capitol to "peacefully and patriotically make your voices heard," and he repeated the word "fight" more than twenty times. "I'll be there with you," he said, though in fact he returned to the White House and watched history unfold on television.

At 1:10 p.m., protesters, including some in flak jackets, helmets, and gas masks, started tussling with the Capitol Police. They raged against the accumulated frustrations—the election, the masks, the economy, the lockdown. An angry man yelled, "Why can't I work? Where's my 'pursuit of happiness'?" Within minutes, the police were overrun at their checkpoints, and thousands of protesters swept toward the Capitol. They stole metal barricades erected by police and used them as ladders to scale the base of the building; they used flagpoles and fire extinguishers and stolen riot shields to crash through windows and doors and poured inside. Videos captured the sight of a lone Capitol Police officer, Eugene Goodman, luring the rioters away from the Senate chamber, in a crucial maneuver that allowed members of Congress to escape. "Where is Pence?" the crowd chanted, ominously. Many had turned their wrath on the vice president because they had a false belief that he could simply stall the certification of votes. When that fantasy collapsed, incensed people roamed the halls in search of him, shouting in naked bloodlust: "Hang Mike Pence!"

The jittery throng coursed through the Capitol, mugging with the statues and lounging at the desks of senators and representatives. They rummaged through drawers and brandished their loot for photographers. A man in a wool Trump hat with a pompom on it, his face in a rictus of glee, carried off a carved wooden lectern bearing the seal of the Speaker of the House. Someone smeared feces on the walls. Aides to Mitch McConnell heard a woman praying outside their door for "the evil of Congress to be brought to an end." A Black member of the Capitol Police later said he was called a racial slur "fifteen times today." Some of the rioters were off-duty police who flashed badges on their way in, and others were far-right celebrities who streamed video as they broke into the capital. One of them was none other than Derrick Evans, the anti-abortion activist who had been elected to the West Virginia House of Delegates. Evans had filmed himself, wearing a helmet and yelling Trump's name, stampeding through the Capitol. (Later, following his arrest, he resigned from the legislature.)

I arrived at the foot of the Capitol shortly after three o'clock, and I looked up to the crowd heaving in and out of the doors on the north side. They collided with police, and both sides doused each other in pepper spray. Protesters crashed their flagpoles onto the heads of the cops, who were wildly outnumbered. The police gave way, and another wave of rioters rushed into the building, chanting, "Treason! Treason!"

As another puff of tear gas wafted out from the melee, Sharon Krahn, a grandmother from Dallas, looked on approvingly. "Our congressmen should be shitting their pants. They need to fear, because they're too posh," she told me. "Their jobs are too cushy, and their personal gain has taken priority over their sense of duty. Maybe they all started off with a good heart, you know, but power corrupts. Our government is proof positive of that."

She wore a plaid scarf and a gray wool hat studded with sequins. I asked if the violence was taking things too far. "Whose house is this? This is the house of 'We the People.' If you do a bad job, your boss tells you about it," Krahn said. She nodded toward the Senate, where the elected officials had already evacuated to safety: "We're not happy with the job you've done." She drew a distinction between the scene in front of her and the domain of enemies she called "Antifa and BLM," who, she said, have "no true aim except destruction and anarchy."

I weaved through the crowd to the grand east staircase of the Capitol, the spot where Abraham Lincoln delivered his Inaugural Address in 1861, appealing to Americans to cherish the "bonds of affection," to recall the "mystic chords of memory." (Six weeks later, the United States was at war.) One hundred sixty years later, the stairs were covered by a leaderless scrum of hundreds, if not thousands, who waved flags for Trump and for the Confederacy. At the top, I watched a bald man in a white shirt and a Trump-style red tie shout into a megaphone, "Our world is broken, our system is broken." I watched a man in camouflage at the base of the steps wearing a tactical helmet of the kind that American soldiers used in Iraq. He shouted up to the top of the stairs, "Who the hell are you?" An armored black SWAT-team truck, which is often posted at the foot of the stairs, had been left marooned and abandoned in a sea of people. A group climbed on the roof and the hood and stuck a sign on the windshield that said "Pelosi Is Satan."

———

As the hours ticked toward 6 p.m.—the start of the curfew announced by Muriel Bowser, the mayor of Washington, D.C.—a white police van, led by a lone cop on a motorcycle, tried to part the crowd below the east stairs, but the crowd converged on it, banging on the metal walls of the van until the driver abandoned the attempt. The guy with the megaphone was still ranting: "We will not allow a new world order . . . If you are truly innocent, you have nothing to worry about."

I introduced myself to a hopped-up guy walking away from the Senate side of the Capitol, and he said, "*The New Yorker*? Fucking enemy of the people. Why don't I smash you in your fucking head?" He made an effort to draw a crowd: "Right there in the blue mask! Enemy of the fucking people!" But the people had other things on their minds, and nobody bothered to join him.

Five years after the Trump era began, a physical assault on U.S. democracy felt both shocking and inevitable—a culmination of everything I'd come to understand about America's political crisis since I'd come to Washington in 2013. On the same grounds, eight years earlier, the tourists from Finland had asked me why the U.S. government had shut itself down, and I had no answer. In the years since, I'd watched Americans gravitate to a president who rejected the notion of a public good; they praised him to me while celebrating the sedition of the Confederate flag and sipping from a coffee cup adorned with a swastika. Others waved away those warnings from the gilded remove of the Gold Coast. The scene unfolding at the Capitol was like an inferno powered by the cynicism, unreason, and deception in U.S. politics. For years, members

of Congress had voted to block gun-control bills; they voiced the demands of the NRA and dismissed the pleadings of parents whose children were coming of age with a nursery rhyme that began *"Lockdown,
lockdown, lock the door."* When, at last, the horror arrived at the doors
of Congress, the elected representatives of the people were hustled to
safety through secret tunnels by their own praetorian guard. Some of
them stripped their congressional pins from their lapels to avoid being
targeted.

As the crowd outside swirled around us, I asked Krahn, the grandmother from Dallas, if she thought Trump's victory had been stolen.
"Absolutely, without a doubt," she said. Why? "Okay," she said, and
started ticking things off on her fingers. "The vote count changing on
TV, the more-votes-than-voters, boxes of blank ballots, and, honestly,
probably the biggest one is the refusal to audit the votes. Because, if
this was fair, if this was a legitimate election, then we should be above
reproach. Just like when the IRS comes in and audits my books, I don't
worry about it."

I asked where she got her news. "You have to be of a mind to dig
through," she said. "So I do not listen to mainstream media anymore. I
like C-SPAN because I want to see it happen and then derive my own
conclusions from it. I do subscribe to *Epoch Times*, and I do read articles
from *The New Yorker* and *The Atlantic*, and I read *The New York Times*,
and I read *The Wall Street Journal*, and I listen to NPR." She added, "I do
not listen to CNN, and I don't listen to Fox, because I've lost all respect.
Hate 'em all."

Krahn's seventeen-year-old daughter, Annalee, wearing a wool
Trump hat and thumbing out a message on her phone, approached with
news. "They found more than one explosive device in the building. My
sister just texted me," she said. Her mom was skeptical: "I think they
want to scare everybody and get everyone out of here." (Molotov cock-
tails were, in fact, discovered in a vehicle near the Capitol, and pipe
bombs were found at the offices of the Democratic National Committee
and the Republican National Committee.)

An hour or so later, after four o'clock, word passed through the
crowd that Trump had put out a video. Two women who had flown in

from Seneca, Missouri, huddled around a cell phone to watch it. Sara Clark owns a gun store that makes custom AK-47s. Her friend Stacie Dunbar is a secretary in a hospital. On the cracked screen of Dunbar's phone, they watched Trump's video, a hasty production seemingly taped in the Rose Garden. "I know your pain, I know your hurt," he told the crowd. "We had an election that was stolen from us. It was a landslide election, and everyone knows it, especially the other side. But you have to go home now; we have to have peace. We have to have law and order."

What do you think? I asked.

"I don't know," Clark said. "It's not going to do us any good to beat the hell out of everything. But we didn't lose. We shouldn't give in."

What do you do now? I asked. Clark turned the question on her friend. "I have no thoughts, honestly," Dunbar said. "I'm at an absolute loss. We're disenfranchised! It just sounded like he just gave up. Our president! Sounded like he just gave up. He gave in."

Why? I asked.

"Because he doesn't want us to do this," Clark said, motioning toward the chaos.

"He doesn't want anyone hurt. That's what he said," Dunbar added. Tears filled her eyes. "I did this for my kids," she said. "I have a son in the Navy, and Trump's done more for our military than any president ever has."

What did you honestly expect would happen by coming here? I asked.

"A win! Four more years," Clark said with a mirthless laugh.

Seriously?

"Yes, absolutely," she said.

"I wanted Pence to do the right thing, but Pence didn't do the right thing," Dunbar said.

As darkness approached, police fired a series of flash-bang grenades to shoo people down from the balconies and steps. A heavyset man in a white "Make America Great Again" hat stood in a crosswalk, watching the crowd begin to move. He was happy. "They sent a message. That's enough," he said. He turned to walk away and added, "Of course, if we come back, it will be with a militia."

TWENTY-ONE

BEHOLD THE LAND

SEVEN AMERICANS DIED in the mayhem and the aftermath of January 6. But the full intensity of the turmoil that day emerged only later, in the details reported by the survivors. One police officer was struck so many times by a taser that he had a heart attack. Another lost an eye after he was gouged with a flagpole. A rioter who collapsed on her way in the door was crushed underfoot before anyone could rescue her. But none of the mayhem carried as much symbolic power as the death of thirty-five-year-old Ashli Babbitt. She was climbing through a broken window, with a Trump banner around her shoulders, when a police officer shot her in the neck.

For two decades, Babbitt's fortunes had followed the course of the country's. In 2002, after graduating from high school, she been drawn to the military, much as Sidney Muller had, in pursuit of a purpose larger than herself. Babbitt enlisted in the Air Force and was assigned to guard the gates at air bases around the world. She served in Afghanistan, Iraq, and the United Arab Emirates. She was discharged in 2016, after fourteen years of bit parts in the twilight war, and she settled near the working-class San Diego suburb where she had grown up. But she struggled to find her way. She worked briefly in security for a nuclear power plant, and then bought part of a small swimming-pool-supply company, but her debts piled up.

As her financial life deteriorated, she poured more of her energy into politics. She filled her social-media channels with paeans to QAnon and Trump, and rants against immigration, drugs, and Democrats. After she died, her brother told reporters, "If you feel like you gave the majority of your life to your country and you're not being listened to, that is a hard pill to swallow."

In its particulars, Ashli Babbitt's life was an uncanny reflection of the population that stormed the Capitol that day. After police had arrested more than a hundred of them, patterns emerged. Nearly 20 percent had served in the military, according to an analysis by NPR. And nearly 60 percent had a history of financial trouble—bankruptcies, bad debts, unpaid taxes, according to *The Washington Post*.

But, in my own encounters that afternoon, I noticed yet another through line, which stayed with me for days afterward: amid their delusions about Satanic pedophiles and a "scamdemic," in between their fears of Black Lives Matter and Antifa, many of the people I met told me that they were on their first trip to Washington, D.C. They might as well have been invading a foreign land.

Donald Trump's insurrection failed because of scattered points of resistance: judges who refused to be insulted by the abuse of the law; an uncooperative secretary of state in Georgia; the impossible bravery of Officer Goodman. When I paused to consider just how far the coup progressed, it often put me in mind of an observation from the Civil War by Abraham Lincoln's secretary of state, William Seward: "There was always just enough virtue in this republic to save it; sometimes none to spare."

Democracy had come closer to failure than many Americans had ever imagined possible, and, for a fragile moment, in the hours after the smoke cleared, it felt as if a fever had broken. Twitter and Facebook abruptly banned Trump from their networks. Lindsey Graham, his most loyal footman in Congress, said, wearily, "Count me out." In a speech to colleagues on the Senate floor, he declared, "Enough is enough." But the moment of reproach ended almost as quickly as it had begun. Within days, as Democrats prepared a second impeachment of Trump, Republican leaders signaled their intentions to defend him—and Graham joined them, in the name of winning above all. "To the Republican Party, if you want to win . . . we need to work with President Trump," he told Fox News in February. "We can't do it without him."

The reaction was similar from many of the people I had interviewed over the years about their support of Trump—in Connecticut, West Virginia, Iowa, New Hampshire. Nobody I spoke to after the insurrection walked away from him. When I asked Ed Dadakis, of Greenwich, if he had any regrets, he said, "While we all have in our own minds that perfect candidate, the fact is that perfect candidate never runs and we are forced to make a choice between two imperfect people. So your question really isn't do I regret voting for Trump but do I wish I'd voted for Hillary. The answer is no. Hillary would've been a disaster." We might as well have been talking four years ago, I thought.

The more I asked, the more people dug in. The truth, I knew, was that any real change, if it was to happen, would start in private. And in that regard, Ed Horstmann, the pastor at Round Hill Community Church who had made no secret of his revulsion for Trump, was optimistic. "For so long, that rhetoric of anger, vengeance, blame had become the only voice in the room," he said. In the weeks after the riot, he had sensed a subtle shift in Greenwich. He said, "There's far more willingness to speak up and speak out, to be more explicit about a core of values that can really build and strengthen the country."

The agonies of 2020 had not snapped Americans out of their divisions; the rifts were too wide and the combatants too entrenched for any easy reconciliation. But the Trump presidency and the Covid pandemic had forced Americans to reckon, more explicitly than at any moment in years, with the costs of inequity, seclusion, and disengagement. Americans were beginning to contend with some of the questions about democracy that had been nagging me since I touched back down in America: Who, among us, deserves what we have—good and bad? How much are we, any of us, in control of our lives? And how did our collective choices lead us here? One way or another, Americans were discovering just how much our destinies were tied to where we lived, places as different as the Golden Triangle, Mud City, and the Jewel of the Hills. Not only did our places shape our schools, our incomes, our values, and our opportunities, but they also shaped our minds, our fantasies, and, above all, our fears.

├────────────┤

On January 13, exactly a week after his supporters tried to overturn the election, Trump became the first president in American history to be impeached twice. The charge was incitement of insurrection. He ignored the proceedings and spent most of his final days soliciting cash from fans. He collected more than $200 million in donations for a "legal defense fund" that would subsidize his life after office. He busied himself on his favorite indulgence: the right to escape punishment. He doled out pardons and clemency to a long list of friends and allies, including his former aide Steve Bannon (accused of fraud), loyalists who had pleaded guilty in the Russia inquiry, and two corrupt allies from Congress: Chris Collins (insider trading), and Duncan Hunter, who had disguised his clothing purchases as gifts for wounded veterans. The pardons were Trump's final salute to impunity, a dispensing of absolution that made a mockery of "personal responsibility" and exhibited the true depth of unfairness in America's system of punishment and forgiveness.

For the rest of those who had put their hopes in Trump, he delivered precious little. Four years after the campaign event where he promised coal miners that they'd be working their "asses off," the industry had 6,400 *fewer* jobs in West Virginia than when he arrived. In a curious coda to Trump's term, his loss had bequeathed West Virginia a moment of more substantive potential: with Democrats suddenly in control of the Senate, a pivotal vote belonged to one of the party's few conservatives—West Virginia's senior senator, Joe Manchin. If his party wanted him to cooperate, Manchin could demand some of the things his state desperately needed, ranging from greater broadband access to workforce training. Around the Capitol, people had taken to calling him "your highness."

For the moment, that potential didn't mean much in Clarksburg. The newsroom at *The Exponent Telegram* had been mostly deserted ever since the declaration of a national emergency on March 13, 2020. John Miller, the editor, was doing his strenuous best to stay positive. "By nature, I'm extremely optimistic, and I remain optimistic," he told me one day as the first anniversary approached. "But at times I've wondered: Is this *ever* going to end?"

It is a painful fact that death lands differently in a small town. Across the country, the death toll from Covid had grown so large that it had become an abstraction, leached of its true horror. Miller didn't have that luxury. When he put the news of the latest deaths into the paper, they weren't numbers; they were people he knew, like Donald Webster, whom everyone addressed by his nickname, "Duck," ever since he'd been a superstar on the high school basketball team, and the senior class president, as well as a Vietnam vet, not to mention the winner of a local political race by such a large margin that even CNN reported on it. "Duck spent twenty-five days in the hospital, on a ventilator," Miller told me. "His family couldn't bring themselves to put Covid in the obituary because he was so determined to beat it." He did beat it, in a sense; he was free of the disease, but it damaged his heart so much that he could not survive.

All Miller could do about it was what he had always done: put the paper out, and carry the numbers around in his head. "Forty-eight hundred cases in Harrison County," he said. "Five hundred vaccines a day." His reporters were working from home, but he couldn't bring himself to let the newsroom go dark entirely. So he still loped into his office every morning with a few other colleagues, working with masks on, even if there was hardly anyone around. "I'm trying to be the cohesive factor," he told me.

Miller was caught in the middle of the political battle, too. "We have people that are very upset that Trump didn't win, and people that are thrilled to death that Biden did—and, trust me, I hear from both," he said. "It's difficult to watch, because, at one point in time, they were friends. But there has just been more heat, more disagreement, more venom."

Not being able to hash it out face-to-face made it worse. "There is the connection—going to a ball game with a couple of thousand people. There's just something there that's therapeutic, and it's missing," he told me. "It's hard to keep the fabric of a community tightly woven when you're not able to get together. The threads start to unravel."

├──────┤

On January 20, exactly two weeks after the insurrection, Trump slipped out of town early, to avoid attending his successor's inauguration. His departure, like his presidency, was a hasty, fractious improvisation, applauded chiefly by his children. The vice president, who had been hunted through the Capitol by rioters, was not in attendance.

On the eve of being sworn in, Joe Biden, Kamala Harris, and their spouses visited a Covid memorial on the National Mall. A nurse named Yolanda Adams sang "Hallelujah" beside the Lincoln Memorial. The reflecting pool was encircled by four hundred lights to honor 400,000 deaths, a toll on par with America's losses in World War II. "To heal, we must remember," Biden said, which reminded me of the poem in my desk. Memory will grow into legend, legend into song, song into sacrament.

Biden's inauguration as the forty-sixth president was the culmination of a long path; sixty years earlier, the success of a fellow Irish Catholic, John F. Kennedy, had inspired a teenage admirer in Delaware to study the Congressional Directory in the school library for clues into how he might achieve the ludicrous ambition to follow him. (His conclusion: law school.) But in his Inaugural Address, Biden spoke less of triumph than of caution: "We've learned again that democracy is precious. Democracy is fragile. At this hour, my friends, democracy has prevailed." *At this hour*—it was an acknowledgment of the risks that remained in what he called our "winter of peril." He dispensed with the euphemisms to speak plainly of the crises before him: "white supremacy, domestic terrorism," and a "cry for survival" from "the planet itself."

He invoked St. Augustine's definition of a people as a "a multitude defined by the common objects of their love," and he listed some basic values: "Opportunity. Security. Liberty. Dignity. Respect. Honor. And, yes, the truth." In another era, that series that might have reminded us of all that bound Americans together. But under the circumstances, the list stood out more for how much those definitions had become contested or hollow. What did opportunity and liberty actually mean in a country where Reese Clark's son Jeremiah was growing up at such risk of incarceration that he wondered if he was going to jail already? Where was the honor in a bankruptcy system that allowed a hedge fund to escape its failed bet on coal by cutting the health benefits of Appalachian retirees? How did the truth become so devalued in the rarified world of Chip Skowron and Gordon Caplan that they squandered their reputations without even noticing that they had passed the point of no return?

Biden turned, over and again, to the prospects for national reunion, what he called "the way of unity": "We can see each other not as adversaries, but as neighbors. We can treat each other with dignity and respect. We can join forces, stop the shouting, and lower the temperature. For without unity, there is no peace—only bitterness and fury."

But if Biden's speech contained one argument above all, it was a belief in the sheer possibility of change. "On this January day, my whole soul is in this: bringing America together, uniting our people, uniting our nation. And I ask every American to join me in this cause." It was a plain appeal to the American idea—a recognition that no president, alone, could change the culture of politics. Repairing the land would fall to the nation entire. "Let's begin to listen to one another again. Hear one another, see one another, show respect to one another," he said. "Politics doesn't have to be a raging fire, destroying everything in its path."

⊢——⊣

In launching his presidency as an argument against the raging fire, Biden would immediately face the hard political calculations of making it real. The previous year, when he was still deep in the competition for the presidency, he had sought out the counsel of the Reverend Dr. William Barber, a pastor of the Greenleaf Christian Church in Goldsboro, North Carolina, an icon in the present struggle for civil rights. Barber was a fellow traveler on the path of unity, but he was vigilant against the trade-offs that could occur in the pursuit. When they spoke, Barber recalled, he told Biden, "Our Constitution does not start with ensuring tranquility. It starts with establishing justice."

"In my tradition, hope is different than optimism," Barber told me when I called him. "Hope has to deal with what caused despair. Trump may have lit some matches in this idea of dividing the country, but Trump inherited an audience that had been prepped and primed for years." In Barber's view, the sources of disunity were not simply incivility or rhetorical excess; they were the underlying facts of injustice, dispossession, and immiseration. "I said, 'Even before Covid, forty-three percent of this country is poor and low-wealth. People are mourning because they don't have health care, wages, and sick leave. They're mourning because of the racism.'"

Since 2017, Barber had cochaired the Poor People's Campaign, which took its name from Martin Luther King Jr.'s 1968 call for a "revolution of values" in America. The campaign thought to "unite poor and impacted communities across the country," including communities of color and, in many cases, poor white people, in a shared pursuit of higher wages, a single-payer health-care system, and voting-rights protections. Barber told me, "In Georgia, for instance, forty-five percent, not of Black people, of *all* people, are poor or low-wealth; one-point-nine million people in Georgia make less than a living wage; one-point-four million people in Georgia are without health care. A third of all poverty is in the South. A third of all white poverty is in the South." When he spoke to Biden, he had advised him, "Speak to *that* in your policies." Barber urged Biden and his advisers to prepare for political fights—over wages, health care, and racism—in pursuit of a larger, more sustainable unity. "It's got to be not just rhetoric and on the surface," Barber told me. "You have to go down to the real level of people's pain, and what folks are experiencing in the country."

⊢────────┤

On February 13, thirty-eight days after the insurrection and twenty-four days after Biden took office, Republicans in the Senate awarded Trump his second acquittal. Seven members of his own party voted to convict, but the tally was far short of the two-thirds needed. The vote itself exposed another hole rusting through America's democratic machinery: because the Senate contains two senators from every state, and so many Americans had left rural America over the decades, Trump's threshold for acquittal—thirty-four Republican senators—represented just 14.5 percent of the U.S. population. The U.S. Senate had become one of the most malapportioned legislatures in the world, behind those of Argentina, Bolivia, and the Dominican Republic.

When it was over, Mitch McConnell, fittingly, concluded the proceedings with a triple axel of cynicism; first, he had delayed the proceedings until Trump left office; then he acquitted him on the ground that Trump was already gone from office; and, finally, in a naked bid to win back queasy donors, McConnell denounced Trump on the Senate floor as "practically and morally responsible" for the attack on the Capitol.

I had come to recognize some recurring patterns in the decisions of some of America's most powerful people—men like Mitch McConnell in Washington, Jim Justice in West Virginia, and Lee Hanley in Greenwich. For one thing, they shared a failure of tragic imagination. In other words, they enjoyed such extraordinary advantages—in wealth, opportunity, security, and redemption—that they miscalculated the trade-offs of lifting a racist candidate to power, or denying the gravity of a virus, or cutting a state's public-health budget. They believed, as Jared Kushner did, that warnings tended to be alarmist; they calculated, as the billionaire Thomas Peterffy did, that avoiding higher taxes and regulation was worth the risks.

Moreover, they shared another habit of mind—a blindness to the ways in which we had supercharged our capacity to do harm. Across American life, we had refined a set of extraordinary tools—for building wealth, firing bullets, and circulating information—that were so powerful, they altered not just the arrangement of American politics, but also the chemistry of it. The AR-15 was as different from a musket as a hedge fund was from a Wall Street bank in the Victorian age; the disinformation on Facebook was not just a digital version of a pamphlet handed out by the John Birch Society; it was, in the wrong hands, a superspreader of lies, engineered with all of the power that Silicon Valley could marshal.

Taken together, our latest tools were differences of kind, not degree, and they were pushing America to the breaking point.

———

By the final months of the "winter of peril," both political and physical, an awareness of fragility had reverberated through every corner of American life. For some, the agonies of the Trump years and the pandemic had exposed more vulnerability than they expected. For others, it had revealed hidden sources of strength. But nobody was left untouched.

On February 3, 2021, Tenesha Barner spent the day at the elementary school where she worked, on the South Side of Chicago, cleaning up and getting ready for students to return to class after months away. In the evening, she joined a cousin on a trip to a furniture store, but on the way back, Barner felt a wave of wooziness pass over her. In the car, she started trembling. She asked her cousin to turn up the heat. But it was already on the highest setting. When Barner reached her front door, she heaved herself into bed, still wrapped in her coat and boots and a hat. By the time she took her temperature, it was 101.4.

A test confirmed the bad news. She had Covid. And, like so many in the neighborhood, her underlying health—diabetes, asthma—put her acutely at risk. Doctors told Barner to keep track of her breathing. The diagnosis terrified her. A few months before, she had watched a relative end up on a ventilator, and Barner started picturing herself in a hospital bed, laced in tubes and wires. To makes matters worse, when doctors told her which medications to buy, she realized there was no safe route for her kids to take to the pharmacy. The nearest Walgreens was a mile and a half away, across hostile territory. Barner called Deirdre Koldyke, the therapist who ran the moms' group. And, for once, she dropped the veil of strength that usually got her through the day. She wept into the phone. "I'm scared," she said. "I don't want to end up in the hospital."

For Barner, quarantine was the culmination of so much of the isolation in her life. She was a single mom in an everything desert who had come of age in surroundings that put her at vastly higher risk of comorbidities, in a neighborhood too dangerous for her kids to cross.

And yet her diagnosis also forced her to see a side of her life that she had not glimpsed until she needed it. In politics, she was among the "forgotten people," as she put it, but she was not forgotten in the world she had made for herself. When word of her diagnosis began to spread, her phone started ringing—there were aunts and uncles and cousins, the mothers of her students, the neighbors across the yard, and the people from church. Even the clerk at the grocery store across the street started texting to check on her. At one point, while she was holed up at home, talking to me on Zoom, the members of her moms' support group started calling to see why she hadn't signed on yet. "If I'm one minute late for our group, I'm getting texts and messages: *'Hey, what's going on?'*" she said, and permitted herself a smile. "That really makes me happy."

Finally, after ten days isolated at home, Barner was cleared by her doctors to take her first steps back out into the world. "I feel okay," she told me four days out of quarantine. She paused to consider that assessment and boosted her own grade a bit. "I feel pretty good," she ventured. Barner had a fragile recovery ahead of her, and very little in the way of money to help her do it. But she had people, and that was enough for now. "I had people backing me, praying for me, calling me, texting me, seeing how I'm doing. And that helps you push, because, you say, hey, I don't want to disappoint them. I've got to get through this. I have people watching me. I have a testimony to tell." There was, she thought, a larger wisdom in that. "That's pretty much how my whole life is."

Listening to her talk put me in mind of a line from "Behold the Land," one of the last great speeches by W. E. B. Du Bois. "You do not stand alone," he told a crowd of young activists in 1946, after a lifetime of struggle. "It may seem like a failing fight when the newspapers ignore you; when every effort is made by white people in the South to count you out of citizenship, to act as though you did not exist as human beings, while all the time they are profiting by your labor; gleaning wealth from your sacrifices and trying to build a nation and a civilization upon your degradation. You must remember that, despite all this, you have allies and allies even in the white South."

Barner had never allowed herself to be forgotten, and she didn't plan to start now. For the first time in her life, she had started to think about relocating. In forty-two years, she had never lived anywhere but Parkway, but in the months before Covid, she had begun to tiptoe farther out into the city. She had gone on some field trips with Deirdre Koldyke and other mothers in the neighborhood, and she had begun to realize how much of the city she had never seen. They had visited the opera and the zoo and a summer music concert on a broad lawn in the suburbs. Some of it was a dud—at the conservatory, she struggled to see the charm in the bugs and the plants and the rain—but other places were a revelation. Nothing awed her like the Art Institute of Chicago. She had walked by it for years, eyeing it from the outside, but it seemed like foreign territory. And now she wanted more experiences like that.

"As I get older, I just want peace," she told me. "Where you don't hear the arguing, the cussing, the fussing, the fighting. That's the type of place I want to be. That might be in the *woods*," she said, and laughed. As long as those woods have no bugs or rain, and, preferably, are south of Thirty-fifth Street. I asked her when she planned to go, but she was still working up to that. "When God is ready for me to go, then he'll make me financially stable enough to leave," she said. She looked at the calendar and realized the next day would mark eighteen years in her apartment. "I feel like my work isn't done here," she said. "Because when I leave, I don't think I'm coming back."

NOTES ON SOURCES

This book effectively began in July 2013, shortly before I returned to the United States. Living in Beijing, Sarabeth and I came to know a retired factory clerk and widow named Jin Baozhu, who lived next door. Jin had never been outside China, but she kept a close eye on the evening news. When I told her we were moving home, she put a hand on my forearm and said, with concern, "America is rich, but it has many guns."

That moment lingered in my mind, not for the specifics—strictly speaking, Jin's portrait was not wrong—but for the way of seeing, the rendering of my country in such stark, simplified lines. It was by no means Jin's fault; she had received a portrait from a scattering of statistics and headlines, unfastened from meaning and history. Once I was back in America, I listened to my countrymen speculate about the motivations and lived experience of people far away—not in China, but in our own nation, in places like Chicago, Clarksburg, and Greenwich. I sometimes thought of Jin Baozhu. Were we really much better in describing ourselves? The alienation from one another reminded me of the impressions conveyed by Morse's telegraph in the nineteenth century—a world "populated by strangers, who knew nothing but the most superficial facts about each other," as Postman had put it.

During the next seven and a half years, I returned to the three places at the heart of this book, with the goal of rendering them in depth and of identifying connections among them that we too often overlook. I came to focus most on nineteen people, whom I interviewed repeatedly, sometimes dozens of times, as their lives evolved through April 2021. I also obtained thousands of pages of court documents and official records. It would not have been possible to produce this narrative without drawing on the expertise of news organizations in each place: *The Exponent Telegram*, *Greenwich Time*, and the *Chicago Tribune*, among others. I am indebted to their journalists, for the work they produce, and for the conversations that many of them had with me along the way. I also received help from a range of scholars, historians, archivists, filmmakers, and government researchers, either in direct communication or through their work. In the notes below, I describe sources that were especially valuable.

PROLOGUE

The natural history of Potter Valley is well described by James R. Welch in "Sprouting Valley: Historical Ethnobotany of the Northern Pomo from Potter Valley, California," *Society of Ethnobiology* (May 10, 2013). Details on the Ranch Fire, which constituted half the Mendocino Complex Fire, were published in "Cal Fire Investigation Report: Ranch Incident," California Department of Forestry and Fire Protection (July 27, 2018). Thomas Fuller, of *The New York Times*, published an exclusive account of the experience of Glenn Kile in the article "He Tried to Plug a Wasp Nest. He Ended Up Sparking California's Biggest Wildfire," *The New York Times* (June 11, 2019). On the accumulating effect of climate change and fire, I drew on Alejandra Borunda, "See How a Warmer World Primed California for Large Fires," *National Geographic* (November 15, 2018).

I first encountered John Gunther's book *Inside U.S.A.* (New York: Harper & Brothers, 1947) thanks to a friend, Charlie Edel, who thought it might inform my return to America; he was right. For biographical detail on Gunther, I was grateful for the work of Ken Cuthbertson, *Inside: The Biography of John Gunther* (Los Angeles: Bonus Books, 1992), and for a splendid recollection by Arthur Schlesinger Jr., "A Man from Mars," *The Atlantic* (April 1997). Steven Stoll's keen observation about history appears in his book *Ramp Hollow: The Ordeal of Appalachia* (New York: Hill and Wang, 2017).

To describe the racial and economic landscape of Washington, I drew on Kilolo Kijazaki et al., "The Color of Wealth in the Nation's Capital," *Urban Institute* (November 2016). For life-expectancy comparisons, I drew on data at the University of California Berkeley's U.S. Mortality Database and official Chinese data as reported in *People's Daily*.

The portrait of evolving perceptions after September 11 relies on a wide range of sources, beginning with a measure of distorted perceptions of Muslim representation in the United States as captured in the survey "Perils of Perception 2016," Ipsos (December 13, 2016), and Scott Shane, "Homegrown Extremists Tied to Deadlier Toll Than Jihadists in U.S. Since 9/11," *The New York Times* (June 24, 2015). The survey of West Virginians on Obama's religion was conducted by Orion Strategies for West Virginia Media and West Virginia Wesleyan College. The mosque attacks were described by Omar Ghabra in "A Small Town in West Virginia Responds to Anti-Muslim Sentiment," Al Jazeera America, March 10, 2014. The comments from Hazem Ashraf were featured in an episode of *Us & Them*, a podcast jointly produced by West Virginia Public Broadcasting and Trey Kay Productions.

On the legacy of guns, politics, and terrorism, I drew on Amy P. Cohen, Deborah Azrael, and Matthew Miller, "Rate of Mass Shootings Has Tripled Since 2011, Harvard Research Shows," *Mother Jones* (October 15, 2014); figures on the armed forces population are from December 31, 2020, Department of Defense, Defense Manpower Data Center; on crime statistics, John Gramlich, "What the Data Says (and Doesn't Say) About Crime in the United States," Pew Research Center, FactTank (November 20, 2020); John R. Lott Jr., John E. Whitley, and Rebekah C. Riley, "Concealed Carry Permit Holders Across the United States," Crime Prevention Research Center (July 16, 2015). The Amtrak announcement, titled "Take Flight, Take Cover, Take Action," is visible online at www.youtube.com/watch?v=wot2FwYCkm8. Television viewership patterns are tracked by various sources, including the Pew Research Center, "Cable News Prime Time Viewership" (March 13, 2006); Rick Kissell, "Fox News Dominates Cable News Ratings in 2014; MSNBC Tumbles," *Variety* (December 30, 2014). In addition to the daily news coverage of the 2013 shutdown of government, its political legacy is well described by David A. Fahrenthold and Katie Zezima in "For Ted Cruz, the 2013 Shutdown Was a Defining Moment," *The Washington Post* (February 16, 2016). Boehner's comment appeared on *Face the Nation*, July 21, 2013. Measures of government demographics and public perception draw from Amy Roberts, "By the Numbers: 113th Congress," CNN (January 5, 2013); Russ Choma, "Millionaires' Club: For First Time, Most Lawmakers Are Worth $1 Million-Plus," Center for Responsive Politics (January 9, 2014); "Public Trust in Government: 1958–2019," Pew Research Center (April 11, 2019); Sam Popkin, *Crackup: The Republican Implosion and the Future of Presidential Politics* (New York: Oxford University Press, May 2021).

1. THE GOLDEN TRIANGLE

I am thankful to Chip Skowron for agreeing to share his story with me over many interviews. In addition, I relied on official documents and interviews with those who had firsthand knowledge of his experience. Other useful background and detail were contained in news coverage.

For enlivening the history of Greenwich, I am indebted to Christopher Shields, the curator of library and archives at the Greenwich Historical Society, who opened his doors to me for repeated visits and suggested a range of essential sources. The brief history told here draws from the writings of Spencer Percival Mead, *Ye Historie of Ye Town of Greenwich, County of Fairfield and State of Connecticut* (New York: Knickerbocker Press, 1911); Frederick A. Hubbard, *Other Days in Greenwich, Or, Tales and Reminiscences of an Old New England Town* (New York: J. F. Tapley, 1913); and from lively recent histories, including Missy Wolfe's *Hidden History of Colonial Greenwich* (Charleston, SC: History Press, 2018).

For the history of the modern era in Greenwich, from the Gilded Age through the civil rights movement, I benefited from Matt Bernard, *Victorian Summer: The Historic Houses of Belle Haven Park, Greenwich, Connecticut* (Novato, CA: ORO Editions, 2018); Karen Jewell, *A History of the Greenwich Waterfront: Tod's Point, Great Captain Island and the Greenwich Shoreline* (Charleston, SC: History Press, 2011); Timothy Dumas, *Greentown: Murder and Mystery in Greenwich, America's Wealthiest Community* (New York: Arcade Publishing, 1998); Andrew Kahrl, *Free the Beaches: The Story of Ned Coll and the Battle for America's Most Exclusive Shoreline* (New Haven: Yale University Press, 2018); and Jane Condon and Bobbi Eggers, *Chardonnay Moms: Jane & Bobbi's Greatest Hits* (Pennsauken, NJ: BookBaby, 2017). Details on the history of local Jewish life and discrimination were contained in the Greenwich Historical Society's exhibit *An American Odyssey: The Jewish Experience in Greenwich*, curated by Ann Meyerson.

The rise of modern finance, including alternative investments, is well described by Sebastian Mallaby in *More Money Than God: Hedge Funds and the Making of a New Elite* (New York: Penguin Press, 2010), and Ralph Gomory and Richard Sylla, "The American Corporation," *Journal of the American Academy of Arts & Sciences: Daedalus* (Spring 2013). Skowron's introduction to the field came from Daniel A. Strachman's *Getting Started in Hedge Funds* (Hoboken, NJ: Wiley, 2000). The account of the changing culture of wealth drew on Patricia Beard's *Blue Blood and Mutiny: The Fight for the Soul of Morgan Stanley* (New York: William Morrow, 2007), and Nina Munk, "Greenwich's Outrageous Fortune," *Vanity Fair* (2006). For fine-grained details on luxury consumption, I was informed by niche news sources, including *SuperYachtFan* and *Bob's Watches*.

For perspective and data on the financial crisis and inequality, I drew on Raj Chetty, Nathaniel Hendren, Patrick Kline, and Emmanuel Saez, "Where Is the Land of Opportunity: The Geography of Intergenerational Mobility in the United States," *Quarterly Journal of Economics* 129, no. 4 (2014); Steven Pearlstein, *Can American Capitalism Survive?* (New York: St. Martin's Press, 2018); Rana Foroohar, *Makers and Takers: The Rise of Finance and the Fall of American Business* (New York: Currency, 2016); and a speech by Lawrence Summers, "40 Years Later—The Relevance of Okun's Equality and Efficiency: The Big Tradeoff," Brookings Institution (Washington, DC, 2015); Jacob S. Hacker and Paul Pierson, *Winner-Take-All Politics: How Washington Made the Rich Richer—and Turned Its Back on the Middle Class* (New York: Simon & Schuster, 2010); and Michael Sandel, *The Tyranny of Merit: What's Become of the Common Good?* (New York: Farrar, Straus and Giroux, 2020).

2. THOUGHTS AND PRAYERS

On campaign finance, James Madison was writing, with Alexander Hamilton, in *Federalist* No. 52 (*The New York Packet*, 1788); on the costs of running for office, "Vital Statistics on Congress: The Cost of Winning an Election, 1986–2018," Brookings Institution (February 2021); Bruce W. Hardy, Jeffrey A. Gottfried, Kenneth M. Winneg, and Kathleen Hall Jamieson, "Stephen Colbert's Civics Lesson: How Colbert Super PAC Taught Viewers About Campaign Finance," *Mass Communication and Society* 17, no. 3 (2014). Ethan Roeder described his experiences in "Want Your Campaign Funding to Be Effective? Diversify," *The Washington Post* (September 27, 2018).

On changes in Washington culture, wealth, and self-perception: Joanne Freeman, *The Field of Blood: Violence in Congress and the Road to Civil War* (New York: Farrar, Straus and Giroux, 2018); David Fontana, "Washington Is Now a Cool City. That's Terrible News for American Democracy," *The Washington Post* (May 7, 2018); Robert Frank, "Washington Welcomes the Wealthiest," *The New York Times* (May 12, 2017); Alec MacGillis, "The Billionaires' Loophole," *The New Yorker* (March 14, 2016); Pete Buttigieg, *Trust: America's Best Chance* (New York: Liveright, 2020).

For research on division and resentment, I drew on Nicholas Christakis, *Blueprint: The Evolutionary Origins of a Good Society* (New York: Little, Brown, 2019); Katherine A. DeCelles and Michael I. Norton, "Physical and Situational Inequality on Airplanes Predicts Air Rage," *Proceedings of the National Academy of Sciences* (May 2016); and Keith Payne, *The Broken Ladder: How Inequality Affects the Way We Think, Live and Die* (New York: Viking, 2017).

On the role and demographics of donors, I relied on a study by Sean McElwee,

Brian Schaffner, and Jesse Rhodes, "Whose Voice, Whose Choice? The Distorting Influence of the Political Donor Class in Our Big-Money Elections," *Demos* (December 8, 2016); and Joshua L. Kalla and David E. Broockman, "Campaign Contributions Facilitate Access to Congressional Officials: A Randomized Field Experiment," *American Journal of Political Science* 60, no. 3 (July 2016). The leaked Democratic slide presentation was reported by Ryan Grim and Sabrina Siddiqui, "Call Time for Congress Shows How Fundraising Dominates Bleak Work Life," *Huffington Post*, January 8, 2013. The history of W. Clement Stone was reported by Dan Balz in "'Sheldon Primary' Is One Reason Americans Distrust the Political System," *The Washington Post* (March 28, 2014), and cited by Jane Mayer in *Dark Money: The Hidden History of the Billionaires Behind the Rise of the Radical Right* (New York: Doubleday, 2016).

To chronicle the triumph of Mitch McConnell, I was aided by his memoir, *The Long Game: A Memoir* (New York: Sentinel, 2016), as well as Alec MacGillis, *The Cynic: The Political Education of Mitch McConnell* (New York: Simon & Schuster, 2014); Robert G. Kaiser, "The Closed Mind of Mitch," *The New York Review of Books* (November 2016); and Steve Coll, "Party Crashers," *The New Yorker* (October 28, 2013).

3. JEWEL OF THE HILLS

The literature on Harrison County, West Virginia, runs deep, and I was lucky to gain two advisers: David Houchin, the Special Collections librarian at the Clarksburg-Harrison Public Library, and Crystal Wimer, executive director at the Harrison County Historical Society. Over many years, they pointed me to sources I would have missed and alerted me when their own hunts produced relevant treasure.

To evoke the economic and political history of coal in West Virginia, I relied on a variety of nonfiction and fiction, including Steven Stoll, *Ramp Hollow: The Ordeal of Appalachia* (New York: Hill and Wang, 2017); John Alexander Williams, *Appalachia: A History* (Chapel Hill: University of North Carolina Press, 2002); Denise Giardina, *Storming Heaven* (New York: W. W. Norton, 1987); Elizabeth Catte, *What You Are Getting Wrong About Appalachia* (Cleveland: Belt Publishing, 2018); Gwynn Guilford, "The 100-Year Capitalist Experiment That Keeps Appalachia Poor, Sick, and Stuck on Coal," *Quartz* (December 30, 2017); Ronald D. Eller, *Uneven Ground: Appalachia Since 1945* (Lexington: University of Kentucky Press, 2008); John Gaventa, *Power and Powerlessness: Quiescence and Rebellion in an Appalachian Valley* (Springfield: University of Illinois Press, 1982); and Anthony Harkins and Meredith McCarroll, eds., *Appalachian Reckoning: A Region Responds to Hillbilly Elegy* (Morgantown: West Virginia University Press, 2019).

On the history of race in West Virginia, the historic election of Mayor David Kates, and the backlash by the Ku Klux Klan, I was informed by interviews with the former mayor Jim Hunt, and the former head of the NAACP local chapter Jim Griffin. Maggie Potapchuk wrote a valuable report on that period, "Steps Toward an Inclusive Community: The Story of Clarksburg, West Virginia," published by the Joint Center for Political and Economic Studies (2001).

I was informed by a number of histories, biographies, architectural accounts, and travelogues, including Henry Haymond, *History of Harrison County, West Virginia: From the Early Days of Northwestern Virginia to the Present* (Morgantown, WV: Acme Publishing Comapny, 1910); William Henry Harbaugh, *Lawyer's Lawyer: The Life of John W. Davis* (New York: Oxford University Press, 1973); "Clarksburg Downtown Historic District," U.S. Department of the Interior: National Register of Historic Places; and *The West Virginia Encyclopedia*, a valuable resource maintained by the West Virginia Humanities Council. The West Virginia Archives has compiled a valuable exhibit on the 1960 presidential election, as has the John F. Kennedy Presidential Library and Museum. The Anti-Defamation League compiled information on the rise and prosecution of the Mountaineer Militia. In addition, I've drawn on reporting by Ken Ward Jr., Eric Eyre, Hoppy Kercheval, Dave Mistich, and others.

The definitive history on the rise and fall of the local glass industry is Ken Fones-Wolf, *Glass Towns: Industry, Labor, and Political Economy in Central Appalachia, 1890–1930s* (Champaign: University of Illinois Press, 2007); additional details were relayed in a perceptive article by Sam Quinones, "Physicians Get Addicted Too," *The Atlantic* (May 2019).

The history of newspapering in West Virginia has been explored by Stewart Plein, Rare Book librarian at West Virginia University, who described the oil-field newspaper competition in a blog post titled "Up in Smoke: The Fascinating Story of a West Virginia Newspaper, *The Volcano Lubricator*" (2016).

For perspective on the collapse of local news and the decline of newspapers, I turned to Margaret Sullivan's vital book, *Ghosting the News: Local Journalism and the Crisis of American Democracy* (New York: Columbia Global Reporters, 2020); a thorough report by PEN America titled "Losing the News: The Decimation of Local Journalism and the Search for Solutions" (2019); Pengjie Gao, Chang Lee, and Dermot Murphy, "Financing Dies in Darkness? The Impact of Newspaper Closures on Public Finance," *Journal of Financial Economics* 135, no. 2 (February 2020); Penelope Muse Abernathy, "News Deserts and Ghost Newspapers: Will Local News Survive?," UNC Hussman School of Journalism and Media (September 15, 2020).

On the intersection of news technology and political dissolution, I drew on the prescient work of Neil Postman and his book *Amusing Ourselves to Death: Public Discourse in the Age of Show Business* (New York: Viking Penguin, 1985); Ezra Klein, *Why We're Polarized* (New York: Avid Reader Press, 2020); Daniel J. Hopkins, *The Increasingly United States: How and Why American Political Behavior Nationalized* (Chicago: University of Chicago Press, 2018); and Jennifer Mercieca, *Demagogue for President: The Rhetorical Genius of Donald Trump* (College Station: Texas A&M University Press, 2020). One of the first glints of the Internet in the world of Clarksburg journalism was in a column by Bob Stealey, "Bob-n-Along: Since I Couldn't Get Online, I Got a Little Bit Outta' Line," *The Exponent Telegram* (February 3, 1999).

4. MUD CITY

The Special Collections Research Center at the University of Chicago holds the papers of Albert Sherer, including clippings from the time of the shooting. In addition, I consulted the digital archives of the *Chicago Sunday Tribune* and other news sources. To find out more on the origins, incarcerations, and descendants of the gunmen, I received indispensable help from Ellen Driscoll and her sister Elizabeth Knight, known professionally as the Ancestry Sisters. They produced documents from Illinois prison records, the Cook County Archives, Cook County Recorder of Deeds, and Cook County Circuit Clerk, among other sources.

On the natural and architectural origins of the city, I relied on William Cronon, *Nature's Metropolis: Chicago and the Great West* (New York: W. W. Norton, 1991); Louis Sullivan, *The Autobiography of an Idea* (Washington, DC: Press of the American Institute of Architects, 1924); Frederick Jackson Turner, *The Frontier in American History* (New York: Henry Holt, 1920); and Robert Herrick, *The Gospel of Freedom* (New York: Macmillan, 1898). The city's battle with the elements was well described by Ron Grossman in "Raising Chicago out of the Mud," *Chicago Tribune* (November 19, 2015). Other valuable reference material was contained in *The Encyclopedia of Chicago*, maintained by the Chicago Historical Society.

In the rich literature on race, class, and geography of the South Side, I consulted the work of Isabel Wilkerson, *The Warmth of Other Suns: The Epic Story of America's Great Migration* (New York: Random House, 2010), and William Julius Wilson, *When Work Disappears: The World of the New Urban Poor* (New York: Knopf, 1996). It would be impossible to convey the Daley legacy without Adam Cohen and Elizabeth Taylor, *American Pharaoh: Mayor Richard J. Daley—His Battle for Chicago and the Nation* (New York: Little, Brown, 2000). Vivid details on Hyde Park and Kenwood draw from Susan O'Connor Davis, *Chicago's Historic Hyde Park* (Chicago: University of Chicago Press, 2013). Her work pointed me to earlier references in Edna Ferber, *The Girls* (Garden City, NY: Doubleday, Page & Company, 1921), and in Le Corbusier, *When the Cathedrals Were White* (New York: McGraw-Hill, 1964). The role of infrastructure is explored by Kevin M. Kruse, "What Does a Traffic Jam in Atlanta Have to Do with Segregation? Quite a Lot," *The New York Times* (August 14, 2019). On current conditions, and the vanishing of employment, I benefited from a superb survey of recent research by Alana Semuels, "Chicago's Awful Divide," *The Atlantic* (March 28, 2018). For comparisons between Chicago and Richmond, I relied on Trevon Logan and John Parman, "The National Rise in Residential Segregation," National Bureau of Economic Research (February 2015); and I learned a good lesson from Ben Joravsky in "Taking *The New Yorker* for a Ride," *Chicago Reader* (March 11, 2010).

To understand mobility, both social and geographical, I drew from Patrick Sharkey, *Stuck in Place: Urban Neighborhoods and the End of Progress Toward Racial Equality* (Chicago: University of Chicago Press, 2012). Other sources include Ben J. Wattenberg and Richard M. Scammon, "Black Progress and Liberal Rhetoric," *Commentary* (April 1973); Julia B. Isaacs, "Economic Mobility of Black and White Families," Brookings Institution (November 13, 2007); and William H. Frey, "For the First Time on Record, Fewer Than 10% of Americans Moved in a Year," Brookings Institution (November 22, 2019). Special thanks to Deirdre and Laird Koldyke, Caitlin Sammons, and the EarthHeart Foundation.

On Obama's rise and his misbegotten campaign in 1999, I was grateful for the work of Ted Kleine, "Is Bobby Rush in Trouble?," *Chicago Reader* (March 16, 2000), and Hank De Zutter, "What Makes Obama Run?," *Chicago Reader* (December 8, 1995), as well as essential writing by David Remnick, *The Bridge: The Life and Rise of Barack Obama* (New York: Knopf, 2010); and Obama's own writings in *The Audacity of Hope: Thoughts on Reclaiming the American Dream* (New York: Crown, 2006).

5. EVERYONE IS DOING IT (TAKE 1)

The official documents in *U.S. v. Joseph F. Skowron III*, and related civil proceedings, lay out a detailed recounting of events and transactions, which were expanded in interviews with Skowron and others. In addition, I was grateful for coverage of his case by Bloomberg, MarketWatch, Reuters, *The Wall Street Journal*, and *Vanity Fair*, including a lengthy report by Chris Pomorski, "A Hedge Fund Ex-Con Finds It's Hard Coming Home to Greenwich," *Vanity Fair* (July 2, 2019).

The building boom, including the rise of Mariani-style homes, was brilliantly described by Nick Paumgarten, "A Greenwich of the Mind," *The New Yorker* (August 26, 2008). Asness relayed his experience of raising kids in the hedge-fund heyday in an interview onstage with Tyler Cowen, distributed as a podcast, and as a transcript on *Medium*, titled "Cliff Asness on Marvel v. DC," *Conversations with Tyler*, November 18, 2015. The Kogan controversy was explored by Michael Idov, "Xanadu, CT," *New York* (May 22, 2009).

My account of the rise of shareholder capitalism draws on Milton Friedman's original article, "A Friedman Doctrine—The Social Responsibility of Business Is to Increase Its Profits," *The New York Times* (September 13, 1970); Michael C. Jensen and William H. Meckling, "Theory of the Firm: Managerial Behavior, Agency Costs and Ownership Structure," *Journal of Financial Economics* 3, no. 4 (October 1, 1976); and Nicholas Lemann, *Transaction Man: The Rise of the Deal and the Decline of the American Dream* (New York: Farrar, Straus and Giroux, 2019).

Changes in partnership and buyback rules are well described by John Carney, "Why Wall Street Abandoned Partnerships," CNBC (November 3, 2010); William Lazonick and Ken Jacobson, "End Stock Buybacks, Save the Economy," *The New York Times* (August 23, 2018); William Lazonick, "Stock Buybacks: From Retain-and-Reinvest to Downsize-and-Distribute," Brookings Institution (2015); "Prepared Remarks of Federal Trade Commissioner Rohit Chopra," Forum on Small Business Financing (May 8, 2019); and Rana Foroohar, "American Capitalism's Great Crisis," *Time* (March 12, 2016). Charles Wilson's testimony to Congress is available online via the Hathi Trust digital library.

Eugene Soltes was generous to me in interviews and follow-ups, and I draw on his book, *Why They Do It: Inside the Mind of the White-Collar Criminal* (New York: Public Affairs, 2016). George Bernard Shaw's observation originated in the preface of *In English Prisons Under Local Government* (London: Longmans, Green, 1922), vii–lxxiii. The vibrant case of Martin Frankel, the neighbor and fugitive, was covered by reporters at the time, including Michael Allen and Mitchell Pacell, "Martin Frankel May Have Fled with $10 Million of Diamonds," *The Wall Street Journal* (July 8, 1999);

Alison Leigh Cowan, "Onetime Fugitive Gets 17 Years for Looting Insurers," *The New York Times* (December 11, 2004). Sutherland's contributions are described in an article titled "Edwin H. Sutherland," published by the American Sociological Association (June 16, 2009). The role of feeders in the Madoff fiasco was covered in the financial press, and Bourke's travails were described by David Glovin, "Bourke to Report to Prison 15 Years After Oil Deal Soured," Bloomberg (May 6, 2013). The term "Rogues Hill Road" was coined by the real-estate blogger Christopher Fountain.

The fallout and implications of financial misconduct were elucidated by David Rafferty, "Greenwich, Gateway to White-Collar Crime," *Greenwich Time* (August 9, 2013); John Bogle, "There Were Once Things One Just Didn't Do," *The New York Times* (March 15, 2012); Andrew Ross Sorkin, "On Wall St., a Culture of Greed Won't Let Go," *The New York Times* (July 15, 2013); Greg Smith, "Why I Am Leaving Goldman Sachs," *The New York Times* (March 14, 2012); and "Goldman Sachs Agrees to Pay More Than $5 Billion in Connection with Its Sale of Residential Mortgage Backed Securities," Department of Justice (April 11, 2016).

6. EVERYONE IS DOING IT (TAKE 2)

Over the five years I've known Reese Clark, he has been patient with my questions on more occasions than I can count. He traced his grandparents' experience back to Alabama, and his own experience through school, the Gangster Disciples, the courts and prison, and, eventually, fatherhood. To ferret out court documents and genealogical history, I received vital help from the Ancestry Sisters.

To capture the evolution and activities of Chicago gangs, I was fortunate to interview Andrew Papachristos and read his work, especially on the Gangster Disciples. In addition, I drew on George W. Knox, Gregg W. Etter, and Carter F. Smith, *Gangs and Organized Crime* (New York: Routledge, 2018). Specifics on the cliques G-ville and Killa Ward were reported by Jeremy Gorner in "Gang Factions Lead to Spike in City Violence," *Chicago Tribune* (October 3, 2012), and "Man Arrested in 2013 Killing Tied to Gang War That Left Tyshawn Lee Dead," *Chicago Tribune* (April 6, 2016). Alfreida Cobb was generous with her recollections at a very painful time in her life. For analysis of the concentration of shootings in specific neighborhoods, I was glad to have a roundup of research by scholars at Northwestern University, published in "Crime in Chicago: What Does the Research Tell Us? IPR Experts Offer Insights and Potential Solutions to City's Violent Crime" (May 28, 2018).

For details on health disparities in low-income neighborhoods, I drew from Jeremy Deaton and Gloria Oladipo, "Mapping the Disparities That Bred an Unequal Pandemic," Bloomberg CityLab (September 30, 2020), and Robert J. Sampson, *Great American City: Chicago and the Enduring Neighborhood Effect* (Chicago: University of Chicago Press, 2013). Ben Steverman summarized Raj Chetty's research in "Harvard's Chetty Finds Economic Carnage in Wealthiest ZIP Codes," Bloomberg (September 24, 2020).

On the history of schools and segregation in Chicago, I relied on multiple sources, including Natalie Y. Moore, *The South Side: A Portrait of Chicago and American Segregation* (New York: St. Martin's Press, 2016); Steve Bogira, "School Desegregation: Is the

Solution to the Public-Schools Mess as Simple as Black and White?," *The Reader* (January 28, 1988); Mary Mitchell, "Déjà vu Sunday for Mount Greenwood Seven," *Chicago Sun Times* (July 15, 2008); Isabel Wilkerson, "The Tallest Fence: Feelings on Race in a White Neighborhood," *The New York Times* (June 21, 1992); Christine Schmidt, "Life, and a Death, in Mount Greenwood," *South Side Weekly* (November 16, 2016); "Schools in Chicago Are Called the Worst by Education Chief," Associated Press (November 8, 1987); letter to the editor from the Fenger High School Local School Council, *Chicago Sun-Times* (September 20, 1991); Maribeth Vander Weele, "Classroom Chaos Seen as Possibly the Worst Ever," *Chicago Sun-Times* (October 1, 1991).

7. YOU PEOPLE

Prison records for Reese Clark and William Wojtkowski keep track of their movements, and, in interviews, Clark elaborated on his experience.

For perspective and data on incarceration and systemic racism, I am indebted to Devah Pager, "The Mark of a Criminal Record." *American Journal of Sociology*, 108(5):937-975, 2003; James Forman Jr., *Locking Up Our Own: Crime and Punishment in Black America* (New York: Farrar, Straus and Giroux, 2017); Elizabeth Hinton, *From the War on Poverty to the War on Crime* (Cambridge, MA: Harvard University Press, 2017); and Toluse Olorunnipa and Griff Witte, "Born with Two Strikes," *The Washington Post* (October 8, 2020).

The history of discriminatory housing, predatory lending, and subprime mortgages in Chicago is informed by Connie Bruck, "Angelo's Ashes," *The New Yorker* (June 22, 2009); Whet Moser, "The *Chicago Reporter* and Lisa Madigan Nail Bank of America on Racial Bias in Countrywide Lending," *Chicago Magazine* (December 22, 2011); Shawn Tully, "Meet the 23,000% Stock," *Fortune* (September 15, 2003); and Ta-Nehisi Coates, "The Case for Reparations," *The Atlantic* (June 2014).

Details on the role and lifestyle of individuals who worked or lived in Greenwich during the mortgage boom are drawn from Bethany McLean and Joe Nocera, *All The Devils Are Here: The Hidden History of the Financial Crisis* (New York: Portfolio, 2010); Gretchen Morgenson, "Mr. Vranos Has a Deal for You," *The New York Times* (July 22, 2007); Susanne Craig, "Lawmakers Lay Into Lehman CEO," *The Wall Street Journal* (October 7, 2008); "Ex-Citi CEO Defends 'Dancing' Quote to U.S. Panel," Reuters (April 8, 2012); Hilary Lewis, "Booted Citi CEO Prince Can't Sell Greenwich Mansion," *Business Insider* (June 18, 2008).

This account of the roots of the Tea Party benefited from the guidance of Theda Skocpol, and from her book, with Vanessa Williamson, *The Tea Party and the Remaking of Republican Conservatism* (New York: Oxford University Press, 2012); and the expertise of Jane Mayer and her book *Dark Money*; I also drew on valuable detail in Popkin, *Crackup*, and from David Remnick, "Day of the Dittohead," *The Washington Post* (February 20, 1994); Joan C. Williams, *White Working Class: Overcoming Class Cluelessness in America* (Boston: Harvard Business Review Press, 2017); and Suzanne Mettler, *The Submerged State* (Chicago: University of Chicago Press, 2011).

The rise of racist conspiracy theories and right-wing militias during Obama's term has been examined in Philip Klinkner, "The Causes and Consequences of 'Birtherism,'" paper presented at the 2014 Annual Meeting of the Western Political Science Association; Ta-Nehisi Coates, "My President Was Black," *The Atlantic* (January/February 2017); Ron Nixon, "Homeland Security Looked Past Antigovernment Movement, Ex-Analyst Says," *The New York Times* (January 8, 2016); and "Militia Movement Rhetoric Elevated to National Level," Southern Poverty Law Center (October 3, 2019).

For history and details of oscillation between the individual and the collective—between the cowboy and the wagon train—I am indebted to the work of Robert D. Putnam with Shaylyn Romney Garrett in their book *The Upswing: How America Came Together a Century Ago and How We Can Do It Again* (New York: Simon & Schuster, 2020). They spoke to me in an interview and shared their perspective on events that developed after their book's publication.

The Luntz session was reported by Chris Moody for *Yahoo News*. The historian Jennifer Burns expanded on her chronicle of Rand's life and influence in "Ayn Rand's Long Journey to the Heart of American Politics," *The New Republic* (August 14, 2012); the scene of the Republican debate in 2012 was mentioned by Popkin in *Crackup*. Ackerman reflected on the political context of war in "Why Bringing Back the Draft Could End America's Forever Wars," *Time* (October 10, 2019); on the origins of Occupy, I benefited from Ruth Milkman, Stephanie Luce, and Penny Lewis, "Occupy After Occupy," *Jacobin* (June 2014). The distribution of war-time casualties, by place of origin, is based on Pentagon data, analyzed by the *Wall Street Journal*, in Michael M. Phillips, "Brothers in Arms: The Tragedy in Small-Town America" (September 22, 2017).

8. GETTING LOADED

This narrative of the lives of Fred Swiger, Freddie Swiger Jr., Christopher Hart, Todd Amos, and Sidney Muller is based primarily on court documents, official witness statements, excerpted VA records, and interviews. I am grateful to family members and friends who spoke with me about very difficult circumstances, including Minnie Swiger, Herman Lubbe, Linda Riggs, Taylor Durst, and Janice Chance. In addition, I was grateful for the assistance of Sam Harrold, Brian Jarvis, and John Miller, and for the cooperation of Sidney Muller.

The description of casualties and events in Sangin draws on Dawood Azami, "Why Sangin's Fall to the Taliban Matters," BBC World Service (March 23, 2017); Taimoor Shah and Rod Nordland, "Taliban Take an Afghan District, Sangin, That Many Marines Died to Keep," *New York Times* (March 23, 2017); "Into the Breach: How Sangin Will Enter the Annals of Marine History," *Military Times* (May 12, 2014).

For details on the evolution of popular attitudes and culture post–September 11, I drew on Roberto Gonzalez, Hugh Gusterson, and Gustaaf Houtman, *Militarization: A Reader* (Durham, NC: Duke University Press, 2019); Ted Galen Carpenter, "The Creeping Militarization of American Culture," a commentary for the Cato Institute; Al Gore, *The Assault on Reason* (New York: Penguin Press, 2007); Phil Klay, *Missionaries* (New York: Penguin Press, 2020); and Jason De León, "The Border Wall Is a Metaphor," *New American Story Project* (no date).

9. BUYING POWER

Jane Mayer brilliantly uncovered the collaboration of Lee Hanley, Robert Mercer, and Patrick Caddell in fostering Trump's candidacy, a project she described in her article, "Trump's Money Man," The New Yorker (March 27, 2017). Alice Hanley, J. William Middendorf II, Roger Stone, and others shared with me their firsthand experiences of the evolution in Republican politics in Greenwich. Middendorf also elaborated on his experience in two accounts of his political career: *A Glorious Disaster: Barry Goldwater's Presidential Campaign and the Origins of the Conservative Movement* (New York: Basic Books, 2006), and *Potomac Fever: A Memoir of Politics and Public Service* (Annapolis: Naval Institute Press, 2011). Galbraith's characterization of the conservative movement was contained in his speech titled "Wealth and Poverty," National Policy Committee on Pockets of Poverty (December 13, 1963). Lowell Weicker's comments were expressed in a speech at Yale University in 1991, and documented by the John F. Kennedy Presidential Library and Museum.

On the rising role and effect of corporate activism in politics, I'm grateful to Rick Perlstein for his insights and for sharing early excerpts of his book *Reaganland: America's Right Turn 1976–1980* (New York: Simon & Schuster, 2020). For details on specific funders and their philanthropic work, I was grateful for insights from Brendan Fischer at the Campaign Legal Center. I also drew on the work of Kim Phillips-Fein, *Invisible Hands: The Making of the Conservative Movement from the New Deal to Reagan* (New York: W. W. Norton, 2009).

For the history of wealth management, and tax and stock policies, I am grateful to the Dartmouth professor Brooke Harrington for her expertise, and for her book *Capital Without Borders: Wealth Managers and the One Percent* (Cambridge, MA: Harvard University Press, 2016); I also returned to Steven Pearlstein's *Can American Capitalism Survive?*, Mayer's *Dark Money*, and Hacker and Pierson's *Winner-Take-All Politics*. Details on the taxes and assets of Tom Foley were reported by Ken Dixon, "Foley Paid $673 in Taxes in 2013," *Greenwich Time* (October 17, 2014).

For details on Prescott Bush and other generations in the family's political dynasty, I benefited from a biography by Mickey Herskowitz, *Duty, Honor, Country: The Life and Legacy of Prescott Bush* (Nashville: Routledge Hill Press, 2003); Jon Meacham, *Destiny and Power: The American Odyssey of George Herbert Walker Bush* (New York: Random House, 2015); and Jacob Weisberg, *The Bush Tragedy* (New York: Random House, 2008). The legacy of Lee Atwater is explored in the film *Boogie Man: The Lee Atwater Story* (2008) and in Beth Schwartzapfel and Bill Keller, "Willie Horton Revisited," The Marshall Project (May 13, 2015).

The culture, growth, and influence of Black, Manafort, and Stone have been documented by Franklin Foer "Paul Manafort, American Hustler," *The Atlantic* (March 2018); and Manuel Roig-Franzia, "The Swamp Builders," *Washington Post* (November 29, 2018).

Steve Bannon and Pat Caddell described their work with Hanley during a dual appearance at the David Horowitz Freedom Center's 2017 Restoration Weekend. The event was held November 16–19 at the Breakers Hotel in Palm Beach, Florida.

10. BALL-LESS PECKERHEADS

Nobody has devoted more time to documenting the business, politics, and practice of mountaintop removal in West Virginia than Ken Ward Jr. of *Mountain State Spotlight*, formerly of the *Charleston Gazette-Mail*. I am grateful for the chance to interview him over the years, and to draw on his reports. The legacy of mountaintop removal is the subject of many important scholarly papers and general-interest publications, including M. A. Palmer et al., "Mountaintop Mining Consequences," *Science* 327, no. 5962 (2010); Melissa M. Ahern et al., "The Association Between Mountaintop Mining and Birth Defects Among Live Births in Central Appalachia, 1996–2003," *Environmental Research* 111, no. 6 (August 2011); Shirley L. Stewart-Burns, *Bringing Down the Mountains: The Impact of Mountaintop Removal Surface Coal Mining on Southern West Virginia Communities, 1970—2004* (Morgantown: West Virginia University, 2007); John McQuaid, "Mining the Mountains," *Smithsonian Magazine* (January 2009); and Steven A. Simon et al., "Ecological Zones in the Southern Appalachians: First Approximation," United States Department of Agriculture Forest Service (December 2005).

The effect of Wall Street attention on coal country is described by Patrick Rucker, "How Big Coal Summoned Wall Street and Faced a Whirlwind," Reuters (August 5, 2016), and Mike Elk, "In the Coal Fields, a Novel Way to Get Rid of Pensions Is Born," *In These Times* (December 31, 2012). Alec MacGillis wrote several times about the effort to remove pension and health-care benefits: see "The Incredible Disappearing Health Benefits," *The New Republic* (February 19, 2013); "Bankruptcy Lawyers Strip Cash from Coal Miners' Health Insurance," ProPublica (October 1, 2015); and "Dealmakers Drop a Plan to Divert Millions from the Health Insurance of Retired Coal Miners," ProPublica (October 8, 2015). The culture of distressed investing is explored in A. Scott Carson, "Vulture Investors, Predators of the 90s: An Ethical Examination," *Journal of Business Ethics* 17, no. 5 (April 1998); Tiffany Kary et al., "Hated by Many, Distressed Debt Brawler Isn't About to Back Down," Bloomberg (June 4, 2018). The sale of the Cohen home received attention in Michelle Celarier, "The Reckoning on Round Hill Road," *Institutional Investor* (June 5, 2017). The turmoil around Patriot Coal was covered in the *St. Louis Business Journal*, *The Wall Street Journal*, ProPublica, and the *Charleston Gazette-Mail*.

The implications of economic distress, declining status, and class discrimination are explored in Jonathan Cobb, *The Hidden Injuries of Class* (New York: W. W. Norton, 1993); Williams, *White Working Class*; Sarah Smarsh, "Poor Teeth," *Aeon* (October 23, 2014); Colleen Flaherty, "(More) Bias in Science Hiring," *Inside Higher Ed* (June 7, 2019); and Lauren A. Rivera and András Tilcsik, "Class Advantage, Commitment Penalty: The Gendered Effect of Social Class Signals in an Elite Labor Market," *American Sociological Review* (October 12, 2016).

11. I SMELL FREEDOM

The political transformation of West Virginia from blue to red has been told from various perspectives. Karl Rove described his strategy in *Courage and Consequence: My Life as a Conservative in the Fight* (New York: Threshold Editions, 2010). Also see

Tom Hamburger, "A Coal-Fired Crusade Helped Bring Crucial Victory to Candidate Bush," *The Wall Street Journal* (June 13, 2001), and Frank Bruni, "Gore Unveils $125 Billion Energy Plan," *The New York Times* (June 28, 2000). Michael Tomasky provided an especially astute analysis of his home state in the essay "The South Creeps North," in *These United States*, ed. John Leonard (New York: Nation Books, 2003).

When I visited Charleston to research the Elk River chemical spill, I was grateful to interview many of the people named in this chapter, as well as others in government who asked to remain anonymous. I benefited especially from interviews with Ward, and from the perspective of Maya Nye, president of People Concerned About Chemical Safety, whose father worked for Union Carbide. For historical detail, I appreciated *Chemical Valley* (1991), a documentary film directed by Mimi Pickering and Anne Lewis Johnson. Among the old clippings, I took special note of a story in 1943 in *The Saturday Evening Post* that pronounced Charleston's chemical industry a "magic valley." Details on the official reporting of the spill and the government's response were gleaned from "COMPLAINT INVESTIGATION FORM Complaint Number: Department of Environmental Protection CH-2010–0261."

In West Virginia, attitudes toward coal, the environment, and climate change are complex. I am indebted to Katey Lauer for my interviews with her and for her writing, including "Making Sense of Crisis: The West Virginia Floods," *Appalachian Voices* (July 6, 2016). Survey data on public opinion drew on Jennifer Marlon et al., "Estimated % of Adults Who Think Global Warming Is Happening," Yale Climate Opinion Maps (August 7, 2018). For history on the role of interest groups, I drew on Richard A. Brisbin Jr., Robert Jay Dilger, and Allan S. Hammock, *West Virginia Politics and Government* (Lincoln: University of Nebraska Press, 2009).

12. OUT OF THEIR SLUMBER

Long before most Americans were waking up to the growth of the white nationalist movement, it was tracked with precision by Devin Burghart and Leonard Zeskind at the Institute for Research and Education on Human Rights; Heidi Beirich, Keegan Hankes, and others at the Southern Poverty Law Center; and Mark Pitcavage of the Anti-Defamation League. In each case, their generous help to me, and their publications, illuminated the full scale of the far-right awakening.

The prehistory of Trump's path to government has been told in many places, and I don't revisit it in depth, other than in details relevant to this narrative. Thanks to Sam Popkin for an early look at his manuscript for *Crackup: The Republican Implosion and the Future of Presidential Politics* (New York: Oxford University Press, 2021), which analyzes a wealth of academic and general-interest accounts of the Republican Party's evolution. Other details were drawn from Karen Tumulty's "How Donald Trump Came Up with 'Make America Great Again,'" *The Washington Post* (January 18, 2017); and from Ben Schreckinger, "'Oh, No': The Day Trump Learned to Tweet," *Politico* (December 20, 2018).

To chart Trump's rise to the top of the Republican Party, I benefited from the recollections of Jeffrey Sonnenfeld at the Yale School of Management; Jim Campbell, the former head of the Republican Party in Greenwich; and many others. Mencken's comments are drawn from "In Defense of Women," originally published in 1918, republished by Project Gutenberg (August 26, 2008); Stone conveyed his philosophy to Jeffrey Toobin, in "The Dirty Trickster," *The New Yorker* (May 23, 2008). Coulter was quoted in Robert Draper, "How Donald Trump Set Off a Civil War Within the Right-Wing Media," *The New York Times* (September 29, 2016). Trump's revealing confession ("They gave it to me") was in an interview with Robert Costa, "Listening to Donald Trump Swear and Talk Politics on His Private Plane," *The Washington Post* (July 12, 2015).

The evolving attitudes on immigration appeared in both on-the-ground and high-level analyses, including Ruy Teixeira et al., "Building an All-In Nation," Center for American Progress (October 22, 2013); Claire Potter, "'As Iowan as Cornfields': How Immigration Changed One Small Town," ABC News (August 12, 2019); Bret Hayworth, "Steve King Anti-immigration Tweet Comes Under Fire," *Sioux City Journal* (June 13, 2018); Janet Adamy and Paul Overberg, "Places Most Unsettled by Rapid Demographic Change Are Drawn to Donald Trump," *The Wall Street Journal* (November 1, 2016); and Bradley Jones, "In Republicans' Views of a Border Wall, Proximity to Mexico Matters," Pew Research Center (March 8, 2017).

The long history of racism in the presidency was noted by David Remnick in his commentary "What Toni Morrison Understood About Hate," *The New Yorker* (August 19, 2019); original sources include Thomas Jefferson, *Notes on the State of Virginia* (Richmond, 1853), 149–52, 155; Tim Naftali, "Ronald Reagan's Long-Hidden Racist Conversation with Richard Nixon," *The Atlantic* (July 30, 2019).

13. UNMAKING THE MACHINES

The weakening of party structures and credibility is a story that applies on both the right and the left. Jane Mayer, in *Dark Money*, provides essential reporting on the eclipse of the traditional Republican Party. The consequences of the fiscal crises in Chicago and Illinois have been closely covered by the *Tribune*, the *Sun-Times*, and other local press.

For an understanding of the extraordinary implications of the killing of Laquan McDonald, and the troubled relationship between African Americans and the Chicago Police Department, I am grateful to Natalie Moore of WBEZ for her time and her reporting. In addition, I drew on valuable details gathered by Christy Gutowski and Jeremy Gorner, in "The Complicated, Short Life of Laquan McDonald," *Chicago Tribune* (December 11, 2015); and "16 Shots," a podcast by WBEZ Chicago and the *Chicago Tribune*.

I benefited from scholarly research into violence and segregation in Chicago, including "Gun Violence in Chicago, 2016," University of Chicago Crime Lab (January 2017), and reporting by Sarah Karp and Becky Vevea, in "How Chicago School Construction Furthers Race and Class Segregation," WBEZ (July 7, 2016).

All too often, political analysis treats the broad community of African American voters as a monolith, and predictions for the 2016 election were prone to that error. But some assessments were prescient, and, later, others identified key turning points in the data. Ta-Nehisi Coates identified the weakness in Clinton's appeal in "The Playboy

Interview with Ta-Nehisi Coates," conducted by Bomani Jones, *Playboy* (June 22, 2016); other insightful pieces included Perry Bacon Jr., "Huge Split Between Older and Younger Blacks in the Democratic Primary," NBC News (May 28, 2016); Philip Bump, "Donald Trump's Risky Plan to Use the Internet to Suppress Hillary Clinton's Turnout," *The Washington Post* (October 27, 2016); Philip Bump, "Mostly Black Neighborhoods Voted More Republican in 2016 Than in 2012," *The Washington Post* (September 25, 2017); and Bernard Fraga, "Why Did Trump Win? More Whites— and Fewer Blacks—Actually Voted," *The Washington Post* (May 8, 2017).

The re-creation of the June 2016 West Virginia flood and its aftermath draws on Ken Ward Jr., "State Flood Protection Plan 'Sitting Dusty on a Shelf,'" *Charleston Gazette-Mail* (July 3, 2016); Brittany Patterson, "After Deadly Floods, West Virginia Created a Resiliency Office. It's Barely Functioning," *Ohio Valley Resource* (January 27, 2020); and Elaina Plott, "The Billionaire and the Flood," *Washingtonian* (May 7, 2017).

14. THE COMBAT MINDSET

Mike Weisser, in our interviews and in his books, elaborated on the evolving cultural role that guns have played in the politics of race, partisanship, and fear. He was generous with his time and his expertise. At the National Rifle Association's convention in Louisville, and in the months afterward, I interviewed several dozen people who research the politics, marketing, and health implications of the modern gun industry, or work in opposition to it, including Richard Feldman, David Hemenway, and Stephen Teret.

The literature on the American sociology of firearms is vast, but I returned most often to Tom Diaz, *Making a Killing: The Business of Guns in America* (New York: New Press, 1999); Pamela Haag, *The Gunning of America: Business and the Making of American Gun Culture* (New York: Basic Books, 2016); Adam Winkler, *Gunfight: The Battle over the Right to Bear Arms in America* (New York: W. W. Norton, 2011); Jennifer Carlson, *Citizen-Protectors: The Everyday Politics of Guns in an Age of Decline* (New York: Oxford University Press, 2015); and Dan Baum, *Gun Guys: A Road Trip* (New York: Knopf, 2013).

On the political utility of fear in ancient and modern culture, I appreciated Martha Nussbaum, *The Monarchy of Fear: A Philosopher Looks at Our Political Crisis* (New York: Simon & Schuster, 2018); Nixon's comments were reported by William Safire in *Before the Fall: An Inside View of the Pre-Watergate White House* (New York: Doubleday, 1975); comments on fear by executives at Cambridge Analytica were reported in "Revealed: Trump's Election Consultants Filmed Saying They Use Bribes and Sex Workers to Entrap Politicians," *Channel 4* (March 19, 2018).

The misinformation about self-defense is described in Michael R. Weisser, *The Myth of the Armed Citizen* (Ware, MA: TeeTee Press, 2015). The children's nursery rhyme about responding to a mass shooter was observed by Georgy Cohen, who circulated a photo on Twitter. The pathways of gun trafficking are described by Chelsea Parsons and Eugenio Weigend in "America Under Fire: An Analysis of Gun Violence in the United States and the Link to Weak Gun Laws," Center for American Progress (October 2016). Underlying data is available from the Bureau of Alcohol, Tobacco, Firearms and Explosives, Firearms Trace Data (2010–2015). Analysis of the frequency of mass shootings was produced by scholars from the Harvard School of Public Health and Northeastern University, Amy P. Cohen, Deborah Azrael, and Matthew Miller, and published in "Rate of Mass Shootings Has Tripled Since 2011, Harvard Research Shows" *Mother Jones* (October 15, 2014).

Trump's harnessing of the combat mindset emerges in a range of sources, beginning with his interview with *Playboy* in 1990 and extending through his interview with the Christian Broadcasting Network shortly before the 2016 election. An accounting of the 158 American families that donated half of all money to candidates on the ballot was reported by Nicholas Confessore, Sarah Cohen, and Karen Yourish, "The Families Funding the 2016 Presidential Election," *New York Times* (October 10, 2015).

The standoffs in Mount Greenwood around Election Day were reported in multiple accounts, including Christine Schmidt, "Life, and a Death, in Mount Greenwood," *South Side Weekly* (November 16, 2016); Jason Meisner et al., "Police Shooting Exposes Racial Tensions in Mostly White Mount Greenwood," *Chicago Tribune* (November 12, 2016); and Ben Austen, "Violence and Division on Chicago's South Side," *New York Times* (December 10, 2016).

15. RADICAL SELF-RELIANCE

I first learned about the subculture of prosperous preppers during a chance encounter with a seatmate on an airplane in 2016. In the months afterward, I benefited from interviews with a range of CEOs and investors who made time to speak with me about their habits and thinking, including Steve Huffman, Tim Chang, Justin Kan, and many others; on the East Coast, Rob Johnson has been an especially knowledgeable adviser on this subject and its larger sociological implications.

On the history of utopian and dystopian thinking, I was aided by advice and readings from the historian Richard White. I also drew from Christopher Jennings, *Paradise Now: The Story of American Utopianism* (New York: Random House, 2016), and Fred Turner, *From Counterculture to Cyberculture: Stewart Brand, the Whole Earth Network, and the Rise of Digital Utopianism* (Chicago: University of Chicago Press, 2006).

The political manifestation of the related concept, the "deconstruction of the administrative state," was described to me in interviews by some of its architects, including Steve Bannon, and some of its critics, many of whom are named in the text. On the history of attempts to restrict the civil service, I drew on the work of Landon R. Y. Storrs, *The Second Red Scare and the Unmaking of the New Deal Left* (Princeton, NJ: Princeton University Press, 2013).

Max Stier and his colleagues at the Partnership for Public Service proved to be an indispensable resource on the civil service and the technical details of its operation. The Trump administration's dismantling of federal functioning, either deliberate or accidental, was reported with such frequency and detail that it's beyond the scope of this note. At times, the details were so abundant that they appeared in otherwise minor mentions. Trump's struggle, for instance, to recall the first name of his fourth national security advisor in three years was contained in a single sentence of a thoroughly informative report by Mark Landler and Helene Cooper, "Bolton Walked Back Syria

Statement. His Disdain for Debate Helped Produce It," *The New York Times* (January 7, 2019).

16. THE BODY OF FACT

To understand the intersection of political violence, belonging, and unreason, I was fortunate to receive thoughtful counsel from many specialists, including Danielle Allen, Larry Diamond, Joanne Freeman, Nathan Kalmoe, Lilly Mason, Robert Putnam and his coauthor Shaylyn Romney Garrett, Jennifer Ratner-Rosenhagen, and Theda Skocpol. Five decades after it was published, the insights of *American Violence: A Documentary History* (New York: Knopf, 1970), by Richard Hofstadter and Michael Wallace, should be more widely known and studied.

On the Lincoln-Douglas debates, I am indebted to Dorothy Wickenden, who helped me develop the connection with the present circumstance, and who shared a portion of her writings in *The Agitators: Three Friends Who Fought for Abolition and Women's Rights* (New York: Scribner, 2021); and to Jill Lepore for her conversations with me and for her account in *These Truths: A History of the United States* (New York: W. W. Norton, 2018). I was fortunate to be writing not long after the release of David S. Reynolds's fine cultural biography, *Abe: Abraham Lincoln in His Times* (New York: Penguin Press, 2020). For accounts of the antebellum Congress, I drew from Freeman's account, *The Field of Blood*.

To illuminate the struggles over reason and intellectual curiosity in the early United States, I was aided by Caroline Winterer, *American Enlightenments: Pursuing Happiness in the Age of Reason* (New Haven, CT: Yale University Press, 2018); Jennifer Ratner-Rosenhagen, *The Ideas That Made America: A Brief History* (New York: Oxford University Press, 2019); and James Perrin Warren, *Culture of Eloquence: Oratory and Reform in Antebellum America* (University Park: Penn State University Press, 2004).

For insights into marketing, persuasion, and disinformation, I drew on Naomi Oreskes and Erik Conway, *Merchants of Doubt: How a Handful of Scientists Obscured the Truth on Issues from Tobacco Smoke to Climate Change* (New York: Bloomsbury Press, 2010); Cailin O'Connor and James Owen Weatherall, *The Misinformation Age: How False Beliefs Spread* (New Haven, CT: Yale University Press, 2018); Susan Jacoby, *The Age of American Unreason in a Culture of Lies* (New York: Vintage, 2018); Jason Stanley and David Beaver, "Beware of 'Snakes,' 'Invaders' and Other Fighting Words," *The New York Times* (May 16, 2019); Gavan J. Fitzsimons and Baba Shiv, "Nonconscious and Contaminative Effects of Hypothetical Questions on Subsequent Decision Making," *Journal of Consumer Research* 28, no. 2 (2001); and "The Success of the Voter Fraud Myth," *The New York Times* (September 19, 2016). The quote from George W. Bush's aide on the "reality-based community" originally appeared in Ron Suskind, "Faith, Certainty and the Presidency of George W. Bush," *The New York Times Magazine* (October 17, 2004).

On the fate of fact in the Trump era, I drew on Kellyanne Conway's interview with Mark Simone of New York's 710 WOR Radio (January 2018) and the heroic labors of the *Washington Post* fact-checker team, including Glenn Kessler and Salvador Rizzo; Michael Lewis, "Has Anyone Seen the President?," Bloomberg (February 9, 2018);

and Andy Kroll, "John Podesta Is Ready to Talk About Pizzagate,'" *Rolling Stone* (December 9, 2018). For valuable accounts of Trump's August 2017 rally in Huntington, I relied on Jenna Johnson, "Why Is Trump Rallying in West Virginia's Huntington? Because He's Mostly Popular There," *The Washington Post* (August 3, 2017); and David Smith, "Why Trump Still Needs the Love of the Crowd: 'This Is Like Medicine to Him,'" *The Guardian* (August 6, 2017).

The search for political meaning and the effects of political nihilism have been examined from a range of perspectives, including Francis Fukuyama, *The End of History and the Last Man* (New York: Free Press, 1992); Thomas B. Edsall, "The Trump Voters Whose 'Need for Chaos' Obliterates Everything Else," *The New York Times* (September 4, 2019); Anne Applebaum, "A Warning from Europe: The Worst Is Yet to Come," *The Atlantic* (October 2018); Damon Linker, "How Right-Wing Populism Overcame Distance," *The Week* (December 1, 2020); James Madison, *Federalist* No. 10: "The Same Subject Continued: The Union as a Safeguard Against Domestic Faction and Insurrection," *New York Daily Advertiser* (November 22, 1787); and Michael Bang Petersen, Mathias Osmundsen, and Kevin Arceneaux, "The 'Need for Chaos' and Motivations to Share Hostile Political Rumors," PsyArXiv (September 1, 2018).

I relied on several studies of political cohesion, including J. J. Messner et al., "Fragile States Index 2018—Annual Report," by the Fund for Peace, and Nathan P. Kalmoe and Lilliana Mason, "Most Americans Reject Partisan Violence, but There Is Still Cause for Concern," Voter Study Group (May 7, 2020). Examples of violent rhetoric by mainstream conservative voices appeared in Jeremy W. Peters et al., "How the El Paso Killer Echoed the Incendiary Words of Conservative Media Stars," *The New York Times* (August 11, 2019).

17. THE ANTIBODIES

For details and perspective on the political implications of the West Virginia teachers' strike, I am indebted to the interviewees named in the text, as well as several published sources, including Charles Keeney, "A Culture of Resistance: The 2018 West Virginia Teachers' Strike in Historical Perspective," *Lapham's Quarterly* (March 30, 2018), and David Dayen, "The New Uprising on a Country Road," *The American Prospect* (September 30, 2019).

On the impact of Christine Blasey Ford's testimony, I was informed by Haley Sweetland Edwards, "How Christine Blasey Ford's Testimony Changed America," *Time* (October 4, 2018). I am thankful to Jamie Miller for an interview on her encounters with Derrick Evans; other details were described in court documents and in West Virginia press accounts; in addition, I was informed by Ruth Bashinsky, "For Women Who Say Derrick Evans Harassed Them, West Virginia Lawmaker's Capitol Assault Arrest Is No Surprise," *Inside Edition* (January 29, 2021).

On the shifting mood among some in finance, I am grateful for an interview with Seth Klarman, and his speech at Harvard Business School on December 1, 2018, titled "Hard Choices: The Importance of Thoughtful Deliberation—and Its Implications for the Future of Capitalism." Ray Dalio was generous with his time on several occasions, and he expounded on his concerns with inequality in several papers, including "Why and How Capitalism Needs to Be Reformed," published in April 2019.

For details on the changing politics of guns in Washington, I referred to Danny Hakim, "At the N.R.A., a Cash Machine Sputtering," *The New York Times* (May 14, 2019); E. J. Dionne Jr., "Opinion: It's the Beginning of the End for the Gun Lobby's Power," *The Washington Post* (December 16, 2018); Scott Smith, "Shootings Prompt Other Countries to Warn About Travel to US," Associated Press (August 8, 2019); Mike Spies, "Secrecy, Self-Dealing, and Greed at the N.R.A.," *The New Yorker* (April 17, 2019); and Maggie Astor and Karl Russell, "After Parkland, a New Surge in State Gun Control Laws," *The New York Times* (December 14, 2018).

I am grateful to Osita Nwanevu for alerting me to the work of Jahmal Cole, who invited me to join his "Explorations" in Chicago. Cole, who also introduced me to Will Hobert, was patient with my questions over four interviews, and he also described his work in a series of self-published books, including *Exposure Is Key: Solving Violence by Exposing Teens to Opportunities* (2017) and *It's Not Regular: How to Recognize Injustice Hidden in Plain Sight* (2019).

18. FACELESS

Trump's first mention of the coronavirus in an interview appeared on January 22, 2020, on CNBC, titled "Trump Says He Trusts China's Xi on Coronavirus and the US Has It 'Totally Under Control.'" Details on the actions and attitudes that defined the response are drawn from a range of government and legal documents, whistleblower accounts, and press reports, including Yasmeen Abutaleb, Ashley Parker, Josh Dawsey, and Philip Rucker, "The Inside Story of How Trump's Denial, Mismanagement and Magical Thinking Led to the Pandemic's Dark Winter," *The Washington Post* (December 19, 2020); Peter Baker and Maggie Haberman, "The President as Bystander: Trump Struggles to Unify a Nation on Edge," *The New York Times* (March 12, 2020). New York's unsuccessful ventilator purchase was reported by Ken Bensinger and Rosalind Adams, "New York Is Still Owed Millions from the Man It Paid $69 Million After He Tweeted at Trump," *BuzzFeed News* (October 12, 2020).

For illuminating connections between poverty and the pandemic, I am grateful for Keeanga-Yamahtta Taylor's piece "Reality Has Endorsed Bernie Sanders," *The New Yorker* (March 30, 2020). The response of white nationalists was reported by Hannah Gais, "Hate Groups and Racist Pundits Spew COVID-19 Misinformation on Social Media Despite Companies' Pledges to Combat It," Southern Poverty Law Center (April 17, 2020). George Packer synthesized the result in "We Are Living in a Failed State," *The Atlantic* (June 2020). The effects of overcrowding on health was explored by Claudia D. Solari, "America's Housing Is Getting More Crowded. How Will That Affect Children?," Urban Institute (April 24, 2019); Christopher Ingraham, "A Stunning Indictment of the U.S. Health-Care System, in One Chart," *The Washington Post* (December 10, 2019). The use of GoFundMe for medical expenses was described by Susan Cahn and Mollie Hertel, "Millions of Americans Donate Through Crowdfunding Sites to Help Others Pay for Medical Bills," NORC at the University of Chicago (November 16, 2009).

In Chicago and Peoria, I appreciated interviews with Reese Clark and Jahmal Cole at a difficult time. Data on the rate of deaths in the Black community draws on Aaron Ross Coleman, "Retail Covid-19 Testing Is a Massive Failure for Black Communities," *Vox* (April 28, 2020). That analysis was based on official data from the city of Chicago, accessible via the COVID Daily Dashboard.

In Greenwich, I'm grateful to a range of interviewees, who spoke with me about political implications of the virus, including Fred Camillo, Michael Mason, Edward Dadakis, Joanna Swomley, and others who asked to remain anonymous. In addition, I am grateful for Ken Borsuk's reporting in "Camillo and Byrne Trade Barbs over Coronavirus Restrictions in Greenwich," *Greenwich Time* (April 21, 2020). The calculation of benefits for high-income taxpayers was produced by the Joint Committee on Taxation of the U.S. Congress and released by members of the Senate, including Sheldon Whitehouse, on April 14, 2020. It was reported by Jeff Stein, "Tax Change in Coronavirus Package Overwhelmingly Benefits Millionaires, Congressional Body Finds," *The Washington Post* (April 14, 2020). The annual performance in the hedge-fund industry was reported in Stephen Taub, "The 20th Annual Rich List, the Definitive Ranking of What Hedge Fund Managers Earned in 2020," *Institutional Investor* (February 22, 2021). The local coronavirus protest was covered by Robert Marchant, "'Money Bags and Body Bags' Protest Rolls Through Affluent Greenwich Neighborhoods," *Greenwich Time* (May 21, 2020).

In West Virginia, Slemp's departure was reported by Michelle R. Smith and Anthony Izaguirre, "Exclusive: Ex-WVa Health Chief Says Cuts Hurt Virus Response," Associated Press (July 10, 2020). The protest at the Capitol was covered by Rick Steelhammer, "Protesters Seek Immediate Reopening of State," *Charleston Gazette-Mail* (April 27, 2020).

My conversation with Biden draws on an unpublished portion of an interview I conducted at his residence in Delaware in July 2020. My discussion of presidents' use of empathy was informed by Colleen J. Shogan's perceptive paper, "The Contemporary Presidency: The Political Utility of Empathy in Presidential Leadership," *Presidential Studies Quarterly* 39, no. 4 (December 2009).

19. ARE WE GOING TO JAIL, DAD?

In interviews, Jahmal Cole, Jim Griffin, Reese Clark, Chip Skowron, and Ed Horstmann shared their experiences of the Black Lives Matter movement of 2020. In Chicago, for details of chronology and official actions, I drew on the city's inspector general's report "Chicago's Response to George Floyd Protests and Unrest," as well as press accounts and activists' assertions.

A wealth of journalism and scholarship has illuminated America's history of systemic racism, segregation, and isolation. I was especially grateful for Daniel Cox, Juhem Navarro-Rivera, and Robert P. Jones, "Race, Religion, and Political Affiliation of Americans' Core Social Networks," Public Religion Research Institute (August 3, 2016); Melvin Oliver and Thomas Shapiro, *Black Wealth/White Wealth: A New Perspective on Racial Inequality* (Abingdon, UK: Routledge, 2006); and Olorunnipa and

Witte, whose article "Born with Two Strikes" provides a powerful statistical backdrop for George Floyd's life.

In Clarksburg, I am grateful to the Harrison County Commission for responding to the request for recordings of hearings on the future of the Stonewall Jackson statue. In addition, I was fortunate to receive a recording from Dave Mistich, and recollections from interviews with attendees. Other details were contained in coverage by *The Exponent Telegram*.

In re-creating the life of William Wojtkowski, a.k.a. William Viete, a.k.a. Willie Ziek, I was fortunate to receive the gracious help of his descendants, who shared recollections, photos, and details of the family history: Leanna Lang Ayoob, Lois Lang, Tony Dorrell, Terri Ogden, and Michael Ogden.

20. THE RAGING FIRE

The historic scale of American wildfires in 2020 was documented by government scientists, as conveyed in multiple accounts: "Northern Hemisphere Just Had Its Hottest Summer on Record," NOAA (September 14, 2020), and Tom DiLiberto, "Over a Million Acres Burned in California in Second Half of August 2020," NOAA (August 26, 2020). Witnesses' statements on the damage and spread are drawn from press accounts produced by CBS and Palo Alto Online, among others.

Accounts of Trump's final months in office—including his Covid diagnosis, his propagation of false scientific theories, and attempts to subvert the democratic election—are informed by press accounts, including Rosalind S. Helderman and Elise Viebeck, "'The Last Wall': How Dozens of Judges Across the Political Spectrum Rejected Trump's Efforts to Overturn the Election," *The Washington Post* (December 12, 2020), and Stephen Wertheim, "How Trump Brought Home the Endless War," *The New Yorker* (October 1, 2020). Details on Facebook's handling of violent material were reported by Ryan Mac, "A Kenosha Militia Facebook Event Asking Attendees to Bring Weapons Was Reported 455 Times," *BuzzFeed News* (August 28, 2020).

Details on the election and events of January 6 are based on firsthand interviews, observations, and press accounts. For especially specific observations, I drew from Emmanuel Felton, "Black Police Officers Describe the Racist Attacks They Faced as They Protected the Capitol," *BuzzFeed News* (January 9, 2021); Edward Luce, "A Bitter US Election That Resolves Little," *Financial Times* (November 4, 2020); and Cassandra Sweetman, "Cleveland County GOP Chair's Facebook Post Condones Violence Morning of Capitol Riot," KFOR (January 12, 2021).

21. BEHOLD THE LAND

Witnesses' and survivors' accounts from January 6 emerged from police officers, rioters, and journalists, as well as staff and members of Congress. News profiles on the background of Ashli Babbitt included Ellen Barry, Nicholas Bogel-Burroughs, and Dave Philipps, "Woman Killed in Capitol Embraced Trump and QAnon," *The New York Times* (January 7, 2021). The high representation of military veterans was reported by Tom Dreisbach and Meg Anderson, "Nearly 1 in 5 Defendants in Capitol Riot

Cases Served in the Military," *All Things Considered* (January 21, 2021); the patterns of financial distress were reported by Todd C. Frankel, "A Majority of the People Arrested for Capitol Riot Had a History of Financial Trouble," *The Washington Post* (February 10, 2021).

For details on the legacy of the Trump years in West Virginia, I drew on the economic portrait by Heather Long and Andrew Van Dam, "West Virginia's Surprising Boom, and Bust, Tells the Story of Trump's Promise to Help the 'Forgotten Man,'" *The Washington Post* (October 30, 2020), and Emily Badger, "West Virginia Has Everyone's Attention. What Does It Really Need?," *The New York Times* (February 8, 2021). For context on the political challenges ahead, I am grateful to the Reverend Dr. William Barber for speaking with me during the busy week of the inauguration; I reached him with the help of Jelani Cobb.

Statistical analysis of the U.S. Senate and its malapportionment draws on the work of Alex Tausanovitch, director of campaign finance and electoral reform at the Center for American Progress, and of Hacker and Pierson in *Winner-Take-All Politics*.

ACKNOWLEDGMENTS

Wildland is a book about public life, revealed in private experiences. Many of the people in these pages agreed to discuss very personal stories in the belief that it might serve a larger good. I am grateful for their trust and candor over many years, even as America's turmoil pushed our conversations into sensitive ground.

At Farrar, Straus and Giroux, I have been especially fortunate to work with Eric Chinski, whose intellectual range and high standards prove that some editors have a cult following for a reason. Nearly twenty years ago, Jonathan Galassi and I started talking about books we might publish, and he has refined every idea since then with keen questioning and patience. Mitzi Angel embraced this project with enthusiasm and lent it the full powers of her team, including Gretchen Achilles, Janine Barlow, Debra Helfand, Na Kim, Spenser Lee, Julia Ringo, Sheila O'Shea, Daniel del Valle, and Sarita Varma.

I am immensely thankful to Jennifer Joel of ICM Partners, a creative, protective friend who also happens to be my agent. Over the years, I have been fortunate to become a friend and client of many of her colleagues, including Chris Silbermann, Ted Chervin, Nancy Aaronson, Nicole Klett-Angel, Michael Glantz, Ron Bernstein, and Tia Ikemoto. Thanks as well to Karolina Sutton and Jake Smith-Bosanquet for bringing my books abroad. In the United Kingdom, I am pleased to be published by Alexis Kirschbaum at Bloomsbury, aided by Jonny Coward.

Everything I write owes a debt, either direct or atmospheric, to my professional home, *The New Yorker*. I am grateful beyond measure to David Remnick, Dorothy Wickenden, Deirdre Foley-Mendelssohn, Pam McCarthy, Nick Trautwein, Michael Luo, Carla Blumenkranz, and John Bennet. They incubated many of the beliefs in this book, and pushed me to probe further and think harder. In Washington, I had the pleasure of working alongside Adam Entous, Susan Glasser, Ryan Lizza, Jane Mayer, Osita Nwanevu, Nicholas Schmidle, and Margaret Talbot.

Since moving back to America, I have had the good fortune to join two institutions that have taught me far more than I have provided: Brookings, where I am grateful to Suzanne Maloney, Bruce Jones, Cheng Li, and Ryan McElveen; and CNN, where I am thankful for the encouragement and trust of Rebecca Kutler and Jeff Zucker.

At various points in this writing, I was aided by vital fact-checking or research from Hélène Werner, Anna Boots, Zach Helfand, Parker Henry, Christina Filipovic, Zach Balin, Jacob Fromer, Will Carroll, James Haynes, Ethan Jewell, Matthew Silberman, and Chang Che.

To describe three places that I love—each complex, distinctive, and changing—I depended on countless conversations with friends whose professional or personal lives give them insights. In particular, Esther Bushell, David Heinzmann, and Ken Ward Jr. also provided close readings of the manuscript with an eye to refining subtle themes and details.

For comfort and laughter in our Washington years, including the plague year, I relied on virtual sustenance from Jonathan Ansfield, John Delury, Gady Epstein, Woo Lee, Phil Pan, Alex Wang, and Ed Wong. Even when we couldn't gather in person, our family depended immeasurably on the help and friendship of Herb Allen, Peter Baker, Amy Brendler, Mike Brendler, Libby Casey, Audie Cornish, Sandy Coburn, Michael Crowley, Charlie Edel, Theo Emery, Jonathan Finer, Eric French, Cyrus Frelinghuysen, Leah Frelinghuysen, Andrew Genung, Susan Glasser, Jorge Guajardo, Sarah Haight, Luke Hartig, Ashley Hernreich, Julia Ioffe, Susie Jakes, Lindsay Jenkins, Patrick Radden Keefe, Adam Kushner, Victoria Lai, Jill Lepore, Rachel Martin, Lauren Mason, Amanda Miller, Richard Nash, Ben Pauker, Jason Perri, Jeff Prescott, Sally Quinn, Michael Riley, Paola Sada, Karim Sadjadpour,

Rikki Schmidle, Chris Schroeder, Bill Shope, Maria Simon, Carla Snyder, Nick Snyder, Sarah Stillman, Monica de la Torre, Tini Tran, Larry Wright, and Howard Yoon.

By birth and marriage, I am blessed to be part of several extraordinary clans. The wisdom and support of my parents, Susan and Peter, run through every page. My sister, Katherine Sanford, her husband, Colin, and their kids—Ben, Pete, and Mae—are a model of love, strength, and intelligent companionship. And I am ludicrously fortunate to have joined the Bermans: Kim, Farzad, Seth, Mandy, Rebecca, Franklin, their broods, and, lucky for us all, Ruth and Harris.

Nobody nurtures my thinking more than Sarabeth, whose energy, humor, and inexhaustible kindness are the fuel that powers our family. I started reporting this book before we had children; I am finishing it in the company of Oliver and Rose. In between, I often oscillated between reasons to despair at our politics and occasions to rejoice at home. By the end, I was writing this book for them, in the wish that they might someday read of a time when their country lost sight of its moral ambitions, and, I hope, began the process of seeing them again.

INDEX

A NOTE ABOUT THE AUTHOR

Evan Osnos is a staff writer at *The New Yorker*, a CNN contributor, and a senior fellow at the Brookings Institution. Based in Washington, D.C., he writes about politics and foreign affairs. He was the China correspondent for *The New Yorker* from 2008 to 2013. His first book, *Age of Ambition: Chasing Fortune, Truth, and Faith in the New China*, won the 2014 National Book Award and was a finalist for the Pulitzer Prize. In 2020, he published the international bestseller *Joe Biden: The Life, the Run, and What Matters Now*, based on interviews with Biden, Barack Obama, and others. Prior to joining *The New Yorker*, Osnos worked as the Beijing bureau chief of the *Chicago Tribune*, where he contributed to a series that won the 2008 Pulitzer Prize for investigative reporting. Before his appointment in China, he worked in the Middle East, reporting mostly from Iraq. He and his wife, Sarabeth Berman, have two children.

DA OCT 2021